When Evil Strikes

african christian studies series (africs)

This series will make available significant works in the field of African Christian studies, taking into account the many forms of Christianity across the whole continent of Africa. African Christian studies is defined here as any scholarship that relates to themes and issues on the history, nature, identity, character, and place of African Christianity in world Christianity. It also refers to topics that address the continuing search for abundant life for Africans through multiple appeals to African religions and African Christianity in a challenging social context. The books in this series are expected to make significant contributions in historicizing trends in African Christian studies, while shifting the contemporary discourse in these areas from narrow theological concerns to a broader inter-disciplinary engagement with African religio-cultural traditions and Africa's challenging social context.

The series will cater to scholarly and educational texts in the areas of religious studies, theology, mission studies, biblical studies, philosophy, social justice, and other diverse issues current in African Christianity. We define these studies broadly and specifically as primarily focused on new voices, fresh perspectives, new approaches, and historical and cultural analyses that are emerging because of the significant place of African Christianity and African religio-cultural traditions in world Christianity. The series intends to continually fill a gap in African scholarship, especially in the areas of social analysis in African Christian studies, African philosophies, new biblical and narrative hermeneutical approaches to African theologies, and the challenges facing African women in today's Africa and within African Christianity. Other diverse themes in African Traditional Religions; African ecology; African ecclesiology; inter-cultural, inter-ethnic, and inter-religious dialogue; ecumenism; creative inculturation; African theologies of development, reconciliation, globalization, and poverty reduction will also be covered in this series.

SERIES EDITORS

Dr. Stan Chu Ilo (St. Michael's College, University of Toronto)

Dr. Philomena Njeri Mwaura (Kenyatta University, Nairobi, Kenya)

Dr. Afe Adogame (University of Edinburgh)

When Evil Strikes

Faith and the Politics of Human Hostility

SUNDAY BOBAI AGANG

Foreword by Ronald J. Sider

☙PICKWICK *Publications* · Eugene, Oregon

WHEN EVIL STRIKES
Faith and the Politics of Human Hostility

African Christian Studies Series 10

Pickwick Publications
An Imprint of Wipf and Stock Publishers
199 W. 8th Ave., Suite 3
Eugene, OR 97401

www.wipfandstock.com

PAPERBACK ISBN: 978-1-4982-3566-2
HARDCOVER ISBN: 978-1-4982-3568-6
EBOOK ISBN: 978-1-4982-3567-9

Cataloguing-in-Publication data:

Names: Agang, Sunday Bobai | Sider, Ronald J.

Title: Book title : When evil strikes : faith and the politics of human hostility / Sunday Bobai Agang ; foreword by Ronald J. Sider.

Description: Eugene, OR: Pickwick Publications, 2016 | African Christian Studies Series 10 | Includes bibliographical references.

Identifiers: ISBN 978-1-4982-3566-2 (paperback) | ISBN 978-1-4982-3568-6 (hardcover) | ISBN 978-1-4982-3567-9 (ebook)

Subjects: LCSH: Christian ethics. | Peace—Moral and ethical aspects—Africa. | Conflict management—Africa. | Peace-building—Africa. I. II.

Classification: JZ5584.A35 A40 2016 (print) | JZ5584.A35 (ebook)

Manufactured in the U.S.A.   06/22/16

This book is dedicated to Christian martyrs across the globe

Contents

Foreword

WHEN EVIL STRIKES BRINGS a new, younger voice from the Global South to the worldwide Christian discussion about how Christians should respond to wrenching situations of contemporary violence, poverty, corruption and injustice. Dr. Sunday Agang is both immersed in the anguished struggles of church and society in his native Nigeria and also trained in theology and ethics in the United States (MDiv, Palmer Theological Seminary; PhD, Fuller Theological Seminary).

Dr. Agang's starting point is the immediate set of problems in his beloved Nigeria: the killing of thousands of Nigerian Christians by the radical Muslim extremist organization, Boko Haram; the failure of the Nigerian government to end the violence; and the broader brokenness of Nigerian society reflected in the widespread poverty and corruption. But Dr. Agang knows that only the details of his Nigerian situation differ from that of people and societies all around the world.

He rightly refuses to locate the fundamental problem, even of the lethal violence, in Islamic extremism. Going much deeper, his ethical/theological reflection correctly identifies the most basic problem as human sinfulness (resulting from the Fall), which is located in every society and every human heart. Christians, just as much as Muslims and adherents of indigenous religions, are all pockmarked with sinful pride and violent grasping for power. (They all also have not been totally destroyed by the Fall and therefore also have the potential for good which brings the possibility of finding solutions to our desperate problems.)

Using the tools of biblical theology and Christian ethics, Dr. Agang wrestles hard with the concrete problems of contemporary Nigeria. This book represents a new generation of Nigerian Christians who are dissatisfied with the past failure of the church to fundamentally transform Nigerian society, but also believe that a more biblical, more profound analysis and Spirit-filled courageous action can in fact reduce the violence, poverty and corruption in their country. That in itself makes this an important book.

But *When Evil Strikes* is important for far more Christians than just those in Nigeria and Africa generally. At a basic level, Christians everywhere face the same fundamental problems. Christians everywhere must decide how to respond to corrupt, ineffective politicians, widespread poverty, and violent threats to peace and justice from militant extremists. Careful listening to how a gifted churchman and theologian/ethicist from the global South struggles with these universal problems will bless Christians everywhere.

Especially interesting is Dr. Agang's wrestling with how to formulate and live a faithful Christian response to the vicious killing of many Christians by religious fanatics. Using the Just Peacemaking ideas of his PhD advisor at Fuller, Glen Stassen, he seeks to understand what it means to follow Jesus' call to love our enemies in a world where those enemies often massacre us. Dr. Agang does not claim to have a final, definitive answer to that question. But understanding how he wrestles with that profoundly difficult problem can help Christians everywhere think more deeply about what is finally a crucial, essential task for Christians everywhere.

Thank you Dr. Agang for this contribution to the global Christian dialogue on what it means to follow Jesus today.

Ronald J. Sider
Distinguished Professor of Theology, Holistic Ministry and Public Policy
Palmer Theological Seminary at Eastern University

Preface

WHENEVER EVIL STRIKES THERE are both casualties and survivors; the old dies and the new gets born. Buckets of tears are drained from the victims, their families and living relations' eyes. Diverse and unimaginable questions are asked and reflected upon. Different claims and conclusions are made: "Those arrogant people who hate Your instructions have dug deep pits to trap me," says the psalmist (Ps 119:85). And the voices of the dead leave their homes in the living.

The world shrinks; and yet divides and subdivides! This is because we live in a world whereby human judgments and actions tend to be guided by evil motives—self-interest, deception and lust for money, sex and power. The existence of cable network makes our world truly a global village: a shrunk world. We get to share the joyful and bitter experiences of the human family. And through electronic press and social media, we read and see the good and the bad of the human race. Although we do not always have the same experiences of the gruesome tragedies of human crises taking place across certain parts of the Majority World, one act of evil makes it looks like evil is a winner over good. Who will ever forget the tragic destruction of over six million Jews during World War II, or the crashing of planes into the World Trade Center in the United States on September 11, 2001, or the abduction of 237 school girls on April 14, 2014 in northeast Nigeria by the Islamic group known as Boko Haram (Western education is forbidden), or the attacks of a Christians Boarding school in Kenya by al-Shabab gunmen on April 2, 2015 which left 148 students dead? Who will forget the suicide co-pilot who crashed a German passenger plane with 48 deaths? These situations of human tragic and gruesome atrocities do cause enormous sense of loss, dread and agony. We get overwhelmed, alarmed and numbed. They are depressing and in most cases cause a deep sense of despair and cynicism. However, as Christians look at what is happening in our world, our response needs to be situated in the context of the cross. We need to specifically remember the first word to the women at the tomb, "Don't be alarmed." This

was the first word the angel said to the first people to learn about the resurrection, the aftermath of a gruesome murder of God's Son, the Messiah. The
first message after the resurrection was a message of hope—a message to
calm people down and assure them that everything was under God's control. This assurance is what helps to push the boundary of possibility for
love, justice and peace in a volatile social context like Nigeria; a country of
tears of sorrows and pains because of the unabated trail of bloodletting. The
dead cannot talk about love, justice and peace for they have gone into the
silence of the grave. But we the living can continue to push for the boundary
of the possibility to help all Nigerians recognize that "The heavens belong
to the LORD, but He has given the earth to all humanity." (Ps 115:16 NLT)
The earth is still the LORD's and all that is in it. But He has assigned its stew-
ardship to all humanity—Muslims, Christians and African Traditional Religionists. This is a fundamental fact: God has not given Nigeria to a single
tribe, ethnic group or a religious community. Rather, He has given Nigeria
to all the over three hundred (300) ethnic tribes or over four hundred (400)
ethnolinguistic groups.

Christians are called to work at living at peace with everyone. Yet,
whenever evil strikes humans only see trouble and sorrow. That is, they
hardly think of the possibility of peace where they feel death wraps its ropes
around them; the terrors of the grave overtake them. In those times they
call on the name of the Lord: "I am under attack, Lord, where are you? Lord,
save me! How long must I wait? When will you punish those who persecute me?" In order to get a grasp of the depth of this kind of reaction, faith
in a hostile society needs critical thinking and reflection. That will involve
carefully analyzing the social milieu where contemporary Christian faith
is supposed to be practiced, what hope it brings to a divided, frustrated,
broken and decaying human world. The book addresses three important
questions to enable Christians who find themselves in situations of human
hostility to appropriately practice their faith in a manner that brings hope
to a hostile society. First, does my Christian faith have anything to say to the
world in which I live? Second, what role should Christians play in defus-
ing or obliterating violence and bringing about peace? Third, why do the
wicked prosper and the innocent suffer? Given that the focus of this book is
the global south, we argue that violence and evil are part and parcel of life
for everyone, existing alongside the good. Violence and evil stem not only
from the socio-religious-economic context of the world we live in but also
from the heart and attitude of humankind; and Christian theologians need
to address those problems.[1] To begin with, I must categorically state that my

---

1. Merton, *Faith and Violence*, 3.

theological reflection on Christian reaction or response to violence is not an ivory tower theology. In 2001 my cousin Rev. Ishaya Bobai was among those murdered by the Muslims in the wave ofShari'a crisis in Kaduna State, Nigeria. The news of his death came crushing like burning coal in my heart. He was a very vibrant servant of God. He got killed at the prime of his life and ministry. I was studying at Eastern Baptist Theological Seminary (now Palmer Theological Seminary) Philadelphia. One of my professors was my prayer partner. When we went to pray I shared with him what had transpired. His reaction was the imprecatory prayer. He prayed asking God to send down fire from heaven to consume the perpetrators of this heinous act of violence. When it was my turn to pray, the Holy Spirit led me to simply ask God to have mercy on the killers of my cousin. I asked God to deliver them from continuing to do this and bring them to his serving knowledge.

I have memories of the parents of the adducted 237 school girls at Chibok, Borno State, Nigeria, by Boko Haram on April 14, 2014. As of October 5, 2014, 219 of them were still missing. I live with the memories of 148 of my kinsmen who were gruesomely murdered and brutally burnt to ashes by Fulani herdsmen on March 14, 2014. Or how does one react to news of brutal murder of a classmate, and an alumnus of a theological seminary one is heading? On September 17, 2014 I got this text message: "Last night [September 16, 2014] Rev. Julius Kurungu and his wife were killed in Fadan Karship by Fulani attack." The Fulani herdsmen have been terrorizing this area since June 2014. Many people have been brutally killed. Rev. Kurungu and his wife were among several of the victims of such carnage. Rev. Kurungu was my classmate at Evangelical Church Winning All (ECWA) Bible College Kagoro from 1980–1985. We were from the same denomination and he served under me as one of the pastors in Kafanchan District Church Council (KDCC). I was the secretary of KDCC for six years (1993–1999). The text message was sent to me by another classmate at the same school, Rev. Nanyak Goifa. I was then the Provost (president) of the ECWA Theological Seminary, which was formerly ECWA Bible College in the 1980s but now has grown to a full-fledged seminary. Kurungu was one of the alumni of the seminary. I knew him and his family. His first wife died and he remarried in 2013. He had young children from both marriages.

When I got the news I thought of reacting to the news, but which of the theories of war can I adopt? How do I avoid making mistakes in choosing the solution to the problem before me? Of course, to me, it is not about the matter of which theory is superior and pious but which theory helps me get on the path of peace, not violence? Perhaps, my primary questions are which theory would guide Nigerians to the path of a humane society? And which approach would be faithful to Christ my Lord? I have several options to choose from: From Origen, pacifism, from Augustine of Hippo, just war theory; and from Glen Stassen, just peacemaking. All of these options are at our disposal to use because "Peace requires the collective effort of many people";[2] and indeed many options. I could not help but ask, if peace is what God desires how does he feel about human hostility, terrorism? God grieves over it, of course. But more than that God is doing something to turn the situation upside down for the benefit of the human race; to create the moral order that gives birth to a humane society, humane social institutions and political systems. Perhaps this is what the psalmist alluded to when he says: "Human defiance only enhances Your glory, for You use it as a weapon" (Ps 76:9–10). The author of Genesis tells us that "The LORD saw how great the wickedness of the human race had become on the earth, and that every inclination of the thoughts of the human heart was only evil all the time. The LORD regretted that he had made human beings on the earth; and his heart was deeply troubled" (Gen 6:5–6 NLT). Human hostility, evil, upsets God! It causes Him to do something: God says, "At the time I have planned I will bring justice against the wicked." For God says, "I will break the strength of the wicked, but I will increase the power of the godly" (Ps 75:2, 10).

As we continue to be bewildered, amazed, perplexed and horrified at the sight of the horrors of death in our planet, we must continue to ask each other "how should we best react to these perplexing and horrifying news of violence and brutality? We must acknowledge the reality: Our world is infested with 'ideologically-fueled violence.'"[3] However, we are not only dealing with ideology but also with competing cultural myths and theological perspectives that have traditionally governed the lives of their adherents for centuries. As I see my brothers and sisters in Nigeria and perhaps around the continent of Africa wrestling with issues and circumstances beyond their comprehension and solution, I do not only empathize with them but I also want to do something that will help them find strength in the Lord their God by *helping them know what the Bible says*. Of course, the Bible is replete with narratives of where things have been and should not have been. For example, the story of Cain and Abel; the Old Testaments narrative of conquests; Isaiah's message about the Messiah; the New Testament account of Jesus' ministry, teaching and violent death and his message of peace to his disciples before and after his resurrection.

The Bible also helps me to understand how to unravel what I mean when I talk about peacemaking and reconciliation. God is the peacemaker

2. Cartwright, *Peace*, 11.

3. Georgia Holmer, USIP Senior Program Officer, presenting her view at the Conflict Prevention and Resolution Forum, US Institute of Peace, Washington, DC, July 8, 2014.

and the reconciler of humanity to Himself. This is exactly what the cross of Jesus Christ teaches us. Jesus Christ's crucifixion has accomplished the requirements for peace and reconciliation of humans with their Creator, God. And now God invites all those with whom He has made peace and reconciliation (restored back to the position of being His children) to participate with Him in the work of telling the world about the Good News of peace and reconciliation with God. As Paul puts it, on the cross God disarmed the powers that be, the spiritual rulers and authorities of the world. He publicly shamed them by Christ's victory on the cross. It then means that as we talk about peacemaking and reconciliation with other faiths in Nigeria, we are claiming the full message of the Gospel which is that Christ is now the head over all rulers and authorities of this world. Our complete confidence in the truth of that scriptural declaration helps us to pursue the work of peacemaking, love, justice and reconciliation as a peaceful and a redeemed community. We are certainly aware of how it seems that evil is winning but we cannot accept such a lie as the whole truth.

Beyond the reality of violent conflicts in Nigeria, there is a flip side of the coin. Therefore, we argue that Nigeria is pregnant with no one to midwife the birth of a new Nigeria. This new Nigeria will not be birthed by violent revolution. For it to be a humane society it must be nurtured by a humane faith, intellectualism and civilization. The ethos of the "new Nigeria" must be founded on the precepts of a God who created human beings in his image and likeness. This is what will birth a new nation; a nation where her leaders intentionally turn away from corruption and "administer true justice"; where ordinary citizens turn away from loving only themselves and money and "show mercy and compassion to one another"; where members of the public "do not oppress the widow or the fatherless, the alien or the poor." Where both leaders and the subjects "in their hearts do not think of evil of each other" (Zech 7:8–10 NLT). Where Nigerians do not only act religious, but they also know and accept the power that could make them godly. Where they are aware that "Religion sets criteria for judging what human beings do with their social life. It insists that not everything human beings imagine or make is good and worthwhile. It questions whether we are right to regard as valueless everything we have not made ourselves."[4] Where Nigerian youths are willing to stay away from people of "depraved minds and a counterfeit faith" (2 Tim 3:8 NLT).

We are not there yet. Instead, we are where social and moral forces are crushing the hopes of many people across the globe. In a world of thick and impenetrable social and moral darkness, scholars seem to be running out

---

4. Davis, *Religion and the Making of Society*, 22.

of adjectives to describe the level of complexity and perplexity humanity faces today. Some have even concluded that God has no business with what is going on. Others, in their pursuit of their self-interest and passion, have concluded that "God is dead." They are therefore answerable to no authority than themselves. All these are some of the pervasive and evasive ways human hostility displays its ugly head in the human race. Job's description of his generation gives a grimy and graphic picture of human hostility against fellow mankind and thereby throws light on the fact that in spite of God's seeming absence, He controls human destiny. Job asks the usual questions that humans anywhere ask when they come face to face with the reality of the brunt of human hostility:

> Why doesn't the Almighty bring the wicked to judgment?
> Why must the godly wait for Him in vain?
> Evil people steal land by moving the boundary markers.
> They steal livestock and put them in their own pastures.
> They take the orphan's donkey and demand the widow's ox as security for a loan.
> The poor are pushed off the path; the needy must hide together for safety.
> Like wild donkeys in the wilderness, the poor must spend all their time looking for food, searching even in the desert for food for their children.
> They harvest a field they do not own, and they glean in the vineyards of the wicked.
> All night they lie naked in the cold, without clothing or covering.
> They are soaked by mountain showers, and they huddle against the rocks for want of a home.
> "The wicked snatch a widow's child from her breast, taking the baby as security for a loan.
> The poor must go about naked, without any clothing. *They harvest food for others while they themselves are starving* (italic mine).
> They press out olive oil without being allowed to taste it, and they tread in the winepress as they suffer from thirst.
> The groans of the dying rise from the city, and the wounded cry for help, yet God ignores their moaning.
> "Wicked people rebel against the light. They refuse to acknowledge its ways or stay in its paths.
> The murderer rises in the early dawn to kill the poor and needy; at night he is a thief.
> The adulterer waits for the twilight, saying, "No one will see me then."

He hides his face so no one will know him.
Thieves break into houses at night and sleep in the daytime.
They are not acquainted with the light.
The black night is their morning.
They ally themselves with the terrors of the darkness.
"But they disappear like foam down a river.
Everything they own is cursed, and they are afraid to enter their
    own vineyards.
The grave consumes sinners just as drought and heat consume
    snow.
Their own mothers will forget them.
Maggots will find them sweat to eat.
No one will remember them. Wicked people are broken like a
    tree in the storm.
They cheat the woman who has no son to help her.
They refuse to help the needy widow.
"God, in His power, drags away the rich.
They may rise high, but they have no assurance of life.
They may be allowed to live in security, but God is always
    watching them.
And though they are great now, in a moment they will be gone
like all others cut off like heads of grain. (Job 24:1–24 NLT)

Hmmm, Job's questions and ours can be very misleading. Such questions have the potential of obscuring the fact that hostility is our human story, it is the narrative of all humans. So if we do not cautiously read our situation of hostility we may likely fall into the trap of making the following assumptions; both of which leads to drumming and stirring up the ego, human pride. One obvious assumption will be the feeling that "I am not in this category of humans who are in the above list." So, an "I versus them" mentality will immediately set in, and lead to pride. The second assumption is a follow up attitude of self-righteousness or holier than thou attitude. Such responses will make it extremely difficult to grasp one of the great truths revealed in the text: God is absolutely in control of human affairs and destiny (Job 24:22–24). However, people of faith who live in overwhelming, perplexing, and hostile societies are dramatically affected and shaped by the worldview of the people around them in that they sometimes relapse into a state of paranoia, despair and cynicism. This book therefore intends to help the reader grasp the whole picture of reality so that they can avoid falling into the trap of human pride, or becoming the devil incarnate!

Acknowledgments

THE JOURNEY FOR THIS book began in 2011. Langham Partnership International had decided to select thirteen of its postdoctoral scholars from the Majority World to participate in a four-year Langham International Research and Seminar Training (IRST). I was fortunate to be among those thirteen scholars selected for the first cohort of the program which took off in 2011. At the beginning of the program I set out to write a book on Christian response to the violence in Nigeria. But as I continued to research on the matter I discovered that I needed to reflect more carefully on the interaction of faith and society, particularly in a context of injustice, corruption and violence. So as I did, I have discovered that what is essentially wrong with the Nigerian society is not lack of religiosity. Rather, it is lack of a religiosity that is embedded in a conception of humanity that is rooted in God's revealed truth about the ultimate roots of human hostility. I also discovered that most books I consulted did not expose, with precision, the ultimate roots of today's hostility and the human family's full participation in the Biblical explanation of the narrative of human hostility. This book fills this gap for the benefit of the human family.

As we do so, we are aware that no one can think for all us! We must each contribute our own quarter to the big picture. That is why no work is solely the product of an individual. Rather it is a consequence of team effort, partnership, collaboration and network, it is a communal achievement. I have remarkably benefited from the insights and works of other scholars. I am overwhelmingly indebted to all the plethora of scholars who have contributed directly or indirectly to the making of this book. First and a foremost, I am profoundly and immensely grateful to those who provided the funds for the Langham International Research and Seminar Training (LIRST). I am also grateful to Prof. Jeffery Greenman who agreed to be my senior mentor during the program and after it. During the times that he was not able to be there, Dr. Ian Shaw also helped me. Secondly, I am very deeply grateful to Professor Ronald J. Sider and Christine Pohl who both carefully

xix

read the manuscript and gave me very useful editorial recommendations. Associate Professor Matthew Michael read the manuscript and made some valuable suggestions for structural improvement—thank you very much for your help. I am also very grateful to Professor Jonathan Raymond, Dr. Audu Tonga Nok and Mr. David Colvin who also read the manuscript and gave me useful suggestions for improvement. Thirdly, Donna Maxfield, Karen Hitchcock, and Wendy Appleby helped me with editing at different stages of my writing. I thank them for all their contributions. Fourthly, ECWA leadership was very kind in allowing me to finish this project. I thank the Board of Governors, management and the entire community of ECWA Theological Seminary Kagoro for supporting me and enduring my absences. My wife Sarah and the children were very kind in bearing with me each time I had to leave and be away for several weeks and months. I praise God for all of his rich graces and for the ability and health to write.

Introduction

The actions of men are the best interpreters of their thoughts.

—Locke

Nigeria's narrative of human hostility knows no monopoly. It is part and parcel of human brokenness in a world that is under siege by sin and death. This is why other contexts are mentioned in this study. Our (humans') contemporary world requires all of us, who are still living on this side of eternity, to live wisely. The reasons are not farfetched. We are surrounded by crippling terror. As this book demonstrates, this terror is in us, within us and outside of us. Human life remains a hidden paradox, elusive. No one, woman or man, living in today's global village can deny the fact that the foundations of human social and moral life are continually getting eroded. Conflicts, war and violence of alarming proportion are wrecking the only human habitable planet, the earth. How can people of faith develop a better grasp of what is happening so that in spite of what the world thinks and does, they can live their Christian life in ways that honor and please their God and Father? The first person who feels the brunt of human violence is the Creator, God. The second is the human race itself and the third is nature. So the context of violence against God, humans and nature invites Christians living in any context of hostility to do deep theological and moral reflections on how to respond.

When we (Christians) look at the magnitude of evil in our world we are often tempted to assume evil is winning. The plain truth is, in times of human crises it is extremely difficult for Christians to continue "to trust [in] the mighty power of God, who raised Christ from the dead" (Col 2:12). However, if they are to survive the danger of a hostile world, they have to cling to Christ: "Let your roots grow down into Him, and let your lives be built on Him. Then your faith will grow strong in the truth you were taught, and you will overflow with thankfulness" (Col 2:6–7). We need to remember that on the cross "He (Christ) disarmed the spiritual rulers and authorities. He shamed them publicly by His victory over them on the cross" (Col 2:15).

A major goal of this book, therefore, is to offer some basic biblical insights that will help the Christians in Nigeria and elsewhere grasp a better and more comprehensive perspective of contemporary social and moral predicaments. By so doing, they will remain humble and dependent on the mighty power of Christ who lives in their lives now. In Africa, people desperately want explanation for every human calamity. To meet this yearning, the book attempts to offer a careful explanation of what has been responsible for the hostility that the human race faces. As we will show in the first chapter, this problem has its origin in the Fall. When man and woman in defiance of God's command chose to obey the Serpent (Satan's sin inducing agent), they believed a lie: "You will be like God." From then on, self-ambition and self-advantage became part and parcel of the human nature. It is as though our DNA[5] was changed after the Fall. Today violence and war have become ingrained in our relationship with God, fellow humans and nature. Someone may say, if evil is part of our nature why then is it the case that not all of us are acting out evil? Why do only some of us react violently to scenes of evil? Evil was not originally part of our human nature. It is a foreign intruder. It is a parasite. It only corrupted and distorted our heart and mind because humans ignored the need to pay careful attention to the commands of the Creator, which the psalmist says, "The commands of the LORD are clear, giving insight for living" (Ps 19:8b).

Whenever the times are evil, the greatest challenge Christians face is securing and safeguarding their Christology (faith in Christ), theology (trust in God) and sustaining their moral vision. What should matter most to a Christian living in a hostile community or society? That is, what is of topmost priority in the Christian life? Based on the biblical discourses of Christ Jesus of Nazareth, his apostles and their co-workers or imitators, one's faith is the foremost precious and valuable asset to be safeguarded against the hostility of the world. Christian faith in Christ is the incomparably great asset that must be tenaciously safeguarded:

5. The scientific meaning of DNA is that it is, "A nucleic acid that carries the generic information in cells and some viruses, consisting of two long chains of nucleotides twisted into a double helix and joined by hydrogen bonds between the complementary bases adenine and thymine or cytosine and guanine" (*American Heritage Dictionary of the English Language*). DNA is simply "a nucleic acid that is the main constituent of the chromosomes of all organisms," which explains their fundamental essence. It is our genetic code and the biochemical basis of heredity and nearly universal in all organisms.

> And now, just as you accepted Christ Jesus as your Lord, you must continue to follow Him. Let your roots grow down into Him, and let your lives be built on Him. Then your faith will grow strong in the truth you were taught, and you will overflow with thanksgiving. (Col 2:6–7)

To safeguard their faith in Christ in difficult times, Christians need to grasp the larger social, economic, political and religious contexts of their generation. The operating and reigning psychology and theology of the day must be grasped. For example, they must try to ask, what is going on in the minds of the perpetuators of excessive evil? Oppressors and the oppressed are engaged in a common phenomenon: They think, reason and conduct themselves according to the assumptions and conclusion they draw from such processes. These assumptions and conclusions then determine their public behaviors and conducts. The summary of the problem of hostility is: Humans assume that they are gods. The psalmist puts his finger where the problem of mankind lies when he said, "The wicked are too proud to seek God. They seem to think that God is dead" (Ps 10:4).

Pride is the root problem of human perpetuation of violent conflict and hostilities across the world. Pride drives humans into conflict with God and with one another. There is an observable pattern which they follow: think, reason, and conduct or act out the assumed conclusions. Humans are deceived by their mindsets: worldview, belief and behavior. "They seem to think that . . . 'Nothing bad will ever happen to us! We will be free of trouble forever!' . . . The wicked think, 'God isn't watching us! He has closed His eyes and won't ever see what we do!'" (Ps 10:4, 6, 11). Then, the next pattern is they speak out their minds. What they speak is deadly: "Their mouths are full of cursing, lies, and threats. Trouble and evil are on the tips of their tongues" (Ps 10:7). They do not only speak out their threats but also act them out: "They lurk in ambush in the villages, waiting to murder innocent people. They are always searching for helpless victims. Like lions crouched in hiding, they wait to pounce on the helpless. Like hunters they capture the helpless and drag them away in nets. Their helpless victims are crushed; they fall beneath the strength of the wicked" (Ps 10:7–10). They act this way because they had thought and now have a rationalized conclusion: "God isn't watching us! He has closed His eyes and won't even see what we do!" (Ps 10:11).

In this book, we argue that human hostility shapes believer or unbeliever. This seems to be one of the gaps in scholars' interpretation of what is happening. For instance, in a book on Islam and Pluralism, the author states, "The history of the world's religions is full of horrible tales of persecution and intolerance. Often times the religious opposition to the beliefs of a people has been used to serve colonialist purposes, as in the treatment of Native American peoples by Christian Europeans."[6] The quote illustrates a secular notion that religion only promotes violence. Of course, colonialists did use religion to justify their evil. Yet, religion is not where evil comes from. This statement is an example of how lack of looking beyond these sentiments has hindered a deeper exposure of the human condition. This book undertakes to expound the fundamental questions of how Christians living in hostile societies should wrestle with and thereby provide authoritative norms for establishing the morality of particular human actions. Part of its intent is to answer the question: What is good and evil? How must Christian moral theologians and ethicists interpret the current situation of hostility across the globe? What is the implication of Christian salvation in the context of hostility? The book offers a commentary on the nature and scope of hostility in the contemporary world with the hope of helping the reader to develop a better and richer perspective on the questions of moral conduct and the implications of Christian salvation.

This book is written in honour of all those whose daily experience is like living a second between death and life. We strive to help Nigerian Christians, and indeed all Christians living in hostile societies to understand how to survive, grow and experience the joy of their faith in spite of such enormous contexts of crippling fear and hopelessness. On this basis, we hope that not only Christians living in such social realities, but also every Christian across the globe will still find it reasonably possible to take pride in their Lord and Savior Jesus to the extent that they conduct themselves in a manner that benefits the Good News about Jesus Christ.

The second purpose of the book is to ask and attempt to examine the question, what could we (humans) be missing in "the war against terror?" A notion that has developed and has gradually become part of our vocabulary in the 21st century is that certain people, and not all, are "prone to evil." We need an alternative narrative to this notion, which will help us to better grasp the fact that terror is an indictment against the human race. If history has anything to teach us, we will all agree that hostility is our human narrative. All human beings are inclined to evil, not just some. However, if we (humans) stop there, we will not grasp the whole narrative of humans: creation and Fall. Based on the first three chapters of Genesis, evil entered the human race through Adam and Eve. So, the correct notion, as we will demonstrate in this book, is that all human beings are capable of both good

---

6. Legenhausen, *Islam and Religious Pluralism*, 1.

and evil. This for us is a better and a more comprehensive assessment of human history. All human beings have the capacity of being hostile and destructive. Of course, these capacities vary; at certain times they are more obvious (explicit) in some and more hidden (implicit) in others.

This book addresses this important gap in the interpretation of the reality of human hostility, violence and destruction. We realize that lack of grasping this gap has led to this situation: The human race is self-deceived and self-destroyed. The world population hit 7,324,782,000 in 2015.[7] Over the years, we can ascertain that as the population increases so also human hostility has tremendously multiplied. That is why, in spite of all the intelligent and creative efforts of human rights advocates, the United Nations (the vanguard and custodian of global human rights), says human hostility has defied simple solution. This is majorly because humans have believed half-truths about the causes of hostility. These half-truths have been packaged nicely in the choice of terms we use to interpret what is happening, which include among other names: religion, ethnicity, identity, tribalism, racism, economy, islamophobia, politics and so on and so forth. The human race, particularly people of faith are paying the price of a belief in half-truth. In this book we argue that human social and moral dilemma has their roots in the biblical narrative of the creation and the Fall of man and woman. In the Genesis account, all humans are descendants of Adam and Eve. All of us humans have, therefore, acquired two natures: good and evil, dignity and depravity. On the evil side of our humanity are: self-interest, deception and lust for power. The summary is pride. That is the immoral behaviour that produces human hostility, resulting in horrific violent and destruction. On the good side of our humanity are: love, right living, compassion, gentleness, making allowances for the faults of others, patience, goodness, peace, joy, kindness, respect for human freedom and so on.

To reduce or even stop violent destruction in our world the true roots of human hostility and violence must be unraveled. For centuries, religious rhetoric and other nouns and adjectives have been employed to cover up the true origins of human social and moral problems. For example, some claim "After centuries of religious persecution, injustice and disregard for human rights, the acceptance of human rights enshrined in the law is one of the greatest achievements of modern history." [8] This is a half-truth! By "religious persecution, injustice and disregard for human rights," the author of the above quote alludes to theistic religion as the problem. This argument

7. "World 2015," populationpyramid.net, http://populationpyramid.net/world/. Accessed March 28, 2015.

8. Gary Saul Marson, "Foreword," xii, in Soloviev, *Politics, Law and Morality*.

is problematic. For one thing, it ignores the positive contribution theistic religion has made to the development of the idea of universal human rights. It also shows a remarkable ignorance of the general problem of humanity: obsessive self-interest, deception and lust for power. If theistic religion is the problem how then can we account for the fact that in spite of the enshrinement of human rights in the United Nations International Laws of the 1940s, our century has been "the bloodiest in human history, and those responsible for the blood have [often] been atheists who explicitly rejected any religious based idea that individual human life is sacred."[9] The problem is not religion, politics, or any other names that men and women have fashioned to keep out of sight the fundamental human ingrained and embedded problem of self-interest, deception and lust for power.

To believe that religion is the source of human woes is to believe half-truths. These half-truths have cost the Nigeria society the unity and integration it desperately desired. Nigerians have continued to play the ostrich to real human cancer: self-interest, deception and the lust for power by trying to use other names to explain away these realities. A case in point is the continuing agitation for the control of oil resources by the Niger-Delta militants and the Boko Haram Shari'a agitation in Northern Nigeria. Money and religion do affect these conflicts. But we argue that these social and moral dilemmas can only be adequately explained by the fact that self-interest, deception and lust for power shape and permeate all human socio-political, socio-economic and socio-religious aggressions. That is where they are embedded. Scriptures point to the fact that human self-interest, self-love, self-passion, and lust for power are the deep rooted social and moral issues at stake. They are products of human pride. The psalmist calls self-interest and the lust for power "HIDDEN FAULTS" and their resultant pride "GREAT SIN" (Ps 19:12–13). In Nigeria, this great sin has continued to cause disunity and destruction of lives and property. A former Minister of Finance and Coordinating Minister of the Economy during President Goodluck Ebele Jonathan administration, Dr. Mrs. Ngozi Okonjo-Iweala puts it succinctly,

> Nigeria has always been complex to govern . . . British colonialists and Nigerian politicians regularly exploited ethnic, religious (Christian, Muslim) and regional differences to divide the country rather than to build a nation. As a result, tensions abounded in the early days of the country. These tensions led to [a] series of military coups in 1966–67 and ultimately to a civil war—the Nigeria-Biafra war.[10]

9. Ibid.

10. Okonjo-Iweala, *Reforming the Unreformable*, 1–2.

These tensions are products of human self-interest, deception and the lust for power. But because we hardly recognize this let alone are willing to confess our weaknesses and repent of our malice and wickedness, the tensions have continued unabated. Human actions, either positive or negative are produced by thoughts. Evil thoughts produce evil actions! We overcome the captivity of self-interest and the lust for power by constant self-criticism and self-repentance. To do so, the psalmist asks a big and a very important question: "How can I know all the sins lurking in my heart?" (Ps 19:12a). Pride originated from the heart of Lucifer, Satan or the devil. The word "lurking" is the same word that God used when He warned Cain of an impending sin if he does not watch out and "do the right thing"(Gen 4:6).

In sum, human beings are caught in the crossfire of a reckless being, Satan, pursuing its excessive self-ambition and an extreme desire to usurp God's right to worship and praise. Those who still reserve a sense of dignity and respect for God are left with the question that Job asks: "Why do the wicked prosper, growing old and powerful? And yet they say to God, 'Go away. We want no part of you and your ways. Who is the Almighty, and why should we obey Him? What good will it do us to pray?' (They think their prosperity is of their own doing, but I will have nothing to do with that kind of thinking)."[11] This is the worst case scenario of human pride. But there are those who actually claim to worship and obey the living and true God; yet, they indirectly behave in the same way like those who say to God "Go away. We don't want to have anything to do with you."[12] Indeed, the general human unwillingness to recognize and reverence God as Lord of their lives makes the earth a hostile region of God's realm. This situation calls for the need to arm Christians with a mindset or a perspective that serves as an antibody to their sinful inclinations and actions in the world. To this we will turn in the chapters that follow.

An Overview of the Book

The method or procedure needs to be set out clearly. We take the approach first of social and historical analysis of the context; then seek to develop a normative ethical framework and a biblical exegesis of some Biblical passages which shed light on the big picture of the main thrust of the book. We approach the work from the perspective of integration. Thus our reading of Genesis, Isaiah, and Acts of the Apostles is that of an ethicist rather than a Biblicist, but it is animated by the desire to help fill in the gap that separates

11. Job 21:7, 14–16 NLT
12. Stob, *Ethical Reflections*, 3.

theology from exegesis today. It provides a preliminary outline which hope-fully will orient other readings and generate reflection on one of the most basic theological problems of our times: to reestablish the relation between faith and practice, so that the dichotomy between them gets collapsed.[13]

The book is divided into three parts. Part one seeks to unmask the truth. The first four chapters are devoted to that purpose. Chapter 1 seeks to open the discussion by placing human hostility where it belongs: The paradox of mankind. All humans, in respective of their race, creed and so on, possess in their essence dignity and depravity, good and evil. We (Chris-tians, Muslims, atheist, Indigenous religionists, etc.) are all capable of doing tremendous good and at the same time capable of committing tremendous evil. Dignity and depravity are our essence. Chapter 2 discusses the reality of hostility in the context of Nigeria's socio-communal crises, which raises theological questions which we address in chapter 3. Chapter 4 discusses the nature and scope of Nigeria's faith communities'—African Indigenous Religion, Islam and Christianity—theological and ideological interactions.

Part two seeks to unmask the current falsehood. Chapters 5 to chap-ter 7 are devoted to that discourse. Chapter 5 discusses and analyzes the myth of violence as redemptive and contrasts it with suffering as redemp-tive. Isaiah's Servant Songs are examined to explain how suffering becomes redemptive rather than the myth of violence becoming redemptive. African presence in some of the scenes of violence is also discussed in this chapter. Chapter 6 argues that the concept of tribe and tribalism is not the cause of human social and moral crises in Africa. Chapter 7 draws attention of the reader to the importance of just peacemaking and its ability to prevent the breeding of insurgents.

Part three seeks to unmask the disguising power of the mission of the church in the midst of human hostility. The last seven chapters of the book are devoted to this subject. Chapter 8 provides a brief reflective reading of Acts of the Apostle from the perspective of the Nigerian situation of perse-cution. It pays attention to the evasive schemes of Satan in those scenes of distraction. The early churchlived wisely. They were always aware of Satan's schemes and were able to resist the temptation to stop the proclamation of the Good News. Chapter 9 focuses on a theological reflection on how Nige-rian Pentecostals and Charismatics epitomize how lack of paying attention to Satan's schemes can cause missiological shipwreck. Chapter 10 discusses the need for a grassroots focus on social justice, particularly, restorative justice, as a panacea for insurgency. It argues that the insurgents are mem-bers of our communities and we should do everything possible to bring

13. Pinkares, *The Sources of Christian Ethics*, 109.

them back to the human family. It takes a cue from the attitude of nursing mother to her violent child. Nursing mothers who get bitten on their
breasts or punched in the face by their nursing babies do not throw them
away. The insurgents are members of our community but they are hurting
us we need to think creatively and intelligently on ways we can get them off
the hook of excessive evil. "Ex-terrorists need rehabilitation and restoration
into participating communities. We argue that Nigerians Muslims should
take a cue from Saudi Arabia that has now created a program to re-educate
extremists about the peaceful principles of Islam and reintegrate them to
mainstream Saudi society. Chapter 11 discusses the seedbeds and models
of just peacemaking in Nigeria by drawing the reader's attention to the
ministry of Bishop Samuel Ajayi Crowther and other contemporary efforts
in Kaduna and Jos cities respectively. Chapter 12 addresses the question of
whether Christians can possibly engage in self-defense. The chapter suggests just self-defense as a possibility. In chapter 13, we discuss and stress the
need for Nigerian Christians to see the mission of the church as a just self-
defense. Chapter 14 describes what the quest for self-defense really mean
to a Christian community that prioritizes mission and the propagation of
the kingdom of God. Chapter 15 discusses how Christian eschatology holds
hope for a persecuted church like the church in Northern Nigeria.

Listening to debates by both Muslims and Christians about the potential sources of war and violence has helped me to realize that we need a better explanation. It is generally assumed that violence is outside the human
race. One can easily pick this assumption in phrases like, "Christianity and
Islam preach and teach peace, not violent conflict or terrorism." But where
does violence come from? The premise upon which this argument is built
is faulty. It is clear that both Christians and Muslims are clueless about the
sources of violent conflicts and wars. Although it is claimed that the two
Abrahamic religions do not teach their adherents violence, we nonetheless
have terrorism and other forms of violence ruining our world. Basically, the
assumption is that violence is outside us. This belief has hindered us from
realizing that violence is part of our fallen nature. This book argues that
religion does not have to preach and teach violence. Violence is right inside
us. We must therefore stop using religion as scapegoat. We must especially
stop naturalistic humanists from seeing religion as the cause of all forms of
terrorism and violent conflict across the globe.

Part 1

UNMAKING THE TRUTH

It has been said that humans are political animals. But we have uncritically accepted the axiom without realizing its far-reaching implication. If we had, we would have long discovered that the human species is the socially insecure and politically jealous and aggressive animal on planet earth. The human story of hostility needs to be exposed and be documented. Part 1 sets out to do exactly that. It focuses on the exposition of the ingrained roots of human hostility with the hope that that will help the human race to recognize its place in the present state of social and moral evil.

Chapter 1

Whose View of Human Hostility Matters?

THIS BOOK PROVIDES AN elaboration of Christian commitment to Jesus Christ and its implications for the broken and decaying world in which Christians live alongside other faiths. As Paul K. Jewett explained, Christian theology is a believing thought which "reflects commitment to Christ as well as reflection upon the implications of that commitment" to other faiths in the human race.[1] With the crises of world faiths—religious communities deeply engage in sociopolitical, socioeconomic and violent clashes on our global world—Christians across the globe need to think carefully, deeply and theologically about just ways of countering violent aggression. Our world is infested with "ideologically-fueled violence."[2] However, we are not only dealing with ideology but also with competing cultural myths and theological perspectives that have traditionally governed the lives of their adherents for centuries. Yet we do not stop to ask, for example, what does God think about terrorism in the world? He obviously grieves over sin and terrorism.

The author of this book has realized that no one person can think for all us. We must each contribute our own quarter to the big picture of what it means to live as people of diverse faith in this only habitable planet, earth. I am glad that the burden of solving the world's problem of revolutionary terror is the collective responsibility of all Nigerians (Muslims, Christians

1. Jewett, *God, Creation, & Revelation*, 5.

2. This expression, "Ideological-fueled violence," was used by Georgia Holmer, Senior Program Officer at the United States Institute of Peace (USIP), while presenting her views at the Conflict Prevention and Resolution Forum in Washington, DC, July 8, 2014.

and Traditionalists). So I see myself dancing in the company of others who have gone before me or are currently here now or will be in the future.

I am aware that at the turn of the new Millennium, many scholarly works have been published on the subject of religious violence and the factors that encourage it. Charles Kimball, writing after September 11, believes that the primary reason for religion becoming an instrument of evil is because its adherents believe in absolute truth. He writes, "Religious ideologies and commitments are indisputably central factors in the escalation of violence and evil around the world."[3] He further notes how the holy books are a major source of the problem: "The Qur'an and the *Hadith* materials make clear that Muslims can and sometimes should take up arms in defense of Islam."[4] Consequently, Kimball concludes, "Grave dangers facing the world community demand focused, intentional, and persistent "striving" together for peace and justice."[5]

There is some truth in Kimball's argument. But I am less satisfied with his conclusion. If the person believes in absolute truth and I do not believe that, how then can I dialogue with such a person? Kimball argues that the solution to absolute truth is to persuade us, people of faith, to reject the idea of absolute truth. But that is impossible, at least in Africa. I dare say that the premise for his argument is faulty. In Africa, both Islam and Christianity hold sway. The adherents of both religions hold tenaciously to the doctrine of absolute truth. Therefore if one begins by denying the existence of absolute truth one loses the credentials for further discussion because no one will pay any attention to what one has to offer. As such, my approach is to help Christians and Muslims as well as traditionalists reflect deeply on their theological stance and how their shared values and understanding can help them recreate a peaceful and a just environment for moral, economic and political aspirations to thrive to the service of human transformation and flourishing.

Harvey Sindima, in his work, *Religious and Political Ethics in Africa*, demonstrates a fine grasp of the embedded factors which encourage religious crises in Africa. He explores the internal and external rivalries which exist between Christianity and Islam in Africa. Both religions have become indigenous to Africa since their early days. He argues that the two religions have different political and religious orientations. On the one hand, Western Christianity, which was introduced to African by Western missionaries, preaches the doctrine of the separation of religion and public life. On the

3. Kimball, *When Religion Becomes Evil*, 4.

4. Ibid., 176.

5. Ibid., 185.

contrary, Islam, like the African indigenous religions, believes that there is no separation of mosque and state. As such, "Islam is a political, economic, and religious force in Africa." He draws his readers' attention to the significant present of Islam on the African continent.[6] Nigeria is among the African countries which have a fair share of Muslim populations. Yet, unlike other African countries such as Northern Sudan, Senegal and Libya, Nigeria cannot be regarded as a Muslim state in Africa. Instead, Nigeria should be considered as a multireligious country with a secular constitution that serves as a bridge between Muslims, African Traditional Religionists and Christianity.[7]

This fact shows the enormous factors militating against the desire for peace and justice in Africa. Both Christianity and Islam are fundamentally missionary faiths. They view each other as rivals, foes, instead of friends, partners. The way each of the groups sees the *other* gives room for mistrust, hatred and destruction. Sindima identifies a number of factors which prevent mutual coexistence between the followers of these religions. He states that they have had difficulty relating with each other: Historically, Christians and Muslims have considered each other infidels to be conquered and controlled.[8]

I would argue that this demonstrates the embarrassing reality of our fallen and broken world. Religion as faith in a transcendent Being does not automatically made us immune to "self-interest and the will to power." Humans seem to be under the grip of competition, rivalry, and the use of violent language toward fellow humans and God. That is why serious stereotyping is the order of the day amongst the two missionary religions in Africa. To compound issues, Nigerian Muslims like their counterparts across the Muslim world hate Western capitalism and materialism. And since Christianity in Africa was brought by Western missionaries from capitalist countries Muslims tend to associate Nigerian Christians with materialism.[9]

Suffice it to say that a lot of assumptions and misconceptions about each other characterize the relationships of the different faiths in Nigeria. One of these assumptions is the comparison of Nigerian Christians with the West and its so-called liberal culture, *amoral culture*. To some extent, Sindima's assertion above provides a key understanding of the major challenge that Nigerian Christians must face: Proving beyond reasonable doubts that Nigerian Christians are not amoral. There is a sense in which Nigerian

---

6. Sindima, *Religious and Political Ethics in Africa*, 139.

7. Paden, *Faith and Politics in Nigeria*, 23.

8. Sindima, *Religious and Political Ethics in Africa*, 141.

9. Ibid.

Muslims are deeply concerned about righteousness and justice in society because they want stability and security. In that case, Nigerian Christians need to convince their Muslim neighbors that they also want morality and social justice because that is what the Bible and Christian ethics teaches. Genuine Christians are not amoral. Therefore, Nigerian Christians need to take heed to Peter's admonition: "Dear friends, I urge you, as foreigners and exiles, to abstain from sinful desires, which war against your soul. Live such good lives among the pagans that, though they accuse you of doing wrong, they may see your good deeds and glorify God on the day he visits us" (1 Pet 2:11–12). In as much as I agree with Sindima, I will argue that Christians have always been persecuted because of the fact that they are seen to represent a worldview that is negative toward society in general. The early church was persecuted for the same reason in the Roman Empire.

Sindima has helped us to understand that Islam was rooted in Africa prior to the coming of Christianity and colonialism. He points out that *Jihad* [Islamic holy war] has been a major source of Islam's growth in Africa, particularly in Nigeria.[10] But I think it is naïve to believe that this is the only primary concern. In this book we must identify something beyond what Sindima assumes. We must investigate other historical facts which are contributing to the incessant violence in Nigeria. Why, for instance, would Nigerian Muslims not see themselves as cousins to other non-Muslim Nigerians but instead see themselves as close cousins with the Arabs?

On the whole, Sindima's work is very important to our efforts in grappling with the situation in Nigeria. It provides a richer background of how adherents of both religions see each other. It will help me to then see what needs to be done to dislodge the threat. But this book attempts to go beyond just historical factors that lead to present situation of violence between Christians and Muslim in Nigeria to include the effect this violence is having on the Christian church itself.

Simeon O. Ilesanmi sees misconception of religious diversity or pluralism as the major problem in Nigeria. He thinks that both Christians and Muslims have failed to grasp the pluralist nature of the Nigerian society. The political biases of the state and its security agencies have contributed to the difficulty. This is the primary reason why evil persists, leading to the destruction of lives and property.[11] He lamented how intellectuals in the academia, by their choice of continuous silence in the face of political injustice, have failed to fill the vacuum created by the state's one-sidedness.[12] Ilesanmi's

10. Ibid.

11. Ilesanmi, *Religious Pluralism and the Nigerian State,* xx.

12. Ibid., xxviii.

work provides us with the means to stress the importance of coexistence. One assumption that is clear from the present circumstance is the idea of having an independent space to flourish and dominate all others. My book attempts to make it categorically clear that both Islam and Christianity cannot possibly enjoy autonomy in the Nigerian social and economic context. Using Ilesanmi's analysis of our pluralistic context, this book underscores the importance of religious freedom, and that the lack of it is the major source of violence. I will argue, both Muslims and Christians need to understand that in a global village no one can stand alone or dominate everyone. We therefore need each other. I like Ilesanmi's work. Nevertheless, his usage or conception of pluralism is not very clear to me. We will need to make sure that pluralism as a term and a concept is explicated in the chapter on the interaction of religion, theology and politics in Nigeria.

Rotgak I. Gofwen (*Religion and Peacebuilding in Northern Nigeria*, 2004) argues that religion plays a vital role in nation building and political development. But with the current religious crisis he sees grave danger: "Religion has become dangerously fused into the nation's body polity, and today has becomes a major centrifugal force threatening the nation . . ."[13] The end result is that it has earned Nigeria the reputation of being commonly "listed among countries in which the chances of a religious war are quite high."[14] Gofwen then catalogues the horrific Muslim and Christian conflicts that have happened in Nigeria. His approach to this issue underlines the impact of violence on the church's mission and theology. My approach similarly, focuses on the impact of violence on church mission and theology and his historical analysis of the events will be helpful.

In the above reviewed literatures, I have noticed a general absence of the role of government policies and implementation in the scheme of things. By government, I mean pre-colonial, colonial and post-colonial governance in Nigeria. I have also noticed a salient lack of paying attention to the African culture, particularly African religiosity, which may also be contributing to the worldview of violence and revenge. These issues must be included in the study of violence and the way forward.

John N. Paden in his work, *Muslim Civic Cultures and Conflict Resolution*, has drawn the attention of African scholars to the need to reclaim the African cultural heritage in the service of human flourishing in the continent. Paden believes that what Nigerians are experiencing is the crisis of relationship. However, the crisis of relationship is not peculiar to Nigerians; it is a global concern. He writes "A crisis of confidence is emerging in the

---

13. Gofwen, *Religion and Peacebuilding in Northern Nigeria*, 6.
14. Ibid.

relations between the Western and Muslim worlds, especially in the aftermath of September 11, 2001."[15] He puts the blame on political leaders in our
world who have failed to educate their people to understand what the issues
are, particularly, "The reality of today's globalizing, interdependent world,
which has clearly entered a new era in international relations."[16] He therefore asserts that what is crucial to a successful war on terrorism is a mutual
understanding of issues at stake. One of the issues he identified is the fact
that "Power politics of the might-makes-right variety are hardly sufficient to
assess the root causes of mistrust and often produce negative reactions that
hinder constructive engagement."[17] Peacemaking is about just engagement
with the other. If we do not understand what the true issues are we cannot
grasp the way to the path of peace, love and justice. Thus
zeroing down on the Nigerian context, Paden believes that the Nigerian government and its people have to realize the pluralistic nature of our cultures
and religions and have the political will to entertain the idea "of multiple
jurisprudential systems (or alternative dispute resolution systems), since the
desire of justice is at the heart of many current grievances exploding into
violent conflict."[18] Paden draws our attention to the fact that the Muslim
community in Nigeria is rooted and rested on a wide variety of cultural
and historical legacies that have over the years been challenged and reforms
been sought.[19]

    In spite of the fact that Nigerian Muslims seem not to connect with
non-Muslim Nigerians, the fact still remains, Nigeria's form of Islam rests
on a solid foundation of African cultural traditions. Paden believes therefore that "there are probably more commonalities among Nigerian ethnoreligious groups than differences."[20] These commonalities need to be explored
so as to ascertain the shared core and concrete values that could be enough
to move us forward and away from a world of failing morality. Paden's conclusion is that what we are experiencing are fundamentally two things: [1]
the forces of religious globalization and [2] reaction to the extreme forms of
secularism that emerged during the cold war; I would add that we need to
pay a critical attention to corruption which illustrates how money trumps
other important social and moral values in Nigeria.

---

15. Paden, *Muslim Civic Cultures and Conflict Resolution*, 16.

16. Ibid.

17 Ibid., 16–17.

18 Ibid., 17.

19. Ibid.

20 Ibid.

Nigerians (Christians, Muslims and African indigenous religions) are slowly learning how to grapple with the different orientations that are driving our postmodern civilization. The old is dying and the new is being born. This is why Paden's work is very critical in helping us to see the need to pay attention to the African traditions and cultures that can help in the effort of grappling with engagement with the *other*. I will argue that there is a need to revisit the traditional means of ensuring that justice works for the benefit of human flourishing at the community grassroots level.

Needless to say the larger perspective of my book allows us to pay attention to what God is doing in our world. It is important to also say that Christianity is a relational faith. That is why we are not surprised to note that in Luke's account of Jesus' ministry after the resurrection, Jesus spent forty consecutive days talking to his disciples "about the Kingdom of God" (Acts 1:3,) the in-breaking of the reign of God. Paden talks about the need for African scholars and theologians to reclaim the African cultural heritage. Based on an understanding of God's reign in all spheres of life, Nigerian Christians can and should pay attention to what God is doing in other faith adherents that are their neighbors. This include, among other things, talking about how African cultures perceive justice and what methods they use to institute justice in grassroots community. Since just Peacemaking is one of the main themes of my book I attempt to see how African culture and Christian theology could provide us with an understanding of the cultural methodology for just peacemaking. This concern has necessitated a chapter on the seedbeds and models of just peacemaking in Nigeria from Bishop Samuel Ajayi Crowther to date.

Nigerian cultures have been significantly shaped not only through engaging with the traditional worldviews but also with the two Abrahamic faiths in Africa—Christianity and Islam. In this case, Nigeria provides a good illustration of the reality of God's reign at work. God has orchestrated the amalgamation of diverse ethno-cultural and ethnoreligious communities into one entity call Nigeria. Grasping this reality is very critical in our search for a resolution of the impasses we continue to face as a people living under one habitable planet, earth. Suffice it to say that *just peacemaking* is talking about the church and its interaction *with* and participation *in* the kingdom of God. Jesus' ministry stresses the importance of human integration and unity in spite of diversity and the temptation to use our difference as a political tool to trample down on other fellow humans in order to climb to the perceived top of the political ladder. Such self-centered attitudes cause frictions, mistrust and hatred. Thus, for Jesus, just peacemaking was nonnegotiable. After his resurrection, in two specific occasions when he appeared to his disciples, he uses the phrase, "Peace be with you" (John 20:19,

26.) During his earthly ministry, Jesus preached and taught much about the kingdom of God. For example, the prayer he taught his disciples to pray, when they asked him to teach them how to pray was a prayer that will constantly keep them abreast with the reality of the in breaking of the Kingdom of God as well as cause them to remember that the kingdom of God is their priority. He furthermore says, "Seek the kingdom of God above all else, and *live righteously*, and he will give you everything you need" (Matt 6:33).

The church is central in Christ's concept of the kingdom of God and its theology. The church is his body and is created to live out the will of God on earth, in spite of the state of affairs. That is why Paul links God's incredible power with the resurrection of Jesus and the final surrendering of all things and authority under Jesus' feet: "Now he is far above any ruler or authority or power or leader or anything else-not only in this world but also in the world to come. God has put all things under the authority of Christ and has made Him head over all things for the benefit of the church. And the church is his body; it is made full and complete by Christ, who fills all things everywhere with Himself" (Eph 1:19–23). Prior to what St. Paul says in Ephesians, Jesus has announced this to his disciples: "Jesus came and told His disciples, 'I have been given all authority in heaven and on earth'" (Matt 28:18). So Ephesians is a commentary on Matthew 28:18. No one who is a savvy reader of the Bible will miss this truth about the centrality of the kingdom of God. So our just peacemaking effort is under the bigger picture of the kingdom of God, the reign of Christ over all of life, cultures, religions, political systems, economic systems and everything we can imagine in the entire creation.

The discourse on human hostility cannot be complete without a brief account of the historic theories of responses to violence and war. In the history of Christianity and the world of politics two responses have dominated the debate about the ethics of war and violence: Pacifism and just war theories. Of course, there has been the case of *holy war* (crusades) as part of the Christian response too. But in the 1990s a group of 23 ethicists and theologians introduced a new category, just peacemaking. The late Glen Harold Stassen played a significant role in launching this initiative. In their book, *Kingdom Ethics,* Glen Harold Stassen and David Gushee in 2003 introduced an important category into the discussion of pacifism and just war theories which has been with the church since the times of Augustine of Hippo. The concept of *just peacemaking* brings a rich category to the issue of war and conflict. Prof. Stassen is among acclaimed Christian ethicists, theologians, and experts in conflict resolution who have produced this relatively new and promising initiative—an additional option to appropriate response to war and conflict violence: the just peacemaking paradigm.

In this paradigm the focus shifts to initiatives that can help prevent war/violence and foster peace. In the wake of cold war and terrorism, Stassen was among the scholars and activists who developed ten key practices and detailed guidelines for peacemaking. Below are ten ways of dislodging vicious cycles of violence in the world which the scholars and ethicists developed in the 1990s: (1) Support nonviolent direct action; (2) Take independent initiatives to reduce threat; (3) Use cooperative conflict resolution; (4) Acknowledge responsibility for conflict and injustice and seek repentance and forgiveness; (5) Advance democracy, human rights, and religious liberty; (6) Foster just and sustainable economic development; (7) Work with emerging cooperative forces in the international system; (8) Strengthen the United Nations and international efforts for cooperation and human rights; (9) Reduce offensive weapons and weapons trade; and (10) Encourage grassroots peacemaking groups and voluntary association.

Stassen and Gushee argue that the theories of *Pacifism* and *Just War* needed an added dimension: "just peacemaking." The doctrine of just peacemaking provides a win-win situation. It recognizes that each side of the conflict needs to be assured of justice in order to ensure sustainable peace. Just peacemaking as a practice has a strong emphasis on ensuring that both parties receive justice. It clarifies the essence of nonviolent direct action. My book explores how Nigerian Christians could learn from these practices tangible ways of engaging their Muslim neighbors in just peacemaking practices.

Walter Wink, in his work, *Engaging the Powers,* a biblical theologian demonstrates a fine grasp of the meaning of "turn the other cheek." Both Wink and Stassen believe that Jesus is not teaching passivity but activity. I appreciate their interpretation because it fits the social and political contexts of Palestine in the times of Jesus Christ of Nazareth. Since my approach is interdisciplinary, I use their methods and principles and those of other ethicists and theologians like Jan H. Boer, Toyin Falola, Jürgen Moltmann, De Gruchy, Desmond Tutu, Martin Luther King Jr., Mahatma Gandhi, etc., to provide answers to the questions the church in Nigeria is asking.

In conclusion, the study of human hostility is the study of human aggressive and excessive violence.[21] A helpful approach to the study of violence is to recognize that religious motivated violence does not happen in a vacuum. It is often a reaction to some perceived threat to a passion or a desire. Violence is often labelled ethnic, political or religious because the people that fight or perpetuate violence are often members of an ethnic, a political or a religious community of faith or claim to be members of a

---

21. Greider, *Reckoning with Aggression*, 25–26.

particular community. Sometimes, approaching the issue from this apparent reality tends to hinder a richer grasp of the ultimate reality of violence. Few scholars have been able to get past "the thinking box" to the ultimate reality of the matter of human hostility. Our book has discovered the critical mass: the gap that needs to be filled if we must correctly interpret our modern phenomenon of human hostilities across the globe. To this missing link we turn in the chapter that follows.

Chapter 2

How Evil Entered the Human Race
The Bible and Human History

*The somber fact is that we are the cruelest and most
ruthless species that has ever walked the earth; and
that, although we may recoil in horror when we read in
newspaper or history book of the atrocities committed by
man upon man, we know in our hearts that each of us
harbors within himself those same savage impulses which
lead to murder, to torture and to war.*

—Anthony Storr, *Human Aggression*

Introduction

Human hostility strives because human beings ignored God's will for their lives. The rejection of God's will breeds violent conflicts. Furthermore, whenever there is no peace God's justice gets ignored. We hardly catch the deceit or impure motives or trickery that goes on in times of war. The war against terror is not an exception. During times of violence and war, our elites and government officials tend to take advance of the state of agitation to perpetuate corruption. Nigeria is one of the countries in the globe where this is true. We live in a country where the political elites assume:

"political power brings much favour." They see it as an opportunity to si-phon public money to their private bank accounts. From May 29, 1999 to May 29, 2015, Nigerian people enjoyed uninterrupted democratic rule. Ironically, during the same period, Nigerians experienced unprecedented bloodshed, which was largely caused by corruption at every level of the so-ciety. Government officials and elites perpetuated corruption at the highest level of society. For example, there were governors whose corruption and money laundering cases were still pending at the time of People Democratic Party (PDP) handing over to All Progressive Congress (APC) on May 29, 2015. These governors included both Christians and Muslims—Mr. Joshua Chibi Dariye (Plateau State), Mr. Boni Haruna (Adamawa State), Mr. James Ibori (Delta State), Mr. Adebayo Alao-Akala (Oyo State), Rev. Jolly Nyame (Taraba State), Mr. Orji Kalu (Abia State), Mr. Bbega Daniel (Ogun State, Mr. Saminu Turaki (Jigawa State), and Mr. Rasheed Ladoja (Oyo State). As of June 2015, some of them were still wanted by UK Metropolitan Police for money laundering. For example, Mr. Joshua Chibi Dariye faces charges of stealing $128 million from Plateau State and Mr. Diepreye Alamieyeseigha for laundering to the tune of £1.8 million among other funds he stole from Bayelsa State.[1] Corruption is one of the worst forms of human hostility. It gives birth to terrorism on global scale.

However, we need to go beyond looking at Nigeria's fundamental problem of corruption from a myopic perspective. For it is easy to look at the above cases of corruption and conclude that the rest of us are innocent of corruption. Many Nigerians talk about corruption as if they are innocent victims of its perpetuators, government officials and the elites. This chapter seeks to correct this wrong impression. It situates Nigeria in the general his-tory of humanity with a view of grasping the fact that what is happening in the country is part and parcel of the human narrative. Nigeria's corruption narrative and its resultant birth of violent conflicts need to be situated in the Genesis account of creation and the Fall. The chapter presents the biblical perspective on the origin of evil and the various local expressions of this problem.

The Cradle of the Human Problem

Since Adam and Eve chose autonomy over dependence on God, the en-tire human history has been characterized by hostility: Whatever positive

---

1. Babs Ajayi, "The End of the Jonathan Kleptocracy (II)," *Nigeriaworld*, April 16, 2015. http://www.nigeriaworld.com/feature/publication/babsajayi/041615.html

progress humans have made they have equally made retrogressive progress.[2] In this chapter we expose the ingrained roots of human hostility. We need to look beyond the mask to unravel the truth: The human race—blacks and whites, Christians and Muslims and atheists and traditionalists—is characterized by self-interest, deception and an excessive lust for power. This isthe human condition that gives rise to humanity's pride, greed and the will-to-rule and to dominate other human beings, making the only inhabitable part of God's creation, the earth, chaotic. Consequently, "There is simply too much chaos, waste, and suffering. . . . There are too many brutalities within nature."[3] How can theologians and missiologists of the contemporary world explain this? We believe that Christian theologians and missiologists owe the human family a better explanation of what is wrong with human history than what the traditional nomenclature—racism, ethnicity, tribalism, identity, religion, economics, poverty, and politics—offers. These terms only keep the roots of human crises and problems hidden. For example, many people think that Islam is wild because its followers believe that it is the superior faith. Yes, that is part of the problem, because the human tendency toward comparison and competition with others invokes war and conflict. Of course, in the Muslims' effort to compare Islam with other faiths, particularly Christianity, Muslims across the globe often conclude that Islam is superior to all faiths, including Christianity; therefore it should be the head not the tail. Muslims think of Islam's superiority on two fronts. First, Allah sent one hundred and twenty-four thousands prophets. They believe the Major Prophets are: Adam, Abraham, Isaac, Jacob, Moses, Jesus and Mohammed, with Mohammed occupying the final and most important place. Second, Muslims believe Islam is superior because of their conquests. Mohammed conquered vast empires during their rapid expansion. However, these reasons are not the whole truth.

Comparing and aggressively competing with others is a symptom of a bigger problem. Therefore, as we look at the unabated social and moral problems, we realize they often lead to horrific hostilities. Comparison, competition, malice and wickedness against fellow humans across the globe, begs the question, "What is the most plausible explanation for today's social and moral dilemmas?" A review of the biblical narrative, found in the first three chapters of Genesis, reveals four great truths about the historical reality the modern world reflects—thus giving a richer insight into the true reality of the human condition.[4]

2. Temple, *Christ and the Way to Peace*, 7.

3. Cooper, *Dimensions of Evil*, 48.

4. See Stott, *Issues Facing the Contemporary World*. See also Smith, *Bible History of*

The first truth is *the Creation*. Scriptures reveals how God is the Creator (Gen 1:1.) When God created the world he used certain descriptive value judgments to describe what he created. He declared what he has created as "good." And after he created man and woman in his image and likeness, he further adds the adjective *very*. He said all that he has created was not just "good" but "very good." This declaration has basically three implications for humanity:

1. In the rest of Genesis 1:2—3 we observe God bringing the material world into being. A "formless and empty" earth is given all it needs for living creatures to thrive (Gen 1:2—3 NLT).[5] God decided to create the earth and made it inhabitable while all other planets, which scientists have discovered to date, have no living creatures.

2. The creation of man and woman culminates God's creational decision and intention. It brought God satisfaction and rest.

3. *Goodness* became part and parcel of humanity: man and woman. Man and woman (Christian, Muslim or African Traditionalist) can do tremendous good because they were created in the image and likeness of a good, and in fact, a perfect God. All humans have the capacity and the ability to pursue and work for peace.

In summary, the greatest theological truth humans have made, from the study of the first three chapters of Genesis, is the discovery of human dignity:[6] Humans—man and woman—are made in the image and likeness of God. But this discovery needs its counterpart, *human depravity*. It is failure to hold the above three truths together that has led to much misunderstanding. During the Enlightenment, the West and North America thought all that humans needed was to create their redemption by using "logical reasoning." As a result, today's secularized human family thinks God is not necessary for success. To correct this impression, Vishal Mangalwadi argues:

> Early Enlightenment philosophers like Descartes made a simple mistake. They presumed that because we have eyes, we can see for ourselves without nonhuman aid. Our eyes are indeed as wonderful as our intellect. But to see, eyes need light. Why would eyes even exist if light did not? If intellect cannot know

---

World Government, 20–23. Smith observed: "To a remarkable degree the remainder of the Bible is an enlargement and elucidation of truths here stated, as it were, in germ" (20–21).

5. Stott, *Issues Facing the Contemporary World*, 64.

6. Mangalwadi, *The Book That Made Your World*, 59.

truth, perhaps it needs the light of revelation. In fact, intellect can know nothing without revelation.[7]

Similarly, the lack of understanding the other side of the human paradox, *depravity*, has led Christians to the pitfall of underestimating the remarkable force of human self-interest and the will to power. Consequently, some Christians tend to believe that "love is a simple possibility."[8] But as we shall see below that is not the case. The second great truth is: *the Fall*. This is the story of how Adam and Eve staged a protest against God's revealed will, openly disobeying and breaking the Creator's command. They chose to obey the fallen creature, Satan. Of course, Satan kept himself out of sight and used the serpent inducer, to sway Adam and Eve to disobey God. William Smith has insightfully described in detail, how it took place. He argued that Satan, keeping himself out of sight got them to focus on their reason instead of focusing on God's commands.[9] Smith asks; "How then did Satan succeed in getting them to eat the forbidden fruit? He accomplished his end by inducing Eve to substitute reasoning for obedience—by making her own reason her guide of conduct instead of God's command."[10] Smith suggests, therefore, that it was not the eating of the fruit that was the fundamental problem. Rather, "The disobeying of God's command was what caused the Fall . . . After examining the tree, they could not find any reason for God's prohibition, so went by their own reasoning, instead of by His word, a thing the human family has ever since been prone to do."[11] The same still happens with Adam's posterity. Human beings are rational beings. As Aristotle would say, "You are born to think." Thus for him, "The unexamined life is not worth living." Reasoning or thinking is not the problem *per se*. However, we need to know that human reasoning is not perfect: human reasoning has been deeply affected by the Fall. Satan still induces us to depend solely on reason as if our reasoning is perfect. For instance, in the eighteenth century, an Enlightenment philosophy led humans into believing that the biblical doctrine of sin is outmoded. Human beings were capable of redeeming themselves from the problems of social and political evil, suffering and pain, if only their minds were developed to think critically.

In the case of Adam and Eve, Satan kept himself out of sight, by using an inducing agent, the serpent to induce Adam and Eve into disobeying God's command. That is, Satan succeeded in getting them to focus on their

7. Ibid., 44.

8. Niebuhr, *The Children of Light and the Children of Darkness*, 148.

9. Smith, *Bible History of World Government*, 64.

10. Ibid., 65.

11. Ibid., 67.

human reasoning instead of God's command. He got them to keep the command of God out of sight and focus on reason. Satan still uses the same method—keeping himself out of sight—to get us to obey the seducer instead of God. Politically correct terms (racism, ethnicity, tribalism, identity, religion, economics, poverty, and politics) do help explain some of what is happening across the globe. But they can also obscure the deeper roots of the human problem: Serving the human ego. It is the excessive drive for self-ambition/advantage, and a distorted desire to acquire the ability to control and dominate others and nature for self-satisfaction and pleasure. Unhealthy comparing of self with others and engaging in unhealthy competition are two of the results.

In summary, the Fall is the historical event which brought evil (the prideful and self-centered character of Satan) into the human race; that is, man and woman acquired evil in their nature. Consequently, every person (Christian, Muslim, or African Traditionalist alike) now has, not only the capacity and ability to do tremendous good, but also the capacity and ability to excessively pursue evil and work for the advancement of self, contrary to their religious claims. According to John Stott, human beings now possess both "dignity and depravity." He refers to this as "the paradox of man." That is a situation where good and evil coexists in the same person. Pride always stands in the way of human efforts. Pride, acting in human self-interest and the desire to dominate, displays its ugly head even in Christian circles.[12]

By and large, when evil entered the human race, it sought to eclipse human goodness. For after the Fall, Scripture says, "The Lord observed the extent of human wickedness on the earth, and He saw that everything they thought or imagined was consistently and totally evil" (Gen 6:5 NLT). In a Bible study on Romans 12:9, "Love must be sincere. Hate what is evil; cling to what is good" (NIV). Stott observed,

> We cannot fail to be struck by the close connection in this verse between love and hatred. Normally we regard them as diametrically opposed to one another. They cannot coexist, we say. Love expels hatred, and hatred love. But the truth is not as simple as that. For Paul immediately follows his command to love with a second command to hate—not of course evildoers (whom he later tells us to love and serve) but evil itself. Whenever love is "sincere" then, literally "without hypocrisy," it is normally discerning. It never overlooked or condones evil. On the contrary it hates it. For love knows both the harm which evil always

12. "Christian Scholars and Scientists—William Tyndale," *Christian History*, http://www.christianitytoday.com/history/people/scholarsandscientists/william-tyndale.html.

does to people, whether the perpetrators or the victims of it, and the blessing which goodness brings them. Therefore, if we love people, we must hate the evil which harms them and cling to the good which blesses them. Otherwise we cannot claim to love them.[13]

Stott's observation should have meaningful insight for Christians living in hostile societies, where horrific wars and violent conflicts are tearing this habitable earth apart; and the most vulnerable members of the human family, women and children are most affected. Love and evil coexist in all humans. War and violent conflict are found in every human society. They illustrate how *self-interest and the will-to-power* are wrecking the earth and trying to make it formless and empty again. Human destructive capability knows no limit. For example, during the Holocaust, which was carried out in a Christian nation, Germany, powerful men killed over one million children, some of whom had their small heads bashed into concrete walls right in front of their mothers.[14] The murderers of those children treated them as "a thing." Human pride led the perpetuators of crimes against humanity to reduce other fellow humans to nothing. If there is any great lesson "the Bible and human history" should teach all humans, it is humility. In other words, there is a connection between the subject of "The Bible and Human History" and biblical humility. It is also our story! When we see ourselves as a part of the human family, in spite of what our new position in Christ is, we will not treat others as "a thing."

The third Great truth: *Redemption.* This is the account of how God came down to rescue humans from the slavery and prison of sin, reconcile and restore them into a reconciled relationship with God and their fellow humans as well as with nature, the created order. Jesus' incarnation points to the fact that in spite of the Fall human dignity is redeemable through the cross. Jesus Christ's death created another possibility for man and woman to get it right with God.

This possibility allows humans to share the incomparable great power of God, which is presently at work in each believer. God's power operating in humans enables them to see evil, accept its reality at work, continually repent and receive God's forgiveness and reconciliation. Finally, God's power will restore believers into a reconciliatory community, while enjoying fellowship with God and other fellow human beings. Jesus gives his disciples the grace to love, not just those who love them but even those who are their enemies. To preach the gospel of peace and not violence is to participate in

13. Stott, "Christian Responses to Good and Evil," 45.

14. Cooper, *Dimensions of Evil,* 48.

the mission of God. God is working to right the world by extracting people from sin's prison.

Interestingly, after all is said and done, because Christians are still on this side of eternity, they still have good and evil as part of their humanity. They have the capacity, capability and ability to do tremendous good, as well as tremendous evil, like any other person born in this fallen world. The major advantage they have is that they recognize and submit to a higher authority, God (2 Cor 12:9–10). In other words, they grasp the fact that the grace of God, working within God's rule of law, is available for them to tap into and use whenever they encounter the challenge of self-ambition, self-advantage, self-interest and the temptation to want to compare and compete with the aim of dominating other human beings. Christians are born twice and die once. On the other hand, unbelievers have no higher law than themselves. Thus, they excessively pursue self-interest and the will to power without restraint. Unbelievers' Adamic sins have not been forgiven; they are born once and will die twice.

Talking on behalf of Christians, Paul says, "Since we believe that Christ died for all, we also believe that we have all died to our old life. He died for everyone so that those who receive His new life will no longer live for themselves. Instead, they will live for Christ, who died and was raised for them" (2 Cor 5:14–15). Humans operate within the law of creation; they are free rational and moral agents. They have free will. Theologians, philosophers and scientists have debated what humans' free will entails. We will not pursue that debate here. Instead, we will say in summary, free will means that the power to reason, think, and act independently, or without God's interference, is ingrained in all humans. We are free moral agents. We are rational beings who are held responsible for every act we carry out on this earth. Within this life span we are free to imagine, reason, think, decide and act according to the urges of our sinful nature. But after this the Hebrew writer says, "[E]ach person is destined to die once and after that comes judgment" (Heb 9:27.) This historical event is about what happens on the other side of eternity. It is a consequence of how we have decided to live our lives on this side of eternity.

This is why Paul cautions: "So whether we are here in this body or away from this body, our goal is to please Him. For we must all stand before Christ to be judged. We will each receive whatever we deserved for the good or evil we have done in this earthly body" (2 Cor 5:9–10). Scriptures caution all humans on how to live on this side of eternity: God first, others second, and self-last! Then we will please God and escape His wrathful judgment. However, a note must be added here. God first means accepting His eternal plan of redemption through the Second Person of the Godhead, Jesus

Christ, the Second Adam. This is what the Law and the Prophets who all the Abrahamic faiths respect, preached and taught. There is no salvation in humanity's effort. It is a gift of God's rich grace to all creation, particularly to the entire human family, Jews and Gentiles alike.

The Paradox of the Human Race

The Bible and the history of the human condition illustrates that without God, humanity's future is "as fragile as spider's web, as flimsy as a shelter made of branches!" (Job 27:18.) The narrative invites all humans to take the biblical theme of *humility* seriously. So far our discussion seeks to point out that human pride, greed, and self-interest or the will-to-power is responsible for human social and moral chaos, suffering, pain and destruction. The Bible and human history invites us to recognize that we are descendants of Adam and Eve. It verifies and affirms the paradox of the human race: dignity and depravity. In other words, it verifies and affirms that our true humanness or essence is characterized by human dignity and human depravity. We are capable of doing tremendous good, as well as equally capable of doing tremendous destruction or evil. As the late Uncle John would say, "We build churches and we drop bombs." Or, I will add, "We build mosques and we drop bombs." We rise in anger to condemn injustice in other lands yet we practice and perpetrate injustice right at our door steps.

Human beings are not immune to sin. If Christians were immune to sin, Paul would not have written Galatians 6 as he did. By paraphrasing to a relevant, contemporary wording, we must see ourselves as children of the same grandparents, Adam and Eve. The reality is that followers of the different religions on earth need to know that their human identity is not based or determined by their religion. It is determined by their creation in the image of God. In this sense, they are children of the Creator, God. As far as human characteristics are concerned, we are brothers and sisters. If one of us is overcome by some unorderly social or moral behavior, those of us who are yet to fall into the same sin should "gently and humbly help that person," bearing in mind that we too may one day necessitate the same kind of help. And (knowing that we are not immune to sin) Paul said, "[B]e careful not to fall into the same temptation ourselves . . ." The terrorists, Boko Haram, ISIS or AL'Qaeda, the insurgents, or whatever name we may call them, have fallen into the temptation of excessive self-interest and the will to power. How should we think of helping them out of the ditch? "If you think you are too important to help someone, you are only fooling yourself. You are not that important" (Gal 6:3). However, while ministering to others in need it also requires us to protect or ensure our spiritual stability too. This is because we are individually going to be held accountable for the way we have conducted ourselves while on this side of eternity. The next time you feel the urge to compare yourself with others, take a look at your fingers and carefully assess how God made them. In spite of the fact that they are not equal, they are not in conflict and war with each other. Each of your fingers does its natural work and finds satisfaction in the effort.

The Genesis account verifies and affirms that the human problem lies in *self-interest and the will-to-power*, manifesting through comparison and competition. It was this act that led to the first murder: Cain killed Abel (Gen 4). That sin did not stop with Cain, but continues to this day. The Genesis account holds the most plausible explanation of what has been the pattern in human history. It tells of two forms of self-interest and the will of power. The first kind is the negative form of *self-interest* and *the will to power* which causes human blindness. It creates a visual tunnel that blinds the eyes of humans into thinking that they are the only species who has a right to live and flourish on earth. They see others as mere things, maggots or worms, and foolishly seek to destroy them as if they are not also part of their species and kinsmen. It works against all human logic, sensibility and conscious-ness. It makes humans wise but stupid and senseless in their conduct toward God and one another. In this state of affairs, humans without the redemptive grace of God are lost in the prison of self-greed, self-pride, self-interest and self-will-to-power. Using logical thinking is not wrong.[15] The second kind of self-interest and self-will to power is positive. The situation described above is correct; it is our story. It is not about them versus us. It is about the reality of the effect of the Fall through Adam on his posterity, the entire human family. It acknowledges that it is okay to love self. For example, it is okay to: "Pay careful attention to your work, for then you will get the satisfaction of a job well done" (Gal 6:4).

Conclusion

There is something more than pride going on with the human race. In other words, the explanation of pride above does not capture all there is in the problem of the human race. We cannot grasp why people like a ninety-one year old President Mugabe of Zimbabwe would cling unto power for thirty-five years; or why President Olusegun Obasanjo of Nigeria would want the constitution of Nigeria changed overnight so that he could go for a third-term in office. The Genesis account reveals why. It tells us the immediate

15. Stott, "Christian Responses to Good and Evil," 43.

implication of the Fall: Human awareness of nakedness, insecurity. Adam says, "I was afraid because I was naked" (Gen 3:8–10.) That is to say, since the time Adam and Eve heard God's voice, ran and hid themselves, the fear of our human nakedness getting exposed has become part of our humanity. The human race fears disgrace, particularly socio-political disgrace. Disgrace is generally the state of having lost the respect or esteem of others, a cause of public shame.

In summary, there is a deep insecurity, which the whole human family faces. This sense of insecurity is what basically causes humans to be extremely hostile. We fight and kill to protect ourselves from being politically, socially, economically or religiously disgraced or humiliated. To be disgraced is to have one's nakedness exposed in public. Therefore, as humans we are not just interested in power, religion, ethnicity, racism and so on; rather, we believe all these will clothe our nakedness. So, one real root of human hostility is the fear of our nakedness getting exposed; thereby bringing us public disgrace, shame and humiliation. We get terrified by the awareness that someone is going to expose our nakedness. Power, particularly political power, seems to provide us with immunity from disgrace. The fear of disgrace (i.e., the misery of experiencing insecurity because our nakedness is exposed) has become part and parcel of the human race. The psalmist captures this fear when he writes these words: "I prayed to the LORD, and He answered me. *He freed me from all my fears.* Those who look to Him for help will be radiant with joy; *no shadow of shame will darken their faces*" (Ps 34:4–5). (All italicized texts are mine). In order for humans to turn away from their secrecy, deception, blind conceit, the psalmist gives this invitation: "Taste and see that the LORD is good. Oh, the joys of those who take refuge in Him! Fear the LORD, you His godly people, for those who fear Him will have all they need" (Ps 34:8–9). This is the only way we can "Turn away from evil and do good. Search for peace, and work to maintain it" (Ps 34:14). The chapters that follow examine, discuss and expose the embedded roots of Nigerian experience of human hostility.

Chapter 3

Why Peace Eludes Nigerians

Introduction

"They have come again!" was the cry of a woman with a 5-month-old baby on her back, running for her dear life. A disagreement during a buying and selling transaction between a Hausa-Fulani Muslim and a non-Muslim in one of the local markets in Kaduna state had just happened. Saturday is the only market day of this community. Both Muslims and non-Muslims share this market. But it is not unusual for a fight to break out in the market over some disputes that have nothing to do with religion, yet will immediately become a religious issue. Her cry caused pandemonium in the market and people ran toward different directions in search of a hide out. People who were visitors to the area might not have grasped the meaning of the phrase, "They have come again." Its meaning does not stop at a previous event of violent conflict but rather includes all other past violent conflicts that have been concurring, even prior to the British colonization of Nigeria. That means that this small incidence brings to memory the larger socio-historical, sociopolitical and socio-religious conflict situations in Nigeria. The word "again" has a deeper connotation than anyone can imagine. Therefore it refutes Robert G. Hamerton-Kelly's assertion that 21st century humans, unlike their counterparts in bible times, are forgetful.[1] In Nigeria we remember past wrongs done to our great-grandparents. We find it extremely difficult to forget the past, even when we cannot define our situation with the precision it requires.

1. Hamerton-Kelly, *Sacred Violence*, 13.

This chapter argues that due to violent conflict, Nigeria is "dancing on the brink." Violence is destroying us but figuring out its nature and defining its theological implications with precision have often been difficult. To overcome this difficulty, this chapter places Nigeria's violence not only in its historical and theological perspectives, but also in its global context. In so doing, it recognizes that conflict violence in Nigeria is not uniquely Nigeria's problem but the problem of a global world in which events in one part of the globe have a way of affecting the rest of the world.[2] Like the rest of the global world, Nigerians are paying an enormous price in lives, money, property, and freedom, thanks to the rising tide of global Islamic jihad. They are incurring intangible costs in loss of freedom, rising fear, and impositions on their way of life.[3] The wind of modernity and postmodernity is blowing across the globe, challenging traditional institutions and systems of the diverse cultures of the world.[4] This chapter, therefore, must explore the impact

2. Falola, *Violence in Nigeria*, 288. See also Ogbu Kalu, *African Pentecostalism*, 189. Kalu maintains that "Everybody is affected by the integration and differentiation of global societies, which not only influences the theory of knowledge but has two other results: the emergence of a new culture and the intensification of culture and value clashes. As cultures as cultures are pressed together, the problem of identity looms large" (*African Pentecostalism*, 189).

3. At times we do not calculate these losses. In his article "What jihad has cost Americans" (*The Counter Jihad Report,* June 25, 2013. http://www.counterjihadreport. com/2013/06/25/what-jihad-has-cost-americans/), Executive Director of ACT! for America, Guy Rogers, enumerates the cost in human lives and other intangible costs, such as the way people are treated at public functions. He also discusses the global Islamist assault on free speech. In Nigeria, it is no longer safe to go to church or public functions. You leave home without the assurance of coming back alive.

4. Marshall Berman documents the account of key events that have shaped our world since the invention of modern technologies. Berman writes:

> The maelstrom of modern life has been fed from many sources: great discovering the physical sciences, changing our images of the universe and our place in it; the industrialization of production, which transforms scientific knowledge into technology, creates new human environments and destroys old ones, speeds up the whole tempo of life, generates new forms of corporate power and class struggle; immense demographic upheavals, severing millions of people from their ancestral habitats, hurling them halfway across the world into new lives; rapid and often cataclysmic urban growths; systems of mass communication, dynamic in their development, enveloping and binding together the most divers people and societies; increasingly powerful national states, bureaucratically structured and operated, constantly striving to expand their powers; mass social movements of people, challenging their political and economic rulers, striving to gain some control over their lives; finally, bearing and driving all these people and institutions along, a n every-expanding, drastically fluctuating capitalist world market. (*All That is Solid Melts into Air*, 16)

of the global phenomena of change that has taken place since the turn of the twentieth century. It analyzes Nigeria's violent situation and some of the pertinent theological issues or questions it raises.

The Nigerian Violent Story

The Beginning of the Story

Nigeria is home to three religious communities: African Indigenous Religions (AIR), Islam and Christianity. Only AIR has the right to claim originality to the Nigerian soil. The two Abrahamic religions met AIR here. Islam spread in Nigeria through two phases. First, it spread across Hausaland through Arab merchants and traveling Islamic scholars in the 12th century. Secondly, Islam spread through Usman dan Fodio jihad of 1804. The jihad took it beyond Hausa-Fulani territory. Dan Fodio's primary motive was to purify Islam.[5] He launched an attack against African indigenous religions and imperfections within Islam. However, what started as Islamic purification quickly turned to desire for economic and political power. The goal of Dan Fodio's jihad's was the establishment of Islamic rule in Nigeria. He could not capture the north central (Middle Belt) and southeast. But the seed of present violence was sown. Consequently, Toyin Falola observes, "A religious divide separates Christians and Muslims, and long-standing intra-religious conflicts further divided the people."[6] The nineteenth century marked the height of Muslim influence, due to the successful jihad of dan Fodio and the establishment of the Sokoto caliphate.[7]

Portuguese merchants brought Christianity to Nigeria through the coast in the 14th and 15th centuries but after they left Christianity could not survive. By and large, the activities of Western missionaries in the early part of the eighteenth century were characterized by failures. However, in the early nineteenth century, Western missionaries made some breakthroughs in mission efforts in Nigeria. They advanced to the interior. According to Falola, "As Islam was spreading in the second half of the nineteenth century, Christianity was just laying its foundation"[8] in the south. When Christianity got to the north, it had to confront Islam as an established religion. Aware of this situation, the early missionary efforts of Christian leaders such as Samuel Ajayi Crowther were diplomatic, emphasizing witness through

---

5. Falola, *Violence in Nigeria*, 25.

6. Ibid., 1.

7. Kukah, *Religion, Politics and Power*, 4.

8. Falola, *Violence in Nigeria*, 27.

dialogue and social action rather than confrontation. But due to the seed of bitter rivalry and violence, the jihad had sown, the end of British rule opened the floodgates of horrific violence.[9]

The Role of British Colonial Administration

During colonial occupation of Nigeria, the British divided the country into three regions—north, southwest and southeast—for their administrative convenience. After the British left Nigeria in 1960, the first national leaders were concerned about building a united, vibrant and stable nation. They worked hard to keep the dream of establishing a unified independent nation. However, the British policy of "divide and rule," which had led to the creation of three regions, became a setback. Regional unhealthy comparison and competition superseded the desire for a united country, to the extent that there was no one unifying national ideology. Instead, each of the three regions became engrossed with the pursuit of regional interest and the desire for political and economic control of the entire nation. It fashioned an ideology that would enable it to favorably win power and control the entire nation. The parochial and aggressive pursuit of regional *self-interest* and *the will to power* killed the dream of a unified independent nation. As a result, Nigeria went into a three-year civil war (1967 to 1970).

Subsequent leaders, who desired to take Nigeria back to the path of a united nation, created more states, assuming that would destroy the aggressive competition. But the strategy has not worked till date. Muslim brothers and sisters see northern Christians as traitors. This misperception stems from their assuming that because Christianity came to the North through the South, northern Christians are collaborators with perceived enemies. Those from, either southwest or southeast, are seen as their competitors and therefore a threat to their *self-interest* and *the will to power*, or desire for control of the so-called "national cake." This is part of the reason northern Christians are targeted. They are caught in the crossfire of unhealthy regional comparisons and competitions. They are denied land to build new churches; and whenever any of the old churches are burnt down during a crisis, they are not allowed to rebuild it. The hatred of Christians has become expanded to include the Muslims' hatred for the West that has become a threat to Islam's expansion and dream of becoming a world power. So it is not only that Christianity is seen as a religion that came from regional enemies, but also from global enemies, the West and North America.

9. Ibid.

However, this story has not ended. An understanding of the human paradox cannot be only visualized from a one-sided picture of the complex problem. Self-interest and the will-to-power is the narrative of all humanity. We must remind ourselves that Hausa-Fulani Muslims in Northern Nigeria are not alone in committing atrocities against fellow humans. How can we exonerate Christian Europe for all the atrocities they committed against humanity? "In recent human history, the Holocaust is a prime example, when babies were among the victims of destruction that humans pursued through pride, greed, self-interest and the will to power."[10] Human pride can steal, kill and destroy.

During this colonial rule, opinions vary as to how the British handled these inter-communal/ religious self-interests and tensions in Nigeria. Scholars seem to argue that the present situation of Nigeria is largely a British colonialists' creation. Yusufu Turaki argues that the British created a society that they believed would not work after independence.[11] Similarly, Falola asserts, "The British administration carefully avoided the creation of a formal or public role for religion. Not that it failed to recognize the existence and spread of both religions, but it chose instead to secularize [it] by introducing the institutions and structures of the new nation-state, which were then transferred to the Nigerian people at independence."[12]

There is no denying the fact that what is today known as Nigeria was a British creation; or better put, God used the British to create a nation, "to the praise of his glory" (Eph 1:14). According to Falola, "By 1860, the British had established a foothold in Lagos, and thereafter began to interfere in the affairs of other areas, most notably the Niger Delta . . . and by 1903, Nigeria was fully colonized."[13] They established two protectorates: Southern and Northern. Lord Lugard amalgamated the two protectorates in 1914. Due to the influence of Islam and the Dan Fodio jihad, the North was politically better established and organized under the Sokoto caliphate than the South. To minimize ethnic and religious tensions, the British adopted two forms of administrative strategies to maintain the peace: direct rule in the south and indirect rule in the north. They adopted the policy of noninterference; missionaries were not allowed to evangelize Hausa, except the Middle Belt, where most of the ethnic groups had resisted dan Fodio's jihad. The British colonialists successfully used the policy of administrative

---

10. Maryam Jameelah, as quoted in Ondigo, *Muslim-Christian Interactions*, 202.

11. Turaki, *British Colonial Legacy in Northern Nigeria*.

12. Falola, *Violence in Nigeria*, 40.

13. Ibid., 51.

convenience—indirect rule—to interfere with dan Fodio aspiration of establishing Islamic rule all across Nigeria.

The Post-Independence Tensions

Prior to independence, Nigeria had decided on a federal structure for its post-independence political system. To manage, intra/inter-ethnic rivalries, the country was divided into three regions: southwest, southeast and north.[14] After independence ethnic protests continued, and to manage that states were created.

Shortly after independence, Nigeria went into serious political and religious crises. As Falola explains, "Interregional relations were characterized by profound hostility and uneven development. Minorities and southern ethnic groups feared Hausa-Fulani domination of the federal government, and every group complained of unequal development."[15] These threats led to civil war from 1967–1970 and the late 1980s religious violence and conflict. Since then, ethnic and religious identities became the political rallying points. Religion was used to consolidate existing identities and to forge new ones.[16]

The Current Violent Arena

The last ten years have been described as "Nigeria's decade of bloodshed." In 2003, Jan Boer has observed that "there had already been over thirty 'violent incidents of riots' in northern states."[17] From 2001 to 2013, a conservative estimate of victims of violence in Nigeria stands at between 50,000 and 60,000.[18] Mutual suspicion and distrust continue to characterize Nigeria's political and religious communities. Jan Boer states, "Both Christians and Muslims in Nigeria speak of each other's grand plans to destroy each other."[19] Nigerian Muslims see Nigeria's secularism as the greatest threat. They assume that the present system favored Christianity. It is on this assumption that Muslims continue to push for the implementation of the Shari'a criminal law. "Both Christianity and Western values are criticized for making

---

14. Ibid., 52.

15. Ibid., 44.

16. Ibid.

17. Boer, *Nigeria's Decades of Blood*, 37.

18. *Reuters*, retrieved on June 19, 2013. http://www.reuters.com/articles/us-nigeria-violence-clashes.idUSTRe6-BR13T20101228.com.

19. Boer, *Christians*, 99.

Nigeria excessively materialist, undignified, and morally decadent."[20] And to many devout Muslims, according to Falola, "the salvation of Nigeria depends on its drawing not on western political models, but from the model of the early *Umma* and its unification of political authority with moral and religious authority."[21]

The Maitatsine crisis of 1980 and the current Boko Haram sect follow the pattern of Dan Fodio's jihad. However, the current Boko Haram insurgency is not only based on the 1804 goal of Islam's purification but also linked to the Arab spring insurgency. The Boko Haram sect is radical Muslim's response to the growth of Christianity in Nigeria. That is why, according to Philip Jenkins, it is "one of the deadliest anti-Christian groups in West Africa" with links to al-Qaeda.[22] It does not spare Muslims who oppose its ideology. From 2009 when the sect started fighting the government and all Western institutions in the country, including Christianity, 3,600 Nigerians and foreigners have been murdered by the group.

Boko Haram, (which means Western education is forbidden) is not just a religious sect but the epitome of using religion to achieve economic and political power. Nigeria's violence has a lot to do with religious and political manipulation. The leaders of different political factions arm unemployed and unemployable youths against their perceived or real opponents. These youth groups eventually become independent of their pay-masters who usually abandon them after achieving their political objectives. They often metamorphose to a militia group, of which Boko Haram is a prime example.[23]

The Communal Dimensions of Violence

Intra-community Violence

The nature of current violence is both inter- and intra-community. This dimension of violence is not limited to Muslim-Christian relationship but also the African Indigenous religions. For example, in May 2013, a cultic group, *Ombatse* ("the time has come"), in Nassarawa state, ambushed and killed 88 secret security servicemen and policemen. *Ombatse* is a traditional and cultural group that exists to counter the incessant attacks by Fulani herdsmen in Nasarawa State.

20. Falola, *Violence in Nigeria*, 74.

21. Ibid., 73.

22. Jenkins, "Third World War," 24.

23. Human Rights Watch, "Criminal Politics," 2.

Islam contains such highly competitive and divergent groups as the Shiites, the Kharajites, the Sunni, and others. The major intra-religious violence was the 1980–82 Maitatsine uprising in Kano which spilled over across the north. Thousands of people were killed. On the whole, the Nigerian Muslims' intra-religious violence is a testament to the fact that Nigeria's Islam, like the rest of the Muslim world, "rests on a wide variety of cultural foundations and historical legacies."[24] In 2005, John N. Paden even predicted that because of the existence of a wide variety of cultural foundation and historical legacies in the Nigerian Islamic context, "many reforms (and reactions to reform) are well under way . . ." in Nigeria.[25] Paden further observed that in a globalized world, "economic globalization creates new winners and losers (or in oil-producing countries, new classes of haves and have-nots)." He then concluded that, "As the pace of change accelerates and uncertainty intensifies, many will return to their spiritual foundations for guidance. Such fundamentalism, or going back to basics, is a worldwide phenomenon and a typical human response to uncertainty. It should not be an excuse for launching a new era of religious wars."[26] The intra-religious violent conflict in Nigeria lends credence to the fact that these complexities are well displayed in Nigeria.[27]

Inter-community Violence

Interreligious violence started before Nigeria's independence. But it only became very explicit in the seventies. Shadrack G. Best asserts that events in the Muslims world, particularly the 1979 Iranian Revolution and the radicalization of Northern Nigerian Islam through its contact with zealous and fundamentalist sects in other parts of the global community made matters worse.[28] Prior to the seventies, Northern Nigerian Islam had interacted with more moderate interpretations like those in Saudi Arabia, Sudan, Egypt, etc.[29] At the turn of the 1980s, Nigerian Muslims watched an uncomfortable trend in Africa, particularly Nigerian Christianity.[30] "Beginning with the emergence in the 1890s of independent churches, fundamentalist and revivalist movements have been strong in Nigeria. Characterized by an

24. Paden, *Muslim Civic Cultures*, 2.

25. Ibid.

26. Ibid.

27. Ibid.

28 Best, "Religion and Religious Conflicts in Northern Nigeria," 63.

29 Ibid.

30. Jenkins, "Third World War," 24.

emphasis on African dignity and pride, and usually controlled by charismatic Nigerian leaders, these churches tend to be uncompromising in their
relations with Islam. The post-1975 Islamic tendency toward radicalism
and fundamentalism have been evident among Christians as well, partly
because the Nigerian state's failure to meet the expectations of its citizens,
and partly because of the increased challenge posed by Islam."[31] Jenkins observes, "One factor driving Islamic militancy in many nations is the sense
that Christianity is growing."[32] They realized it interferes with their goal of
returning Islam to its past glorious civilization.[33]

Theological Reflections

We now examine five major theological questions raised by the violence
over religious domination in Nigeria. We compare two biblical texts—Genesis 4:1–8 and James 4:1–3—to give a thick definition of violence. To have a
thick theological reflection on violence, we need to see it as a whole package,
a system not a single event. Hamerton speaks of it as, "the system of sacred
violence."[34] Paul is helpful in discussing violence. He draws Christians' attention to the schemes of the devil in Ephesians 6. Conscious of the schemes
of the devil, Jürgen Moltmann says, "Before religious communities can contribute anything to world peace, they must themselves become religions of
peace and overcome tendencies in their own traditions to hostility and the
destruction of enemies."[35] Firstly, what is the root of violence? In biblical
and theological studies Christians have traditionally seen violence as the
consequence of sin and the Fall. Violence is rooted in fallen human interaction with one another, in a world of needs and unsatisfied desires. Genesis
4:1–8 records that the first death in the Bible was a violent murder by Cain
of his brother Abel—he "attacked his brother and killed him." Rene Girard
speaks of violence as driven by "deformed mimetic desire." Hamerton observes that "Girard's particular contribution is the identification of violence
as the energy of the social system."[36] Cain's approach of seeking the favour
of God that Abel had without doing it God's way, illustrates the pathology
of violence against those who stand in the way of getting what is wanted or
desired.

31. Falola, *Violence in Nigeria*, 47.
32 Jenkins, "Third World War," 23.
33. Ibid., 24.
34. Hamerton, *Sacred Violence*, 15.
35. Moltmann, *The Politics of Discipleship*, 132.
36. Hamerton, *Sacred Violence*, 17.

Girard again speaks of violence proceeding from someone preventing another "from appropriating the object they all desire through physical or other means."[37] Girard's theory of violence confirms that covetousness and jealousy, what he calls, "mimetic desire," pervades human relations.[38] In the sin-fractured society of Genesis 4 we also see violence is rooted in human pride. Marjorie Hewitt Suchocki explains, "This pride is the inherent desire within fallen humanity to be like God, not in terms of character, but in terms of power."[39] Human beings live in a state of continual conflict and rivalry because of deformed desire and pride.

Secondly, "deformed mimetic desire" (that is a distorted desire) is seen within Christian communities. David P. Nystrom explains the intra-Christian community violence suggested in the James 4:1–3 passage: "James says that disputes come from the desires (*bedone*) within them . . . This image is not unknown elsewhere in the New Testament. 1 Peter 2:11, Romans 7:22–23)."[40] I-Jin Loh and Howard A. Hatton suggest that this desire is related to anger and hatred.[41] This is why in verse 2 James says, "You kill and covet." This is perhaps a reference to Genesis 4:1–8. As in Genesis, where the reason for the killing includes anger rooted in covetousness and jealousy. Therefore, Nystrom concludes, "James is explaining that violence is never a solution worthy of pursuit. To choose the path of violence is to place oneself within a vicious cycle of retribution."[42] The situation in Nigeria is not just about threats from outside the Christian community, but also from within. By and large, the greatest threat that the Church in Nigeria faces is not Boko Haram, but human pride. This pride is characterized by doubt and lack of faith in the God who can do far more with and through those who believe in him than those people can ask for or even think about (Eph 3:20). It is also seen in intra-Christian confusion of essential and the nonessential aspects of biblical doctrines. For example, an essential doctrine of the Christian church is the belief that Jesus Christ is the Son of God. So, no one can claim to be a true believer and yet deny that Jesus Christ is the Son of God. A nonessential doctrine is a debate about such thing as what to wear to church. Every denomination is free to choose what to wear to choose. But because of pride Christians have despised other Christians on the basis of the nonessential doctrines of their denominations.

---

37. Girard, "Mimesis and Violence," 9–19.

38. Girard, *Violence and the Sacred,* cited in Mark McEntire, *The Blood of Abel,* 1.

39. Suchocki, *The Fall to Violence,* 29.

40. Nystrom, *The NIV Application Commentary on James,* 223.

41. Loh and Hatton, *Handbook on The Letter from James,* 138.

42. Nystrom, *The NIV Application Commentary on James,* 224–5.

Thirdly, what issues does the Love to Neighbor Principle of Jesus create? Humans are created for community life with others. The principle—"It is not good for man to be alone"—illustrates this truth. In this community life they are always encountering challenges. The love principle is given with the awareness of the schemes of the devil. What we need is what Paul speaks of as "love with faith" (Eph 6:23). As Desmond Tutu affirms, "We are human because we belong. We are made for community, for togetherness, for family, to exist in a delicate network of interdependence."[43] But in a violent society where trust has broken down, what are the implications of "love your neighbor . . ."? To love our neighbors include loving our enemies, even a suicide bomber. This love is anchored on the concept of God's love, justice, forgiveness, reconciliation and peace.[44] In recommending that we love our neighbors as ourselves, God wants us to affirm the humanity of the other. We are able to love the enemy because we also stand in need of love and have experienced Christ's love. Whenever Christians who are faced with the situation of the threat of violence and how to response are confronted with the Jesus' call, "turn the other cheek" it seems to be a command coming from the theologians or the super Christians.[45]

Fourthly, how are we to understand and apply the principle of forgiveness in this socially charged context?[46] Richard Rice-Oxley asserts, "Forgiveness stands at the heart of Christian faith and life. Jesus taught his disciples both to ask for and to offer forgiveness."[47] Similarly, Casiano Floristan and Christian Duquoc remind us, "The practice of Christian forgiveness cannot be reduced to a mere ethical attitude. It is entry into the mystery of God's saving love, whose kindness goes beyond all justice."[48] But how do you forgive people who do not believe they are doing anything wrong, but rather they think you are the one in the wrong? How do you forgive people who will never stop stigmatizing you as infidels? Of course, we must also ask whether Christians also stigmatize Muslims. The narratives of Jesus and Stephen are our models. Jesus did not wait for the people who crucified him to confess before he prayed to the Father to forgive them.[49] Stephen did not wait for those who stoned him to ask for forgiveness before he prayed to God for their forgiveness. Leonardo Boff observes that forgiveness is power

---

43. Tutu, *No Future without Forgiveness*, 154.

44. Gruchy, *Reconciliation*, 22.

45. Hamerton, *Sacred Violence*, 14.

46. Rice-Oxley, *Forgiveness—the Way of Peace*, 3.

47. Ibid., 3.

48. Floristan and Duquoc, *Forgiveness*, x.

49. Tutu, *No Future without Forgiveness*, 220.

and enablement. Forgiveness creates a new social community. "God's forgiveness re-establishes our community vertically towards heaven; the forgiveness bestowed on those who have wronged us restores our community horizontally in all directions."[50] No wonder, Desmond Tutu asserts that the future depends on forgiveness.

Fifthly, what are the implications of the understanding of violence raised by Islamic theology? Islamic theology represents diverse opinion on these matters, which are largely based on the interpretation of Qur'an and the Hadith. In the Shari'a, according to Ibn Tamiyyah, "The goal is not to know God, but to obey him perfectly. The devout do not love God's essence (dhat) but his command (Shari'a)."[51] But Muslims have two different views of what God's commands mean. On the one hand, there are Muslim who do not support what the radicals are preaching and promoting. They often refer to surah 73:10, 11; where Muhammad, at the early days of his mission, urges his followers: ". . . be patient toward those who deny the truth . . ." and in surah 41:34 he says, "Repel (evil) with what is better."

On the other hand, there are Muslims in Nigeria whose ideologies are based on radicalized Islam.[52] To urge their followers to fight and kill, they often refer to the "Sword Verses": "Fighting is prescribed for you . . ." (Qur'an 2:216). It is based on this attitude that Falola argues, "Islam has a tradition of militancy. While many take a quiescent approach to gaining converts and fortifying the faith, some believe that jihad is the only way to purify Islam and overcome paganism entirely. To Muslims bent on jihad, coexistence and accommodation are unnecessary, and even unacceptable."[53] This section of the Muslim community is posing a challenge to the Christian community. Their theology does not have a place for other religions to coexist with Islam. What an impasse to the cause of social justice and love!

Conclusion

In spite of the rigid position of some Muslims, God is calling Christians to a deeper social and historical understanding of the past and present situation in Nigeria, and profound theological reflection to develop God-honouring ways of responding to this crisis which prevent an escalation of violence. All too often violence in Nigeria is compounded because ethnic and religious groups in Nigeria "use" theology to justify their own position and get power

---

50. Boff, *Onze Vader,* quoted in Floristan and Duquoc, *Forgiveness,* 9.

51. Quoted in Hunt, *Muslim Faith and Values,* 129.

52. Hunt, *Muslim Faith and Values,* 3–4.

53. Falola, *Violence in Nigeria,* 46.

for themselves. Their political actors who control the states seek the means to profit from religion in a variety of ways—by using it to acquire power, stabilize or destabilize politics, consolidate political constituencies, and reinforce ethnic and religious identities. There is a need to find theological tools to undermine the roots of "deformed mimetic desire," or human "pride." There is an urgent need for the Christian community to understand the theological implications and take the path of healing.

Chapter 4

Religious Fragility and Failing Symbiotic Interactions

Introduction

In spite of the incessant violent conflicts in Nigeria there could still be some positive religious symbiotic interactions happening, which could foster hope for the country. How can Nigerians turn fragile symbiotic interactions into positive interactions? This chapter examines what may be needed to make that achievable. Undoubtedly, Nigerians—African Traditionalists, Muslims and Christians—encounter each other on a daily basis at different spheres. We board the same public transportations, our civil servants encounter each other at work every week day, and our entrepreneurs share office spaces or are even colleagues, partners and collaborators and so on with people of other faiths in Nigeria and beyond.

The plain fact is that religion is not just a thing or an *it,* but it is like a human entity. Religion tends to involve all the social characteristics of human beings. Therefore, some have concluded that religion is a human social institution. It is dynamic. That is why it is "an important component in many conflict zones and can be a powerful tool for preventing violence."[1] An Islamic expert, John N. Paden, who has studied the Islamic culture of northern Nigeria, once observed that Nigeria is one of the countries in the

---

1. David Smock, in "Religious Peacebuilding: Approach of USIP David Smock, Marc Gopin, Susan Hayward & Palwasha Kakar," YouTube video, 1:02:07, filmed at The Rumi Forum, Washington, DC, Sep 23, 2014, posted by "RumiForum," Oct 10, 2014, https://www.youtube.com/watch?v=yvyDNTT2nU0.

world where one finds not only a large Muslim population but also an almost equally large Christian element: about fifty percent Muslim and fifty percent Christian (and ten percent traditional religious believers). This state of affairs makes Nigeria a very potential social context for research on how multireligious communities can symbiotically interact. However, as we have demonstrated in this book, the interaction of Islam and Christianity in Nigeria has been very fragile and divisive. As a result, today Nigeria is one of the states of fragility in the world.[2] The challenge that each passing Nigerian political system often faces is how to bridge the religious identity divide.[3]

However, in spite of this obvious difficulty, this chapter reviews the interaction of Nigeria's religions and argues that beyond the violent conflicts that have besieged the Nigerian society, there might still be some positive interaction happening. That is, it is clear that each of the religions—African Traditional Religions, Christianity and Islam—has evolved ways of exerting some pervasive influence on the others. Therefore, there is the need to pay careful and purposeful attention to the resiliency and dynamism of the impact each of the religions is exerting on the others. To do so certain assumptions must be highlighted. First, it has been argued that Africans are incurably religious. This assumption usually makes it look like non-Africans are not religious. Yet, we believe that not only Africans are incurably religious; rather all human beings are incurably religious.

Our hope in discussing religious symbiotic interaction and not just interfaith issues in this chapter is to push the boundary of possibility for peaceful harmony forward by examining how such positive interactions could lead to human flourishing. We recognize the difficulty faith communities have in accepting and celebrating difference. Faith communities in Nigeria tend to insulate themselves. They adopt a separatist and reformist posture in that they hardly see human difference as a gift from God, the Creator of all human beings, the natural world and the galaxies. On the one hand, in our interactions as religious communities, particularly in Northern Nigeria, the human problem of self-interest, deception and lust for power, and money put us in an enormous state of anxiety. This situation is due to self-centered ambitions. Of course, it is very obvious that there are no religious adherents in Nigeria who are without self-ambition. Our religiously based selfish-ambition makes us want to be ahead of the other faiths instead of working in partnership and collaboration with them for the common good of society. In the effort to be ahead of the others we tend to see them

2. Lauren Herzer Risi, "What's in a Name? States of Fragility and Adjusting Aid to Conflict Zones," *New Security Beat* (blog), April 13, 2015. http://www.newsecuritybeat.org/2015/04/whats-name-states-fragility-adjusting-aid-conflict-zones/

3. Paden, *Faith and Politics in Nigeria*, 17.

as a threat to attainment of our perceived goals. Nobody says we should not have self-ambition. However, we should not allow such ambition (s) to cause us to build a wall of resistant to positive symbiotic interpersonal interactions which could make our nation safer for all of us to thrive.

As we look across our nation, we can see a small cloud of the workability of this kind of positive interactions right at our door steps. The Yoruba Muslims in southwest Nigeria provide a redemptive example of the possibility of African Traditionalists, Muslims, and Christians having meaning interreligious interactions. The Yoruba Muslims are not separatists and reformists. In other words, they do not have the separatist and reformist spirit of Northern Nigerian Muslims. As such, in the southwest, African Traditional Religionists, Muslims and Christians share each other burdens and joys. It is quite natural to see a church and mosque sharing boundaries. However, in Northern Nigeria such healthy relationships are seen as taboos. Northern Nigerian peoples rarely see each other as possible partners.

On the other hand, the divisive nature of religious communities in Nigeria has given many Nigerians politicians (either Muslims or Christians) the opportunity to pit the poor masses against themselves. In Northern Nigeria, the religious sentiment experience in our day to day interpersonal relationships trickled down to the political arena, resulting in the politics of exclusion, discrimination and elimination. In order for the poor to overcome this and experience true socioeconomic and sociopolitical transformation they must be willing to learn how to avoid getting drawn into the politics of exclusion or elimination. Change is a possibility! For example, in the March 2015 Presidential elections we saw some lights at the end of tunnel. Nigerian electorates, members of ATR, Muslims and Christians bounded together and elected Rtd Gen. Muhammadu Buhari as their president instead of the incumbent, President Goodluck Ebele Jonathan. The Electoral umpire, Independent National Electoral Commission (INEC), had to allow their votes to count. It was incredible to see Nigerians making sure that nobody ascends to political position through the determination of a few disgruntle political elites. The next thing we desperately need is to place loyalty to God above all else and national loyalty above ethnic, religious or regional ones. This would involve a repositioning of religion and allowing our religious moral values, ethical virtues to permeate all of life—private and public. It will also involve reorienting Nigerians (ATR, Islam and Christianity adherents) toward a comprehensive understanding of the idea of citizenship. Muslims in the southwest are able to interact freely with other faiths in the region because the Yorubas do not allow religious sentiments to trump other moral values that make religion serve God's eternal purposes for human flourishing. In so doing they avoid the lethal nature of religious divisiveness which the northern region has been experiencing. Embracing the idea of citizenship and national unity will provide a solution to violence. In the event of threat to life and property, citizens will be able to, like St. Paul, appeal to their citizenship (instead of their religion) for government intervention.

We—ATR, Muslims and Christians—need to respect the God-given freedom in each person. God who has the power to coerce us into obedience doesn't do it because He respects the free will He has given each of us. If God doesn't coerce us into obeying him, why do *you* a mere fellow human being think you can do it? Religion is voluntary, not force! This is the idea of interaction we envision for Nigeria, particularly in the northern region.

African Traditional Religions in Relationship to Christianity and Islam

Over the years, Islam, Colonialism and Christianity have tended to wage war against African Traditional Religion (ATR). In other words, ATR has come under severe attacks from three fronts—Islam, colonialism and Christianity—but ATR survived all of those attacks.[4] A basic survey of how colonialism, Christianity and Islam attacked ATR is essential. To this survey we now turn.

African Traditional Religions and Christianity

Christianity's encounter with ATR was brutal. Christianity was introduced to Nigeria via the south by the collaborative efforts of Western explorers, merchants, administrators, imperialists, and missionaries. The introduction of colonial rule in Nigeria opened her up to so-called Western civilization. Joseph Omosalde Awolalu points out how this phenomenon brought about the introduction of a "new system of government, law and order, and new religions."[5] All these foreign forces mounted vigorous campaigns against the indigenous cultures, particularly religion, which they "regarded as heathenish, paganish, uncivilized, and of the evil one."[6] Given that Europe and North America were Christian continents then, the explorers, the administrators, the merchants, and the missionaries were convinced beyond reasonable doubt that it would be best to have Nigerians converted to Christianity.[7] Beneath this conviction, however, was an economic motive. It was believed

---

4. Awolalu, "The Encounter between African Traditional Religion," 11.

5. Ibid.

6. Ibid.

7. Ibid.

that Christianity was going to make wild Africans tamable for the administrative conveniences of the colonialists. Therefore they encouraged their
home governments not only to send capable administrators to maintain
law and order but also zealous Christian missionaries to preach the gospel
of Jesus Christ. The missionaries were backed up and given protection by
the colonial administrators. In consequence of this, there was a solid collaboration among the merchants, the administrators and the missionaries
to suppress the indigenous religion and to impose Christianity.[8] Whatever
the motive, as Paul would say, at least the Good News of Jesus Christ was
preached to Nigerians and those who were walking in darkness saw the
great light of God.

The abolition of the slave trade fostered the aggressive evangelization
and introduction of Christianity in the southern part of Nigeria. As we will
show in chapter thirteen, liberated slaves who returned to West Africa and
who had embraced Christianity in servitude preferred to continue Christian
worship rather than return to the old traditional mode of worship . . . in this
way, Christianity began to challenge African traditional religion.[9] Awolalu
argues that the greatest and most effective weapon used by Christian missionaries to disrupt traditional beliefs [and Islam] was Western education.
As missionaries claimed that they were working for the spiritual salvation
of the people, so also did they claim to be working for their material well-
being. Of course education was a very good thing. What was problematic
in the exercise, however, was that all new converts were taught in the mission houses and were encouraged to look down upon their culture. That
approach would later become the seedbed of ethnic and religious conflicts.
Mission schools and colleges soon sprang up in many places; and men and
women were taught the Scriptures, reading, writing, and arithmetic. Eventually those who were educated along this line became converted and bade
adieu to the old faith. Some of them who were knowledgeable in the Scriptures became powerful preachers against the "idolatrous practices" of their
people. In this way, "traditional life was deeply undermined, and the family
structure was disrupted."[10] As a result, today it is not only Boko Haram that
is fighting back but also traditional religionists who were not happy with
what colonialism and Christianity did to indigenous religions.

8 Awolalu, "Continuing and Discontinuity," 7.

9. Awolalu, "The Encounter between African Traditional Religion," 113.

10. Ibid., 114.

African Traditional Religions and Islam

Although Islam was in the country several decades before colonialism and Christianity, it had an apparently tolerant beginning. Yet, Muslims had a hidden agenda. The Muslim merchants waited not only until they were strong enough to stage a jihad, but also until they had studied the weaknesses of Northern Nigerians. Islam was introduced to the Hausa and Fulani in northern Nigeria by Muslim itinerant traders. They were clever enough not to demand a sudden break with the traditional religion. They targeted the community leaders or rulers. The rulers, in turn, influenced their subjects and encouraged them to say the Muslim confession of faith: "I believe there is no god but Allah, And Muhammed is the prophet of Allah."[11] Thus between the 14th century and the 18th centuries very few converts were made among the adherents of traditional religion called the Maguzawa. Those who confessed the Muslim faith were still practicing traditional religion. Sacrifices were offered by the Maguzawa to a number of iskoki (spirits) found everywhere—in the sky, forest, hills and bodies of water. Iskoki do possess worshippers, and such spirit possession is called bori. But a radical change came in the 19th century when Uthman dan Fodio, a Fulani born in Gobir who became an enthusiastic Muslim teacher, felt disgusted at the way his fellow Muslims were compromising with the adherents of ATR. He quickly organized some of his followers into a fighting force and waged a holy war (jihad) against those who did not accept Islam, or those who were compromising with the traditional religion. In this way, Uthman dan Fodio forced many Hausa people to abandon the traditional religion and accept Islam. He, therefore, purified Islam. He conquered the Hausaland and gained a foothold in Adamawa and Nupe areas of the north and got entry into Ilorin, which is the gateway to the Yorubaland in the southwest.[12]

In short, Christianity and Islam are seen by many Africans as the two foreign forces which undermined the ATR. They both divided the community into two camps—the converts (either Christian or Muslims) looked down upon the old traditional religion and the loyal adherents of the traditional religion. They also looked down on each other. Thus it can be asserted that from the middle of the 19th century to about the middle of 21st century, there has been a continuing struggle between the imported religions and the indigenous religion held by Nigerians.[13]

11 Ibid.

12. Ibid., 114–115.

13. Ibid.

ATR and Renewed Modern Tensions

ATR is the indigenous religious heritage of the pre-Islamic, pre-colonialist/ Christian Africa. Although there are no pervasive shrines, gods and goddesses as before, ATR still exerts enormous and pervasive influence upon the adherents of Islam and Christianity. Besides, there has been concerted effort by the remaining adherents of ATR to take back its lost territories. Traditionalist fight back: Cultural Revolution of the 1970s: Since tradition worldview is part and parcel of the African mindset and worldview, Christianity and Islam did not continue to hold undisputed sway. Rather about the middle of the 20th century, when most countries in Africa became politically conscious and eventually achieved independence, there was a huge hostile response. For example, Nigeria attained independence in 1960; and this affected many aspects of Nigerian life, including culture in general and religion in particular. There were many nationalists who associated the foreign religions with imperialism and colonialism and who wanted to see Christianity and Islam supplanted and replaced by ATR. The only saving grace was that, at the time of independence, there were strong Nigerians who were devoted Christians and Muslims. But Nigerians were forced to reexamine their stand vis-à-vis ATR. In the wake of the reevaluation of Nigerian culture, indigenous languages, style of dressing, art, music, drumming, dancing, and observances of traditional festivals, received a boost.[14]

In pursuing the Cultural Revolution, undue attention was given to the revitalization of the indigenous culture, particularly religion. In consequence, "traditional religion came to be recognized as a religion that Nigerians could embrace without a feeling of inferiority among the adherents of the foreign religions."[15] ATR became equal to Islam and Christianity in the eyes of governments and Nigerians. This led to universities in the country changing their divinity departments to religious studies departments.[16]In sum, indigenous religions and their counterparts, Islam and Christianity, as well as civic culture have been the seedbeds of religious hatred and division which are disrupting the social and political landscape of the country. The spirit of looking down and despising other people created by the forces of the so-called foreign religions continued to bear fruit and to be perpetuated. All three religious communities in Nigeria have their enthusiasts, thereby creating unhealthy and lethal competition and war.[17]

14. Ibid.

15. Ibid.

16. Ibid.

17. Caillois, *Man and the Sacred*, 170–171.

It is important to realize that war does produce dramatic change. For example, when the civil war ended in 1970 there was a new Nigeria. Nigerian Christians came out with a new desire to see the nation socially, spiritually and politically transformed. That gave birth to a revolutionary movement with the motto: "I Found It!" This experience unfortunately did not last as we shall discuss in the chapter on Nigerian Pentecostals and Charismatics' theology of public engagement.

The Nigerian experience of sour relationships amongst the three religions—ATR, Islam and Christianity—is a tip of the iceberg. In the next section we must see Nigeria's experience of war and violence in the light of the global community. This will help us to understand the historic or classic Christian approaches to war.

Recurrent Problems on the Path of Symbiotic Relationship

Four issues need to be clarified to help us understand the symbiotic nature of the interactions of the three Nigerian religions—ATR, Islam and Christianity. First, it has been argued that Africans are incurably religious. This assertion usually makes it look like non-Africans are not naturally religious. However, all human beings are incurably religious. In a brief definition of religion, A.K. Rule defines religion as "the acknowledgement of a higher, unseen power; an attitude of reverent dependence on that power in the conduct of life; and especial actions, such as rites, prayers, and acts of mercy, as peculiar expressions and means of cultivation of the religious attitude."[18] We would argue that what the world needs today, if it must overcome the temptation of self-destruction, is a humane religiosity.

Second, there is the perennial question of the relation of Christianity to other religions. Over the centuries, the Christian view of other religions has sometimes seemed almost entirely negative. There was a time when all that was important was to talk about the true religion, Christianity, and ignore others which were categorized as superstitions. This attitude has its roots in the Old Testament where "the worship of Baal or Astarte is denounced by the prophets as worship of nothings." It was a false religion. Augustine's argument in the City of God was an argument aimed at demonstrating the nothingness of Roman religion.

Third, these reactions to other religions have made it very difficult for Christians to understand the nature and theology of those religions let alone tolerate their right to exist.[19] But with recent concern about terrorism

18. Rule, "Religion, Religious," 426.
19. Hastings, "Religion," 604.

we cannot continue to avoid taking other religions seriously. The attitude of seeing them as false and good for nothing has prevented Christians in Africa from recognizing the pervasive influence of African Traditional Religion and Islam on Christianity.

Even in the Old Testament, we see other religions affecting Israel's religion. For example, Hastings states, ". . . the religious development of Israel is seen as having been deeply influenced by the beliefs of neighboring (Canaanites) peoples. Distinctive as the Israelite tradition undoubtedly was, it cannot be understood in isolation."[20] Self-reflection, self-criticism and self-repenting all depend on our awareness of the world around us. God does use other people and their faith to rebuke us. This is true with Christianity which is an incarnational religion. Christianity has been influenced by Judaism and Christianity has influenced Islam and vice versa. Christians would do themselves much good to wrestle with the nature of other religions and how they might be mutually interacting with each other. We need to enter into conversation with them. We see an example of that heritage in the Alexandria School of Theology where Clement and Origin wrestled with Platonic and Gnostic thought.[21] Hastings concludes that "A Christian theology of religion needs somehow to hold together the import of two seemingly contradictory NT texts: 'There is salvation in no one else [than Christ], for there is no other name under heaven given among men by which we must be saved' (Acts 4:12). And 'God our Saviour desires all men to be saved' (1 Timothy 2:4). 'No other name' on the one hand, 'all men' on the other . . ."[22] That does not mean that an unselfcritical alliance of world religions is necessarily an alliance for righteousness or that all religions "really" teach the same moral or social code.

Fourth, Christians and other faiths have some shared understanding and/or core values perhaps more than they often realize. Of course, there is no denying the fact that Christianity has given to the world what other faiths or religions have not. Edward Grant pointed out that during the latter Middle Ages (AD 1050–1500), God used the Bible to create a peculiar religious person, called the schoolman or scholastic. This peculiar religious person used the Bible as his primary tool to study theology and society.[23] As a result, Mangalwadi states that no earlier culture had created such a rational man with the intellectual "capacity for establishing the foundations of the nation-state, parliaments, democracy, commerce, banking, higher

---

20. Ibid., 605.

21. Ibid.

22. Ibid., 607.

23. Grant, *God and Reason in the Middle Ages*, 1.

education and various literary forms, such as novels and history,"[24] With
these clarifications, we need to now turn to an elaboration of the concrete
interaction of Christianity and other faiths and their adherents in Nigeria.

The All-embracing Nature of the Christian Faith

The point the foregoing analysis has stressed is that religion is all embracing.
It involves belief in transcendent, worldview and praxis.[25] The New Testament described Christianity as a religious faith which is rooted in the life,
teaching, and death by crucifixion, and resurrection of Jesu of Nazareth. The
doctrine of Christianity is the life wire of its adherents' life: claims, beliefs
and practices. For instance, in Nigerian Christianity there are texts that are
very fundamental in terms of living a life of public and private integrity,
particularly in situations whereby interpersonal relationship becomes extremely difficult. People intentionally treat you unfairly just to see what you
will do. Jesus told Christians what to do in such circumstances: Forgive.
Forgiveness is humanly difficult but it is not impossible if we know why we
have to do it. Thus Jesus gives the reason in this text: For if you forgive men
their trespasses, your heavenly Father also will forgive you; but if you do not
forgive men their trespasses neither will your Father forgive your trespasses.
(Matthew 6:14–15) Nigerian Christians are taught to live in harmony with
one another, to be compassionate and humble. And given that they have
tasted God's love and forgiveness, they are unconditionally required to forgive even those who are unforgivable—their enemies. When they do, they
are directly achieving two important things: (1) they are imitating God who
forgives our trespasses and (2) they are reciprocating God's forgiveness.

Another important text that helps Christians in their daily relationships with other Nigerians is Luke 14:11: For everyone who exalts himself
will be humbled, and he who humbles himself will be exalted. A Christian
who takes the Word of God seriously will do everything possible to avoid
the temptation of pride which invariably leads to despising other fellow humans and assuming that you can reduce them to nothing. In some sense,
the Christian life of forgiveness is rooted in humility. We cannot forgive
others when we are proud and always want to make even. In the early 60s,
Apostle Peter wrote to a persecuted Christian community these words to
remember it of Christian life and duties: "Do not repay evil with evil or insult with insult, but with blessing, because to this you were called so that you
may inherit a blessing" (1 Pet 3:9). These texts unraveled what is absolutely

---

24. Mangalwadi, *The Book that Made Your World*, 77.

25. Frame, *The Doctrine of the Christian Life*, 56.

needed if Christians in Nigeria will ever be able to push the boundary of possibility for harmony, love, justice and peace in the Nigerian context of multireligious communities. Somebody has to stake his or her neck out to do "the dirty job" of cleaning up the socioreligious and sociopolitical messes of our nation. The Christian call to costly discipleship requires such service. By and large, the Christians Holy text, the Bible claims that "With God all things are possible!" This phrase simply means that if we trust God and not our anxieties and fears we can push the boundaries of the possibility for some meaningful interactions in Nigeria amongst the faiths communities.

To do so, one critical obstacle needs to be addressed. There is the assumption that Christianity is a proud religion because it claims to be the only true religion in the world. This impression about Christianity might not be entirely true. It is not Christians who have made that claim. Rather, that is Christianity's founder and Savior, Jesus Christ told one of His disciples, Thomas: "I am the way, the truth, and the life. No one can come to the Father except through Me" (John 14:6 NLT). So, Nigerian Christians are claiming and living what their Lord, Master and Saviour has taught them. Of course, in Nigeria, the only religion that does not claim superiority to the other faiths is African Traditional Religion. But Muslims also claim that Islam is a superior religion because its prophet and founder, Mohammed, is the last prophet and has the last message from God.

The point here is that in as much as this challenge is critical and definitely needing attention, pursuing such discussion will only lead to social derailment. Therefore, in order to move forward, each religion in Nigeria needs to try to relearn the nature, scope, theology and ethics of its neighbour. In doing so, the adherents of each religion need to recognize that it is God who has given the earth to all humanity; and by extension God has given all Nigerians—ATR adherents, Muslims and Christians the right to live and move freely in the country. All religions in Nigeria have the right to life, shelter and community. They have the right to live and flourish. The psalmist says: "The heavens belong to the LORD, but He has given the earth to all humanity." Therefore, religious freedom is the right of every Nigerian. The church's teaching on creation includes the creation of all humans in the image of God. All living things are created. God along deserves worship and awe. The psalmist says, "The heavens proclaim the glory of God. The skies display His craftsmanship" (Ps 19:1). Creation can be studied; nature cannot be worship and/or be feared. But you see, in African Traditional religions nature is feared and worship.

Human Failings and the Scripture

An analysis of the interaction of religious faiths in Nigeria will be incomplete without a careful elaboration of what constitutes sin. All religious adherents share the original sin of the first human ancestors, Adam and Eve. As we have observed in chapter 2, their rebellious attitude against the clear instructions of God led them into sin, that is, the conscious breaking of God's moral law. What constitutes this sin can be gleaned from the biblical text. Adam and Eve believed Satan's lie that eating the fruit of the forbidden tree will actually make them wise like God (Gen 3:1–17). This was the sin of pride, greed and lust, as it were. C. J. Mahaney commented that the account of Satan in Isaiah 14:13 underscores the fact that pride is what constituted the earliest sin. For the motivation behind Satan's rebellion is exposed thus: "You said in your heart, 'I will ascend to heaven; above the stars of God I will set my throne on high.' Led by the prideful Lucifer, powerful angelic creatures possessing beauty and glory far beyond our comprehension arrogantly desired recognition and status equal to God Himself. In response, God swiftly and severely judged them."[26] Mahaney argues, "Pride not only appears to be the earliest sin, but it is at the core of all sin."[27] Similarly John Stott states that pride "is more than the first of the seven deadly sins; it is itself the essence of all sin."[28] All religions have a dose of the problem of pride. Pride is at the center of religiously motivated violence and destruction of human life and the natural world. For as Mahaney commented, "Pride takes innumerable forms but has only one end: self-glorification. That's the motive and ultimate purpose of pride—to rob God of legitimate glory and to pursue self-glorification, contending for supremacy with Him."[29] This is the primary reason why the Christian Scriptures tell us that God opposes the proud (James 4:6; 1 Pet 5:5). Pride is what causes disunity amongst religious faith communities. The desire to have an edge over and above other faiths is not only driven by fear of domination but also by pride. In his discussion of The Trinity of Sin, Christian social ethicist and theologian, distinguished Prof. Yusufu Turaki observed that "Pride . . . works more on the soul and spirit. Pride is drawn to status, fame, honour, pomp and power, and it corrupts our thoughts and imagination by filling them with images of what we could enjoy and persuading our minds that we deserve them."[30] This is

26. Mahaney, *Humility*, 30.

27. Ibid.

28. Stott, "Pride, Humility & God," quoted in Mahaney, *Humility*, 30.

29. Mahaney, *Humility*, 32.

30. Turaki, *The Trinity of Sin*, 92.

why our minds can hardly have room for the love of God or love for our neighbors. In addition to pride is the hidden concern for security. As we have argued in chapter II, human beings dread disgrace, public exposure of nakedness. Since Adam and Eve hid from God when they heard His voice because they were naked, the sense of self-insecurity has become our lot in life. Still, pride alone does not explain all there is in human hostility.

Our pervasive human sense of insecurity causes us to act contrary to God's plan for human flourishing: diversity, harmony and interdependency.[31] All human beings are sinners in need of God's saving grace, the finished work of Jesus Christ on the cross. Thus the Christian teaching of salvation and redemption becomes critical to all faiths.[32] In sum, humans are created by a personal, rational, and thinking Being. Thus, Christians and other faiths have some shared understanding and core values more than they often realize.[33]

On the other hand, there is no denying the fact that Christianity has given to the world what other faiths or religions have not. In order to give humans a vision of an alternative community of moral-virtue character and vision, a community that nurtures human flourishing, God decided to disclose himself to the human race through Jesus Christ's incarnation— the virgin birth of Christ demonstrates God's love of the human race and the natural creation. Jesus took on the human flesh in order to judge sin, thereby affirming the possibility for repentance, reconciliation, restoration into divine and physical relationship. Indeed, all things, including humanity is meant and created to proclaim God's glory![34] It is important to say that the whole of Christian doctrine and theological interpretation rest on the foundation of this primal affirmation of Scripture. Christian affirmation of Scriptures is derived from a biblical awareness of God not only as the source of all truths but also as the Truth in and of himself.[35] Christianity's belief in the incarnation not only distinguishes it from other faith, but also helps it to grasp a better perspective of humanity: human dignity. If God can take on human flesh it means that humans are indeed created in His image and likeness; the human person is not a thing, a worm, so to speak. Humans are created with dignity, in imago Dei.

---

31. Jewett, *God, Creation, & Revelation*, 5.

32. Ibid., 5.

33. Orr, *The Christian View of God*, 4, as quoted in Erickson, *Christian Theology*, 21.

34. Erickson, *Christian Theology*, 17.

35. Mangalwadi, *The Book that Made your World*, 82.

Conclusion

In conclusion, Nigerian religiosity is real! In spite of the various ongoing violent conflicts, Nigeria's religious communities are interacting with each other. For better and for worse they are influencing each other. Nigerian theologians and ethicists need to find a way of helping these communities recognize their relationship and the social dynamics involved. Nigerians need to be told that one of the primary reasons there is lack of respect amongst the various faith communities is because politics and religion are compromised, misguided, abused and mismanaged. Finally, if Nigeria must move forward, Paul says,

> Love must be sincere. Hate what is evil, cling to what is good. Be devoted to one another in brotherly love. Honor one another above yourselves. Never be lacking in zeal, but keep your spiritual fervor, serving the Lord. (Rom 12:9–21)

This means that all Nigerians, irrespective of their religious affiliations, should pursue peace and maintain it. The Christian God is the God of love, justice and peace. To pursue peace is to serve the Lord of peace through participation in peacemaking. The next chapter examines Nigeria's role in peacemaking.

Chapter 5

Classical Christian Approaches to Violence

Introduction

Violence and war are undesirable elements of our social life. Violent conflicts constitute an entire phenomenon that exalts and transforms human societies. It does so at the cost of great suffering and pain. In other words, war's destruction is unimaginable and limitless. It is all embracing. This is why we must strive for peace. Christians have taken many approaches in deciding how they should act according to their faith. In this section, we will summarize the following major approaches: pacifism, crusade, just war, and in the 1990s, just peacemaking. Generally speaking, all approaches draw upon four sources—that is, four places to look for the vision, values, and rules that can provide answers to the questions: "What does God want of us and how shall we live?" TheseSources are the Bible, Church tradition, reason, and experience. Christian ethics begins with a careful reflection on the Bible as a record of God's word to God's people who have gone before us. Christian tradition includes resources such as creeds, Church declarations, canon law, sermons, histories, lives of the saints, and writings of theologians.

This chapter defines and elaborates some of the classic perspectives on war. It begins with an examination of various Christian approaches to violence. It draws upon these varieties of approaches in order to help the process of peacemaking and initiatives. However, since we live on this side of eternity, conflict, violence and war abound. There is no nation that does not face this challenge, except Switzerland. Yet we must not miss the paradox of war and violence. We must understand, why it happens and what are the desired outcomes.

Pacifism and Violence

Faced with violent suffering, early Christian pacifists chose a remarkable alternative to violence. They rejected the killing of one human being by another. The Christian believed such violence totally opposed the foundations of Christian faith.[1] They knew by experience that the Spirit of Christ was not the same spirit which inspired social relationship in their pagan society. This power of love in their midst freed them from the need to rely on raw force. They replaced the need for war with this thought: "Every word which [goes] out of our mouth in faith and love shall tend to bring conversion and hope to many. They themselves had experienced the presence of God's kingdom marked by the power of love. They trusted both the providence and the protection of God for their life and survival in this world."[2] They were perhaps guided by the following basic principles and convictions:

1. First, peace for those who confess the Christian faith, cannot be defined simply as the absence of conflict, strife and war. The word *shalom,* as it is used in the Bible, expresses the wholeness of full human life in a community of mutual sharing and affirmation. It includes prosperity, happiness, and respect among friends, and all that belongs to personal fulfillment. For a community, it means the flowering of its common life in all respects. It is the fulfillment of the promises of God. As such it is a dynamic concept which demands ever-new realization in personal and social situations (Ps 128:5–6). It includes not only the constant renewal and transfiguration of the individual person's outlook and inner being, but also the constant reexamination and, if necessary, radical refashioning of the external social, economic and political structures of societies.

2. Peace is therefore inseparable from the achievement of justice in human life, provided that justice be understood in the biblical sense, not as the administration of a set system of laws but as the activity of God, raising up the poor and outcast, vindicating the victims of oppression

---

1. Driver, *How Christians Made Peace with War*, 60–61.
2. Ibid., 60–61.

and saving people from their sins for new life with each other and with him.[3]

The foregoing two points demonstrate that nonviolence is a belief which is theologically grounded. The early church had a perspective on nonviolent self-defense, rooted in a strong dosage of faith in the activities of God in the world, particularly on the cross. Christians were not passive as it is often construed today.[4]

In sum, pacifism is against all forms of violence. It draws our attention to the fact that violence is not only an enemy without, but also within persons. We may not have to go into a physical war. Yet, we must fight the spiritual battle. We must observed that the debate on the efficacy and the applicability of pacifism tends to eclipse the main subject: Imitation of Jesus Christ. A particularistic concern for justice has distorted our Christian minds in that we can be likened to the Jews and the Greeks of Paul's day. Their moral and philosophical worldviews blinded their eyes. Paul had to work hard at dislodging their mindsets so that the Gospel would take root in their hearts.[5] In order to create an alternative narrative, Paul points both Jews and Greeks back to the person of Christ.[6] Pacifism asks Christians who find themselves in an environment of horrific human hostility to not allow that situation to deprive them of the foundation of faith in a risen Lord, Jesus Christ.

Just War Theory and Violence

Augustine of Hippo has been tagged as the originator of the Just War theory. His work on the City of God seems to reveal why this was a subject that he was concerned about. The main thesis of the City of God is two loves: The love of God which eventually leads to the love of one's neighbor and the love of the self. He was not someone who was interested in politics, but because he was deeply concerned about the issues of order and peace, and realized that human beings cannot act peacefully until they are forced to do so, he suggested that government must sometimes wage war for the sake of peace and for the perfection of the state. In suggesting just war as a theory, Augustine was responding to the overwhelming situation of his time, whereby the Roman Empire was experiencing unprecedented unrest owing to the many

3. Committee on Society, Development, and Peace, *Peace—The Desperate Imperative*, 9.

4. Ibid., 13–14.

5. Pinkares, *The Sources of Christian Ethics*, 110.

6. Ibid., 115.

attacks on the empire by so-called "barbarians" from outside. Yet what we tend not to realize is "Augustine is strikingly nuanced in his views about war. Although he considers military force morally justified in certain cases, he never stops lamenting the fact that such violence has to be used at all."[7] Augustine says, "No one is fit to inflict punishment save the one who has first overcome hate in his heart. The love of enemies admits of no dispensation, but love does not exclude wars of mercy waged by the good."[8] This statement shows that he was deeply disturbed by the circumstances confronting society at that time. So he has to come to term with the fact that to avoid indiscriminate wars, just war must be used in the service of peace and unity of the empire.

With the Just War Theory in mind, Christians today raise the question: should Christians defend themselves when attacked by Muslims? If yes, what would self-defense involve? I will explore the answer further in the chapter on Christian Just Self-defense. Here, however, we will point out some cultures seem to idolize and promote violence. For example, culture of honour and shame often promote violence. Plato (c. 427–c. 347 BC) lived in a Greek culture of honour and shame; this was a culture where courage was sometimes valued above and apart from the other classical virtues of temperance, wisdom, and justice. Some of the Greeks of his day valued war as a means of teaching and testing courage in war was sometimes valued above classical virtues of temperance, wisdom, and justice. Plato reflects these values only in measure, for while he proposes that children learn courage from watching the courageous example of their soldier-parents in combat, he places limits on plunder and the enslavement of defeated peoples. Plato privileged peace. He believed that war, whether eternal or civil, was not the best . . . but peace with one another, and good will are the best gifts to the human race. In short, Plato's culture of shame and honor determined his proposal for war. Yet, he privileged justice. The only problem is the efficacy of applying it at the social level, which is often complicated and more complex than we often realize. Justice is not a simple possibility in social settings.

---

7. Reichberg et al., *The Ethics of War*, 70. This is to say, "Augustine is not enthusiastic about political affairs and the accompanying necessity of waging war" (ibid. 71). Unlike Aristotle who "emphasized the intimate connection between political institutions and human flourishing, Augustine was less sanguine about the value of the temporal order for human happiness."

8. Quoted in Windass, *Christianity Versus Violence*, 97.

Just Peacemaking and Violence

Just peacemaking was born during the Cold War. It evolved from the United Nations' (UN) peacekeeping concept. The nation has been in the forefront of many peacekeeping operations in the world. Nigeria was in the forefront of pre-independent agitations in African; and during the Cold War Nigeria participated in peacekeeping missions across the globe, from Congo to Bosnia Herzegovina.[9] When it comes to regional and continental peacekeeping in Africa, Nigeria is a country that has totally committed itself to the efforts of ensuring peace and order. Just peacemaking is not the same with peacekeeping. Just peacemaking (as we have observed in the next chapter) refers to the efforts that policy makers need to make to prevent the breaking down of law and order in the first instance. It provides an added ingredient to the theories of pacifism and just war. Its primary concern is how to ensure justice on both sides of the parties in conflict. In the chapters that follow we will try to engage the implicit biblical thought behind the idea of a nonviolent just self-defense.

Conclusion

Christian history has given a world characterized by moral failure three categorical theories of resolving war and violence—pacifism, just war and just peacemaking. Since all three are proposed by saints whose faith seeks understanding of how to live out the gospel truth, we cannot approach the matters of war and violence as if those principles do not exist. We must deploy the three principles for the service of the human race common good. We must seek to make the world a conducive place for the common good and of human flourishing. This goal will primarily help Christians to see nonviolent direct action as another redeeming example of self-defense, which is at the heart of Jesus' ministry of preaching, teaching and social action.

9. Sanda, "Nigeria's Global Role in Peacekeeping," 79.

Chapter 6

Christian Nonviolent Just Self-Defense

To do an evil act is base. To do a good one without incurring danger is common enough. But it is the part of a good man to do great and noble deeds though he risks everything in doing them.

—Plutarch

Violence is a part of life, so everyone says. War is inevitable. Killing is everywhere. The abnormalities of violence and war, so drastically opposed to life as God intended it, have become so normal that the world cannot imagine anything else. The world cries out for alternatives. The world needs an imagination. Therein lies a portion of our task.

—John R. Yeats

Introduction

This chapter argues for Christian only option for self-defense taught by the master, Jesus Christ: nonviolent just self-defense. It raises and discusses some fundamental questions that contemporary Christians wrestle with as

CHRISTIAN NONVIOLENT JUST SELF-DEFENSE   57

they face on daily basis the threats of Islamic persecution or terrorism in Nigeria. The following important questions are examined: Does the Bible have a message on Christian self-defense that pastors do not want lay members to know? If yes, what kind of message does it have? In the context of a biblical perspective, Christian self-defense takes a different dimension than what it is in a liberal democracy. It involves critically and carefully thinking, reasoning, and drawing a different conclusion from those of the enemies. As we think and reason about self-defense, we need to pay attention to how God works. The enemy thinks "God is dead." There are, of course, certain enemies that believe that God exists and that they are actually fighting His battles. For example, the Lord's Resistance Army (LRA) in Uganda, Boko Haram in Nigeria and Islamic State (IS) across the Middle East, all think that they are fighting for God or the true religion of Allah. Yet, their destruction of innocent people demonstrates that they think like the wicked who say "God is dead!" In such contexts, the Christians who pay attention to God can trust in God instead of human efforts. He or she will be able to realize the reality: "But the Lord is in His holy Temple: the Lord still rules from heaven. He watches everyone closely, examining every person on earth. The Lord examines both the righteous and the wicked. He hates those who love violence" (Ps 11:4–5). It is very instructive to pay attention to what the psalmist reveal here: God who does not have favorites, "examine both the righteous and the wicked." And any one of them "who love violence" He hates. In other words, both the righteous and the wicked are under the scrutiny of God. Whoever loves violence—the righteous or the wicked—the Lord hates. This makes the issue of Christian self-defense very delicate. First of all, we need to recognize that if we (Christians) do wrong God who hates violence will not spare us: "He will rain down blazing coals and burning sulfur on the wicked, punishing them with scorching winds" (Ps 11: 6).

Israelite Wars with the Canaanites

They did not conquer the land with their swords; it was not their own strong arm that gave them victory. It was Your right hand and strong arm and the blinding light from Your face that helped them, for You loved them. You are my King and my God. You command victories for Israel. Only by Your power can we push back our enemies; only in Your name we can trample our foes. I do not trust in my bow; I do not count on my swords to save me. You are the One who gives us victory over our enemies;

You disgrace those who hate us. O God, we give glory to You all
day long and constantly praise Your name. (Ps 44:3–8)

This is a very helpful reflection about the Canaanite war and all the
wars that Israel fought with their neighbors. Our cry for self-defense is okay.
But it must not lead us to where we will deny God what He desires and deserves in creating us: Giving Him all the glory and praise. In the above cited
psalter, we see Israel recognizing and intentionally focusing on why God
gives victory: "We give you praise and glory all day long" (Ps 43:3). Paul also
says, "Always be full of joy in the Lord. I say it again—rejoice" (Phil 4:4). The
reality of the violent conflicts and destruction of innocent lives is happening
at various complex levels. Much of the violence is connected to the fact that
corruption renders governments across the globe community insensitive to
the plight of the poor.

Human Dignity and Non-Violent Self-Defense

One of the greatest discoveries of Western Christianity is "human dignity."
This discovery came as result of a careful reading of the creation of man and
woman in the image and likeness of God. *Nonviolent Just self-defense* in this
chapter is defined as doing what you can to ward off attack nonviolently. It
is a proactive approach to self-defense in that you are thinking not only of
protecting your own life but acting like a true friend and servant of God
who doesn't give up on anyone. That is you try all you can to save the life
of the aggressor. It is an attempt to value both your life and the life of the
aggressor. It is the ability to remind yourself of the fact that you have rights
and responsibilities. One of those responsibilities is the moral obligation to
equally value and protect the life of the other. Jesus' incarnation has a lot
to teach us. It elucidates the fact of our human dignity. Our bodies are not
just dust and ashes; they are the image of God. So God values them to the
point of taking up human flesh in order to rescue us from the prison and
pit of sin: hopeless pride, excessive self-interest and the desire to dominate
others, which all lead to all kinds of disorderly behaviours in the form of the
following tendencies: greed, lust, malice, evil and wickedness.

Avoiding Truth-twisting

In order to objectively interpret how the concept of just self-defense might
contribute to pacifism, just war and just peacemaking, we approach the
issues at stake as a double advocate. We also look at the issue from the
perspectives of God as a God who allows humans to freely exercise their

God-given freedom. We do our theological and social reflections paying attention to the fact that Christians are called to be apostles of love and peace in an age of hate. Therefore, it is crucial to do a theological reflection on the meaning of peace. However, before doing so, we must remind ourselves of the fact that one of the serious crimes against God and the human family is the sin of twisting the truth. God sharply rebuked Job's friends saying to Eliphaz the Temanite: "I am angry with you and your two friends, for you have not spoken accurately about Me, as My servant Job has" (Job 42:7 NLT). This game of truth-twisting has led humanity to the situation it finds itself today. The level of hostilities and conflicts that are wrenching out of place the fabric of human social and moral life are generally products of truth-twisting. In Nigeria they are destabilizing human communities and societies, thereby creating very grievous humanitarian crises and insecurity on an alarming scale.

Self-criticism Needed

Those of us who teach and preach nonviolent resistance to evil need to make sure that our love for God's people is sincere. First, one of the ways to know that is self-criticism and examination. For instance, we may need to ask ourselves: "Have I rejoiced when disaster struck my perceived enemies, or become excited when harm came their way?" Second, we need to check what we claim the Scriptures say about the subject of peace. For instance, if in an attempt to preach the gospel of peace and nonviolent resistance to evil we fail to give the human family the whole truth about the God of the Bible, we are doing great disservice to Jesus Christ and His Church. In fact, we will make it look like we have skeletons in the cupboard to hide or we are concealing some truths in Scripture which our people may have read or will read. Third, we must remember this fact: If God chooses to allow every mess that happened in human history, particularly, the history of the Jews in Scripture, we have no reason to seek to protect Him. There are Scriptural passages that talk about violence and about Him as a violent God.

Furthermore, we (Christians) need to realize that challenges of life elicit response. Therefore, speaking as a double advocate, I would say categorically that if contemporary Christians anywhere in the globe want to go to war or violently respond to their persecutors, they have some basis in scripture to do that—both in the Old and New Testaments. On the one hand, God is portrayed in the Old Testament as a God who is violent and supports violent destruction of humans by fellow humans. There is a red thread of that in the New Testament as there is a red thread of nonviolence in the Old Testament. One biblical scholar has carefully counted the number of times the Old Testament explicitly mentions the word violence in general as well as in connection to God. He computed and came up with the following statistics: "The Old Testament contains 600 passages of explicit violence, 1000 verses attributing violent action to God—both stories of God ordering killing and of God killing others."[1] For example, in Exodus 15:5 Moses described Yahweh as a warrior. Habakkuk 3:9, 11–12 point out how the Lord uses weapons. In Lamentation 2:5 the author, Jeremiah, tells of how God goes as far as fighting actively against the chosen people. If we accept the Bible as the word of God, which we do, then we cannot deny these texts as being part of the Christian Bible that we hallow and respect as God's revelation to the human family.

In the New Testament where we have more teaching on nonviolent resistance to evil, we also have passages that lend themselves to the view of Christians who would want to argue in favor of violent response to the challenge of injustice or war. A familiar passage which is frequently quoted is Jesus' cleansing of the temple as recorded in Matt 21:12–14; Mark 11:15–17). We are told that Jesus entered the temple to pray and instead of finding worshipers praying to God He saw money changers buying and selling thereby distracting the attention of people who have come to worship God. They were distracting people from the real purpose of the temple: House of Prayer. At this sight, Jesus became angry. He immediately overturned their tables and chairs, even using a whip according to the account in the gospel of John (2:13–16).[2] Again, in Matthew 10:34 Jesus made a statement that has been regularly used to argue for violent resistance of evil. He said, "I have not come to bring peace but a sword" (Margot Kässmann explains that this passage can be seen in a different light; we will note that later).[3]

Several points are important.

1. We must not avoid the challenge of the Old Testament's frequent teaching on war. "OT contains many statements that have been used to support participation in armed conflict. The words of Moses in such passages as Deuteronomy 7:16 constitute a warrant for Israel to engage in aggressive "holy" wars to seize the Promised Land. In Deuteronomy 20:10–18 rules to conquest are given that command the Israelites to exterminate all those who live within the Holy Land.

1. Schwager, *Must There Be Scapegoats?*, 46–47. Quoted in Kässmann, *Overcoming Violence*, 25.

2. Kässmann, *Overcoming Violence*, 28.

3. Ibid.

Deuteronomy chapters seven and twenty, along with the war narratives of Joshua, Judges, and Samuel, make it clear, as Peter Craigie shows, that aggressive wars were carried out "at the command of God, in the name of God and with the help of God. And even if it is argued that the biblical 'historical' narratives have a legendary character to them, and that the wars of conquest described therein did not actually take place, still the problem remains. For although the historical reality of the wars of conquest may perhaps be removed in this manner, the theological ideal remains."[4]

2. If contemporary Christians want to violently respond to the challenge of persecution today they will definitely have many examples from history to emulate. Christianity has had a long trajectory of experiences which includes the narrative of Christian atrocities prior and during the Reformation. One of the Christian heritages is the crusades: This was the history of over 200 hundred years of series of military campaigns that Christians in the Middle Ages undertook to recapture back the Holy City of Jerusalem from the Muslims who, in 1076, captured Jerusalem and built a mosque. The Christians who fought those wars saw themselves as Christian pilgrims. They actually saw themselves as carrying out the mission of God. Thus the "taking of the crux" all the way to Jerusalem symbolized their vows that would only be fulfilled upon reaching their destination. In sum, those encounters were messy, brutal and bloody on both sides.

3. If contemporary Christians choose to reject nonviolent resistance to injustice or persecution, they have the long Christian tradition of Just War theory. This theory was developed by the church fathers like Augustine of Hippo and later leaders like Thomas Aquinas. The church started as a pacifist church but added the theory of just war after recognizing the reality of human nature and the need to ensure freedom and order in society. Many things came together to prompt the shift from pacifism to just war. The church's alignment with the state starting with Constantine led to Augustine and others arguing that pacifism was not enough. Augustine specifically believed that due to human nature humans are naturally violent and to keep them in check force has to be used. Nonetheless, to avoid chaos, this force must be regulated by a legitimate body, the government. In other words, to avoid indiscriminate and arbitrary use of force, it was suggested that only an

4. Craigie, *The Problem of War in the Old Testament*, 50. Quoted in Clous, "The Christian Church and Peace through the Centuries," 69.

authorized body can enforce order. In their reading of Romans 13 they saw government fitting that role. If government, in the pursuit of law and order starts a war every loyal citizen is free to participate fully to bring law and order in society. However, realizing that human governments are not flawless, they created criteria for when citizens should support government for going to war or for citizens opposing a war.

Glen Harold Stassen gives a summary of the criteria based on the U.S. Catholic bishops' definition in *Challenge of Peace.*

a) Probability of *success:* To kill and maim people is wrong even for a just cause, if after all the deaths, the just cause will be lost anyhow.

b) Just *cause:* War may be fought only to protect innocent life, preserve conditions necessary for decent human existence, and secure basic human rights against a real and certain danger. The position of the side to be defended must be more just than the adversary's position.

c) Last *resort:* All peaceful alternatives must have been exhausted.

d) Just *authority:* War may be declared only by those with responsibility for public order.

e) Just *means:* War must not directly attack noncombatants but only military targets. "Under no circumstances may nuclear weapons or other instruments of mass slaughter be used for the purpose of destroying population centers or other predominantly civilian targets." Just means and cost/benefit proportionality apply both to the decision to make war and to conduct during the war.

f) *Cost/benefit proportionality.* The cost of the war to people and to the international community must not exceed the good expected if it is fought.

g) Just *intention:* The purpose of war may not be conquest, enslavement, revenge, or an ideological crusade but only the pursuit of peace and justice. Unnecessarily destructive acts or unreasonable conditions such as unconditional surrender must be avoided.

h) *Announcement:* The intention to make war and its just causes must be clearly announced by the legitimate authority, so that the adversary is aware of the seriousness of the situation and of what he must do to avoid war, and so that the people can judge its justice.[5]

5. United States Conference of Catholic Bishops, *The Challenge of Peace,* 85–109,

The genocidal conflicts in Nigeria and other parts of Africa are not conventional. The only thing they follow in the above list is the last point: *announcement*. They sometimes send letters to announce their coming to attack. However, they fail the criteria because they do not give terms of peace. So, Christians who want to respond to genocidal conflicts by adopting this principle may not find it very helpful to them.

4. But we must ask whether contemporary Christians who are overwhelmed by genocidal violence and want to respond to that challenge by violence are ignoring the teaching of Jesus in Matthew 5–7 and other passages which seem to condemn the use of violence. If we stop at the above analysis, however, we have not done justice either to the whole of Scripture or to the history of Christianity. Contemporary Christians must not forget the fact that Israel was a theocratic nation when it fought the Canaanites wars. Israel went to war with God as their king. Other nations today are not in the same situation. Second, much of the OT teaching emphasizes peace as well as war. In Isaiah 2:4 and 9:5–6, Micah 4:1–3, and Zechariah 9:9–10 the prophets refer to the Redeemer of Israel, the future Messiah, as one who would begin a new government of Israel and would end the militaristic ways of the world by establishing a pacifist society. These texts indicate that military industries would be converted to the production of agricultural implements and that existing weapons and armaments would be destroyed. God "causes wars to end throughout the earth. He breaks the bow and snaps the spear; He burns the shields with fire" (Ps 46:9). In the NT, Jesus reinforced His teaching that violence is no solution to human problems when He was arrested by the Roman soldiers. Peter, wishing to defend Him, drew his sword and struck the servant of the high priest, cutting off his ear. "Put your sword back in its place," Jesus told him, "for all who draw the sword will die by the sword. Do you think I cannot call on my Father, and he will at once put at my disposal more than twelve legions of angels?" (Matt 26:51–53).[6] The answer is obvious: the LORD of heaven's armies is here among us; the God of Israel is our fortress" (Ps 46:7, 11).

5. If the contemporary Christians who are overwhelmed by their situation of hostility want to respond in violence, they will need to reconsider their decision in the light of the definition of peace. Peace

147, quoted in Stassen, *Just Peacemaking*, 232–33.
6. Yeats, "Peace in the Old and New Testaments," 70.

is variously defined by scholars. Peace means more than the absence of war. It is now generally accepted that peace does not mean that we will completely do away with all negative aspects of social life. The central tenet of peace is not an utopian concept. Rather, peace is about well-being that is possible even in the midst of circumstances that are beyond human control. Another important fact is that peace is not limited to humans only but also involves the well-being of the entire creation. Finally, peace is not brought about by the effort of mere humans. It is the act of the God of peace. Peace is God himself. This is very important because it means that if God is not recognized and acknowledged as the source of peace we cannot find peace. So peace is not about us, it is about God and our human response to Him in obedience. God is the focus. He should therefore be the focus of our self-defense. The cross gives us a bigger picture of how God is truly the foundation of self-defense.

Putting the Christian perspective on peace in the light of the cross gives us a better grasp of the state of human affairs. *Baker Evangelical Dictionary of Biblical Theology* defines peace by its etymological roots in the Hebrew and Greek. First, it argues that the English word "peace" conjures up a passive picture, which needs to be corrected. It is therefore observed that peace is not just "an absence of civil disturbances or hostilities, or a personality free from internal and external strife." Rather, the Bible goes beyond that picture to demonstrate that based on the Hebrew root *slm*, peace means "to be complete" or "to be sound."[7] This implies that if contemporary Christians are not interested in peacemaking they must reexamine their theological soundness, which, as Paul says, includes the fact that our faith, love and salvation are the primary key concerns of Christian self-defense. These—faith, love and salvation—are what we need to protect above all else: "But let us who live in the light be clearheaded, protected by the armor of faith and love, and wearing as our helmet the confidence of our salvation" (1 Thess 5:8). Therefore, if Christians choose to abandon this truth, it may show that they have not grasped the fundamental truth of their faith in Christ. For one of the key issues about peace is the work of Christ on the cross of Calvary. We must be willing participants in the eternal plan of God for humanity and creation as a whole. We are not the ones who cause peace to happen. God has already paid the price for the peace we are asked to preach and practice. He broke down the wall of hostility which used to separate humans from each other and humans and their Creator, God. It is in this light that one can better understand what Jesus meant when he declared, "Do not suppose

7. Schaefer, "Peace."

that I have come to bring peace to the earth. I did not come to bring peace, but a sword" (Matt 10:34). That is, because not everybody is going to be willing to live a righteous and just life. Generally, even those who profess Him as their Lord and Savior are not going to completely surrender to the life of right and just living, which is the foundation of peace. The blessing of being a peacemaker lies in the fact that we have the option of living to please our sinful nature but we instead opted for a life of right and just living, the way of peace. In other words, we don't pursue peace because we run out of options for violence, but because we realize whose we are: the children of the God of righteousness, justice and peace. We a united with the Prince of all peace, Jesus Christ! And Paul wrote, "The God of peace will soon crush Satan under your feet" (Rom 16:20). By becoming Christians, whether contemporary Christians like it or not, they have signed up for peace. You can't go back! For in the New Testament, peace is at the heart of every aspect of the message of the gospel. In order to bear witness to the gospel, Christians are called to exhibit peace in their relationships. Moreover, the biblical message of peace is comprehensive, relating to all of life rather than limited to the context of military violence. Peace describes the well-being of the person and the nation—both political well-being and a secure relationship with God. "The Bible portrays peace as integral to all of this life as well as the life that lies beyond."[8] With the foregoing clarification of the issue of peacemaking, let us now turn to how the idea of just self-defense contributes to the discussion of pacifism, just war theory, and just peacemaking.

Further Reflections on Nonviolent Just Self-Defense

Given that ideas have consequences, what consequences would a Christian quest for nonviolent self-defense have in a world where people think it is naïve not to defend yourself with violence in the face of an attack meant to harm you or loved ones? We need to ask where, how, why, what, and when, should we talk about nonviolent just self-defence?

1. The context of talking about nonviolent just self-defense needs to be clear. We live in a generation that is increasingly violent and hostile. The unprecedented sophistication of the hostility that today's Christians face makes their faith fragile. The level of Christianity's fragility is unimaginable in the sense that the number is enormous. For out of the world's over 7 billion people, "More than 1 billion people live in countries affected by armed conflict or by the fragility

---

8. Yeats, "Peace in the Old and New Testaments," in *Peace Reader,* 16.

of their societies. Fragile states are often vulnerable to conflict because their populations tend to see their governments as ineffective, illegitimate, or both. As a group, they are the ones that lag behind in achieving the United Nations' Millennium Development Goals."[9] Some people blame the failure of society on the lack of living a way of life that pleases the Supreme Being. For example, in this category, we have some Muslims who in the effort to appease Allah want to implement the Muslim criminal law, Shari'a, to the letter and thereby establish an Islamic State (IS). They assume that this is what will enable Islamic countries to retrieve their historical and power of past fame. They want their kinsmen to believe that they are fighting to protect the interest of *the religion of Allah* as allegedly superior to all others. But we know that[10] many contemporary religious groups and communities that are fighting other religions are doing so primarily for economic and political reasons. Thus, today we have widespread terrorism. Their approach to war defies all conventional ways of engagement. They break all the international standards of particularly just war theory by using random attacks on soft targets and destroying innocent civilians and property. Our discourse on any kind of self-defence must bear this situation in mind. The reality is we live in a world where violence and lawlessness are on the increase. Our cities and villages are overcrowded. Many people, particularly the young, are out of work or in dead-end jobs, and most can see little light at the end of the tunnel. They are alienated from the traditional stabilizing forces of family disciplines, and they are fed with Nigerian TV Nollywood violent movies and unattainable sex, where the role models are often muscle-bound supermen, and the major motivations are greed, lust, rage and revenge.[11]

2. We need to know exactly when it is appropriate to talk about self-defence. Should Christians wait until there is an attack before they respond? Or should they attack first if they seem threatened by hostile people?

3. People living in fragile contexts usually do not wait for government to help them because the government officials, who are supposed to provide them security, freedom, order and justice, have been failing

9. United States Institute of Peace (USIP), "States of Fragility: Post-2015 Ambitions." Retrieved on March 23, 2015. www.usip.org/events/states-of-fragility-2015-ambitions

10. Cameron et al., *Globalization and Self-Determination*, 218.

11. Wiseman, *The SAS Self-Defense Handbook*, 8.

them. If the church fails to help them articulate their perspectives on self-defense their random responses will be grievously disastrous.

4. We need an alternative to self-defense, which *nonviolent just self-defense* fits. Nonviolent Just self-defence is an attempt to listen to the voices of people living under perpetual threat of genocide, annihilation. It is also a way of asking, are there no more options than pacifism, just war theory, or crusade? We need to pay careful attention to several examples from the historic peace churches. Each of the examples below show a difference approach to the issues of the day and one common thread is nonviolence approach to the issue: *Example from Swiss Anabaptism*: The historical narrative of Anabaptism shows that they were opposing the unhealthy social, political and religious situation of their time. For example, in Switzerland Zwingli's followers had to part ways with him because of his unwillingness to break away from the Catholic tradition, particularly the unhealthy marriage between the church and the state. "The first re-baptism of 21 January 1525 may have been about bringing the practice of baptism in conformity with a New Testament pattern . . . Within a few short years, those who accepted re-baptism were choosing to enter and to build a church that chose its own leaders without regard for the authorities in Zurich and that practiced economic sharing as an alternative to a property-based security protected by the sword."[12] They opposed tithe because the tithe was used to pay pastors who will not serve the interests of the marginalized but the established church and the state. While it was said that Anabaptists were killed for practicing rebaptism, what actually got them killed was defying the authorities that presumed to establish the church and defying the state church established by civil authorities for the whole of society.[13] Here lies an important clue in nonviolent just self-defense that was all nonviolence and had such an impact in the society. It birthed a church that was willing to remain true to the faith in spite of the many hardships. Their faith, love and their confidence in Christ's salvation made them resolute and resilient in the face of persecution. The greatest self-defense that the church needs today is: Faith, love and confident in Christ's salvation.

By and large, the general idea of self-defense is loaded with many assumptions which might need to be unpacked. For example, there is the assumption that one can overpower the person who intends to inflict harm

---

12. Manchala, *Nurturing Peace,* 33.

13. Ibid., 34.

without personally getting hurt or harm in the process. Furthermore, self-defense is a legally defined term/concept. This means that when the matter comes to a court of law, *in order for what you do to be considered as self-defence, your actions must stay within legal standards and boundaries.* If you cross these legally spelt out standards by the judicial institution—and it doesn't matter *why*—then you are no longer legally defending yourself or others. The definition of self-defense rests on the following arguments. Every human being has a right to life, that is, not to be killed.[14] The logic is that when an aggressor comes to harm or kill you or a loved one, he/she has legally forfeited his/her right to life and can be killed by you who still has the right to life and to protect your life or the life of a loved one.[15]

The challenge of making sure the life of the aggressor is protected presents fundamentally two challenges.

1. Identify and address by the early church fathers. The early church fathers, like St. Augustine of Hippo and St. Thomas Aquinas understood that human beings, because of what they are by nature, if left without specific guidance self-defense can easily metamorphose to self-revenge and self-vendetta. Some of the people who assume that self-defense is going to just be what it is legally defined above are naïve about the paradox of humans: the capacity to do tremendous good and at the same do tremendous evil. That is why Augustine taught: *We do not seek peace in order to be at war, but we go to war that we may have peace. Be peaceful, therefore, in warring, so that you may vanquish those whom you war against, and bring them to the prosperity of peace.*[16] Augustine taught that the passion for inflicting harm, the cruel thirst for vengeance, and unpacific and relentless spirit, the fever of revolt, and the lust for power, are rightly condemned in war.[17] Similarly, St. Thomas Aquinas taught that if a man in self-defense uses more than necessary violence, it will be unlawful: whereas if he repels force with moderation, his defense will be lawful . . . Nor is it necessary for salvation that a man omit the act of moderate self-defense to avoid killing the other man, since one is bound to take more care of one's own life than of another's.[18]

14. Rodin, *War and Self-Defense*, 3.

15. Ibid., 4.

16. *Letter to Boniface*, clxxxix, quoted by Tonti-Filippini, "Self Defense and Just War Theory," 5.

17. Ibid.

18. Ibid.

2. Self-defense involves violence. Therefore, we have to face the difficulty of defining violence. Violence is a very challenging term to define because it does not have borders. It is generally a denial of space for the other to coexist. It is refusing to acknowledge the humanity of the other. It is ignoring the following faith convictions:

- That all human beings—male and female—are created in the image of God

- That human life is intricately interrelated with the rest of God's creation, and that human relationship with God is experienced and lived out in mutually interdependent relationships.

- That human beings are called to uphold the integrity of God's creation, [and respect and protect human dignity and right to shelter, life, and participating in the mainstream society].

Violence has been described as violation and harm against all striving to be part of a free and equitable relationship in God, with each other, and with all of creation. It is an assault on life as gifted to us. Nonviolent just self-defense and just peacemaking as a Christian calling thus minimally involve opposing and transforming forces of violence that undercut the ability of people to live in freedom and dignity and optimally involves strengthening all efforts that work for the furthering of life for all.[19] Why defining violence is proving difficult is because definition entails creating parameters and limits. But violence does not fit into the category of borders.[20] Violence is borderless, so to speak. The borderlessness of violence can be illustrated with the narrative of violent attacks in Nigeria. Whenever there is violent conflict it is not only the people that are at the specific location of the crisis get killed, but also those who are passerby. The humans and the environment also get destroyed.

Conclusion

As we contemplate a reflection on these matters, we must not forget that it is part of our calling to clarify issues so that they human family benefits from our partnership with God, who says, "Let there be light," and there was light. God calls his people in every generation and dispensation, who armed themselves with the attitude of His Son, Jesus Christ, to work with him to

19. Manchala, *Nurturing Peace,* 64.

20. Ibid., 10.

bring peace to fruition. In the dispensation of Israel they were called to align with God's agenda of punishing the Canaanites for ignoring him and worshiping the gods and goddesses of their own imagination. But as we have seen elsewhere in this book, one still sees the motif of peace flowing through the pages and narratives of the Israelites. Our dispensation started with Jesus declaring "peace be with you" to his disciples. We are not the Israelites who needed a promised land. It is a dispensation wherein the weeds are allowed to grow with the good seeds. We see a God who through Jesus Christ "defeats violence and war and human brutality of all kinds with fierce and undying love."[21] This is the God we are called to align with today. Peace in general and defenselessness in particular have their most profound source in Jesus Christ, his cross and resurrection. As such, it is a challenge to every person who professes faith in Jesus. "The good news about Jesus Christ is the gospel of peace."[22] Sometimes we think what we are going through is so unique that it requires a fresh approach than what we read in the Bible and in the history of the church.

Given Jesus' teaching in the Sermon on the Mount, particularly Matthew 5:43–48, violent self-defense is not an option for the Christian. Jesus clearly advocated nonviolent self-defense in the entire block of the Sermon on the Mount (Matt 5–7). Nonviolent just self-defense as strategy means the ability to know the defense techniques that can do you good in time of attack. One of the strong nonviolent just self-defense principles is information. When people are well informed about who the enemy is that is enough to know what nonviolent just self-defense strategy to adopt.[23] For example, several churches in Kaduna and Jos cities have realized that their proximity to the Muslims make them very vulnerable to attack. Therefore, what they have decided to do is to collaborate with their Muslim neighbors to feed the hungry and cloth the naked. In so doing, ECWA Lemu Road which is right at the heart of a Muslim community has decided to reach out to the Muslims to meet some social needs the Muslim community. The pastors and the church elders of identified the Muslim community leaders and contacted them with the intention of working together to meet any critical social need the Muslims have. In one of the crises in the city, the Muslim youth in the vicinity protect the church from being burned down by youths from other Muslim communities. This strategy which the church adopted worked. It goes to confirm that nonviolent just self-defense is refusing to see nonvio-

---

21. Ibid., 17.

22. Ibid., 23.

23. Maslow, *Motivation and Personality* , 195, quoted in Wilson, *A Criminal History of Mankind*, 10.

lence as passivity. Nonviolent just self-defense is about Christians who are resolutely committed to Jesus Christ's teaching on nonviolent self-defense: "Pray for those who persecute you." Nonviolent self-defense is all about being creative and engaging in intelligent gathering as well as being proactive.[24]

Describing the process, Paul says, "We use the weapons of righteousness in the right hand for attack and the left hand for defense" (2 Cor 6:7). Of course, the context of self-defense is the context of suffering. Yet, as recent scholarship shows "Paul's apostolic witness was not only that the life, death, and resurrection of Jesus changed individuals' status before God, but also that through Jesus Christ God is bringing about a new world, a new society, a new kind of human relationship, based on peace and reconciliation rather than on fear and antagonism."[25] This requires us to combine nonviolent just self-defense with all the other theories: pacifism, just war and just peacemaking. The life of Jesus Christ is a model and an empowerment for a renewed and reconciled society that challenges the warring habits of the present order. This is what the gospel represents. Peace is a gospel.[26] The next chapter discusses the above subject in terms of the mission of the church.

24. Groves, "Revisiting Self-Suffering," 221.

25. Mast and Weaver, *Defendless Christianity*, 15.

26. Yoder, *The Politics of Jesus*, cited in Mast and Weaver, *Defendless Christianity*, 15, 16.

Chapter 7

The Contemporary Quest for Self-Defense

But the believers who were scattered preached the Good
News about Jesus wherever they went.

—ACTS 8:4 NLT

Self-interest and happiness can never go together.

—ANONYMOUS

All truth is safe, and nothing else is safe; and he who keeps
back the truth, or withholds it from men, from motives of
expediency, is either a coward or a criminal, or both.

—ANONYMOUS

Introduction

Whenever evil strikes every fabric of social life and spirituality gets shaken. This chapter wrestles with the reality created by decades of corruption, persecution and bloodshed. It evaluates how decades of bloodshed and destruction in Nigeria, generally fueled by share financial unfaithfulness and corruption of governmental officials in Nigeria have tended to eclipse Nigerian Christians' conception of the mission of the church. I discuss how Nigerian hostility undermines the church's mission. Christians who have been bearing the dreadful state of affairs are overwhelmed and crippled by fears. Some of them are even getting radicalized by the other faith communities—Muslims and African Traditional Religionists—in Nigeria. This is because they fear the possibility of been decimated by "religious terrorism." So some think they can't help but resort to violent self-defense. I argue that the Church needs to remember it has a mission. As in Acts of the Apostles, the persecution which resulted from the execution of Stephen, ("a man full of God's grace and power . . . full of the Holy Spirit" Acts 6:8; 7:54–59) scattered the disciples of Jesus Christ, who were known as people of *the Way*, the church. They were forced to leave the comfort of Jerusalem. Yet, they did not forget the mission of the church. The scattered band of disciples was a people with a clear mission from the Master, Jesus Christ. Thus, we read: "But the believers who were scattered preached the Good News about Jesus wherever they went" (Acts 8:4 NLT). If Nigerian Christians will do same today, they must grasp the connection between corruption and persecution.

The Politics of Corruption and Persecution

Persecution is a situation whereby fellow human beings seek the utter destruction of the lives of their fellow brothers and sisters. In our contemporary world, excessive lust for power and corrupt acquisition of public resources for self while in public office are the bedrock of persecution. We live in a continent where the political elites assume that siphoning public money to their private bank accounts is the smartest thing to do.[1] Corruption prevents God-given resources in a society benefiting everybody. Few elites that have access to the resources enriched themselves with public fund with impunity to the detriment of the masses; thereby create a situation of disaffection and disillusionment. The members of society who experience and suffer the hardships, humiliation and powerlessness so created can't help but react in a revengeful manner.

In her recent book on what is happening in the Middle-East and Nigeria, Sarah Chayes examines what emerges: "Afghans returning to the Taliban, Egyptians overthrowing Mubarak government (but also redesigning Al-Qaeda), and Nigerians embracing both radical evangelical Christianity

---

1. Babs Ajayi, "The End of the Jonathan Kleptocracy (II)," *Nigeriaworld*, April 16, 2015. http://www.nigeriaworld.com/feature/publication/babsajayi/041615.html

and the Islamist terror group Boko Haram. In many such places, rigid moral codes are put forth as an antidote to the collapse of public integrity."[2] Chayes identified the unexpected link: *corruption*. Thus, Chayes argued, "Since the late 1990s, corruption has reached such an extent that some governments resemble gloried criminal gangs, bent solely on their own enrichment. These kleptocrats drive indignant populations to extremes-ranging from revolution to militant puritanical religion."[3] The disturbing reality of this situation is that innocent people get killed. Thus who are looking for opportunity to revenge the humiliation that has been perpetuated against them or against their relatives become easy prey to opportunists who desperately want to create a power vacuum so that they too can achieve their own self-interest, and lust for power. In order to achieve their goal they use religiously motivated rhetorical language to flare up the state of affairs. Chayes work is extremely important. But it has a gap that must be filled. Corruption is not just what government officials or a few elites in society do. It is part and parcel of the human family. As we have pointed out in this book (see chapter II), since the fall, humanity has been affected with excessive self-interest, deception and lust for power. Thus the mission of the church is very necessary!

The Challenge of the Contemporary Church in Nigeria

The incarnation of Jesus Christ has made it possible for humans whose nature is ingrained with self-ambition, deception and lust for power to live for the common good of humanity. Christ restores humans to their original state of goodness to the extent that they can walk the talk: The mission of the church is living as children of light and truth in a corrupted and twisted generation. As we have argued in this book, Christians are still capable of doing tremendous evil like all other humans beings. The surest way of safeguarding themselves is to remember Paul's caution: "Live no longer as the Gentiles do, for they are hopelessly confused. They live for lustful pleasure and eagerly practice every kind of impurity" (Eph 4:17–19 NLT.). One of the things that should guide Christian's thinking on any matter is, would it cause sin to control me: "Don't sin by letting anger control you" (Eph 4:26 NLT). Paul further invite Christians to "speak the truth in love, growing in every way more and more like Christ, who is the head of His body, the church?" (Eph 4:15 NLT). The Christian community in Nigeria can't ignore all these exhortations in its pursue of self-defense.

2. Chayes, *Thieves of State*, front page cover.
3. Ibid.

As Christians continue to face the challenge of national terrorism, self-defense is seen as an inevitable option. Thus, from the onset, two broad statements need to be made.

1. If we see and treat the discourse of self-defense within the confines of missions, that is, the *Mission of God*, we will be better prepared to take advantage of every opportunity persecution offers for spreading the Good News to a broken and dying world. We need to objectively articulate the issues at stake and be as frank as possible in the discourse.

2. People who do not think about self-defense do not have a strategy for self-defense. It is one thing to feel the need for self-defense but it a whole different ball game to know what self-defense entails. Several decades ago, particularly in the early 1970s and 1980s, it would have been unthinkable to hear Nigerian Christians talking about self-defense. The mindset of Nehemiah and his people was what they knew: "Our God will fight for us" (Nehemiah 4:20). Today, however, things have changed. Without a good picture of the crippling fears that Christians living in a violence-prone society face, you cannot grasp why things have changed. Nigeria's violent conflict is multifaceted: economic, political, ethnic, and religious corruption. Thus, the question of self-defense becomes complicated. Christians, particularly the youth, have for more than three decades and a half ago discovered that they will not survive if they don't do something to defend their churches and their communities. They argue that the spirit of self-defense has been with the Church since the unhealthy marriage of the Church and the state (the Roman Empire) during the reign of Constantine. Self-defense is a widespread phenomenon. As we listen to the biblical witness we should be willing to expect a twist: What if God says self-defense is what works what will that entail or not entail?

Christians who faced the daily reality of violence are sincerely seeking answers to the problem of insistent attacks. They are forced to ask God, "I am being attacked; how long must I wait. When would You punish the perpetrators of destructions of innocents lives?" They think that those of us who write about nonviolent responses to aggression have not been in a situation where we feel like we are a second between life and death. They feel we are clueless and absolutely have no idea what we are talking about.[4] Of course, they feel that way because they think we are asking them to be passive.

4. Culliton, *Nonviolence,* 6–7.

People reject nonviolence because they assume that nonviolence proposal encourages the perpetuation of evil. Culliton shows that is mistaken. He says, "Christian nonviolence does not leave one totally defenseless nor does it give aggressors an unimpeded opportunity to do whatever they choose."[5] In summary, nonviolence is not a situation where you let evil thrives. Rather it is a strategy whose aim is to obliterate and/or uproot violence nonviolently. But to achieve peace is to participate in nonviolence.

There is the need to think concretely about the situation of violence and the quest for self-defense in Nigeria so that we will be able to turn our darkness into light: hope, grace, and peace. A question to ask is, would self-defense give our people hope, grace, and peace? Jürgen Moltmann reminds Christians that the concrete reality is that "overcoming violence nonviolently is possible. But it can also require martyrdom. We think of Gandhi and Martin Luther King, Jr.; we think above all of Christ himself."[6] We can find guidance in what Peter told his audiences who were perhaps going through a similar situation like ours: "So then, since Christ suffered physical pain, you must arm yourself with the same attitude He had, and be ready to suffer, too. For if you have suffered physically for Christ, you have finished with sin" (1 Pet 4:1 NLT). Peter had a firsthand experience of persecution. I bet he had not forgotten his imprisonment and all that he suffered in Acts. He and other apostles were flogged by the council: "The apostles left the high priest's council rejoicing that God had counted them worthy to suffer disgrace for the name of Jesus" (Acts 5:41). He also understood the context of his audience. What was going on at the time of Peter's writings, were some of the most horrific tortures devised by man. At the time of Nero (Caesar of Rome), Christians were being used as human torches to light his palace. They were also being thrown to the lions, and all kinds of wild animals in the Coliseum. The pagans of the Roman Empire considered Christians worse than they were. Christians were thought to be cannibalistic because of the communion remembrance, as well as incestuous because they called each other brothers and sisters. Christian publicly confessed Christ even though they understood the consequences.

So, 4:1 is Peter's way of defining Christian self-defense. No surprise! Our Redeemer's life is an embodiment of what attitude and shape Christian self-defense should take. Peter elaborates what he says in 4:1 with 4:12: "Do not be surprised at the painful trial you are suffering, as though something strange were happening to you" (4:12), NIV). If there is anyone in Nigeria who should have a good grasp of what is happening and the reality of

5. Ibid., 8.

6. Moltmann "Political Theology and the Ethics of Peace," 41.

persecution, it is the Christians. Christ has told every Christian what to expect. He said, "A slave is not greater than his master . . ." Christ further said, "If they have persecuted me, they will persecute you also." Yet we need to take the whole counsel of Scriptures. 1 Peter 5:9 says, "But takes your stand against him (Satan) solid in the faith, knowing that the same things in the way of suffering are being accomplished in the entire association of your brothers in the world." Christians across the globe are suffering persecution for their faith in Christ. For instance, in Middle Eastern countries it is common for Christians to have their hands cut off for distributing gospel tracts. Contemporary Christians cannot simply talk about self-defense in the way the world perceives and defines it. It must be a self-defense of a different kind. We also need to take the time to seriously deal with the underlying issues of which violent conflicts and wars are but symptoms. We must understand the underlying social, economic, political and religious issues, which are fundamentally destabilizing communities and nations across the globe.

Jesus and Christian Self-defense

The Bible, however, provides the essential framework for these conflicts. And the Bible provides answers to questions of social justice and human oppression. As J. Andrew Kirk writes, "The starting point of any theological interpretation must coincide with the bias of the Christian gospel itself ("good news to the poor . . . releases to the captives . . . liberty to those who are oppressed," Luke 4:18) . . . There is no option; theology must be done out of a commitment to a living God who defends the cause of "the hungry" and who sends "the rich empty away" (Luke 1:53).[7]

To arm ourselves with the attitude of Christ, the Beatitudes and the Sermon on the Mount should be read in the context of social injustices and overwhelming human oppression. Therefore, the social world of the audience of Jesus' day needs to be understood so that we would not be using our social lenses to interpret what he said in the Sermon on the Mount. It is only by so doing that we can catch the remarkable transforming power of his statements in the Sermon on the Mount. Luke saw Jesus as: A Bringer of Good News to the poor. Jesus ministry confirmed that title, particularly as He went to villages and towns to teach and preach that Good News. When He read the portion of Isaiah 61:1–2 in Luke 4:18–19 at his inaugural speech, scholars believe He saw Himself as fulfilling those words. Seeing Himself as one who has been anointed to bring Good News to the poor, Jesus generally confronted the establishment and exposed the social structures of

---

7. Mott, *Biblical Ethics and Social Change,* xii.

systemic evil. For example, his table fellowships with outcasts—prostitutes, tax-collectors, sinners, lepers and so on—were times where He openly and freely ate with those who were considered religiously and socially untouchables. Jesus audacity to eat with them was to expose the social injustices of the Jewish holiness code and thereby restore a sense of human dignity in a people whose society has made them think and believe that they were less than nothing, not even human beings. It is in this larger context that we can better grasp some of the statements that Jesus made in the Sermon on the Mount. You may be wondering how all the foregoing connects with the issue of self-defense. To grasp the connection one needs to follow Jesus profound statements in the Sermon on the Mount, particularly related to the issue of nonviolent just self-defense.

Jesus said, "If someone slaps you on the right cheek, offer the other cheek also (Turn the other cheek)" Matthew 5:39. Many people think Jesus teaches his audience to passively endure social abuses. As a result, contemporary Christians living in hostile societies often openly reject this command. Perhaps the fear of death makes the statement sound suicidal to them. Such fear blinds their eyes from carefully paying attention to the concrete principle of transforming initiative that is based on Jesus' deliverance mission to the socially disinherited. Scholars tell us that in the Jewish culture of Jesus' day the audience, which were his disciples and the poor, would catch what Jesus meant. I personally believe that if the statement meant what some think (i.e., passive reception of evil), the poor would have risen up in protest and stoned Jesus to death. But they didn't because that was not what Jesus meant. Walter Wink and other New Testament scholars and ethicists tell us that in that culture, there was a way of slapping people that would either indicate honour or dishonour, equality or inequality. For example, masters backslap their slaves (with the back of their hand) to show their inequality. And you can only use the back hand of your right hand to slap someone standing in front of you on that right cheek. If anyone in society backslaps his fellow brother or sister it shows that that person intends to dehumanize or humiliate the person so backslapped. Notice that Jesus says, "If someone slaps your *right* cheek." This definitely shows that the person is backslapped with the intention of being reduced to nothing. But if the person who is backslapped offers or turns the other left cheek, the aggressor has no choice but to use his fist (not the back of his hand), which shows the aggressor has failed in achieving his or her intention of humiliating the person. And that means he is treating the other person as an equal, not someone inferior. And when that happens the person that was backslapped gains equality. The process of deliverance has begun. In other words, by simply turning the other cheek he or she is saying I refuse to be humiliated or dehumanized any longer. See I am your equal. I am a human being just like you; so treat me as such. All this is implied in turning the other cheek when your oppressor backslaps your right cheek. Again Jesus said, "If you are sued in court and your shirt is taken from you, give your coat, too" (Matt 5:40). This thought fit the context of humiliation, injustice and dehumanization. Jesus is saying if an oppressor takes you to court and sues you and takes your outer garment, then pull off your inner garment too and strip naked to shame the oppressor and show how unfair he is being.

The Jewish culture is like African culture where it is considered shameful and even a taboo to see the nakedness of someone. Therefore, by the poor creditor giving both garments to the creditor before the judge, he/she stands naked before those in the court that day and then he/she runs out of the court naked so that those who are standing outside listening to court cases sees him/her running out naked. Such scene will engender outrage from those standing outside and they will turn against the oppressor because their injustice against the poor has been exposed. This act nonviolently discredits the oppressor and the court system which is now seen as a system that is not favorably disposed towards the poor.

Jesus further said, "If a soldier demands that you carry his gear (back pack) for a mile, carry it two miles" Matthew 5:41. Jesus' audiences were under Roman occupation. They were the conquered people. The Roman government had a policy that allowed soldiers to ask people from the conquered cultures of the Empire to carry their military back packs in order to remind them of their humble place in society. But due to abuses of this policy, the soldiers were only permitted to have the person carry the pack one mile. It was illegal for the Roman soldier to force someone to carry his pack two miles. It is in this context that Jesus told his audience at the Sermon on the Mount to go a second mile. This means, when the person who has been asked to carried the soldier's pack or gear reaches the one mile limit, the soldier reaches out his hand to take back his backpack. But the person refuses to give it and continues to walk towards a second mile. At this point the soldier is thrown off balance. That act puts him in confusion and recognition of getting into big trouble with his superiors. Again, the nonviolent response is not passive. The oppressed person actively asserts his dignity! In this process the soldier discovers the humanity of the person carrying the backpack; he suddenly recognizes that he is dealing with an equal, not just, a nobody. As we look at Jesus' approach in the Sermon on the Mount, we are left with the ground for nonviolent just self-defense as part of just peacemaking. The Sermon on the Mount is to be seen in the context of God's grace. We are participant in the delivering grace of God because of what happened on the cross:

> For Christ Himself has brought peace to us. He united Jews and
> Gentiles into one people when, in His own body on the cross,
> He broke down *the wall of hostility that separates us.* . . . He
> made peace between Jews and Gentiles by creating in Himself
> one new people from the two groups. Together as one body,
> Christ reconciled both groups to God by means of His death on
> the cross, and our hostility toward each other was put to death.
> [And remember] He brought this Good News of peace to you
> Gentiles who were far away from Him and peace to the Jews
> who were near. (Eph 2:14–16 NLT)

This is the ground of just peacemaking and nonviolent just self-defense. Jesus says, "You have heard that it was said, "Love your neighbor and hate your enemy. But I tell you: Love your enemies and pray for those who persecute you, that you may be sons of your Father in heaven. He causes the son to rise on the evil and the good, and sends rain on the righteous and the unrighteous. . " (Matt 5:43–48). Jesus who taught us to pray for our enemies did it himself even when he was hung upon the cross. Jesus defined our enemies as those who curse us, hate us, and exploit us selfishly. Nigerian Christians can love and pray for their enemies (Muslim terrorists) because Jesus asks Christians (including Nigerian Christians) to love their enemies and pray even for those who persecute them. Given that Christian love originates from the heart, and not just an emotion, Jesus has the right to command us to love our enemies. What Jesus is asking us is not burdensome because we have each personally benefited from it. He loved us when we were his enemies too (Rom 5:10). Loving and praying for our enemies demonstrates how much we appreciate how much God has loved us and through Jesus Christ brought us near to himself. The idea of praying for our enemies is a strategy: When we are able to pray for our enemies we will find it easy to love them. Prayer takes the "poison" out of our attitude. In Matthew 5:43–48, Jesus did not leave us in darkness about why he is commanding us, his disciples, to love and pray for our enemies. These reasons include, among other things, the following:

1. This love is a mark of maturity, proving that we are sons of the Father, and not just little children.
2. It is Godlike. The Father shares his good things with those who oppose him. Matt 5:45 suggests that our love "creates a climate" of blessings that makes it easy to win our enemies and make them our friends. Love is like the sunshine and rain that the Father sends so graciously.

3. It is a testimony to others. "What do ye more than others?" is a good question. God expects us to live on a much higher plane than the lost people of the world who return good for good and evil for evil. As Christians, we must return good for evil as an investment of love.

When Jesus talked about the need for Christians to be perfect in Matthew 5:48 he does not imply sinlessness. What he simply means is that we will be doing what God does: "The Father loves His enemies and seeks to make them His children, and we should assist Him!"[8] This shows that God's grace is not cheap, as Bonhoeffer reminds us. Bonhoeffer argued that if we don't expect suffering we are expecting cheap grace. This kind of grace is "grace without repentance, grace without concrete change in our way of relating to others, grace without cost to us. It is 'easy believism,' which characterizes many who claim to be Christians (Matt 7:15–27)."[9] Bonhoeffer challenged Christians living in hostile societies to embrace a "costly grace":

> Costly grace is the gospel which must be *sought* again and again, the gift which must be *asked* for, the door at which a man must *knock*. Such grace is *costly* because it calls us to follow, and it is *grace* because it calls us to *Jesus Christ*. It is costly because it costs a man his life, and it is grace because it gives a man the only true life . . . Above all, it is *costly* because it cost God the life of his Son: "ye were bought at a price," and what has cost God much cannot be cheap for us. Above all, it is *grace* because God did not reckon his Son too dear a price to pay for our life, but delivered him up for us. Costly grace is the Incarnation of God.[10]

It is a pity that it has been many decades since Bonhoeffer wrote these words; yet the church is still not willing to embrace this gospel of costly grace. This is why when contemporary Nigerian Christians talk about self-defense they are actually thinking of a self-defense that is costless. they have no clue that cheap self-defense is "unity without responsibility, forgiveness without repentance, equal treatment without restitution, harmony without liberation, conflict resolution without relational healing, peace without God."[11] The price of cheap self-defense could be as devastating as the price of cheap grace was for Germany.[12] We should not underestimate the complex-

8. Wiersbe, *The Bible Exposition Commentary*, 1:25.

9. Bonhoeffer, *Cost of Discipleship*, quoted in Stassen and Gushee, *Kingdom Ethics*, 36.

10. Bonhoeffer, *The Cost of Discipleship*, 44–45, quoted in DeYoung, *Reconciliation*, xvii-xviii.

11. DeYoung, *Reconciliation*, xviii.

12. Ibid.

ity and the depth of the fragmentation of the Nigerian society.[13] Yet we must not succumb to fear and discouragement and give up on the possibility of nonviolent just self-defense. Our task is to participate with God in breaking down the walls that separate human communities: *Self-interest and the will to power*. If God has not given up on us why should we (Christians) give up on the Muslims? The truth is that generations of Nigerians face a terrible failure if we do not embrace just peacemaking and/or nonviolent just self-defense that is "life changing, society transforming, and long-lasting."[14]

Further Reflections on Self-Defense

The book of Acts reported, "But the believers who were scattered preached the Good News about Jesus wherever they went" (Acts 8:4). The ripples of what happened in Acts are still being felt today in contexts where Christians realize that "[G]reat challenges present great opportunities."[15] That was exactly what it meant for the early church. If contemporary Christians do not see the mission of the church as the surest self-defense, there will be no way they can take advantage of the subtle opportunity that persecution often offers. We need to pay attention to the following distracting assumptions and rationalizations, which Christians invariably do offer, that tend to eclipse a healthy view or perspective about what God can do in spite of the persecution:

- We often assume that we are *the sinned against* (and not also sinners) and so the problem entirely the fault of others and so we do not have much to do with peacemaking.

- We assume we are marginalized in that we have no credentials that qualify us to be peacemakers.

- We assume the language of peacemaking in the Bible is for certain kinds of Christians but has nothing to do with us.

- We tend not to realize that peacemaking is first of all God's mission.

- We tend to forget that peacemaking is the big vision of God for the church and the entire human race (Rev 7:9).

- We tend to also assume that regional and international bodies like the African Union (AU), Community of West African States (ECOWAS), World Health Organization (WHO), the New Partnership for Africa's

13. Ibid., xix.

14. Ibid., xi-xii.

15. Okonjo-Iweala, *Reforming the Unreformable*, 4.

Development (NEPAD), the United Nations (UN), Food and Agricultural Organization (FAO), and The World Trade Organization (WTO) are responsible and capable to bring world peace without our doing anything.

Just peacemaking is saying to each other, "Look, you and I both belong to God. I, too was formed from clay. You don't need to be afraid of me" (Job 33:6–7a). I don't have to worship you, but God alone. I don't have to be afraid of you like a god! Let us agree that only "God is greater than any human being" (Job 33:12). To be sincere with each other we need to declare to each other that: All of us have "sinned and twisted the truth, but it was not worth it" (Job 33:27). Therefore, we need to make peace with one another. To stop unhealthy comparison and competition we need to tell each other the truth about our humanness: For God created both the Christians and the Muslims in Nigeria. This is the primary identity marker that links all humans in one family, and not religion, ethnicity or any other markers humans tend to use to justify the destruction of lives and property.

Furthermore, Christians do not have any reason for comparing themselves and competing with any other person or creed. God's incomparably great power, which he exerted when he raised Christ Jesus from the dead is at work in them (Eph 1:18–23). In fact, Jesus Christ says, "I have been given all authority in heaven and on earth" (Matt 28:18 NLT) This implies that everything is already there for the benefit of the Church: "God has put all things under the authority of Christ and has made Him head over all things for the benefit of the church" (Eph 1:22). God puts everything at Christians' disposal not for them to brag about but so that they can freely share the Good News with the rest of the world that is not there yet. For the early Christians, persecution was not going to shut their mouths. Whenever God allows a situation He doesn't stay aloof. Rather, He is always interacting in human affairs. As he does, we see him using ugly situations and turning them out for the benefit of the human race. For example, Christian experienced terrible persecution for several decades in Communist China. But in spite of that, the church grew and today Christianity is flourishing in China.

Conclusion

God is still in the business of tearing down the walls of hostility and making room for the Good News to be preached. The church in Nigeria needs to understand this dynamic so that she will participate in the harvest of lost souls. Satan wants us to forget the mission of the church so that we will be captive of fear. Violence is a symptom, not the real problem. As Christians reflect on violence and how to respond to it they must realize that "hatred and revenge only intensify over time . . . Only repentance heals the cancer of hatred . . . Nigeria is more than a place and a nation; it is an attitude,"[16] corruption. Nigeria is like many other corrupt societies in the world where the masses are looking for an opportunity to vent their frustration. Corruption and happiness can never coexist. Corruption has reduced our society to religious bigotry and stereotyping in that our political and religious elites use it to pit the poor masses against each other. Our identities—"social, religious, linguistic and ethnic—are used as instruments in the struggles for power and wealth on the one hand, and for justice and dignity on the other."[17] These settled attitudes impact our theological reflections in no small measure. If we will really help the church to participate in the mission of God, we need to encourage Christians to: "wrestle with the 'dilemmas of power,' [corruption], and the challenge of seeking 'unity amid increasing diversity; consider the theological relevance of affirming 'human vulnerability and the church's option for a kenotic existence' and emphasize the need 'to heal the trauma of violence' as an important way of overcoming the vicious cycle of violence."[18] This book has pointed us to the deeper problem of evil in society. Finally, it results from the Fall and the fact that all people are sinful, selfish and evil. We have recognized the seriousness of evil. All human beings can potentially do tremendous evil. Our world is saturated with self-interest, deception and excessive lust for power. Therefore, eradicating corruption is not a simple possibility. It requires more than good political decisions and systems. It requires divine help. And that means: We must pray! In Paul's prayer formula we see a picture of how we can pray to make things that are impossible a simple possibility. Paul writes,

> I urge you, first of all, to pray for all people. Ask God to help them; intercede on their behalf, and give thanks for them. Pray this way for kings and all who are in authority so that we can live peaceful and quite lives marked by godliness and dignity. This is good and pleases God our Saviour, who wants everyone to be saved to understand the truth . . . In every place of worship I want men to pray with holy hands lifted up to God, free from anger and controversy. (1 Tim 1:1–4, 8)

---

16. This is a commentary on Obadiah 1:10, which says, "Because of the violence against your brother Jacob, you will be covered with shame" (NIV). The lesson here is that until Muslims and Christians in Nigeria recognize each other as human beings, they will never stop killing each other.

17. Manchala, *Nurturing Peace*, 7.

18. Ibid., 7.

This helps us understand what we should do in prayers and the result we should be looking for in a context of corruption. If we understand how much the sin of corruption is killing and destroying us, we will not play with prayer. Paul understood what could happen if people and their rulers are not prayed for: they will continue to harm us. But if we pray for them, they may have a life-changing encounter with God or overcome their destructive tendencies.

Part 2

UNMASKING FALSEHOOD

THE SOCIAL, ECONOMIC, AND religious problems plaguing nations of the world have created a psychological challenge. We feel like we are in siege: constant state of agitation. In Nigeria, the Boko Haram, and lately, Fulani herdsmen and farmers' deadly clashes, have led to the death of thousands as well as crippling socio-economic life across the nation.[19] In spite of all the technological advances humans have made in the 20th and 21st centuries and efforts to contain human violent aggression, human history is still characterized by a situation where "bloodshed follows bloodshed" (Hos 4:6). And because of unending decades of violence and insurgency, Nigerians have continued in what should be described as a constant state of anxiety, crippling fear and hopelessness. This constant state of agitation has not allowed the Nigerian people to stop and think about the broad issues of their national needs, which will usher in a truly new Nigeria. They have failed to realize that what is actually happening in the country and in the globe is that "the old is dying, the new is being born." Nigeria is an expectant mother. But lacking a qualified midwife, Nigeria is having great difficulty in childbirth. Human beings fight and destroy each other because they assume that is what will bring them peace and wholeness, progress in life and the progress of their religion. This has given birth to the myth of redemptive violence. Humans kill their fellow human because they believe a lie. This lie must be debunked to create room for humane social, religious and political order. To this project we now turn.

19. Balarabe Alkassim, "Northern governors vow to tackle insecurity in the region," *Daily Trust,* March 26, 2014. http://www.dailytrust.com.ng/daily/news/20049-northern-governors-vow-to-tackle-insecurity-in-the-region

Chapter 8

The Suffering Servant in Isaiah
and the African People

Introduction

This chapter argues that if Nigerians are to overcome their current social, political, ethnic, and religious predicaments, they will need to grasp the general human context, not just their own parochial, Nigerian context. They must reflect on the situation of violence; what in fact causes it? Perhaps many Nigerians who have been most hit by the reality of human violence against fellow humans; and in fact have in one way or the other contributed to it would say injustice is the primary cause. They may say that everywhere you turn there is one cry: "Give us justice and peace!" The awareness of injustice or unfair treatments creates a situation of frustration, exasperation, and aggression, which by and large often result in violent destruction of life and property. This act is assumed to be the only necessary response to protest real or perceived injustice in society. Generally, human excesses and injustices often lead to the belief that violent response will bring about the desired result: justice and peace.

We humans live in a world where every person strives to move to the top, ahead of others. We strive for the so-called "autonomy." This situation is nowhere illustrated than by the separatist and reformist posture of the Muslims in Northern Nigeria. It is also demonstrated in the ethnic game of stereotyping and despising other ethnic tribes in Nigeria and elsewhere in Africa. These attitudes are largely the result of the assumption that if one wants to forge ahead one must treat them unjustly and unfairly. This is partly why as we advance in our science and technology so also we are accelerate our desire for autonomy. Consequently they forget that if we rapidly accelerate we will derail. Whenever a train derails there are always negative consequences: causalities. On May 12, 2015 Amtrak Train 188 traveling from Washington, DC to New York City derailed in Philadelphia, USA. Over speed caused the derailment. The train rapidly accelerated 65 seconds before the crash from 70 MPH to 106 MPH. One second before the derailment the engineer applied an automatic break in order to avoid derailment at the curve. But that was too late. The train derailed, killing eight passengers on board and leaving many of the 240 passengers on board seriously injured. This pathetic incidence illustrates the human life. We think that in order to move ahead we have to push other fellow humans to the bottom of social life. It is in this context that violence is often seen as redemptive. That is, we move ahead by using every available means, including violence, to accelerate to the top. Jesus' life revealed a different route to the top.

Through Adam and Eve's disobedience to God's revealed truth, humanity had derailed. So the essence of Jesus' coming into the world is to put humanity back on track. He came to help us slow down so that we will not derail by rapidly accelerating. Jesus alludes to this problem of rapid acceleration when He responded to the mother of James and John request; and the subsequent indignation of the ten disciples. When the ten disciples eventually learned of what transpired they flared up. However, Jesus called them together and said, "You know that the rulers in this world lord it over their people, and officials flaunt their authority over those under them. But among you it will be different. Whoever wants to be a leader among you must be your servant, and whoever wants to be the first among you must become your slave. For even the Son of Man came not to be served but to serve others and to give His life as a ransom for many" (Matt 20:25–28 NLT). That is, whoever wants to be ahead must not unfairly treat others by demanding service but must humbly serve others instead. This situation flies in the face of a generation that is rapidly accelerating in science and technology but lacking behind in the spirit of humility and service. Jesus draws our attention to the fact that there is a better way to the top: Humility and service. This is the picture we have in the Isaiah Servant Songs. In this section of Isaiah prophecies, Jesus is set as the model for human flourishing, harmony and integration. After the resurrection Jesus announced to the disciples that he has not just gone to the mountain top but God has actually handed over everything in heaven and on earth to Him: "Jesus came and told His disciples, 'I have been given all authority in heaven and on earth.'" Paul picks that discussion further by announcing that "He (Jesus) is far above any ruler or authority or power or leader or anything else—not only in this world but also in the world to come. God has put all things under the authority of Christ and has made him head over all things for the benefit of the church (Eph 1:21–22). Jesus Christ became the head of all things nonviolently. He has taught us that to get to the top we must be willing to absorb pains and sufferings. We can actually get to the top without necessarily treating other people unfairly. We do not have to become violence in order to get ahead. This falsehood is exposed by Jesus' willingness to absorb violence: Jesus has become the head of all things not by treating others unfairly but by absorbing the unfair treatment meted to him by others.

The point here is that Jesus promotes nonviolence in the Gospels. In the Old Testament, the prophets had predicted how he will promote nonviolence by absorbing suffering. In order to create an alternative and transformational narrative in Nigeria, we use the theme of the Servant Songs of Isaiah, which underscores the theme of justice and its resultant peace. This approach will not only provide a critique of the myth of redemptive violence, but also point to the potentiality and possibility that Nigeria may have a new beginning from the God of all creation, the God of Isaiah's Servant songs. God promised a new exodus to the Israelites after their Babylonian 70 years exile. God promised that the Israelites will experience times of refreshment from the Lord, the author of all of life: "Look at My Servant, whom I strengthen. He is My Chosen One, who pleases Me. I have put My Spirit upon him. He will bring justice to the nations" (Isa 42:1). To paint a different picture of Christian response to violence this chapter engages in a detailed exegesis of the Servant Songs of Isaiah and to their link to the Master, Himself. We can counter the world's view of violence as redemptive by arguing that God views the servant suffering's mission as redemptive suffering.

Revisiting "the Myth of Redemptive Violence"

People fight back not only to get even but also because they actually believe that violence is redemptive. Walter Wink borrowed the term "the myth of redemptive violence." He argued that this perception of violence exists in all faith communities across the globe. The world believes that violence is redemptive because it misses the fundamental and root cause of violence: sin. Because of this gap, the view that violence is redemptive spreads like wild fire. But we need to counter this lie and address these questions: what is redemptive about violence? Violence is sin; can sin be redemptive? What is the mission of the Church, the body of Christ? How can the church become the servant of God in an era when violence is viewed as redemptive?

Wink has brought the attention of the world to a belief about violence which has been raging for centuries. His basic argument is that violence persists in the world because the world believes it is redemptive.[1] Wink uses Paul Ricoeur's commentary on the Babylonian creation story mythology. In the Babylonian myth, creation itself is an act of violence: Tiamat, ("mother of them all,") is murdered and dismembered; from her cadaver the world is formed.[2] And the human race is also a result of the blood of a god. According to Wink,

> After the world has been created, the story continues, the gods imprisoned by Marduk for siding with Tiamat complain of the poor meal service in their jail. Marduk and Ea therefore execute one of the captive gods, and from his blood, Ea creates human beings to be servants to the gods.[3]

Wink notes that the logical conclusion in this myth is that "Humanity is created from the blood of a murdered god. Our very origin is violence. Killing is in our blood. Humanity is not the originator of evil, but merely finds evil already present and perpetuates it . . . Human beings are thus naturally incapable of peaceful coexistence; order must continually be imposed upon us from on high."[4] Although this is a myth that my Nigerian tribal creation narrative does not share, the belief about violence is very potent, alive and well in my tribal group and other ethnic groups in Nigeria. Nigerians, however, believe in similar myths that encourage violence. One of such myths is, Allah yace tashi in taimake ka (that is: God says if you get up and act He will help you to succeed). In times of threats to life, this myth gets catapulted into the imagination of violent response without mincing words. By default, Wink's particular narrative of the Babylonian myth about the origin of violence in the cosmos and humanity has become the religion of this world. Little wonder, bloodshed follows bloodshed. According to Wink,

1. Wink, *The Domination System,* 14.

2. Ibid.

3. Ibid.

4. Ibid., 15. This is the view that makes it impossible to resist the temptation for revenge. There are theologians like Augustine of Hippo and Reinhold Niebuhr who believed that humans can only be tamed by coercion. As Wink concluded, humans believe that we can only achieve peace through coercion. "Peace through war, security through strength: these are the core convictions that arise from this ancient historical religion" (*The Domination System,* 17).

> Violence is the ethos of our times. It is the spirituality of the modern world. It has been accorded the status of a religion, demanding from its devotees an absolute obedience to death. Its followers are not aware, however, that the devotion they pay to violence is a form of religious piety. Violence is so successful as a myth precisely because it does not seem to be mythic in the least. Violence simply appears to be the nature of things.[5]

This is true in Nigeria. I have heard people say that "if the enemy knows that I have an AK 47 gun, he will not come to fight me." In other words, "The threat of violence, it is believed, is alone able to deter aggressors. . . . We learned to trust the Atomic Bomb to grant us peace."[6] Of course Wink is not saying that this is the only reason why violence has refused to be conquered. Based on our discussion of the Bible and human history in chapter two of this book, I believe that violence spreads in the world because humans have twin traits (natures) in the human race: dignity and depravity. They have the potential of doing tremendous good and at the same time of doing tremendous evil. That means that even without a myth of redemptive violence they will still find a way of pursuing their agenda: warding off the danger of disgrace—a pervasive sense of self-insecurity. The significant contribution Wink has made is to tell us that the Church has been called to work for peace at a time when many people out there believe that violence is redemptive.

We can debunk this belief by demonstrating from the Servant Songs of Isaiah; and arguing that in God's economy, suffering and not violence is redemptive. In the Servant Songs of Isaiah 52:13–53:12, the Servant absorbed violence into himself and in so doing neutralized it. The Servant Songs of Isaiah reveal how God willingly took away our fear of disgrace by himself accepting to suffer disgrace on the cross. Human hostility, as we have argued in chapter two, is rooted in the human fear of disgrace, i.e., public exposure of our human nakedness, ingrained self-insecurity. Of all that human beings extremely dread, the fear of our nakedness (a sense of self-insecurity) and being publicly humiliated before our peers or other fellow humans overshadows them all. We still replay the dramatic scene of Genesis 3:10: we run and hide our ingrained awareness of insecurity and nakedness. This flight from being discredited or shamed is exhibited and displayed in violent aggression, competition, and pride. The primary root of human hostility therefore is the evasive effort to hide our human insecurity and nakedness. If Nigerian Christians understand what every human being dreads, they

5. Ibid., 17.
6. Ibid., 13.

will grasp the radical nature of what Jesus faced on the cross; and what it meant for Jesus to be crucified. To be disgraced is to be abandoned, rejected, ignored and humiliated by your fellow human beings. Jesus faced what was even more terrible He was not only abandoned and humiliated by us human beings, the very people He created and is sustaining by His power, but he also experienced what felt like His Father abandoned Him. However, in reality, God the Father never abandoned Jesus at the cross. Jesus felt what we usually felt when in grievous pains and sufferings. We tend to feel the absence of God's presence. That is why the loud cry of all humans is: "Do not abandon me, O LORD. Do not stand at a distance, O LORD" (Ps 38:21). Jesus did not just teach nonviolence, He faced the worst violence: abandonment; He felt the experience we often and apparently face of the absence of God's embracing presence. As a result, it is hope raising to note that what humans fear and dread in their relationship with their fellow humans and God, Jesus experienced fully. In doing that, He brought an end to the shame and dishonour that we humans all unbearably dread. He made it categorically clear that the Trinity is always present at the site of our sufferings. That is to say, the Trinity was fully present at the cross. When Christians suffer for doing God's will the Trinity is fully present with them.

The Four Servant's Songs in Isaiah 40–66

The suffering Servant's narrative falls into the section of Isaiah prophecy that begins from Isaiah 40–66. This is the last half of the Book of the Prophet Isaiah. John Goldingay and David Payne have noted that there is an interrelationship between this part of Isaiah and the rest of the book (chapters 1–39) and with other parts of the Hebrew Bible, such as the books of Hosea, Jeremiah, Lamentations, Zechariah, and Psalms.[7] The Tyndale Concise Bible Commentary nicely introduces the whole section of the Servant Songs of Isaiah (chapters 40–53).[8] This section is known as the consolation sec-

7. Goldingay and Payne, *Isaiah 40–55*, pp. 2–3.

8. Hughes and Laney, *Tyndale Concise Bible Commentary*, 265. This commentary points out that the prophets of Israel, Isaiah in particular, were exhorted to speak words of consolation to God's people in the Babylonian exile. A herald announced the coming God among his people (Isa 40:3). The "voice" (Isa 40:30) was revealed by the New Testament to be that of John the Baptist (Matt. 3:3), the introducer of Jesus, the Messiah. The divine plan of the Messiah's coming depended on God, not man (Isa 40:6–8). Given that the people have waited decades for deliverance without anything happening, they have to be reassured of the possibility of the fulfilment of this promise. Thus Isaiah 40:12–26 demonstrates the awesome power of God. Nothing could hinder God's coming to the people of Judah. He is incomparably greater than any foe! "Who has measured off the heavens with his fingers" (Isa 40:12) refers to a "span," which is the distance between the

tion of the book.[9] Its main thesis is that the time has finally come for God's people and the nations to enjoy God's magnanimous favour. The opening verse of chapter 40:1 says, "Comfort, comfort, comfort my people, says your God." This tells of a people known by the speaker (God) who needed comfort. Biblical scholars generally agree that this refers to the nation of Israel, who had been captives for several decades because of their own failure to keep faith with God. They have experienced ugly circumstances that require them to be comforted. "Thus" as Goldingay points out, "Chapter 40 begins by affirming the earlier chapters' account of the people's failure and punishment but also the promise of a day of comfort, of a revelation to God's splendor, and of the coming of God as deliverer."[10]

Many biblical scholars affirm that the four servant's songs describe the Servant's Career. Kaiser adds a fifth song (Isa 61:1–2). The first song (Isa 42:1–9) emphasizes the Servant's special divine commission to establish justice (Isa 42:1–4) and deliver those who are imprisoned (Isa 42:6–7). This song clearly points out that this individual designated as "the Servant of the Lord" is not going to bring justice violently. In fact, it portrays the Servant as one who does not draw attention to himself (Isa 42:2) and who refrains from oppressing those who are already downtrodden (Isa 42:3a). The second song (Isa 49:1–13) develops these themes, describing in more detail the servant's special status (Isa 49:1–3) and his commission to deliver the exiles from bondage (Isa 49:5–12). This song also indicates that the servant would experience some discouragement and rejection in carrying out his task (Isa 49: 4, 7), thus paving the way for the main theme of the third and fourth songs, the servant's rejection and suffering.

It is important to note that the Servant songs of Isaiah reveal that the Servant of the Lord receives the Spirit of the Lord, the Spirit of power and of justice, and that "he will bring justice to the nations" nonviolently. For, "he will not shout or cry out, or raise his voice in the streets. A bruised reed he will not break, and a smoldering wick he will not snuff out." Instead of violence and coercion, "In faithfulness he will bring forth justice." He will do

thumb and little finger, about nine inches. The "circle" (Isa 40:22) of the earth referred to the sky that appeared to be a canopy.

9. Goldingay, *The Message of Isaiah 40–55*, p. 9. Goldingay asserts that 40:1–11 "have links of their own with marker chapters earlier in the book that relate to the destiny of Jerusalem, notably chs. 1; 12; and 35. The book as a whole begins by addressing "my people"—or rather by avoiding addressing them in order to refer to them in the third person, complaining *about* them before the ears of the entire cosmos (1:2–3). Now Yhwh once against addresses heaven (?) about them, but to more hopeful import. It is not merely to bring them or anyone else a message, but to implement a purpose. Yhwh is not merely speaking but acting."

10. Goldingay, *The Message of Isaiah 40–55*, p. 9.

so with courage, tenacity, and resiliency: "He will not falter or be discouraged till he establishes justice on earth. In his law the islands will put their hope." These opening words of the first Song have already anticipated the last song where we clearly see the commitment of the Servant of the Lord to nonviolence and the willingness to absorb violence in his own body.[11] As I reflect on the Servant Songs of Isaiah, I see their appropriateness to Nigeria's situation. Because the God who spoke about the Servant's ministry is the Creator of all nations, Nigeria is His nation too. Like the Israelites, Nigeria has been in some form of captivity. Yes, what Nigeria needs is a new Nigeria, a nation with justice and peace for all its citizenry. So I will pay attention to the Servant Songs to see how I can use them as a critique of those in our society who believe that violence is redemptive.

Behind the opening words of the first Servant song lies a hidden reality: suffering. We may ask, what does suffering have to do with justice and peace? But we must wait until we come to the fourth servant song, where at last the servant of God is able to achieve justice for the entire human race through absorbing suffering nonviolently. This may sound depressing and indeed unacceptable to the modern and post-modern reader. But the reader must be patient and wait till we get there. For now, God declares through Isaiah that he has decided to do a new thing on earth; a novel and fresh thing. In Isaiah 42:9 he says, "See, the former things have taken place, and new things I declare; before they spring into being I announce them to you." In the Servant Songs of Isaiah we see God doing a new thing. These songs should be read within the context of God's salvific programme and as an announcement of and a desire to introduce a new thing in the world: redemptive suffering.

The Meaning of the Fourth Servant Song

We need to note that the context (chapters 40–66) of the fourth Servant Song of Isaiah (Isa 52:13–53:12) demonstrate that the sin-factor is more than a breakdown of relationships between humans; it includes the Creator of all the galaxies. Israel had what could be called a "dangerous opportunity." If she had used the opportunity, she would have been what God intended her to be: servant of God to the world. But because she missed it, she had to face the consequences: 70 years of Babylonian exile. In other words, the background reminds us that Israel had missed her calling to be a light to the nations and had to face the consequences of straying away from her covenant relationship with Yhwh (the LORD, God Almighty). However,

---

11. Goldingay, *The Message of Isaiah 40–55*, p. 153.

God had not given up on his people and the entire creation. In his infinite, compassionate love he had decided to deliver Israel. So the larger background of the Servant Songs is "Israel's future deliverance and restoration to the land," which "is portrayed as a second Exodus (Isa 43:16–21, 44:26–27; 48:20–21; 49: 9-12; 51: 9-11; 52:10–12)."[12] This is called a second Exodus because in the first Exodus, "God delivered Israel by making a way where there was none . . . The Exodus from Egypt was also a creative event whereby God formed a new nation out of the chaos of bondage and oppression (Isa 43:15)."[13] The old died and the new was born!

Similarly, living in a world of the myth of redemptive violence, most of the Jews of Jesus time expected a human Messiah, a hero who would defeat his enemies by military prowess and establish his kingdom. But Henri Blocher argues, "The way of triumph for this Messiah, the way by which his everlasting kingdom would be set up, was not military prowess; he would defeat his enemies, as Isaiah foresaw, by surrendering himself to an atoning death."[14] Even when Jesus was tempted and enticed by Satan to take a shortcut to glory, he refused and rather decided to go the way that the Father had shown him: "the Servant pattern which the Father has revealed to him."[15] Jesus chose to follow the way of the Father rather than the way of the world. "The Servant prophecies were in his mind. He added significantly that the way to glory in his kingdom is just the reverse of what it is in the world: for earthly rulers, the exercise of authority means trampling down others, but the first among the followers of Jesus must be servants of all. And then came the desired statement: "The Son of man also came not to be served but to serve, and to give his life as ransom for many." This is the theological meaning of the last Servant Song in a nutshell, with, again, that typical word "many" (Mark 14:24).[16]

Goldingay points out that suffering and persecution tend to disfigure people. So it was with the man in the vision (Isa 53:14). People were shocked and appalled at the sight of him. He himself knew this, and had to live with it (Isa 53:3). He knew what he looked like, and he knew how people felt about him, so he avoided them and thereby in a sense saved himself the pain of rejection.[17] When he came in contact with people, he found out that

12. Zuck, *A Biblical Theology of the Old Testament*, 325–33. See also Blocher, *Songs of the Servant*.

13. Zuck, *A Biblical Theology of the Old Testament*, 325–33.

14. Blocher, *Songs of the Servant*, 15.

15. Ibid., 16.

16. Ibid.

17. Goldingay, *God's Prophet, God's Servant*, 141.

no-one would look at him or acknowledge him. He was ignored, treated as if he did not exist.[18] This is still the social stigma that the ugly of this world suffer.[19] In short, the four Servant Songs reveal a God who has decided to comfort his people because of the enormous destruction the myth of redemptive violence is causing to humanity and the entire creation; a world rife with the miscarriage of justice. Jesus was a victim of this miscarriage of justice himself.[20] Yet Jesus yielded himself, uncomplainingly, to unjust punishment.[21] The fourth Song introduces the Servant of the Lord and his attitude to suffering which has become redemptive.[22] The Servant Songs are an open invitation to humans to return to God for forgiveness, salvation and also, as God's co-workers, participate in God's program of redemption, with a voluntary commitment to the service of His new exodus. Jesus said to his disciples: "I have set you an example that you should do as I have done for you" (John 13:15). God wants those who will be willing to take up their crosses and follow him like Jesus Christ. Africans like us have shared in the process of God salvific programme. That is, Africans have actively played a significant role in the service of God's purpose and desire to have his creatures bring him glory. Therefore, at this junction, it will be good to also make the point that all the evidences of the African presence in Scripture are linked to bearing witness to redemptive suffering. Four Africans have emerged at instances and at scenes of redemptive and creative suffering. And some of the direct victims have willingly share in the impact of the violent suffering they have had to endure. The African presence at the scene serves as God's opening invitation for us to share in Jesus Christ's redemptive and creative suffering instead of participating in what the world terms, "redemptive violence." These Africans become members of the special group of God's peoples known as "the servant of the Lord." The mission of the Nigerian church today must be understood from the perspective of the Old Testament concept of "the servant of the Lord." The question therefore: how have Africans fared in this path. That is, how have Africans participated in the story of the servants of the Lord? To this question we now turn.

18. Ibid.
19. Webb, *The Message of Isaiah*, 211.
20. Blocher, *Songs of the Servant*, 15.
21. Ibid., 58.
22. Ironside, *Isaiah*, 296.

The African Presence in the Vision of the Servant of the Lord

In God's economy, those who are determined to absorb the impact of suffering are God's servants and specialists of change. They are catalysts of a different tomorrow and a new thing that is yet to happen, which is necessary to break down the vicious cycle of violence we are all witnessing in Nigeria and other nations of the world. The relationship between Nigerian Christianity and "The Vision of a Servant Church" needs to be elaborated. When we think of the servant song, we have to remember that it is not just about Israel, the chosen people of God but also about the whole human race. Therefore, it is striking that when the epistles in the New Testament speak of Jesus in the terms we have analyzed above, the context is concern not merely with a right understanding of Jesus, but with his followers' willingness to walk the way Jesus walked. "Christ . . . left you an example, so that you might follow in his steps . . ." (1 Pet 2:21); "the attitude you should have is the one Christ had . . ." (Phil 2:5 GNB). The Servant Songs of Isaiah offer a vision of what God wants to do and can do with someone who is prepared to be his servant: "my servant will act wisely; he will be raised and lifted up and highly exalted" (Isa 52:13). The poem, as some biblical scholars call it, is a job-description. Or it is a challenge to the reader as to whether he is prepared to be a servant of this kind . . . The vision is fulfilled by Jesus. Yet "It is still God's vision for his people, and God's challenge to them."[23]

In the above analysis, the concept or the motif of the servant of the Lord can apply to more than one person. It refers to several people, including ordinary human beings like Israel, Israel's remnant and Isaiah the prophet of the exile himself. It perfectly fits the description of the Servant Songs of Isaiah, is Jesus Christ. But God's vision is not just for Jesus but also for all humanity. Jesus said to his disciples: "I have set you an example that you should do as I have done for you" (John 13:15). God wants us to realize that he wants us to be willing to take up our cross and follow him like Jesus Christ. African Christians know that Africans have actively played significant roles in the service of God's purpose and desire to have his creatures bring him glory. It is important to see the many instances where Africans in Scripture are linked to redemptive suffering. Four Africans in the Bible have emerged at scenes of redemptive and creative suffering. And some of the direct victims have willingly absorbed the impact of the violent suffering they had to endure. In this section we pay attention to how these Africans participated in redemptive and creative suffering instead of participating in what the world terms, "redemptive violence." This will help us learn how

23. Goldingay, *God's Prophet, God's Servant*, 156.

these Africans are members of the special group of God's people known as "the servant of the Lord." We hope to later in the book argue that the mission of the African church today must be understood from the perspective of the Old Testament concept of "the servant of the Lord."

As we have seen, the theme of the Servant Songs of Isaiah points to what God expects his people to do on behalf of others. God seems to be interested in people who willingly offer themselves to his service of rescuing, delivering and redeeming others from the path of danger to the path safety. They create an environment for the work of salvation to be birthed and be nurtured. They indirectly share in the absorption of the impact of violent suffering that is part of God's larger picture of creative and redemptive suffering. Throughout the pages of the Old and New Testaments we see a pattern of Africans who mysteriously found their ways into the narrative of God's chosen people, participated in God's delivering justice and compassionate love. Then they had a part in absorbing the impact of the violence in the world. They serve as redemptive examples of how God would like humans to act in the face of violence, adversity, calamity, suffering and pain. We shall consider four such Africans in the Bible.

First, Ebed-Melech: His name means servant of the king. He was an Ethiopian eunuch and found his way into the palace of King Zedekiah of Judah. He pushed for the deliverance of Jeremiah from an empty cistern into which his kinsmen, (who were not happy with his prophecy in the midst of Babylonian threat) had thrown him and left him to die. They found his advice to surrender to the Babylonians insane and offensive (Jer 38:1–13). Ebed-Melech was one of the Africans who was a proselyte and yet rose to a position of prominence in Israel. The law of Moses made specific regulations regarding the admission into the Jewish faith of such as were not born Israelites (Exod 20:10; 23:12; 12:19, 48; Deut 5:14; 16:11, 14). The entire narrative of how he helped rescue Jeremiah demonstrates how God uses weak things for the accomplishment of his plan. In the life of Ebed-Melech, God demonstrates his ability to surprise us.[24]

---

24. David Wiseman, "The Integrity of Ebed-Melech." http://david.wiseman.ca. Accessed March 21, 2014. Put another way, the Jewish leaders of Jeremiah day hated him because his prophetic messages were anti-Jewish establishment. The Jewish leaders who served in the court of King Zedekiah assumed that Jeremiah was in support of the Babylonian invasion. They perhaps arrived at such conclusion because Jeremiah announced the imminent destruction of Jerusalem. Jeremiah was arrested by a group of royal officials and thrown into an empty well. This happened during a time of great famine in the land. The Cushite Ebed-Melech happened to find himself serving at king Zedekiah's court. Ebed-Melech was the only official of the royal court who saw the evil of throwing a human being into a dry well during famine time. He objected to Jeremiah's gruesome execution. He tactfully protested Jeremiah's effective execution

The second African is Hegai. He was a eunuch of the Persian king, Xerxes, who was in charge of the royal harem at the time when the seat of Queen Vashti became vacant.[25] He played a vital role in the selection of Esther, who later rescued her people from the plot of Haman. He won the trust of Esther when she was preparing for her meeting with Xerxes (Esth 2:3, 8, 15). Esther was placed in his custody before she was called to appear before the king. He was a facilitator of her successful selection as the rightful replacement of the dethroned Queen. He coached Esther on what to do in order to win the attention of the king. When Esther went to the king she followed his instruction and was selected as a suitable replacement of the Queen.[26] Hegai was a conduit of God's saving grace to the Israelites. Esther played a tremendous role in saving the lives of her people. She put her life on the line to save them from the destruction Haman had planned.

The third person is Simon of Cyrene, (Cyrene is a city in Libya, in northern Africa). He played a tremendous part in giving Jesus help with the crosspiece on his way to Golgotha. Some scholars have suggested that he later became a strong witness for Christ. He was said to be one of the leaders of the church in Antioch. He was nicknamed "Black," Niger. Others, however, no doubt the two people are the same persons.[27] Whatever may be the case, we know that Simon of Cyrene was an African. In allowing him to carry the crosspiece behind Jesus, God demonstrated his sense of creative and redemptive humor: A stranger, an African, was indirectly drafted to share in the burden of carrying the impact of cruel suffering, while the chosen people were maltreating the Messiah of the world. Simon is an epitome of discipleship. As Paul John Isaak said, "Simon of Cyrene, carries the cross behind Jesus (Luke 23:26). This action illustrates the nature of discipleship, which involves taking the cross and following Jesus (Luke 9:23; 14:27). It also illustrates who Jesus is: one who goes before and opens the way for others to follow. Jesus has gone before the disciples (Luke 19:28); now they are to follow after him in the way he has opened. Simon of Cyrene is a model for disciples who share Jesus' trials."[28] Simon was compelled to carry Jesus' cross to the place of crucifixion (Matt 27:32).

---

with the king by pointing out the famine as a major reason why Jeremiah should be rescued from the well. King Zedekiah allowed him to go ahead and rescue Jeremiah. Ebed-Melech's action pleased the Lord. As a result God awarded Ebed-Melech with survival of the Chaldean invasion (Jer 38:7, 39:18).

25. Martin, "Esther," 704.

26. "Hegai," in *Easton's Bible Dictionary,* Bible History Online. http://www.bible-history.com/eastons/H/Hegai/

27. Douglas, *The New Bible Dictionary*, 1188.

28. Isaak, "Luke," 1248–49.

The fourth African is the Ethiopian Eunuch. The climax of the narrative of Africans who, in spite of all odds participated in God's creative and redemptive suffering is the account of the Ethiopian eunuch. He was a highly placed government official in his own country. His pilgrimage to Jerusalem shows that as a Gentile he was a devout Jewish proselyte. It was not easy for eunuchs to have access to worship. "The law prohibited eunuchs from entering the Lord's assembly (Deut 23:1)." However, through Isaiah the prophet, God has announced that he was doing everything new. This new thing includes radical reversals. Isaiah 56:3–5 actually predicted that eunuchs will be included in the great blessings that God promises in the future, particularly at the Millennial Age. The Ethiopian eunuch in Luke's account is a foretaste of the coming blessing but also the climax of God's dealing with the Gentiles, represented by the different persons of African descent participating in scenes of violent opposition and danger and being conduits of blessing. They were part of the journey that leads to a perfect salvation God has planned for all humanity. Although he was not perhaps allowed to worship in the assembly of the Lord as a full-fledged proselyte (Acts 8:27), he was able to have the test of the most important portion of the Servant Songs of Isaiah. That the quote was perplexing to the eunuch is not a surprise. The whole narrative of the Servant song is itself perplexing.[29]

The Ethiopian Eunuch had been in Jerusalem and was going home. He was reading a portion of the fourth servant song of Isaiah. No wonder, as Craig Keener noted, "Luke devotes nearly as much space to the conversion of this one foreigner, who can function as an indigenous witness in his own culture, as to the revival in Samaria."[30] He was a wealthy and highly placed government official. Yet he was thinking about worshipping the God of the Israelites. And as God will have it, he got the right portion of the Servant Songs. Luke's narrative of the Ethiopian Eunuch underlines the significant role of Africans' presence in Scripture and their participation in God's salvation and thereby reaping the fruit of God's creative and redemptive suffering through Christ.[31]

Conclusion

This chapter has presented a fundamental argument that will inspire Nigerians to overcome their current social, political, ethnic and religious predicaments. The reflection on the situation of violence raises questions. One of

29. Hubbard, "Ethiopian Eunuch," 346.

30. Keener, *The IVP Bible Background Commentary*, 345.

31. Ibid., 346.

such questions is, "What in fact causes it?" Many Nigerians have been most hit by the reality of human violence against fellow humans; and in fact have in one way or the other contributed to it. This category of Nigerians believes that the primary cause of violent conflicts is injustice. The awareness of injustice or unfair treatments creates a situation of skepticism, frustration, exasperation, and aggression, which by and large often result in violent destruction of life and property.

The narrative of Isaiah Servant Song has helped us to realize that God's promised Messiah present alternative picture to all other traditional models of responding to violent attacks. Jesus readily absorbed violence into himself to the extent that he became disfigured beyond recognition. In God's incomparably great wisdom, through Jesus' nonviolent response to the worse form of injustice ever meted to humans, God conquered the greatest enemies of the human race: sin, corruption and death.

To absorb violent injustice nonviolently is a human possibility. The eunuch Ebed-Melech in Jeremiah, Hegai, the superintendent of the harem with Esther, the Ethiopian eunuch and Simon of Cyrene, who carried the Cross after Jesus are great witnesses to the possibility of living up to God's new vision for humanity. Like Jesus, they each somehow absorbed violence into themselves and in so doing neutralized it. Someone may argue that these are only individuals who each bore the shame of the Cross and so shamed their tormentors, but that that is much harder to achieve at a corporate level. Yes, that may be true, but it is not impossible. The Servant song of Isaiah invites Christians in Nigeria to enter into the service of "the servants of the Lord" in a world that believes in the "myth of redemptive violence."

All the scenes of the African presence provide a strategy that could help Nigerian Christians to confront the violence in our nation and other nations of the world. They are an illustration of a life consecrated to the destruction of the devil's work. They were following the path of their Master, Jesus Christ: "He canceled the record of the charges against us and took it away by nailing it to the cross. In this way, He disarmed the spiritual rulers and authorities. He shamed them publicly by His victory over them on the cross" (Col 2:14–15).

Chapter 9

Tribes, Tribalism, and the Christian Faith

Introduction

Nigeria's woes include a crisis of ethnicity or ethnic differentiation. This reality of the effect of the Fall on humanity has made it difficult for Nigerians to live and enjoy satisfying interpersonal relationships. Human desires corrupt the earth (2 Pet 1:4). To have moral excellence we need to supplement our faith with excellent knowledge, self-control, patient endurance and love for everyone (2 Pet 1:5–7). So, we argue that if Nigerians were to grasp how to celebrate each other and live as just and righteous neighbors to one another in a multi-diverse country, Africa and the global community will immensely benefit. This chapter places Nigeria in the larger context of the African cultural structures that must be brought to the service of "the path of peace." It argues that the general threats to human life and property that tribal identities, political and religious wars and conflicts pose in the twentieth and twenty-first centuries, have distorted Nigerian concept of tribes and tribalism as well as the whole question of human neighborliness. This problem bedeviled the whole of Africa and indeed the rest of the global south. As a result, anthropologists have suggested the elimination of the term "tribes" and "tribalism" in our vocabulary and instead replacing it with ethnicity.[1]

One can see how some form of "tribalism" has led to great evil. For example, the two world wars (World War I and II), the Cold war, the current ongoing battles in the Middle East, violent conflicts in Africa and across the globe. This has led experts in the field of violent conflicts to speak of: "clash

1. Andrew Walls, interview, Wycliffe Hall, Oxford, September 17, 2012.

of civilization,"[2] or "clash of identities."[3] But that is not the whole story. In many parts of the world, Africa in particular, it is unthinkable to say that tribes and tribalism are all evil; therefore let us replace them with something politically correct and convenient. As we will show in this chapter, tribes and tribalism are not necessarily the cause of violent conflict in the world. Rather, the deeper problem is the sin and selfishness in the heart of every man and woman.

This chapter is a theological discussion of the concept of "tribes" and "tribalism" and how these concepts (archaic to the Western mind) might help Africans grasp their place in the human community and celebrate their differences and interconnectedness. It attempts to look at the concept of *tribes* and *tribalism* in a way that facilitates a better answer to the question, "Who is my neighbor?"[4] It pays attention to the following key issues: (1) The biblical teaching on our common humanity; (2) use of "tribes" in Scripture and modern Africa; (3) roots of tribal conflicts in "Christian" majority countries; (4) crisis in identity: tribal and Christian loyalties; (5) the concept of being brothers/sisters, neighbors, extended family; (6) and tribalism and racism.

The truth, as Stone and Dennis observe: "Our global society is more closely interdependent than ever before and failure to recognize the common humanity of all the peoples of the planet will be a costly mistake."[5] African ethicists and theologians need to spend more time thinking of how to dislodge ethnic prejudices as well as mutual suspicion, fears and hostilities. Revisiting the discussion on tribes and tribalism and the whole question of who is my neighbor holds hope for this need. We need educational strategy that will help us raise up a new generation of youth with excellent "moral vision and moral character"[6] who will be ready to say no to bloodshed. We need a shift in mindset and attitude, which a positive view of tribes and tribalism could give us.

Our Common Humanity in Biblical Thought

The biblical account did not argue for the proof of God's existence. It simply affirms that everything, including human beings, exists because of God

2. Huntington, *Clash of Civilization,* 183.

3. Abdu, *Clash of Identities,* 31.

4. Agang, "Tribes and Tribalism: 'Who is My Neighbor?,'" paper presented at the Langham International Partnership Research Seminary, Wycliffe Hall, Oxford, September, 2012, pp. 15–17.

5. Stone and Dennis, *Race and Ethnicity,* 7.

6. Hauerwas, *A Community of Character,* 9.

(Gen 1:1—2:3). The word "tribe" does not have a straightforward definition. Anthropologists give it various definitions, which include the following: "A social division in a traditional society consisting of families or communities linked by social, economic, religious, or blood ties, with a common culture and dialect, typically having a recognized leader: indigenous Indian tribes."[7] This definition is not enough, though. It does not tell us anything about the origin of tribes and God's intended purpose for tribes. Moreover, the definition of tribe is limited to traditional society. We need a more profound definition of tribe that gives us a better picture of who we are in the community of humans. Any definition of tribe that we give should be one that enables us to overcome the continuing situation of ethnic cleansing and genocide. The dictionary definition of tribe is focused on political arrangements. It does not allow for a rediscovery of the source of tribes: God. We need to realize that tribes are God's creation. As such tribal differences ought not to be a problem.

We need to recognize that the starting point for any discussion the significance of tribes, tribalism and good neighborliness is God's creation. The human author of Genesis writes, "In the beginning God created the heavens and earth" (Gen 1:1). Looking back to this text, Paul writes, "Everything comes from God, everything exists by his power, everything is intended for his glory" (Rom 11:36 NLT). John Gladwin states that "Christian faith sets man in the context of divine creation."[8] It is extremely important to understand this: Every person—and every Muslim, Christian or African Traditional Religionist in any group or tribe—on planet earth comes from God, exists by God's power, and is expected to bring God glory and praise. It means that the message of our common humanity must be preached without reservation. We may have different political constituencies, governments, states, regions, countries, currencies, languages, cultures and religions, yet we are all God's creatures and exist by God's power, depending on and benefiting from the earth resources, which God has created for human flourishing and survival.

The Use of Tribe in Scriptures and in Modern Africa

Lamin Sanneh has observed that "So much of the Bible is weighed down with tribal matters." All tribes share in the consequences of fallen human nature. And because of Christ's death and resurrection all tribes share equal

7. From *Oxford Dictionary & Thesaurus*.

8. Gladwin, *God's People in God's World*, 62. The word "man" not only covered the idea of man and woman, but tribe and tribalism, race, and so on.

access to "the benefits of God's intervention in Christ."[9] The modern rejection and hatred of the term "tribes" and "tribalism" can be reversed by a positive and systematic elaboration of what it means to be human and how humans were intended to see their fellow humans in their relation to God, the Creator of all the galaxies. In this section we will provide this elaboration via the Old and New Testaments.

The Old Testament Trajectory of Tribes and Tribalism

The narrative of tribes and tribalism follows the creation account found in the first book of the Bible: Genesis. This book provides the beginning of what happens in the whole of the canonical Scripture (both Old and New Testaments). As such the importance of tribe and tribalism is traced throughout the whole biblical corpus. Therefore our account of tribes and tribalism, either positive or negative will be inadequate if it does not connect with the creation of all things and the human race in particular, as recorded in Genesis.

Genesis makes it clear that persons are created for community. "It is not good for man to be alone. I will make him a helper suitable for him" (2:18). The statement was made when Adam was not alone. He had all the animals with him in the Garden of Eden. In fact, to demonstrate that the animals were not the suitable companions Adam needed, God asked Adam to name them. It was like God was saying to Adam, see whether you can in the process of naming the animals find a companion for yourself. Of course, Adam discovered that none of the animals fit his crucial need for companionship. So, when God finally removed Adam's rib and created a woman out of it and brought her to Adam, he shouted: "Finally, this is now bone of my bone, and flesh of my flesh." Adam here acknowledged her suitability for companionship and for fellowship and intimacy. This is an expression of a sense of embrace, satisfaction, completeness and interconnectedness. We can safely say, God made humans for companionship both with him and with one another. Nothing else on earth can fill that need. After this happy moment, we do not know how long Adam and Eve enjoyed each other. The next story about them is the story of exclusion.

The Fall of Adam and Eve created a new beginning. A deep rift was created between them and God and between them and each other. Adam could not now call Eve "bone of my bone" and the "flesh of my flesh." He now sees her as a threat: "This woman that you gave to me, she made me eat the tree." Sadly, Adam and Eve began a legacy that has been extremely

---

9. Sanneh, "The Significance of the Translation Principle," 38.

difficult for humans to break: self-interest and obsession with power, wealth and domination at the detriment of other fellow human beings. Their son, Cain copied it. Cain attacked and killed his brother Abel. Interestingly, he did this not because of tribalism or tribal rivalry and loyalty but because he did no longer saw Abel as "bone of his bone and flesh of his flesh." When God asked him about the whereabouts of his brother, he could without mincing words say, "I do not know. Am I my brother's keeper?" Companionship demands moral obligation and responsibility for the mutual welfare of each other. But the Fall changed that grasp of human relationship. Humans became more and more violent toward God and toward each other until all the first descendants of Adam, except Noah and his three sons, were destroyed in a forty days and forty nights flood. The violence that led to the destruction of the first human race absolutely has nothing to do with tribalism or tribal identity clashes. What we do find in Genesis is what God reveals as the problem the Fall has brought to the human race: All persons (Muslims, Traditional African Religionists, or Christians or even none of the above) have hearts that are corrupt without God's grace. God said about man, "Every inclination of his heart is evil from childhood" (Gen 8:21). That is very instructive. Even without tribes and tribalism in Africa, there will still be people who will have other reasons for attacking and killing others. In summary, there are three important things we can glean from the forgoing analysis: 1) created as communal beings, we need something like "tribes"; 2) but sin leads us to distort the good side of "tribes" and use them for violence against other tribes; 3) still, God uses "tribes" (e.g., especially Israel) for his redemptive purposes.

God has not forgotten that "it is not good for man to be alone." When we come to Acts 2 a new community is birthed. In Acts 2, the scattered languages and the tribes that developed out of human sin are brought back together once again. We may not speak the same language or live in the same country. We are brothers and sisters to each other. Our tribal differences and diversities, if rightly grasped, can enhance our ability to celebrate and worship God's gift of tribal identity. The need for an awareness of our common humanity is underscored in the gift of spiritual gifts as explained by St. Paul.

New Testament Trajectory of Tribes and Tribalism

The Old Testament story of Israel seems to ignore most of the other tribes and nationalities as if they existed without God. And even Israel, which is made up of the twelve tribes was also not stable. In Judges they destroyed each other. Eventually before the end of the Old Testament the nation was divided between North and South. As a Jewish, Jesus belonged to a particular tribe. But his message was for all "tribes"—not just for the nation of Israel but all nations. "Therefore go and make disciples of all nations, baptizing them in the name of the Father and of the Son and of the Holy Spirit." That underscores the intention of God to bring all things together. Transformation in Christ will bring all tribes and languages together. We notice that the baptism is not in the name of one's tribe but in the name of God the Father, God the Son and God the Holy Spirit. (Matt 28:19–20). One might think that the text suggests the disappearance of tribes. But God showed his positive view of tribes and tribal identities when the Holy Spirit poured out God's grace on every tribe present at Pentecost. One thing is obvious: the unification of the tribes in Acts 2:1–12. The scattered tribes of Genesis 10 are again in Jerusalem and able to understand each other after such a long time. The Holy Spirit comes upon the disciples and they are given the ability to speak a foreign language that so that everyone can understand: "Each one was hearing them speak in his own language" (Acts 2:6, 8).

This happened to show that God was reuniting all tribes and languages from every nation under heaven. The tribal differences and diversity did not disappear though. They did not need to because they are not a threat to our relationship to God and to one another. As long as, we are united in God. Tribes did not disappear because they all come from God, exist by his power and are intended for his glory (Rom 11:36). Revelation 7:4–10 then picks up the theme of the tribes. The twelve tribes of Israel and all other tribes outside Israel are gathered together to worship God: "After this I looked and behold, a great multitude that no one could number, from every nation, from all tribes and peoples and languages, standing before the throne and before the Lamb, clothed in white robes, with palm branches in their hands, and crying out with a loud voice, "Salvation belongs to our God Who sits on the throne, and to the Lamb!" (Rev 7:9–10).

This is the chief goal of human creation to together bring God glory out of a common fellowship. Christ is the center of tribal unity. Rev. Ronald Nathan says, "As a Christian my understanding of God, the Scriptures, and the church could be enhanced or limited by my cultural perceptions. Hence my theology is not shaped by the traditions and dogma of my denomination alone."[10] He cited Nida who says, "No one cultural manifestation of the Christian life, (including our own) has arrived at perfection, but each has its unique contribution to make and each should be permitted to make it."[11] In

10. Nathan, "Issues for the Black Minister," 11.

11. Nida, *Customs and Cultures,* cited by Nathan, "Issues for the Black Minister," 28.

his article, "Race relations in Britain: Possibilities for the future" Rtd Revd. Patrick Kalilombe writes, "The crucial factor is that the presence of these new cultures, races, religions, and colours is DEMANDING a change of the traditional way people relate to DIFFERENCES."[12] In the past, persons of a different colour, race or religion could be accepted or even welcomed as "strangers" or visitors. They could be tolerated fairly easily because their presence did not challenge the local cultures, people or power. Sooner or later they would return to where they came from and leave the local people in peace. Moreover, the "different stranger" was expected to behave like a guest: somebody who seeks favour and consideration, and is in no position to dictate terms. This state of affairs changes dramatically when the different "other" claims to have equal rights as a fellow citizen."[13]

One of the most important freedoms we can experience is the freedom of knowing how much I need others. This is the reason why Ecclesiastes says, "Two are better than one" (4:9–10). God in his wisdom gives humanity the privilege of living with different tribes because if one falls the other can help him or her out. The spiritual gifts are diversely given to us to keep us from claiming autonomy or independence. What Paul says about spiritual gifts could equally be said about tribal differences. All tribes are from God like all gifts are from the Lord: "There are different kinds of spiritual gifts, but the same Spirit is the source of them all. There are different kinds of service, but we serve the same Lord. God works in different ways, but it is the same God who does the work in all of us. A spiritual gift is given to each of us so we can help each other" (1 Cor 2:4–11). The purpose of tribes, as in spiritual gifts, is the same: different tribes are given us so we can help each other. We have many choices available. The only thing that we cannot choose is the tribe into which one should be born. The choice of where anyone of us is to be born belongs to the Lord. But what God has graciously given to all of us is the ability to learn, understand and speak other tribal languages. In Africa, no human being is really human without others. As John Mbiti puts it, "I am because we are. And because we are I am."[14] Tribes are our window to the human community. Our tribes are the link to the real world. This is not only true in Africa but also in the rest of the world. For example, in 2001, my former schoolmate, her husband and I visited New York. While in New York, we used the opportunity to visit where records of early immigrants who entered the United States were kept. She had been told that her great-grand father came from France to the States about a century or

---

12. Kalilombe, "Race Relations in Britain," 39.

13. Ibid.

14. Mbiti, *African Traditional Religions and Philosophy,* 200.

more ago. She checked to see if that was true. His name was in the record! When she found his name on the record, she jumped with a shout of joy. That discovery gave her a new cultural identity; a sense of belonging. If this happened in the US, how much more in Africa where tribal identity is still very significant? To belong to a tribe in Africa is to be a true human being.

Tribal Conflicts in "Christian" Majority Countries

If the description of tribe above is true, why do we find tribal conflicts in Africa, even in Christian communities? Africa's problems are multidimensional. Richard Werbner states, "The story of ethnic difference in Africa threatens to overwhelm the larger debate about the postcolonial identity politics across the continent. It is as if an old narrative, once told in terms of tribe and now in terms of ethnicity and ethnogenesis, is still spell-binding. Yet ethnic identities are merely a small fraction of the many identities mobilized in the postcolonial politics of everyday life."[15] Werbner's argument points to the fact that ethnicity is not the problem that causes ethnic conflict in Africa. In fact, as we have argued so far, tribe and tribalism are not the root of our human hostility. Rather, it is the paradox of humanity: good and evil co-exist in all of us. So it does not matter what name we use. We will not find the solution to our problem until we place it where it belongs: The reality of the Fall.[16] This is the reason political independence did not perform its expected magic of bringing freedom to Africans. Instead, Africans succeeded in taking the colonialists off their backs only to replace them with their cousins and kinsmen who were the same humans like the whites with self-ambition, deception and the lust for power.[17]

As result the state leaves many survivors alienated from their nation-state.[18] The reason, as we have noted elsewhere, is an overwhelming sense of self-insecurity and thereby fear of disgrace. African leaders assume that political power will protect them from public disgrace and shame. So, when they get power, which is the most important that every human being wants to have on this side of eternity, they find it extremely hard to relinquish it.

---

15. Werbner and Ranger, *Postcolonial Identities*, 1.

16. Ibid., 2. Werbner further notes that the cultural politics of identity act dynamically upon that palimpsestual tension. It uses the not-now to negate, renegotiate, or playfully compromise present authority. In turn, it also reaffirms authority, or its possibility, by counteracting the traces of colonial and pre-colonial sociality within the postcolonial. In it multiple shifting realities, the postcolonial encompass contradictory complexity and times out of time.

17. Ibid., 12.

18. Ibid., 13.

They literally become captives of the sinful nature: self-interest, deception, and excessive lust for power. Consequently, they become socially, religiously and morally corrupt.

Caught in overwhelming circumstances of human self-interest, deception, lust for power and pride, which all lead to competition and destruction of lives and properties, Christians across Africa are commonly faced with the difficulty of responding nonviolently. Tribal and ethnic confrontations in African are indeed bloody. In those situations, Christians' nakedness—spiritual weakness—always gets exposed. They often find out that they lack the moral, ethical and theological skills that will help them overcome the temptation to murder either their fellow Christian brothers and sisters or non-Christians. The wars between the Tivs and the Jukuns in Nigeria's Middle-Belt and between the Fulani and Berom in Jos, Nigeria, are all prime examples. As Francis Ayul Yuar has observed, in most of these cases, it has become clear that Christians lack moral values that will help them to say no to violence against fellow human beings and stand for peace, reconciliation and intimacy.[19] Scripture teaches that when Christ suffered, died and was resurrected from the dead, he broke the walls of hostility, by making the two—Gentiles and Jews—one. Paul writes,

> For he himself is our peace, who has made the two one and has destroyed the barrier, the dividing wall of hostility, by abolishing in his flesh the law with its commandments and regulations. His purpose was to create in himself one new man out of the two, thus making peace and in this one body to reconcile both of them to God through the cross, by which he put to death their hostility. (Eph 2:14–16)

Yet, Christians are still building walls of hostilities, excluding others from their circle of moral obligation (to borrow a phrase from David Gushee, *Righteous Gentiles*). Christians are called to engage the cross and mirror divine peace, coherence, and integration within themselves and the world.[20] But this confirms the truth of what Genesis 8:21 says about every human being: "[E]very inclination of his heart is evil from childhood" (Gen 8:21). God created us with the capacity to choose. We have largely used our capacity to choose for self-interest and desire to power. This has devastated human flourishing.

19. Yuar, "A Critical Evaluation," 11.
20. Dreyer, "The Soul's Journey into God," 120.

Crisis in Identity–Tribal loyalties and African Christians

Crises in identity abound in the African continent. Given Africa's interactions with diverse cultures—political, religious and otherwise—identity crises are a common place in the continent. John S. Mbiti had predicted that because of rapid political changes happening in Africa in the 1950s and 1960s, Africans were going to face crises of identity. What that means is that things are changing fast beyond Africans imagination.[21] The reality is that nationhood does not give one the basic ingredients of tribal identity.[22] Tribal identity is thicker than national unity. In Nigeria, the Hausa-Fulani and others on the Plateau, particularly in Jos and its environs have been destroying each other since 1994.

Africa is experiencing crises in identity because many people are replacing their non-functional political identities with traditional tribal sources of unity and identity. Human beings from other tribes are seen as things and dehumanized by their fellow brothers and sisters. Ethan Steyn observed that in Rwanda, Tutsi were called *cockroaches* by Hutus, and in Vietnam, Montagnards were called *moi,* meaning "dog," by the Vietnamese. In Nigeria tribal loyalties often distort the Christian faith. It does reveal that Christians are not immune to *self-interest and the will to power*. Each tribe has both superiority and inferiority complexes. It has a certain way of seeing itself and distinguishing itself from the other tribes.[23] Fears, assumptions, perceived and real threats and the mechanism for self-defence, all contribute to what is known as a "they" versus "us" dichotomy. To reinforce tribal loyalties, tribal communities engage in categorization and stereotyping of each other, hoping to have an edge over the others.

In a seminar I attended in August 2012 on "Healing the Wounds of Conflicts in Jos," the facilitator divided us into a group of five and asked each group to discuss the question: "Why do we fight each other?" Each of the groups consisted of diverse tribes in Nigeria; the general group included someone from the United States. After 1:30hrs of brainstorming and interaction, all the five groups came to one conclusion: we fight each other because of tribal and individual pride. This pride distorts the ethnic group's concept of tribal identity and Christian identity. In spite of the fact that Scripture teaches humility, sometimes it feels like many people in the church are happy to continue with the Christian culture but not Christian

---

21. Mbiti, *African Traditional Religions and Philosophy,* 216.

22. Ibid., 217.

23. Alexander E. Hopkins, "Protest and Rock n' Roll During the Vietnam War," *Student Pulse* 4, no. 11 (2012), http://www.studentpulse.com/articles/713/protest-and-rock-n-roll-during-the-vietnam-war.

faith and its virtues and moral values. The tribal loyalties are like having a log in our eyes. The way of seeing ourselves in comparison to others affects our ability to view them as human beings. This distortion makes it look like it is okay to kill.[24]

People get abused to the extent that they are manipulated. For example, opportunists manipulate something as good as tribalism to satisfy their self-interest and the will to power. Christopher Shuabu Abashiya, a native of the Hausa tribe of Northern Nigeria, became a Christian at an early age. Most people in his native tribe are Muslims. So when he became a Christian he was persecuted and had to leave the comfort of his biological family and his tribal kinsmen at a very tender age. The missionary that led him to Christ took him to a Good Samaritan from the Jaba tribe of Southern Kaduna who gladly took him in for safety. He grew up and became assimilated to his host community to the extent that it never again crossed his mind that he was a stranger in that community. In fact, his host family not only adopted him but actually gave him the same treatment they would give their biological children. They trained him up to the doctoral level. After graduation he got employed by the state government. Eventually, when it was the turn of a Jabaman to be appointed as one of the commissioners in the state, he was appointed to represent the Jaba people. Suddenly, he realized that he did not really belong. People in the community and the tribe protested his appointment, arguing that he was not a true son of the soil. They were jealously saying "How can a stranger be giving a position that is the share of the Jaba tribe?" Ironically, they forgot that he was a human being and Christian like them. Their reaction was not only motivated by suspicion and mistrust, but by an individual in the community who had manipulated the situation for his self-interest. They failed to see him as a brother, neighbor and member of the extended family of God.

Neighborliness and the Human Family

The idea of neighbor is a helpful picture of the unity that God desires among tribes. Being good neighbors to each other shows an understanding that we are not independent of each other. True understanding of humans and the necessity of neighborliness diffuses and dislodges division. It encourages the celebration of difference and encourages unity in diversity. This is the expressed concern of Jesus' prayer in John 17:2. The *American Heritage Dictionary* defines neighbor in terms of proximity: someone who lives near another. But a better definition that is close to what Jesus meant when he

---

24. Gülen, "In True Islam, Terror Does not Exist," 7.

answered the question, "Who is my Neighbor?" is that a neighbor does not have to necessarily be someone close to us. Rather, a neighbor is someone whom you recognize as a fellow human being and are called to serve his interest as you would serve yours. This revolutionary thinking is in line with the passage in Matthew 19:19 that urge love of one's neighbor. One fundamental trouble Christians face today is over-familiarization with the narrative of the Good (or as Glen Stassen says, "The compassionate") Samaritan. We pretend to understand what Jesus teaches without living it in daily life.

While in reality, one of the fundamental causes of our social disintegration in the churches today can be traced to the fact that Christians do not fully grasp how Jesus defined neighbor. He did not define a neighbor using the definition of our English dictionary. Rather, he gave a narrative that poignantly drove home the message: being neighbor means recognizing the humanity of the other and reaching out to him or her as a fellow human being who deserves to be treated as a dignified fellow human being.[25] Jesus took the question beyond the parochial understanding to God's original intent:

> [Jesus] moves beyond the more exclusive concept of Judaism in regard to the definition of neighbor and fills it with new meaning. The Good Neighbor of the Kingdom is not bound by local, racial or geographical implications, but rather is motivated by love and compassion wherever he meets need. The Samaritan in the parable had no problem recognizing a neighbor in the man who fell among thieves, and acted generously (Luke 10:35) because it was neighbor love which motivated him . . . The living faith of the Christian believer is grounded in love and calls for action to be the good neighbor to all men [and all tribes].[26]

Both the priest and Levite did not see the man dying in the ditch as a fellow human being created in the image of God, with all that other human beings have: dignity. The priest and the Levite examples of people who ignore their fellow human beings—other tribes or individuals—and think that they can claim to love and serve God. Christians today still follow the bad example of the priest and the Levite.

I was in the US in June 2012. My friends came to where I was staying to take me out for dinner. On our way, I saw two young people standing at a stop light begging for something to eat. Everybody was driving past them as if they were not human beings. They were ignored by their fellow human beings. This happens everywhere in the world today. We ignore our fellow

25. Banks, "Neighbor," 451–52.
26. Hunt, "Good Neighbor," 267–68.

human beings who need our help for a meal or other things. The concept of neighbor means seeing other individuals or tribes as fellow human beings. The Bible uses the concept of "brother keeper" and "one another" to illustrate the fundamental truth of our common humanity. The existence of tribal diversity does not mean we can exist without one another. Paul writes, "Just as each of us has one body with many members, and these members do not have the same function, so in Christ we who are many form one body, and each member belongs to all others" (Rom 12:4–6). Because we need each other God has given us the capacity to show compassion and cooperate with other fellow human beings. As Ilchi Lee says, this is possible, in spite of the fact that: "Human beings can be horrible to one another, perhaps even more menially cruel and violent than the most vicious animal. Yet human beings can also be incredibly kind and generous. In times of crisis, we are capable of demonstrating behaviors that defy a "survival-of-the-fittest" view of human society. Every culture on earth values acts of putting others before self and kindness before cruelty."[27]

In March of 2012, there were multiple bomb explosions in two urban cities of Kaduna State: Kaduna and Zaria. A Muslim hid the children of his Christian neighbor while the parents were trapped at work by the violent conflict that erupted after the bomb blast. All the family belongings got burned. But the Muslim neighbor succeeded in rescuing and hiding the children of his Christian neighbor from the Muslim youth who were setting Christian homes ablaze, burning people and their property. After the police and soldiers successfully brought the chaos to an end, the parents reached home and found that everything was burned to ashes. They thought that their children were also burned to ash. But their Muslim neighbor secretly told them that their children were safe and alive. Why did he do that? He did that because he did not see them as Christian infidels but as fellow human beings; and needing neighbor's help. Out of human love and compassion, he risked his life to save them.

We are Neighbors to each other. "In reality, the level of our understanding and appreciation of one another depends on how well we recognize the qualities and riches that each person possesses."[28] To be our brother's and sister's keeper is to be good neighbors to each other. Gustavo Gutierrez states, "A spirituality of liberation will center on a conversion to the neighbor, the oppressed person, the exploited social class, the despised ethnic group, the dominated country."[29] He argues that "Becoming a neighbor to

27. Lee, *Earth Citizen*, 13.

28. Gülen, *Toward a Global Civilization*, 6.

29. Quoted in ibid., 48.

another is the result of an action, a commitment, of approaching another and going out of one's way. Gustavo Gutiérrez encourages us to learn that the neighbor is not someone whom we find in our road, but rather our neighbor is someone in whose road we place ourselves.[30] Love is our shared core value as humans in a planet of diverse needs. Glen Stassen explains why love is key in human relations: "Love is not a one-way street running from God to us, in which God has no motive, does not seek any return of love from us and is unaffected by our love or unfaithfulness. Rather, God wants mutual love, personal communion in which we give love back to God."[31] In the same way, human love is mutual or reciprocal. Neighbor love is not opposed to justice but "leads to community-oriented affirmation of justice."[32] Neighborliness in Africa is sacred. To understand this, South Africans use the concept of UBUNTU to describe it. Ubuntu means common or shared humanity: "I exist because you exist. Without you I fail to exist."[33] This meaning cuts across Africa. Nussbaum tells of how it was this concept of shared humanity which underpinned the work of the Truth and Reconciliation Commission in South Africa, led by Co-chairman Bishop Desmond Tutu. Another important concept is the idea of extended family. The African concept of extended family has the idea of seeing those who are not in your immediate biological family or circle of obligation as part of your family. All tribes are members of the extended family. This fact is helpful. My parents used the concept of extended family to teach me good ethics and morality: everyone in my community is either, my sister or brother or uncle my aunty. The idea of "them" versus "us" could be destroyed if we taught ourselves the African concept of the extended family.

Tribalism, Racism, and the Christian Faith

Tribalism and racism are not the same. Racism is racial segregation and supremacy, while tribalism is the pride of a tribal group. It refers to tribal organization and love for one's tribe. It is a state or fact of being organized in a tribe or tribes.[34] Therefore tribalism, if used carefully can bring much needed blessings. But what is the real problem? The real issue is human sinfulness in a fallen world. This is why both religion and tribal identities (which are not bad in and of themselves) have been abused; and Africans

30. Quoted in ibid., 117.

31. Stassen and Gushee, *Kingdom Ethics,* 330.

32. Ibid., 331.

33. Nussbaum, "Ubuntu," 21.

34. See *Oxford Dictionary & Thesaurus.*

are paying the heavy price of losing our young men and women. In the name of race and tribal identities, Christian brothers and sisters have turned against each other, killing children, adults and destroying property worth millions of dollars every month. Yet, not all violent conflicts and wars are tribally or racially motivated.

In the name of race and tribal identities, Christian brothers and sisters have turned against each other, killing children, adults and destroying property worth millions of dollars every month. Yet, not all violent conflicts and wars are tribally or racially motivated. Scholars have argued that what we see happening in Africa today is not limited to tribal competition and rivalry. Rather, it is linked to the British colonial legacy of helping so-called majority tribes in a region to dominate the minority tribes. Yusufu Turaki has been one of the proponents of this view. Turaki argued that the real issue in Africa tribal conflicts is the lack of having right moral and ethical structures in place which was caused by a combination of the British colonial legacy and the missionaries' approaches to ethical teachings in the early days of Christianity.[35] John Mary Waliggo writes,

> The Christians missionaries who came to evangelize Africa in the nineteenth century presented a limited and defective Christology. They came with ready-made questions and answers. They came with Christology developed in Europe throughout the centuries. It was highly conditioned Christology, made to respond to specific situations and peoples. They did not pause for a moment to ask: What is Jesus Christ for you Africans? What do your African religions and cultures say about the Jesus Christ of faith? How do you conceive salvation?[36]

He concludes that "Defective Christology produces defective ecclesiology." Tribal labeling and belittling is still taking place in Christian communities across Africa. A 17-year-old, Adaobi Tricia Nwaubani from Nigeria narrates her nasty experience of the negative side of tribalism.[37] She met a young man from the Yoruba tribe of Southwest, Nigeria. Adaobi is Igbo from the Southeast of Nigeria. They became interested in each other and started talking about getting married to each other. With great excitement, Adaobi took her boyfriend to her parents for introduction. When her parents heard that he was Yoruba they gave their daughter a look that showed her something

---

35. Turaki, "Christianity and African Traditional Religion," and *British Colonial Legacy in Northern Nigeria*, 24.

36. Waliggo, "The African Clan as the True Model of the African Church," 111.

37. Adaobi Tricia Nwaubani, "Nigeria tribalism: a personal love story," *Guardian*, September 18, 2010.

was wrong. After the young man left, Adaobi's parents sternly warned her not to have anything to do with him. The father bluntly told her. "You must never get involved with a Yoruba man. They are wicked!" Adaobi could not get it. Why would her parents say that she cannot marry the man she so loved? Later she discovered that most of her people, the Igbos, viewed the Yorubas as "cantankerous traitors" because the Yorubas did not keep their promise of supporting them against the Hausa-Fulani during the Biafran war of 1967 to 1970. Therefore, the Igbos brainwash their children and discourage them from intermarrying with the Yorubas. Adaobi eventually, had to break off with the young man. But she later went to a University in Yorubaland and discovered a more shocking revelation about the bitterness that existed among the two tribes. She said, "I met Igbos convinced that everyone speaking Yoruba in the vicinity was conspiring against them. And the Yorubas were provoked whenever an Igbo dare to contest a school election; and Igbos deserting Yoruba in favour of Igbo brides. And Yorubas horrified when offered an Igbo meal. It was all quite pitiful." The situation created mutual suspicion and fear. The Christian faith is supposed to dislodge these bitter experiences in African. But they still abound.

Conclusion

The present picture of tribes and tribalism is not encouraging. But since tribes come from God, tribes and tribalism have the potential of helping us to achieve the goal of true humanity. Tribes are good means of recognizing our common humanity. First, we must recognize and identify ourselves as a people that come from God, exist by his power and are intended for his glory and hold that identity superior to any identity of nationality, tribe, or religion. Second, we need to reinterpret our life's goals and refocus them on the concept of being "one another's keeper" by "finding ways to fulfill material needs while also honoring"[38] the Creator of the galaxies and celebrating our common humanity. African Christians need to learn how to own some responsibility for whatever is going wrong or right in Africa. This attitude will help ". . . to restore hope and confidence in each other by building mutual trust and love" in all African tribes.[39] Christians from all tribes need to be reminded that on the cross Jesus broke the walls of hostilities between the Jews and Gentiles, creating one new humanity, out of all our divided humanities.

38. Lee, *Earth Citizen,* 14.

39. Yuar, "A Critical Evaluation," 27.

Tribal diversity can be fun, if we are willing to embrace and embody Jesus' ethics of loving other tribes as our own tribe. Through Luke's Gospel, Jesus reveals the human problem and tendency of hating, excluding and insulting each other. That this situation persists means that there is a defect with our Christian upbringing. It demonstrates a lack of sound biblical, theological, moral and ethical foundation—"one that would guide a Christian's moral response to ethnic or socio-political crisis."[40] In the 21st century, these racial and tribal loyalties still "play a significant role in denying the feuding communities a chance to see the Christian moral values of humanity and humility toward those they disagree with."[41] Superior love is Jesus' call to his disciples. The disciple's standard of love is to be greater than that of the average person's love. Love involves going the extra step. Love may require enduring injustice. Love means seeing other as we would like them to see us. Love means serving without strings attached or expecting response.[42] The standard of one's evaluations is determined by one's own treatment and evaluation of others. This theme of justice in the eschaton anchors the entire exhortation in a context where disciples are accountable to God for their actions. Love and mercy dominate the subunit, with judgment being tied to mercy.[43] Love includes mercy, following God's own example. This attitude produces a hesitation in judging others, as believers realize that God will treat them in the way they have treated others.[44] G. B. Cair explains that Jesus calls his disciple to a radical agape love. Finally, Nigerian Christians need a rediscovery of the message of Christ's Great Commission: "Go ye and make disciples of all nations." This means that our interest must go beyond the tribe or the individual. We must stand for the interest of our nation and all nations. Our ethics must go beyond tribal identity to include national and global identity. Christ's salvation is not only for individual tribes but for all tribes. We need men and women of selfless service to humanity!

---

40. Ibid., 14.

41. Ibid.

42. Bock, *Luke*, 586.

43. Ibid., 587.

44. Ibid., 560.

Chapter 10

How to Handle our Destroyers

Introduction

Nigeria's military approach to the war on terror can eclipse the fact that impossibilities do happen in circumstances of persecution and hardship. Our Christian faith and love flourish in such times. Yet, in some ways the reality of what is happening in Nigeria cripples faith and hope, particularly in the Boko Haram insurgency. The more one hears, sees and reflects on the human loss that the Boko Haram sect is causing in Nigeria, The more there is an overwhelming sense of helplessness and powerlessness. This particular circumstance brings us face to face with the true nature and scope of human hostility, which is rooted in and produced by the paradox of Man: dignity and depravity, good and evil. In this situation, what hope do Nigerian Christians have for the perpetuators of evil and the victims of this evil? This chapter offers suggestions on the way forward for all Nigerians to create room in their hearts for the members of the Boko Haram. Christian Nigerians should be especially able to do this. Based on the Bible, God does not give up on us. The God who pursued us and found us is capable of pursuing members of the Boko Haram and finding them. God has called Christians in particular to love everyone, even enemies.

Zechariah's hymn in the first chapter of Luke can help us. Through the prophet Zechariah, God promises to "guide our feet to the path of peace"; that is, the feet of those who turn to Jesus Christ for salvation, so that in spite of their circumstances they will serve Him "in righteousness and holiness." Zechariah is aware of the fact that "the only way to walk righteously is to follow the path God sets."[1] We can't help but admire Zechariah's courage and attempt to come to grips with his circumstances: needing salvation from "the hand of all who hate us," not able to serve God "without fear, in holiness and righteousness"; and being among "those who live in darkness and in the shadow of death." This is much like the difficult circumstances God sometimes puts into our lives, which we must come to grips with through an attitude of faith, trust and hope.[2] The hymn reminds us that we are saved in order to participate in the path of peace. So when many people are urging military action against Boko Haram, Nigerian Christians' language is the language of peace, justice and love. The genuineness of this language is tested in the context of horrific violence.

That Islamic extremism and terrorism have put our global world at risk is not debatable. So we must face a difficult question: *How shall we rid ourselves of this risk?* A follow-up question that must be addressed in a world come of age in a time of terrorism is this: *How may God be guiding our path toward peace?* This is the question to which we now turn in this chapter— first, by defining Boko Haram; second, by proposing a moral vision through a discourse of the efficacy and applicability of Glen Stassen's just peacemaking practices in the context of terrorism; and finally, by suggesting other contextual ways of moving forward.

The Boko Haram Insurgence

Boko Haram is an Islamic revolutionary group targeting not only what the group perceives as representatives of a putatively oppressive regime in Nigeria, but also ordinary citizens living under that regime. The group began in 2002 as a small Salafist faction based in northeastern Nigeria, led by a chain of charismatic but poorly educated preachers, namely Mohammed Ali, Mohammed Yusuf and Abubakar Shekau. These leaders believe that British colonialism and the Nigerian state that resulted from it imposed an un-Islamic way of life on Nigerian Muslims. This led the group to oppose Western-style education, which is how the sect came to be known as Boko Haram. The phrase, *Boko Haram*, which translates roughly to "Western education is forbidden,"[3] was a label given to the group by outside observers. But the group calls itself by the Arabic phrase, *Jama'atu Ahlus-Sunnah Lidda'Awati Wal Jihad*. This phrase has been translated as "People Committed to the

---

1. Bock, *Luke*, 77.

2. Ibid., 75.

3. Loimeier, "Boko Haram."

Propagation of the Prophet's Teachings and Jihad."[4] Such commitment to violent jihadi ideology is what makes the group a terrorist revolutionary movement.[5]

The Boko Haram insurgency in Nigeria forces us to re-evaluate terrorism. Can any form of terrorism be morally justified? What is in the mind of terrorists? The term "terrorism" has its origin with the French Revolution, a time when the French government acted violently against its own people. It has also been used to describe the violent activities of labor organizations, anarchists, nationalist groups, minority political organizations, and religious movements. In the twenty-first century, "terrorism most frequently referred to the acts of non-state agents (individually or collectively) acting against another group, be it a government, a multinational corporation, or a dominant religious hierarchy."[6] Most scholars agree that terrorists are indiscriminate in their actions.[7] One of Nigeria's biggest challenges is how to avoid playing the game of the terrorists. Beyond the current military approach to the insurgency, there is need for a moral vision that will help Nigerians find a creative way to transform the situation, and a way forward.

The Origin of the Boko Haram Sect

The Antecedents of Boko Haram

Hasty characterization of the Boko Haram sect as a terrorist group might cause us to miss important information about them. With the kidnapping of the Chibok girls on April 14, 2014, Boko Haram has attracted global attention. But what are its antecedents in the history of Islam? We have to look at the history of Islamic thought and the key ideas that have dominated that history. I have found Basheer M. Nafi's history of the rise of Islamic reformist thought and its challenge to traditional Islam very useful in helping to navigate the nuances of Islamic radicalism and intellectualism. Some of his arguments seem to fit the big picture of Boko Haram.[8] The intellectual history of Islamic scholars and theologians is a catalogue of various schools of thought. Prominent among them is the salafiyya (reformist school of thought) founded by Ahmad B. Taymiyya (1263–1328). Nafi notes

4. Walker, "What Is Boko Haram," 1.

5. Walzer, "Terrorism," 294.

6. May et al., *The Morality of War*, 293.

7. Walzer, "Terrorism," 294.

8. Nafi, "The Rise of Islamic Reformist Thought," 28.

that "Central to Ibn Taymiyya's reformist project was his emphasis on the primacy of the original Islamic texts, the Qur'an and hadith; beyond which he saw only the consensus of the Prophet's Companions and the Companions' Followers as binding."[9] Taymiyya was driven by a search for unity and the desire to confront foreign influences on Islamic culture. He endeavored to re-establish the ultimate authority of the earlier, unadulterated views of Islam.[10] His project has influenced many Muslims, including Usman Ibn Fodio of Nigeria (1754 to 1817), who used those ideas to construct an Islamic framework compatible with the Qur'an and Sunna for emerging societies in non-urban environments with strong local traditional vestiges. Ahmad B. Taymiyya and Usman Ibn Fodio laid the groundwork for the continuing challenge to traditional Islam to deal with western imperialism and capitalism, and a desire for urgent renewing of the moral fabric of society and a new era of *ijtihad*.[11] Boko Haram is an offshoot of the revivalist mission of the eighteenth century, but it is also fueled by the social background of the nineteenth-century reformists.[12] In this revivalist mission the reformists see Shari'a as "the only path for restoration and renewal," because "the Shari'a is the prescribed organizer of life." If that is the case, no limits were prescribed for laboring within its framework. It thus follows that *ijtihad* was not only desired or recommended, but also required and imperative for Muslims in every age and place, through which the position of the *Ummah* (the Muslim community) in the world is continuously redefined.[13]

Boko Haram is agitating for a return to Islamic Shari'a law. It is important to observe here that, prior to colonial rule in Nigeria and throughout the period of British rule (1903 to 1960), northern Nigerian Muslims had largely followed the Maliki School of Jurisprudence.[14] However, with independence the situation changed. John N. Paden described the enormous impact of this change. Paden tells of the role Sheik Abubakar Gumi played in the paradigm shift in northern Muslims' intellectual quest. In his effort

9. Ibid., 30.

10. Ibid.

11. Zuhur, *Precision in the Global War on Terror*, 55. Zuhur explains that "*Ijtihad* is the eighth verbal form of j-h-d, (the root of *jihad*) and intensifies the root meaning of "striving" to a special process of creative reasoning. It is one of the sources of jurisprudence, or Islamic law-making, which was, historically, abandoned by Sunni jurists, though it remains a part of the Twelver Shi'i tradition. A cleric could be trained and certified in *ijtihad,* thus earning the rank of *mujtadhid.* Modernist Muslims and liberals rather frequently call for *ijtihad,* or "a return to *ijtihad*" as a means of reform from within Islam.

12. Nafi, "The Rise of Islamic Reformist Thought," 40.

13. Ibid., 42–43.

14. Paden, *Muslim Civic Cultures and Conflict Resolution,* 162.

to revive the Islamic law, Shari'a, in Nigeria, Gumi used his connection with Saudi Arabia to reevaluate "the historic legacies of both the Maliki and Sufi traditions in northern Nigeria."[15] According to Paden, "Gumi focused on going back to the original sources in the Qur'an and was one of the first to interpret the Qur'an into Hausa language. Until his death in 1992 he served as a symbol for challenging the cultural legacies of Islam in northern Nigeria, insisting on Qur'anic-based reformation."[16] Gumi became a mentor to many of the younger generation of educated northerners, and Kaduna, as capital of the northern region and a "new" city, became identified with his *Izala* (anti-innovation) movement. Gumi's links with the Saudis' intellectualism eventually strengthened Nigerian Muslims' ties to the custodians of the holy places, and weakened those with the traditional West African roots of Islamic culture.[17]

The Evolution of Boko Haram

Boko Haram came out of Gumi's Izala sect in Nigeria. Since Boko Haram mutated from the Izala group to a full-grown rebellion movement in 2002, it has continued to metamorphose. The ingredients that fuel the fire of Boko Haram include, among other things, the way security agencies in Nigeria have handled the group with blunt force. It has been said that "Christians are like nails; the harder you hit them the deeper they go." But I would like to say that by default all human beings behave similarly; the harder you hit them the deeper they go. The Boko Haram sect is clear evidence of this fact. Kyari Mohammed has identified three overlapping historical phases of the movement. The first phase, according to Mohammed, is the Kanama phase (2003 to 2005). During this phase the group unsuccessfully waged war on the Nigerian state. It was repelled with casualties on both sides. The leader of the group of this first phase was Mohammed Ali, a Nigerian who was radicalized by jihadi literature in Saudi Arabia and was believed to have fought alongside the *mujahedeen* in Afghanistan. The second is the *dawah* phase. With the suppression of Boko Haram in July 2009, the group went into hiding and devoted itself to proselytization, recruitment, indoctrination, and radicalization of its members. This phase was characterized by intensive criticism of the secular system; debates with opposing *ulama* (other Muslim clerics) on the propriety or impropriety of Western education, Westernization, democracy, and secularism; and unceasing criticism of corruption

15. Ibid., 162.
16. Ibid.
17. Ibid.

and bad governance under Governor Ali Modu Sherriff (2003 to 2011) of
Borno State, as well as the conspicuous consumption and opulence of the
Western-educated elite in the midst of surrounding poverty. According to
Mohammed, the third phase began with the taking over of the leadership
by Abubakar Shekau. After the 2009 suppression of the movement and
the killing of its leadership in gory and barbaric form by Nigerian security
agencies, Boko Haram again went deeper underground, only to reorganize
and resurface with a vengeance in 2010. Since then the group has not only
attacked perceived enemies but has also indiscriminately attacked security
officials, politicians and businessmen and women, bombing high-profile
targets in Abuja such as the Nigeria Police Headquarters and the United Nations offices in June and August of 2011. As the military crackdown intensi-
fied, the group became even more aggressive and militant. It has resorted to
more desperate measures, which include burning school buildings, kidnapping students, attacking telecommunications stations, blowing up bridges,
kidnapping and slaughtering foreigners and so on.[18]

Boko Haram lacks morality in its war tactics. This is demonstrated
by the aimless and indiscriminate slaughtering and bombing of innocent
citizens. Understanding the intellectual and social psychology of Boko Haram will help us to grasp the many facets of the group's social life, thoughts,
feelings and behaviors towards Muslims and non-Muslims, and the impact
of its attitudes on the Nigerian people in general. One place to start is the
group's specific demands: (1) it wants certain aspects of Western Education
obliterated in Nigeria (2) it wants to establish a caliphate in Nigeria, and
(3) it wants to replace the Nigerian constitution with the Islamic legal law,
Shari'a. From the sect's outlook, its objective is a political one, even though
it calls for the abolition of politics altogether and the replacement of the
modern state by Islamic Shari'a jurisprudence. Yet it has a comprehensive
program which integrates religion, the economy and politics.

Boko Haram and Failed Negotiations

Nigeria is facing its defining moment. Like Prof. Wole Soyinka has observed,
this moment is more important and critical than the civil war of unity that
Nigerians fought in the late 1960s.

From all indications, the Nigerian government cannot engage the
Boko Haram sect in meaningful just peacemaking. The government has
had several failed attempts. Therefore, knowing why past efforts at engaging
Boko Haram have failed will help in the present effort. The first attempt

18. Mohammed, "The Message and Methods of Boko Haram," 10.

at dialogue was in September, 2011. The group identified two key people, former president Olusegun Obasanjo and Babakura Fugu, the brother-in-law of the late Boko Haram leader, Mohammed Yusuf, in Maiduguri, Borno State. During the process of dialogue, Babakura Fugu was mysteriously assassinated. The core Boko Haram sect denied responsibility for the murder. Prior to this, Boko Haram had always claimed responsibility for any atrocities it committed against the Nigerian people. The second attempt at dialogue happened in March, 2012. The group identified the president of the Supreme Council for Shari'a in Nigeria, Sheik Ahmed Datti, to mediate between it and the Nigerian government. Sheik Ahmed Datti initially accepted the responsibility but later declined, as he felt the government was not able to keep the discussion secret and would instead prematurely release information to the media.[19] Akinola Ejodame Olojo believes these were significant signs that the group was willing and ready for dialogue. But Andrew Walker believes that there were two groups within the sect—moderate and a radical, or hard-core group—which made engaging the group a complex and difficult task. Walker suggests other factors that also contributed to the difficulty. For example, the Nigerian police are often led by corrupt or incompetent officers who fight for their own fiefdom rather than work together for the interest of the nation.[20] As Walker observed, negotiation would be difficult to foster because some of Boko Haram's stated demands are practically impossible to realize and are often contradictory. For example, it wants to break Nigeria into two, north and south; but they desire also that the whole of Nigeria should come under Shari'a law and convert to Islam. It has also demanded that Goodluck Jonathan should convert to Islam. However, there are other demands that might serve as a window for dialogue and just peacemaking. The group has demanded that senior members who have been arrested by the government should be released, all property that has been taken from its members should be restored, and the people responsible for the execution of Mohammed Yusuf and other members of the group should be punished. "These are political demands and could be part of a negotiation," says John Campbell.[21] It is also difficult to see how any meaningful negotiation would be carried out. The group has on several occasions murdered its own members who have attempted it, and the group's cell-like structure is vulnerable to faction and splits. There would be no guarantee that someone speaking for the group is speaking for all of

19. Akinola Ejodame Olojo, "Engaging Boko Haram: Militarization, Mediation, or Both?" *Global Observatory,* September 26, 2012. http://theglobalobservatory. org/2012/09/engaging-boko-haram-militarization-mediation-or-both/

20. Walker, "What Is Boko Haram," 7.

21. Ibid., 11–12.

the members.[22] Given that as reality, can we really talk of a way forward at a time when things appear to be not only falling apart but getting worse? The courage to talk about a way forward must come from an understanding of the mission of the Church as the mission of Jesus Christ: peacemaking.

Boko Haram and Just Peacemaking

Using the work of the late Glen Harold Stassen at this point, this section seeks to[23] test the applicability of his vision of just peacemaking in a terrorist context like Nigeria, and to advocate the need for practices providing a moral vision which can shape the fight against Boko Haram insurgency. Based on his Anabaptist roots, the late Stassen and his colleagues worried about the world's lack of attention to practices that have been effective in preventing war. They argued that "A new paradigm needs to be justified by its bringing to attention important dimensions of concern that previous paradigms overlooked, or did not articulate as clearly as needed."[24] Just peacemaking practices, Stassen and his colleagues argued "Can enable us to see conflict situations from a new and fruitful angle." In my estimation, just peacemaking as proposed by Stassen and his colleagues[25] can provide additional concrete steps to resolving the Boko Haram impasse in Nigeria. For example, Nigerian ethicists and theologians can use the ten practices Stassen proposed to interpret specific social, cultural and religious contexts of Nigerian society and its grassroots communities. I affirm the efficacy and utility of just peacemaking because of its focus on practices that prevent war or terrorism from happening in the first place. But even after it has happened, the practices, because of their focus on justice as Jesus' ethics,

22. Ibid., 12.

23. This chapter was originally written in honor of Glen H. Stassen, who was an ardent advocate of just peacemaking as a critical supplementary theory to the two other theories of Christian response to war—pacifism and just war theory (see Stassen, "The Unity, Realism, and Obligatoriness," 171). He argued that "Just peacemaking is a new paradigm for Christian ethics alongside just war theory and pacifism. It answers a different question than just war theory and pacifism: not the question of justification but prevention." The Nigerian government mishandled the Boko Haram insurgency. If the government had had this vision it would have done better in preventing it before it got out of hand.

24. Stassen, "The Unity, Realism, and Obligatoriness," 171–94.

25. See Stassen, Just Peacemaking, 156. The ten practices that prevent war have been fashioned out by twenty-three interdisciplinary scholars who took a decisively realist turn when they rejected defining just peacemaking theory in terms of principles or ideals, and instead decided to focus on practices that are in fact demonstrating their effectiveness in the realistic conditions of present history.

can give confidence to the parties involved. For as Adrian Guelke observes, "Common reasons why people resort to violence are the perception that they will continue to be denied justice under the existing political system . . ."[26] The cry for justice is a key cause for the emergence of Boko Haram. Since Nigeria returned to democracy in 1999, northern Muslim politicians have generally felt alienated and marginalized.[27]

Stassen saw just peacemaking as one of three theories—pacifism, just war and just peacemaking—which hold hope for dislodging violence and war. He believed just peacemaking was rooted in the practice advocated by the Prince of Peace, who wept over Jerusalem because it did not know the ways that make for peace. He argued that in these radical practices, "Jesus gives us a powerful way of deliverance from the vicious cycles that lead to violent death and destruction."[28] He was among those who firmly believed that Christians should direct their energies toward finding a set of criteria and a model for just peace instead of continuing to argue only for pacifism and just war.[29] He contended that just peacemaking practices have worked because they are Christ-like, transforming initiatives. They are practices that are first and foremost aimed at preventing the occurrence of war or violence by concentrating on justice and seeking to win both parties to the side of justice. Furthermore, his belief in the workability of just peacemaking principles is based on how practitioners like Mohandas Gandhi, Martin Luther King Jr., and Nelson Mandela successfully deployed just peacemaking practices in the extreme conditions of colonial India, racist United States of America and apartheid South Africa.

One may wonder though whether just peacemaking can work in situations of Islamic extremism and terrorism. Stassen would say yes, it can, because its ideas are practices that are faithful to Christ's nonviolent direct action in the Sermon on the Mount (Matt 5–7). In fact, he would argue that just peacemaking practices are some of the most "effective war-preventive practices . . . in the wake of the threat of terrorism . . ."[30] Inasmuch as I resonate with his argument, the practices must be applied in each context by careful analysis of the situation and clear understanding of the mindset of those involved in the conflict. Stassen and 22 other just peacemaking ethicists and theologians have helped us by proposing the following ten practices: (1) Support nonviolent direct action; (2) Take independent initiative

26. Guelke, "Negotiations and Peace Processes," 56.
27. Paden, *Muslim Civic Cultures and Conflict Resolution*, 171.
28. Stassen and Gushee, *Kingdom Ethics*, 150.
29. Stassen, *Just Peacemaking*, 2, 5.
30. Stassen and Gushee, *Kingdom Ethics*, 169.

to reduce threats; (3) Use cooperative conflict resolution; (4) Acknowledge responsibility for conflict and injustice and seek repentance and forgiveness; (5) Advance democracy, human rights, and religious liberty; (6) Foster just and sustainable economic development; (7) Work with emerging cooperative forces in the international system; (8) Strengthen the United Nations and international efforts for cooperation and human rights; (9) Reduce offensive weapons and weapons trade; and (10) Encourage grassroots peacemaking groups and voluntary association.[31] Space will not allow us to delineate each of the proposed ten practices. However, the next two points are some contextual ways Nigerians can engage Boko Haram in just peacemaking.

Theological Reflection

Engaging Boko Haram in just peacemaking must start with humble recognition of our common humanity with terrorists: human aggression. All just peacemakers need to begin by recognizing their participation in the essentially human nature of competition, aggression and revenge. Storr puts it concisely when he writes:

> That man is an aggressive creature will hardly be disputed. With the exception of certain rodents, no other vertebrate habitually destroys members of his own species . . . The somber fact is that we are the cruelest and most ruthless species that has ever walked the earth; and that, although we may recoil in horror when we read in newspaper or history book of the atrocities committed by man upon man, we know in our hearts that each of us harbors within himself those same savage impulses which lead to murder, to torture and to war.[32]

These succinct words of Storr about the true nature of humans give us a clearer perspective that would go a long way in guiding our feet toward the path of peace in Nigeria. Human aggression is an inborn impulse which is not the monopoly of insurgents but a reality that all fallen humans struggle with.[33] It is necessary to recognize and focus on aggression because

31. Agang, *The Impact of Ethnic, Political and Religious Violence*, 262.

32. Storr, *Human Aggression*, ix.

33. Ibid., ix. Storr writes that one of the difficulties we face when it comes to defining aggression is that there is no clear dividing line between those forms of aggression which we all deplore and those which we must not disown if we are to survive . . . The desire for power has, in extreme form, disastrous aspects which we acknowledge; but the drive to conquer difficulties or to gain mastery over the external world underlies the greatest of human achievement. Generally speaking, paranoid persons deny their

it can also be used to bless humanity. This approach will enable us to begin thinking of ways we can retrain both adults and children to use aggression positively for the benefit of humanity. Aggression has two sides, like a coin. Kathleen J. Greider calls the two sides of aggression the paradox of "violence and vitality." In her search for a solution to the problem of violence, Greider believes that a way out of the impasse that violence presents in our contemporary history is to pay attention not only "to decrying and devising solutions to it" but also "to give equal attention to ways we can help individuals and whole communities cultivate the enormous vitality required to live ethically and empathically and thereby decrease violence."[34] The big question that must be addressed is how do we constructively redirect the energy of violent aggression into vitality (nonviolent aggression) for the protection of the human race? Just peacemaking is an option that can help Nigeria to rechanneled Boko Haram's aggressive energies toward national transformation.

To indirectly engage Boko Haram is to also address the social and cultural conditions that create the breeding grounds for recruits. Studies conducted by Freedom C. Onuoha in 2013 showed that Boko Haram is recruiting Nigerian youths who feel distressed, alienated, discontented, and generally uncertain about their future because of the unfavorable sociopolitical, socioeconomic, sociocultural and socioreligious conditions in Nigeria.[35] Onuoha argued that these conditions make it enormously possible for insurgents to recruit young men in Nigeria.[36] Therefore, the Nigerian government must embark on robust programs that would block Boko Haram through strengthening standards of education, providing youth with job training and creating job programs, promoting peace education and embarking on a campaign of zero tolerance for corruption at all levels of society.

Boko Haram is a child of corrupt social, political and economic systems. The Nigerian youths, particularly from the Islamic community, are sick and tired of waiting for a turn of event that will give them hope for a future. The Boko Haram sect has been watching the corrupt lifestyle of Nigerian elites and for lack of knowing how to bring change blame it on Nigeria's secular status. Boko Haram sect uses the corrupt lifestyle of Nigerian Muslim elites as an example of what is wrong with the secular status

---

hostility and attribute it to other people (100).

34. Greider, *Reckoning with Aggression*, 1.

35. Freedom Onuoha, "Why Do Youth Join Boko Haram?," United States Institute of Peace, Special Report 348, June 2014, p. 1. http://www.usip.org/publications/why-do-youth-join-boko-haram

36. Ibid., 1.

of Nigeria. They preach reformation of the system to a generation of youth that is bearing the hardship, which corruption has birthed in Nigeria. Boko Haram promises the Muslim youth a change that will only happen if strict Islamic law—Shari'a—is introduced; and Shari'a is the law of the land. And the youth are convenienced that this indeed will bring hope to them.

Boko Haram has easy access to a disenfranchised and estranged populace: A few elite recycling powers within themselves to the detriment of the larger populace. For a new Nigeria to be birthed we need political elites who are willing to share power and encourage all and sundry to participate in the affairs of the nation as dignified stakeholders. To save Nigeria from terrorism, we will need to understand that there are fundamentally two types of power: power over (access power) and power with (collaborative power). At present, things are not working in Nigeria because of the quest for power over: We need power *with* and not power *over*.

Why corruption thrives in Nigeria is because corruption is the conduit for power over. People, who are bent on using power *over*, will invariably birth insurgents. They are aware that human psychology demonstrates that constant state of agitation doesn't allow one to stop and critical think of other broad issues of our needs that could lead to challenging the status quo and thereby bringing transformation. They have realized that crises allow them to ruin Nigeria's treasury with impunity. Today, peace is fragile in Nigerian communities because the communities have to bribe the law enforcement agents—the military and the police—to protect them. Nigerians get overwhelmed by protracted crises cause by the activities of bloodthirsty men and women in the country. However, Christians who know God's incomparably great power should help Nigerians regain patience and hope. Therefore, as we (Christians) see the overwhelming nature of corruption in Nigeria, we must avoid falling into the trap of Satan by thinking that there is no hope for the country. We need deep intellectual fair-mindedness: unbiased, neutrality and acquiesce. This would involve the ability to see Nigerian elites (Nigerian oppressors) and the general public beyond their actions. That is, in spite of their wickedness and evil, they still have the imago Dei (the image of God). Therefore, we need to prophetically remind Nigerians of the fact that they still have potentials of goodness, dignity, honesty and the ability to live above reproach. If we must have ministry of hope among Nigerians across all faiths, we must see them as God sees them: Jesus sees people beyond their action.

In spite of the situation of Boko Haram and other violent conflicts across Nigeria, God is doing something new. The plain truth is crisis happens when the old is dying and the new is being born. It is like a pregnant woman. The crisis is the process of birthing a new born child, the process of transformation that is necessary to give birth to the new baby is painful and distressful. If the process of transformation is missed decay will happen. The corruption and terrorism crises in Nigeria are part and parcel of the pivotal moments in the history of Nigeria. What Nigerian Christians need to ask is how we can be part of the process of making it possible for a new Nigeria to be born. First, we will need to go back and look at the historical pivotal moments of Nigeria: Usman Dan Fodio's 1804 Jihad, colonialism, independence, the civil war, the election of a Christian president, the ASSUU seven months strike in 2012, etc.

Second, we need to know that, according to the Christian Scriptures to aspire to a public office is an honorable desire (1 Tim 3:1). However, for such a person to be an agent of midwifing a new Nigeria, he or she must live above reproach. And since money and sex and power—pride—are the major problems of public officials' moral-failures, they will need to imbibe the flowing alternative moral vision:

- they must live above public and private reproach
- they must be faithful to their spouses;
- they must exercise financial and sexual self-control;
- they must live wisely, and have a good moral reputation;
- they must enjoy the practice of hospitality, and they must be able to teach their families and peers how to live a healthy moral life;
- they must not be drunks or be violent;
- they must be gentle, not quarrelsome;
- they must not be money lovers;
- they must be able to manage their family well, and train their children to be obedience and respectful;
- they must not become proud so that the devil would not cause them to fall;
- the governed must speak well of them so that they will not be disgraced and fall into the devil's trap;
- they must be well respected and have integrity among their peers and the general public;
- they must not be dishonest with money;
- they must be committed to the ministry of their faith communities and must live their faith with a clear conscience;

- They must invariably do self-examination and must create a working system of checks and balances;

- their spouses must behave in a way that the public will find it a lot easier to respect them, rather than slandering them;

- their spouses must exercise self-control and be faithful in everything they do; and

- they must create honest ways of giving incentives and rewarding hard work and faithfulness;

These God's revealed moral lifestyles through the Christian Scriptures will crush insurgency. They are the weapons of self-defense that Nigerian Christians need to employ, use and hold public servants from all religious divide to practice. As Christians do so they should not forget that transformation needs negotiation, education, skills and prayers.

It is only when we are willing to pray faithfully that we can dream of a birth of a new Nigeria. Nigerians must be encouraged to create functional community (civil societies), family and a nation that is not going to be taken advantage of. One major thing that we need to be aware of is: the paradox of man: good and evil, dignity and depravity.

Conclusion

As an Islamic terrorist movement, Boko Haram now constitutes one of the biggest threats to Nigeria's stability and security.[37] The group continues to cause widespread emotional and psychological trauma. Even so, researchers need to step aside and take a careful look at what is happening and what else needs to be done to ward off this threat. Just peacemaking is the moral and ethical vision that should shape today's attempts to resolve violent conflicts. Advocating the need for engaging Boko Haram's sect in just peacemaking is simply a call for trying all the options humanly available. Just peacemaking brings a rich option and alternate solution to war and violent conflict. In this paradigm the focus shifts to initiatives that can help prevent vicious cycles of war/violence and foster peace. It argues that in engaging insurgent groups

37. Boko Haram is doing everything possible to re-establish the caliphate in northeast Nigeria and eventually the whole country through a vigorous violent campaign for a stricter observance of the Islamic legal law (Shari'a). Non-Muslims want them to focus on an agenda for national integration and unity; but integration is not their dream. Rather, their target is the conversion of a "pagan" (infidel) world to Islam. Of course, this "infidel world" includes the West and North America. As a way of dealing with insurgency, we advocate the need to include a general understanding of human aggression.

and ethnic militias, we must not stop at the level of the symptoms but dig deep into the real issues that cause the sickness. It is a paradigm that enables its practitioners to engage in critical thinking and analysis;[38] it analyzes the assumptions, the threats and the fears that usually make it extremely difficult to forge ahead in the effort to bring about the desired reconciliation and transformation of any situation that breeds insurgent groups and ethnic militias. Finally, no matter how challenging the circumstances we face in today's world, there is a way forward because God is always willing and able to "guide our feet into the path of peace." Based on his experience, John Paul Lederach explains that the key to significant change will come not when we are capable of producing a hard, factual, objective view of a situation and the predictable outcome; rather, it comes from a kind of naiveté that suspends the lens of presented reality, and with a commonsensical approach asks questions and pursues ideas that seem out of line with reality as presented.[39] "Terrorists aim to rule and murder is their method."[40] We must be willing to resist the temptation to play the terrorists' game[41] by resorting to just peacemaking. Just peacemaking principles can encourage Muslims and Christians to work together to create a Nigeria that is free from terrorists. Its focus on win-win-win situation makes it possible for Nigerians to be able to work at addressing social injustices before they ever get out of hand.

38. These virtues are proposed by Philip E. Dow, *Virtuous Minds*, 28–61.

39. Lederach, "Cultivating Peace," 36.

40. Walzer, "Terrorism," 304. Andrew Walls argues that "terrorism involves the killing of innocents, in that the difference between (just) war and terrorism is that in the former innocents are not targeted but (routinely) killed while in the latter they are targeted and killed" (quoted in ibid., 325). In that case his conclusion is that "terrorism and war are not so morally different from each other" (quoted in ibid.).

41. Walzer, "Terrorism," 304.

Chapter 11

Creative Models of Just Peacemaking in Nigeria

Introduction

Nigeria is an epitome of the proverbial animal farm where all animals are equal but some animals are more equal than others. No wonder, the northern region is replete with cases of horrific human bloodletting, destruction of property and the environment. In such an environment, just peacemaking is complicated and complex. To start somewhere, this chapter traces the efforts of some of Nigeria's famous peacemakers and their contributions to just peacemaking in Nigeria and beyond. To show that Nigerian Christians do not lack models of just peacemakers and for lack of space, the chapter selects few models like Bishop Samuel Ajayi Crowther and other current cases in Kaduna and Plateau States. This chapter discusses the narrative of Samuel Ajayi Crowther and concluded that unlike most modern pastors, missionaries and the larger church, Crowther saw peacemaking as a colossal and plethora part of his missionary journey. It also discusses the other models of just peacemaking in Kaduna and Jos and concluded that just peacemakers are not born but made.

The Story of Bishop Samuel Ajayi Crowther

With Christians and Muslims holding dominance in different regions [of Nigeria], religion frequently raises political and constitutional issues for the

Nigerian secular state. But what is really happening is not religion, instead it is self-interest and the will-to-power. For example, at a consultative meeting held on May 7, 2009 with Northern States Governor's Forum, Christian Association of Nigeria (CAN) Northern States raised the following questions:

> Do those who call themselves Northerners, see themselves as having equal rights and access to justice, power, freedom of worship, land etc.? Are those of us in the north treated with equal dignity as human beings or are there some who have more rights and should be treated with more dignity than others? Have we and can we come to terms with the stark reality that we are a heterogeneous society and are willing to live and let others live? Can a north, which has been built and so far, sustained on a foundation of injustice, suppression and deceit by an elite ever remain strongly united since it is still within the grip of such an elite? Can a north, which has refused to create a level playing ground for its people to worship the one true God in freedom and without molestation, ever hope to receive blessings from God? How can a north, which appears to glory in the shedding of blood as a result of religious intolerance, which is glaring systematic, ever hope to be united? Are we, as northerners, willing to take to heart, observation of the former Kaduna State Governor (Ahmed Mohammed Maikarfi) when he said "for Muslims, the Koran is supreme, for Christians the Bible is supreme, but in Kaduna State, given our diversity the constitution of [the] Federal Republic of Nigeria should be supreme? Are we willing to ensure that the constitution of the Federal Republic of Nigeria is implemented to the letter or are we going to continue on the path of using and interpreting it only when it suits some sections of our society?"[1]

CAN's series of questions tell the story of a region that segregates and discriminates against her citizens. It is a story of horrifying experiences of betrayal and destruction happening since pre-modern to modern Nigeria. "They betray [and destroy] their friends for their advantage" (Job 17:5). The entire northern region is reaping the seedbeds of selfishness, malice and wickedness it has been sowing. In fact, part of what is happening in Northeastern Nigeria—Boko Haram saga—today is proving one fact: Their (northern Muslims') own schemes are eventually becoming their down fall. Yes, "How can a north, which appears to glory in the shedding of blood as a result of religious intolerance, which is glaringly systematic ever hope to be united?"

1. Jatau and Dogo, "A Position Paper by Christian Association of Nigeria," 1–2.

Nigerian Christian peacemakers need to give the situation its proper perspective—the paradox of man—for the reason that no realistic and serious consideration and commitment to Christian mission can take place without, not only equal commitment to love, justice, righteousness and peace but also equal awareness of their own inclination toward the same paradox of man: good and evil. Indeed, from the narrative of Archbishop Samuel Ajayi Crowther (1809 to 1891) we will grasp this dimension of the human society. We ought to say that we (human beings—Christians or Muslims) all betray our friends for our advantage. The story of Henry Townsend and his collaborators, Samuel Ajayi Crowther's white colleagues, is a prime example. In pursuance of their selfish ambition and the drive for power and control, Townsend and his supporters caused Crowther to be frustrated and miserable to the extent that he died of a stroke. And after Crowther died in 1892 no African ever became bishop until sixty years later. Olson writes, "All but three of the Niger Mission's 15 Africans were fired. When Crowther protested, he was charged with violating his code of office. He died shortly thereafter, and a white bishop was put in his place. The continent would not see another African Anglican bishop until 1952, sixty years after Crowther's death."[2] This confirms to us that Christians are not immune to the temptation of doing what the sinful nature craves: self-interest and the drive for power or domination of others. Thus Christian mission needs to include and employ *just* peacemaking in the service of human well-being and the creation of healthy relationships.

Crowther and the Pioneering of Peacemaking

The context of peacemaking in Nigeria is very complex and hard to interpret. Of course, we are aware that Christian peacemaking did not start nor end with Samuel Ajayi Crowther. Nigerian communities have at different times and levels been involved in peacemaking. Both the religious and secular communities of Nigeria have in one way or the other, locally, national or internationally been involved in peacemaking.[3] However, this chapter focuses on the peacemaking that is based on Christian principles and values distilled from Jesus' ministry of just peacemaking. This sort of peacemaking sees the work of peacemaking as the mission of the Church, a realization of

2. Olson, "Bishop Before His Time," 15:

3. Paden, *Muslim Civic Cultures*, 28. What Paden has said about the Muslim communities in Nigeria can be said about Christianity. He writes, "The Muslim communities in Nigeria have played a major role in keeping the country together since independence in 1960 and in avoiding outright failure of the national political systems."

the centrality to and the linkage of the concept of peacemaking to the cross and resurrection of Jesus Christ. It is on this basis that the starting point of the chapter is Bishop Samuel Ajayi Ade Crowther. As we will demonstrate below, Crowther demonstrated an unusual ability to engage his captors in just peacemaking even when he had the opportunity to take revenge when he became part of the Niger expedition later.

Crowther was born and brought up during the years when slavery was seen as a legitimate business by many people whose economic self-interest and the desire for power had twisted their minds. In the eighteenth and nineteenth centuries slave trading was at its peak and provided important sources of revenue and access to items such as guns and European luxury goods that contributed greatly to the consolidation of wealth and power in many states. In the states of the northern savannas and the Sahel, the institution of slavery had deep roots, and had connections with Arabs' trans-Saharan trade routes where markets for slave exports had existed for several centuries. The Islamic religion which came to Nigeria in the fifteenth century[4] brought with it inhumane trade of human beings: slave trade. Thus as the main trans-Saharan trade routes moved east in the fifteenth and sixteenth centuries, coinciding with the expansion and consolidation of the Hausa states and the Borno empires, tensions between these states, in which the taking of slaves for eventual sale in the trans-Saharan markets became both a tactic and a goal.[5]

Crowther had first-hand experiences of the evil of slave trade and thereafter mistreatment from the hands of his fellow white racists or colleagues from the Church of England.[6] He was a teen ager when his native Yoruba village of Osugun fell into the hands of Fulani slave raiders. He was among those captured alive and sold into slavery. He was sold to five or six different African masters before Portuguese traders purchased him and placed him on a slave ship to cross the Atlantic.[7] On his way to the land of no return, their ship, *Esperanz Felix,* was rescued by an antislavery squad ship; and by the then British policy Crowther was not supposed to be sent back to Nigeria. Thus he was sent to the recently established colony of Sierra Leon.

While in Sierra Leon, he was among the first students of a recently established first university in Sub-Sahara Africa, the famous Fourah Bay College where he had the privilege of acquiring the best education and

4. Falaranmi, "The Nigerian Islamic View of the State," 73.

5. Falola and Heaton, *A History of Nigeria*, 39.

6. Olsen, "Bishop Before His Time," 10.

7. Ibid.

preparation for a life of service to God's world, particularly the African continent. Crowther reported that in six months he learned to read the New Testament and that he became "convinced that [he] was a sinner, and desired to obtain pardon through Jesus Christ."[8] He eventually became part of an expedition to Nigeria through the Niger British Company, whose primary goal was to introduce legitimate trade and commerce that would eventually supplant the illegitimate trade in human beings. Upon his returned to Nigeria via the Niger Company, Crowther encounter the Muslims whose kinsmen had sold him into slavery. Instead of revenge, Crowther, a genuine disciple of Jesus Christ decided to engage them in peacemaking. Archbishop Crowther traveled the length of the Niger River every year until he was eighty-forty years old.

The famous Christian mission historiographer, Andrew Walls, paints a picture of how Crowther really did it. Walls analysis is a great reminder that Nigeria's journey to peacemaking goes back to the interaction of Christianity and other faiths in the nineteenth century. During Crowther's time, it was clear that because Christianity is an incarnational faith, Christian missions requires careful interaction and engagement with other faiths: African Traditional Religion (ATR [which is sometimes call African Indigenous Religion—AIR]) and Islam. Andrew Walls stresses the fact that the story of Nigeria's peacemaking cannot be complete without giants like Bishop Samuel Ade Ajayi Crowther. Crowther is believed to have conducted what was perhaps the first positive Christian dialogue with African Indigenous Religionists and African Muslims.[9] Walls observed, "Crowther sought common ground . . . He enjoyed courteous and friendly relations with Muslim rulers, and his writings trace various discussions with rulers . . . [Crowther said] 'After many years' experience, I have found that the Bible, the sword of the Spirit, must fight its own battle, by the guidance of the Holy Spirit.'"[10]

Crowther's captors and rescuers had no idea that they were participating with God in the making of a man of intellectual courage, intellectual fair-mindedness, intellectual carefulness, intellectual curiosity, intellectual tenacity, intellectual honesty, and intellectual humility.[11] Crowther was the

---

8. Crowther and Schön, *Journals of the Rev. James Frederick Schön and Mr. Samuel Crowther*, 371–385, quoted in Climenchaga, "Heathenism, Delusion, and Ignorance," 661–681.

9. This article, from the *International Bulletin of Missionary Research*, Jan. 92, Vol. 16 Issue 1, 15–21, is reproduced, with permission, from *Mission Legacies: Biographical Studies of Leaders of the Modern Missionary Movement* edited by G. H. Anderson *et al.*

10. Walls, Samuel Ajayi Crowther, 28, quoting Crowther, *Experiences with Heathens and Mohammedans.*

11. Dow, *Intellectual Virtues*, 19–20.

epitome of just peacemaking in Nigeria. He clearly illustrates what peace-making entails: True peace, the kind Jesus came to give us, is only attainable through discrimination against untruths! His entire approach and attitude to Islam and AIR reminds us of the fact that the only way to achieve true peace in one's life is to learn to discriminate against untruths—lies. That is what Jesus means when he said, "Ye shall know the truth, and the truth shall set you free." Being a peacemaker requires both positive and negative activity. On the positive side, we are told in Ephesians, Chapter 4 to associ-ate with people who, like us, "make efforts to guard the unity of the Spirit through the adhesive nature of spiritual peace." In Hebrews 12:4, we are told to "pursue peaceful relationships with everyone." These instructions must be followed if we seek peaceful living on a public level. Crowther illustrates this in his just peacemaking style.

Crowther's Style of Peacemaking

The West African religious scene of Crowther's day necessitated engage-ment with followers of Islam and ATR or AIR. From her careful study of Crowther's journals and letters, Alison Fitchett Climenchaga gleaned the complex nature and scope of Crowther's inter-religious encounters. Crowther had different approaches to just peacemaking with the two religions that Christianity met in West Africa. From his choice of words and vocabulary in his published journals, letters and treatise as well as his unpublished works preserved in the Church Missionary Society, Climen-chaga was able to detect his different approaches. In his approach to just peacemaking, Crowther demonstrated a remarkable ability to tell the truth with caution and sensitivity. In general Crowther recognized the existence of both Islam and ATR as a distraction from the true worship of God, which Christianity should seek to correct and perfect. He recognized the fact that Islam posed greater challenges to conversations with Christianity than AIR because Islam made its adherents difficult to accept the revealing and trans-forming power of the Gospel. Crowther used negative terms to describe Islam and AIR. Some vocabularies or terms he applies solely to traditional religion. For example, he reserves the term "heathenism" to describe many different forms of traditional religion, but never applies "heathen" to Is-lam.[12] He saw and described African Traditional Religionists as "gross idola-ters" for while they acknowledged the "worship of the only true God" they also worshipped lesser deities, whom they believed God created for their benefit. He rejected this perspective and denounced the lesser deities as

---

12 Climenchaga, "Heathenism, Delusion, and Ignorance," 667.

"devices of Satan" designed to keep the Yoruba apart from God. In his dealing with Muslims, Crowther occasionally calls them "superstitious" because
to him, the Muslims have a "superstitious regard" for the Qur'an and that
leads them to wearing charms. He removes a charm from the neck of one
of his Muslim students in Sierra Leon because "such superstition was not
countenanced in any Christian school."[13] Climenchaga noted how Crowther
applies a few choice terms especially to Islam. For example, he often associates Islam with ignorance, lamenting the difficulty of convincing "ignorant
bigoted Muhammedans" through reasoned argument, for they are "unedu-
cated people."[14] This alludes to the Muslim recitation of Arabic phrases that
they do not fully understand. If one stops here, one would conclude that the
use of these terms does not show Crowther to be a peacemaker at all. But
we need to patiently move forward. Crowther treated both Islam and AIR
based on their wide coverage. For example, given Islam's sophistication and
global reach, he views it in a slightly more positive light than he did ATR.
While he sharply criticizes Islam, particularly for the perceived ignorance
and deceit associated with it, he claims that it is superior to traditional religion. He cites awareness that "Mohammedanism . . . is superior to the
religion of the heathens" as the reason that heathens have embraced Islam.[15]
Part of the reason Crowther accorded Islam superior rating was because of
its monotheism, which led some of Crowther's contemporaries to conclude
that Islam represented a more advanced stage of religious development.
Some even believed that it could serve as a potential aid to the spread of
Christianity because it prepared Africans to receive Christianity, the pinnacle of human development and religious truth.

The Role of Scriptures in Crowther's Peacemaking Efforts

In spite of these vocabularies and the choice of words to describe African
Traditional Religion and Islam, Crowther was able to still engage both in
just peacemaking because of his respect for humanity, humility and trans-
parent truth-telling. Crowther's reflection on other religions was deeply
rooted in the Bible, which provided him with several different nuances and
lenses through which he perceived them and grasped his own role of Christian just peacemaking. Crowther had an exceptional ability to insightfully
connect his understanding of both African Traditional Religion and Islam

13. Crowther and Schön, *Expedition up the Niger,* 7.

14 Ibid.

15. Crowther and Taylor, *The Gospel on the Banks of the Niger,* 171, quoted in Climenchaga, "Heathenism, Delusion, and Ignorance," 673.

with what he gleaned from Scriptures. For example, quoting Joshua 14:12, he compares the "cities great and fenced" with the "strongholds of Moham-medanism and heathenism," and he prays that for the sake of the mission he will be able to conquer these strongholds.[16] In his interaction with Muslims he made it categorically clear that the Bible does not refer to Islam and Mu-hammad. Once, a group of Muslims visited him at Zogoshi, saying:

> We understand that the Anasaras [Christians] do not like Mohammed's name to appear in their book, as the names of Abraham, Moses, David, &c." I replied, that Mohammed had not been born till six hundred years after Christ, and after the close of the Anasaras' Bible . . . could not be mentioned there.[17]

Crowther set a record of everyday interreligious encounter with the three religions that are firmly rooted in Nigeria: Indigenous African re-ligious traditions, Islam and his own religion, Christianity. He genuinely recognized the legitimate existence of African Traditional Religions and Islam in the African continent. His approach and methodology were such that he made effort to stay as closely as possible so as to give them every op-portunity to the means of grace. Because of his curiosity, Crowther, (though no great scholar or Arabist) developed an approach to Islam in its African setting that reflected the patience and the readiness to listen that marked his entire missionary method. Avoiding denunciation and allegations of false prophecy, he acceptance what the Qur'an says of Christ. Crowther looked to the future with hope; and because of his expository teaching of the Bible the average African Christian knew the Bible much better than the aver-age African Muslim knew the Qur'an. And he pondered the fact that the Muslim rule of faith was expressed in Arabic, while the Christian faith was in Hausa, or Nupe or Yoruba. The result was different understandings of how the faith was to be applied in life.[18] He also recommends Isaiah's "ex-posure of the folly of image-worship" (Isa 44:8–20) as a useful model for condemning idolatrous worship, and he likens practitioners of traditional religion to those in Romans 1:22–25 who "worshipped and served the crea-ture more that the creator." More charitably, he portrays liberated Africans playing the role of Moses speaking to his Midianite father-in-law, Hobab, approaching their countrymen with the invitation, "Come with us, for the

16. Crowther, *Letter from February 26, 1883,* quoted in McKenzie, *Inter-religious Encounters in West Africa,* 78. Cited in Climenchaga, "Heathenism, Delusion, and Ig-norance," 670.

17. Crowther and Taylor, *The Gospel on the Banks of the Niger,* 36, quoted in Cli-menchaga, "Heathenism, Delusion, and Ignorance," 670.

18. Walls, "A Second Narrative of Samuel Ajayi Crowther's Early Life," 14.

Lord has promised good to Israel" (Numbers 10:29). Perhaps Crowther uses this passage to indicate that he perceived Africans as potential recipients of the blessings intended for God's people. Moreover, both this and the Isaiah passage cast the Christian evangelist as an individual sent by God to lead God's people.[19]

Crowther's Trailblazing Quest in Just Peacemaking

To appreciate Crowther just peacemaking effort we must go beyond the words he used to describe AIR and Islam above. Like Climenchaga observed, "More plausible explanations lie in the history of Christianity's engagement with Islam and traditional religion and Crowther's own perceptions of the role Christianity ought to play in the West African religious scene." In his just peacemaking with traditional religion, Crowther rejects the idolatrous aspect of the religion but believes that local traditions and customs are what give a people their identity and roots. For Crowther, Christianity's role is to perfect rather than destroy local traditions. Speaking of both Islam and traditional religion, Crowther declares that "their false doctrines have to be exposed, their errors corrected, and they . . . led and directed to Him who is 'the way, the truth, and the life.'"[20] For the Muslims, he ensures that they were given their due respect as human beings created in the image of God. Well aware that his ability to preach and establish mission stations in some areas depended on the good favor of Muslim officials like the Emir of Ilorin, Crowther sought to cultivate cordial relations with them. Especially in the latter portion of his career, rather than leading with denunciation of the Qur'an's revelatory status or of the Prophet Muhammad's character, Crowther sought to build his proclamation on common Christian and Muslim commitments to monotheism and shared reverence for figures like Jesus, Mary, and Gabriel. These characteristics have led Andrew Walls to see Crowther pioneering a distinctive "African Christian approach to Islam," one firmly Biblicist in character and buoyed with the confidence that empowerment of the Holy Spirit and the power of vernacular preaching could transform the hearts and lives of even the most stubborn Muslim audience.[21]

---

19. Climenchaga, "Heathenism, Delusion, and Ignorance," 671.

20. Crowther and Taylor, *Gospel on the Banks of the Niger*, 236.

21. Walls, "Africa as the Theater of Christian Engagement with Islam," 163, quoted in Climenchaga, "Heathenism, Delusion, and Ignorance," 679.

Principles and Lessons from Crowther

Meaningful just peacemaking occurs in the context of careful biblical reflection and respect of the God-given human agency of freedom to reason, think and decide. Through trials and errors, Crowther perfected his just peacemaking principles. He has left us several lessons which could guide today's peacemakers in Nigeria. The situation he encountered might not be directly the same with ours but nothing much has changed. Indeed, since the days of Crowther or even prior, Christian peacemakers in Nigeria have had to deal with the reality of ATR and Islam. In Ilorin and Nupe land, Crowther encountered northern Nigeria Islam with its focus on power and authority. The underpinning center of Nigeria's Islamic customs and controversies has been its ideological aspiration and hope: power and political control of the entire country. For instance, Sir Ahmadu Bello, Sarduna of Sokoto is credited as saying, "The new nation called Nigeria should be an estate of our great grandfather Othman Ibn Fodio [dan Fodio was the Fulani jihadist who in 1804 conquered Hausa-land and most of southwestern Nigeria and supplanted AIR/ATR with Islam]. We must ruthlessly prevent a change of power. We use the minorities in the north as willing tools and the south as a conquered territory and never allow them to rule over us; and never allow them to have control over their future."[22]

As Crowther said, Nigerian just peacemakers need to expose such errors. For it was Blaise Pascal who once said, "Men never do evil so completely and cheerfully as when they do it from religious conviction."[23] Many Nigerian Muslims share these insinuations and feelings. People who try to create divisions and problems on the basis of religious or social affiliation are not serving the Lord, God of love and peace. In the Church we also have people who are serving their feelings. That is why Paul says, "Brothers and sisters, I urge you to watch out for people who create divisions and problems against the teaching that you learned. People like that aren't serving the Lord. They are serving their own feelings. They deceive the hearts of innocent people with smooth talk and flattery" (Rom 16:17–18).

To be people of integrity and complete honesty, Christians are supposed to live not for their own feelings. As Paul enjoins us, "We don't live for ourselves and we don't die for ourselves. If we live, we live for the Lord, and if we die, we die for the Lord. Therefore, whether we live or die, we belong to God" (Rom 14:7–8). If we live for God, he is called the God of peace. If we know God as the God of peace, "Each of us should please our

22. *Parrot*, October 12, 1960, recalled by *Tribune*, November 13, 2002.

23. Quoted in Colson, *God & Government*, 47.

neighbors for their good in order to build them up. Christ didn't please himself, but, as it is written, *The insults of those who insulted you fell on me.* Whatever was written in the past was written for our instruction so that we could have hope through endurance and through the encouragement of the scriptures" (Rom 15:2–4). This is what just peacemaking means: upholding justice and righteousness no matter what challenges may come up. The narrative of Crowther calls our attention to God's grace at work in a world of gargantuan greed and terrible suffering, where appalling human sacrifice is confronted by astounding self-sacrifice. Himself a former helpless slave, Crowther, "became a world-class explorer, a distinguished linguist, and exulted statesman and a revered man of God. It is a story of godly men making sad but honest mistakes, of visionary statesmen and political intrigue on two continents, and of legitimate human aspiration pitched against age-old economic sharp practice."[24]

Crowther saw his mission work as part and parcel of his just peacemaking and as "the means of [God's] grace" which would induce his heathen countrymen to come within reach of the means of God's grace and hear the Word of God.[25] That is why, "While early on, Crowther was biting in his criticism of Islam [which was embraced by many chiefs of the Upper Niger] he later changed his approach. He came to realize that a Muslim "by kind treatment may be led to read and study the Christian's Bible, which by the blessing of God may lead him [or her] from the error of his [or her] way." Andrew Walls has called his work on the Niger Expedition the "First sustained missionary engagement with African Islam in modern times."[26] Crowther demonstrates high spirit of flexibility, great patient, a political will, and utmost sincerity of purpose. This is perhaps necessitated by the fact that Crowther realized the totality of human experience over the ages has shown in practical reality that there can be no societal development and human security without love and peace.

The narrative of Crowther stresses the importance of paying attention to interreligious encounters in Nigeria and the need for such encounters to include African Indigenous worldview, particularly the religious traditions of ATR, Islam, and Christianity. We tend to ignore the indigenous religions when we think about religious encounters and dialogue in Nigeria.[27] We often forget that Nigeria offers one of the best multireligious research contexts in the world, with no single religious group or tradition holding

24. Decorvet and Oladipo, *Samuel Ajayi Crowther*, back cover.

25. Olsen, "Bishop Before His Time," 13.

26. Ibid.

27. Conteh, "Traditionalists, Muslims, and Christians in Africa."

the majority. Crowther's narrative also opens our eyes to the need to carefully investigate the everyday inter-religious encounters in Nigeria. For any meaningful interreligious encounters, the reality of the human condition should be taken seriously so that as peacemakers we are compassionate and patient enough to believe in a future with the possibility of hope for peace in spite of what is presently the case. The narrative of Crowther showed how he was a man who had a deep appreciation for God's linguistic gift in a world many languages. He realized the incarnational power of the Word of God and thereby developed interest in learning foreign languages to the extent that his linguistic work was thorough and extensive. He studied not only English but also Latin, Hebrew, Greek and Arabic. And when he became a teacher in one of the Freetown villages, he learned the local language of Temne.[28] What Crowther faced might not be the same thing with what we are facing in Nigeria today. But it is the same human condition, which the biblical doctrine of sin calls original sin that we all face. As J. N. K. Mugambi argued, "effective dialogue across religious and cultural traditions is possible only when the parties involved have mutual respect and reciprocal treatment between each other. Such conditions have not prevailed, owing to Western missionary patronage and condescension towards peoples of other faiths and cultures."[29]

Crowther's narrative is very revealing. In it there are two important aspects that should help us in analyzing the turn of events in Nigeria and elsewhere in the world: The paradoxical situation of the danger of pride and the blessing of humility cannot be missed in the account. The summary of the account is that those who set their hearts on seeking the Lord God of creation are a source of blessing to every nation. They are the people who make it possible to still have some good in every ethnic group in Nigeria. They introduce their neighbors to the means of grace. On the other hand, evil is often perpetuated by those who do not set their hearts on seeking the Lord God, their creator. Instead, they serve their feelings as a substitute of serving God's kingdom and upholding his justice and righteousness. In other words, those who indulge in evil are people who do not set their hearts on seeking the Lord. Those who set their hearts on seeking the Lord cannot despise their fellow human beings whom God has created in his own image and likeness.

Finally, as Climenchaga observes, Crowther's interactive encounter with traditional religion and Islam is instructive in the context of the global church today. First, Crowther provides a model for doing inculturation,

28. Decorvet and Oladipo, *Samuel Ajayi Crowther*, 94.

29. Mugambi, "Missionary Presence."

particularly through his concern to balance fidelity to the gospel with openness to the symbols and practices meaningful in particular context. As he matured as a pastor, he developed a cautious respect for African customs, and he advocated for a moderate, gradual evangelistic approach toward both Islam and traditional religion. He practiced careful discernment—rooted in both his engagement with the Christian tradition and his experience ministering in West Africa—concerning the relationship that elements associated with non-Christian religions might have with authentic Christian belief and practice. Second, Crowther's life illuminates the dynamics of interreligious dialogue. Although contemporary theological discourse often conceptualizes interreligious dialogue and Christian proclamation as different or even contrasting activities, Crowther's example reveals the way that the two have often overlapped in Christian missionary practice. In Crowther's work, dialogue and proclamation were deeply interwoven with each other, such that it is impossible to speak of Crowther's interreligious dialogue apart from his efforts to proclaim the gospel.[30]

As has been noted above, white Christians, represented by Henry Townsend, in pursuance of their self-interest and the will to power frustrated Crowther until he died of stroke. And after his death no African ever became a bishop of the Anglican Church in the continent until after sixty years of Crowther's death. These were the same people who have given him remarkable benevolent treatment right from the time he was rescued and sent to Sierra Leon. Although some of those missionaries from the Church of England who mistreated him knew that "the attitude and conduct of a missionary in relationship with potential and actual converts greatly influences their response to that missionary's teaching" they still maltreated him.[31]

Yet God is able to turn evil to be good. Christianity spread widely among Southern Nigerian peoples. For example, disillusionment with missionary acts produced various "African" Churches in the 1890s, but a major schism was averted. Since the First World War (1914 to 1918) indigenous Churches stressing prophecy and healing (the Yoruba name for there is *aladura*, "praying people") have developed a model of the Church distinct from that introduced by missions, but alert to the life-situation of Nigerian worshippers. The period since the Nigerian Civil War (1967–70) has produced many new charismatic Churches and evangelistic movements. Various Nigerian Churches have missions abroad, including Britain and

---

30. Climenchaga, "Heathenism, Delusion, and Ignorance," 681.

31. Mugambi, "Missionary Presence," 1.

the USA.[32] These churches, however, have become seedbeds of disunity and competition within and without to the extent that we need just peacemaking not just with other faiths but also within the Body of Christ, the Church.

Contemporary Just-Peacemaking Efforts after Crowther

Each generation of Christians and/or their missionaries should not only follow the legacies of its forbearers or forerunners but has to also be creative and adopt ways of transforming its structures of social and institutional violence. Over the years, Nigerian Christians and their missionaries have had to adopt methods that, looking back, can be seen as just peacemaking. That is, they employed methods that enabled them to still share the gospel in a hostile and volatile context like Northern Nigeria, where Islam holds sway. Northern Nigeria in the 1900s was an area dominated by Islam and Indigenous African Religions. That is why missionary efforts at converting the Muslims and Indigenous African religionists were met with stiff resistance. This resistance was harsher in the Muslim dominated parts of the northern region of Nigeria to the extent that the British did not even have direct rule in Northern Nigeria. To neutralize and pacify the seedbeds of structural conflicts, sown by Islam and the British administration, the missionaries, both expatriate and nationals adopted a subtle but also acceptable method of indirectly reaching the Muslims and the non-Muslim with the gospel message. They concretely identified areas of needs in Northern Nigeria which were obvious. These included basic needs like education and health care services. That is, they concretely engaged in providing humanitarian, social actions which were critically needed in a region that was left behind from participating in the community of nations who were moving towards modernizing civilization. Ayuba Mavalla has argued that Nigerian missionaries, both national and expatriates played a vital role in development projects such as education and health services. This served as means of prosecuting their Christian calling and gaining converts, thereby unexpectedly starting the process of transforming structural violence in the then colonial Northern Nigeria.[33]

As such the Christian missionaries of the 1900s had to wisely choose their methods so as not to create an impasse. Thus they "primarily used Western education and medical services as tools for gospel propagation but—perhaps as an unintentional by-product—these services became empowering agents of change among the marginalized, thus transforming

32. Cross and Livingstone, *The Oxford Dictionary of the Christian Church,* 1162.

33. Mavalla, *Conflict Transformation,* 32.

the structural violence in Northern Nigeria and in Kaduna and Jos cities in particular."[34] Before the Muslims could discern what was really happening and work towards thwarting it the impact had been felt. This should be seen as the seedbeds of contemporary Shari'a and Boko Haram violence. When the Muslims discovered the secret, it created deep seated hatred and mistrust to Western missionaries and their collaborators, Nigerian converts to Christianity. The present situation of persecution is a reaction to past events as well as the Muslims' efforts to stop the continuing growth of the gospel by instilling fear and despair in the minds of Christians. That means, the game has changed and the Christians today need a different approach with the aim of just peacemaking. This must include what Apostle Peter calls, "arming yourselves with the attitude of Christ (1 Pet 4:1): Christ's attitude of nonviolent approach to suffering and pain. The situation of mutual distrust has metamorphosed to a situation where Christianity is seen as *haram* (i.e., a forbidden religion in Nigeria) by some people in Northern Nigeria. Christians need a strategy that could include dialogue. Rev. Fr. Dr. Cornelius Afebu Omonokhua observes that "Dialogue has been used in Nigeria to help people resolve long-standing conflicts and to build deeper understanding of contentious issues."[35] Dialogue, as a contemporary strategy for just peacemaking is not about judging, weighing or making decisions, but about understanding and learning. Dialogue dispels stereotypes, builds trust, and enables people to be open to perspectives that are very different from their own.[36] But do you really dialogue with someone who does not even see you as a human being? A theological reflection is needed if we must answer this question correctly. The context of Nigeria's peacemaking theological reflection, particularly in Northern Nigeria is that Nigeria is the land of bloodshed. In this land, Christianity is *haram* (forbidden), not just by Boko Haram. Therefore, for the sake of millions of Nigerian Christians, Muslims and Indigenous religionists, I research and write on the need for peacemaking as the panacea of living in God's vision for humanity: Living in love, peace and harmony. I tell the story of the past atrocities not to create despair, fear and hopelessness but to look at history not only with a human face but from the perspective of God and seek transformation and transition into the vision of God for humanity.

To familiarize myself with the historical details, I have read the accounts of some of the horrific situations of barbarism in Northern Nigeria,

34. Ibid.

35. Cornelius Afebu Omonokhua, "The Need for Inter-Religious Dialogue," Carefronting. http://www.carefronting.org/the-need-for-inter-religious-dialogue/. Accessed October 30, 2014.

36. Ibid.

supported and perpetuated by leaders who were supposed to ensure freedom, order and justice in our society. But because they have agreed to a lie and the blindness cast by the devil, they have assumed that God does not want Christianity and Christians in Nigeria, particularly in Northern Nigeria. A few of such stories should be enough to demonstrate this fact.

The Story of Ekklesiya Yan'wa a Nigeria (EYN)

Bitrus V. Z. Debki, a member of Ekklesiya Yan'wa a Nigeria ([EYN] i.e., Church of the Brethren in Nigeria) was an eyewitness of the Kaduna State Shari'a law crisis of 2000. He tells of how even prior to this incident, there were other numerous attempts to eliminate Christianity in Northern Nigeria by a group of people in Northern Nigeria who assumed "Christianity has no reason to co-exist with Islam in Nigeria." For instance, between the years 1980 and 2000 alone, there were an estimated nineteen different incidences of attacks specifically directed against northern Nigerian Christians speared headed by northern Muslims. Ironically, these same Muslims would fight to protect the interests of nations that do not even share boundaries with Nigeria. For example, after the American invasion of Afghanistan, Nigeria Muslims took to the street and attacked fellow Nigerians who are "the Christian brothers and sisters" of Americans and live in Kaduna and Kano. The same thing again happened in Kano when America attacked Iraq. The Muslims in Kano reacted and again killed Christians. While the world thought of Osama Bin Laden as a murderer, a terrorist, Nigerian Muslims saw him as their hero, to the extent of making and wearing Bind Laden t-shirts and bomber stickers.[37]

One of the questions that have baffled many Nigerians is, why was it that during the military rule, when northern Nigerian military officers were in power the Muslims did not succeed in the demand for Shari'a until when a Christian came into power under a democratic government? Gen. Muhammadu Buhari, Ibrahim Badamasi Babangida, Sani Achaba and Abdullahi Salami were all Muslims who ruled the country. Yet the Muslims did not succeed in their demand for Shari'a. Of course, the seedbeds of Shari'a were sown during those years, particularly during Babangida's presidency. And so, as soon as Rtd. Gen. Olusegun Obasanjo, a southwestern Baptist Christian, became the civilian President of Nigeria, the governor of Zamfara State got Shari'a law passed into law by the State House of Assembly. Many northern states followed suit. Muslims in Kaduna State also decided to pursue the matter of Shari'a implementation in a state where both the

37. Debki, "Crisis in Kaduna," 88.

Christian and Muslim faiths are evenly divided. Yet, on Tuesday, December 14, 1999, Muslims in Kaduna State submitted a letter to the State House of Assembly requesting for the full implementation of Shari'a law. Bitrus Debki tells of how the State House of Assembly appointed a committee of eleven people—five Muslims and five Christians, with a Muslim as the Chairman—to deliberate on the feasibility and plausibility of the request. The Chairman of the Committee shrewdly asked the Muslim members of the committee to write down in detail the reasons why they want Shari'a implemented; and he also asked the Christian members of the committee to write in detail why they did not want the implementation of Shari'a. But his insincerity was soon discovered. It was a complete set up. For while the Christian members of the committee were still trying to consult with their people, the State House of Assembly ignored the committee and started pushing for the passing of the implementation bill into law by force. To make it look like it was because of outside pressure, the Chairman of the committee secretly mobilized Muslims across the local government areas of the state to come to the State House of Assembly and they went there local government by local government. They took two consecutive weeks doing this. According to Debki, each of the local government representatives of the Muslim community that came to the State House of Assembly was fully covered by the media and what they said was reported publicly to the hearing of everyone in the state. In short, all the local government officials said they endorsed the implementation of full Shari'a law in Kaduna State. The issue of a committee set up to sample the general public opinion was bypassed. It was very obvious to every Christian in Kaduna States that the Muslims were determined to implement Shari'a by force.[38]

All alone, the Christians were silently watching the unfolding event. When it was very clear to them that the Muslims were committed to implementing Shari'a law in the state by all means, the Christians decided to stage a peaceful procession with a letter clearly spelling out why they did not want the implementation of Shari'a law in the state. On February 21, 2000, the Christian Association of Nigeria (CAN) organized a peaceful procession to the State House of Assemble and to the governor's house to present a letter indicating Christians' rejection of the Shari'a law in Kaduna State. The major reason being that in Kaduna State no one religion (Islam or Christianity) can claim majority. Already the Muslims saw the Shari'a law as a case of *do or die* affair, jihad or holy war. So when they saw the Christians marching back from the State House of Assembly and the Governor's house peacefully, they came out in numbers and attacked. On that first day hundreds of

38. Ibid., 89.

Christians, particularly those who were from the northern part of the city, were horrifically murdered. Some of them were burned to death. Interestingly governor, Alhaji Ahmed Maikarfi flew out of the country. Some people said that he heard of the plan to attack the Christians. So the deputy who was a Christian could not do much to protect Christians. The fact that there was no military intervention and the Muslims had three field days of killing and burning Christians goes to confirm that there was a set up.

Later, however, when the Christian youth realized that that would be killed if they did not do something to protect themselves from the onslaughts; they started killing Muslims who were living among them in the southern part of the city of Kaduna. That incident led to a permanent division in Kaduna city. All the Muslims that survived the carnage moved to the northern part of the city while all the Christians from the northern part that survived the carnage also had to move to the southern part of the city. The same situation repeated itself in May 2000. After both incidents, every side of the religious community started regretting the loss incurred. Every side suffered great loss. Both Muslims and Christians realized that if nothing is done to seek for peaceful resolution of the crisis survival will be extremely difficult in the state. It was now time to talk about dialogue, confession, forgiveness and reconciliation. It was against this backdrop that the Interfaith and Mediation Center was established in Kaduna with the help of people from Britain and United States of America.

The Story of Peacemaking Efforts in Kaduna

In Northern Nigeria there are groups and individuals who have grasped the need to be ambassadors of peacemaking across the religious divide. The basic conviction that leads people to encourage involvement in peacemaking is generally this: *Development cannot take place without peace.* This is not only the view of economists and analysts who have been watching events across the globe, particularly in Asia, Africa and Latin America, but also of God's word. "Put the sword back in its place," Jesus said to Peter, "for all who draw the sword will die by the sword" (Matthew 26:52 NIV). We must observe that just peacemaking should go beyond parochial economic reasons. We need peacemaking that is based on obedience to God's vision for humanity: living in love and harmony. Economic reasons are some of the basic causes of the violence. Nigeria as a nation has been the site of perennial violence between Muslims and Christians, especially in the Middle Belt and in the northern parts of the country. Here, the two religions have co-existed—and sometimes competed for converts and the control of the soul of Nigeria: politics and economics—for over a century. Given this situation, Kaduna has produced two peacemaking ambassadors: a Pentecostal preacher, Rev. James Movel Wuye and Muslim Imam, Muhammad Nurayn Ashafa. They came together to contribute their quota to the peace efforts in the country, particularly in the Middle Belt. They both believe that religious peace and cooperation are a prerequisite to sustained economic development and growth. A Voice of America reporter Isiyaku Ahmed writes:

> For decades, religious strife between Christians and Muslims in northern Nigeria has claimed property and lives. Recurring flare-ups between members of each group have left thousands dead, wounded, and homeless over the years. The violence contributes to political instability, which in turn deters development. For example, providers of essential services have often been Christian migrants from the south and east of the country. But many of them have fled the area, or avoid settling there out of fear of violence. The same applies to foreign investors.[39]

Why is the issue all about politics and economic concerns? What does God think about the violence? In asking such questions, Rev. Wuye and Imam Ashafa have found the best way of responding to this protracted situation of horrific violence in Kaduna States. They have adopted two methods: Muslim-Christian Dialogue Forum and the Inter-faith Mediation Center. Both Rev. James Movel Wuye and Imam Muhammad N. Ashafa were at first people who were hunting for the heads of each other based on the religious divide. But when their eyes got opened to a different reality of life, they were willing to put their swords back in the sheath and they embraced just peacemaking as a way of life that will ensure a way forward. Together, they have become catalysts of peacemaking in Kaduna and across the country. From their website we found this excerpt:

> For years Nigeria has suffered from violent conflict between religious and ethnic communities, with extensive loss of life and damage to property. In 1995, two leaders of opposing factions— one a Muslim, Imam Muhammad Ashafa, the other a Christian, Pastor James Wuye—helped found Nigeria's Interfaith Mediation Centre. Its mission is to create a peaceful society through non-violent and strategic engagements in Nigeria and elsewhere in the world. The two men were brought together in a quest for peace and have become world-renowned peacemakers.[40]

39. Boer, *Nigeria's Decades of Blood*, 24.

40. "The Interfaith Mediation Centre, Nigeria," LenCD. http://www.lencd.org/case-story/2011/interfaith-mediation-centre-nigeria. Accessed March 7, 2015.

The website further states that the Interfaith Mediation Centre evolved from the ideas of a few passionate individuals into an internationally respected non-governmental organization. It uses advocacy to influence key legislation, and develops innovative tools for interfaith dialogue. For nearly 15 years, the Centre has flourished as a faith-based organization. It has carried out more than 180 successful interventions in Nigeria as well as in Sudan, Kenya and Iraq. Among its achievements are the signing of the Kaduna Peace Declaration of Religious Leaders, after which Kaduna enjoyed nearly a decade of peace, and the Yelwa Shendam Peace Accord, which brought peace to feuding communities. It also contributed to the establishment of the Government of Kaduna State's Bureau for Religious Affairs.[41] From the above account, we can see that the God of love and peace is able to use both Christians and Muslims to bring about peace in a world of hatred and horrific destruction of life and property. The narrative of Rev. Wuye and Imam Ashafa is a credible testimony to this fact. In fact, the narrative of a host of other Nigerian peacemakers lends credence to this truth, as we shall consider below.

The Story of Peacemaking Efforts on the Plateau

The Bible teaches that God is a God of love and peace (2 Cor 13:11). What confirms that we believe this is true is: Just Peacemaking. Just peacemaking, however, is not an automatic reality for all Christians. Just peacemakers are not born but made. They begin with an overwhelming sense of human natural insecurity and fear. Thus they begin where every one of us is, saying: "It is impossible to live in peace with Muslims." They start with doubting the capability of Muslims to pursue peace, while their holy book, the Quran teaches violence, holy war, or jihad. They usually believe, like most of us do, that the best we can do with Muslims is to fight back if the strike us on one cheek. So, to be a just peacemaker requires a belief in the biblical worldview that teaches that in spite of all odds it is possible to live in harmony and peace with each other. Rev. Yakubu Pam Narrative: In some ways, the narrative of Rev. Pam is like that of the Apostle Paul. Paul did not start as a saint; rather he started as a persecutor and destroyer of the Christian faith. However, he became a just peacemaker when he had a refreshing life-changing encounter with Jesus Christ; he got genuinely converted. His worldview and mindset got renewed and transformed into the worldview of the God of love and peace. The narrative of Rev. Yakubu Pam and a host of other peacemakers

41. Ibid.

in Nigeria, vividly illustrate this point. Pam's story lends credence to the fact that just peacemakers have to have a renewed mindset. They start with an overwhelming sense of insecurity and fear, but then when they recognize their weaknesses and come to grip with the transcendent reality of God's incomparably great power which is at work through those who are willing to trust God's declaration that it is possible to live in harmony and peace, they can accept the fact that God says, "My grace is enough for you. For my power work best in weakness" (2 Cor 12:9).

Rev. Pam was a leader of the Christian Association of Nigeria (CAN) in his home state, Plateau. This was a time when Christians in Nigeria, overwhelmed by decades of horrific persecution were overcome by fear, had become radicalized and started mimicking the disorderly behaviors of their murderers. They were saying: "Violence must be met by violence." Rev. Pam was among the Christian leaders who were saying, "If the Muslims kill a Christian the Christian must make sure the revenge by also killing Muslims." The Christians had found the principle of "an eye for an eye" more palatable than Jesus's teaching in the Sermon on the Mount on "Turn the other cheek" or "Love your enemies! Pray for those who persecute you! In that way, you will be acting as true children of your Father in heaven. For He gives His sunlight to both the evil and thee good, and He sends rain on the just and the unjust alike" (Matt 5:43–45). Perhaps, the Christians opted for the "An eye for an eye" principle because it best fit the human desire to make even by meeting evil with evil and good with good.

It was in the midst of such a situation that Rev. Pam had a life-changing encounter with Jesus in a very subtle way. In 2001 Muslim Fulanis attacked a village in Yelwa Shendam, in the Southern part of Plateau state, killing several hundreds of Christians and non-Christians alike. In a reprisal attack the Christians and non-Christians also launched an attack on the Muslim Fulanis, killing several hundred of them. The then Nigerian president, President Olusegun Obasanjo made a trip to Jos, Plateau State to have a first-hand assessment of what had transpired and to perhaps console those who lost their beloved ones and property. The president decided to consult with community and churches leaders on a way forward. Since Rev. Pam was one of them, he also attended the meetings and as a spokesman for the Christians in Plateau state. During this interactive session with the president, Rev. Pam sought to know why the President didn't visit Plateau State when the Christian were murdered by the Fulani Muslims until when he heard that Christian attacked and killed Fulani Muslims. Carmen McCain similarly narrated what really happened. According to her,

In late February 2004, dozens of Tarok Christians were killed in Yelwa, a village in southern Plateau State. Two months later, hundreds of Fulani Muslims were killed in reprisal attacks. Just days after attack against the Muslims, then-President Obasanjo visited Plateau State. As the state chairman of the Christian Association of Nigeria (CAN), Rev Pam was selected to ask the President three questions regarding the crises in Plateau State, one of which was why he had not visited the area two months ago when Christians were killed.[42]

The president did not like that public insult and thereby responded by calling Rev. Pam an "idiot" and the Christian Association of Nigeria on the Plateau, "CAN my foot." The president's reaction and response to Rev. Pam's question had ripple effects. On the one hand, it was a public humiliation to Rev. Pam. On the other hand, it made him a hero among his peers. For after this incident, some United Nation officials from New York visited Jos, Plateau State for a fact finding mission. While in Jos, they met with Rev. Pam. In their interaction with him they recommended to him the possibility of getting trained for peacemaking in New York. Rev. Pam reluctantly accepted the offer and in 2006, the UN invited Rev. Pam to the Youth Assembly on Global Peace that met every August for three years. At the program, people from around the world shared their experiences of violence in their local communities. Rev. Pam was shocked to learn that other places were also experiencing violence similar to that of Plateau State, places like Rwanda and India. Hearing testimonies of conflict by people from different nations, ethnic groups, and religions helped Rev. Pam change his thinking from focusing on the welfare of just Christians to instead thinking about the welfare of all human beings, regardless of their religion or ethnic group. Over those years he was attending the UN programmes, Rev. Pam was also thinking about what he could do within Jos to foster peace. In early 2009, Rev. Pam met with some key leaders to discuss a new organization that would engage the youth to be leaders in bringing peace to their grassroots communities. The organization was named the Young Ambassadors for Community Peace and Inter-Faith Foundation (YACPIF).

Suffice it to say that the whole experience turned out to be the stroke that broke the camel's back. Rev. Pam found out that the God of love and peace had orchestrated the UN training package to help him grasp God's vision of peacemaking for a new Plateau. Perhaps we can say Rev. Pam had his "aha moment" during those years of training in peace-making. It also looks

---

42. Carmen McCain, "Radical Peacemaker" published by Weekly Trust on 31 March 2012.

like those UN officials from New York were sent to Nigeria like Ananias was sent to Saul, saying, "But go, for Saul is My chosen instrument to take my message to the Gentiles and to kings, as well as to the people of Israel. And I will show him how much he must suffer for my name's sake" (Acts 9:15–16). God showed Rev. Pam how much he wants him to do for peacemaking on the Plateau.

For instance, after the episode of his interaction with President Obasanjo and the embarrassing answer he got from the President, Carmen McCain tells of how "the relationships that Rev. Pam developed with the Muslim neighbors in his community indeed yielded great fruit. The Muslim neighbors have protected Rev. Pam's church from being burnt in at least three separate occasions when youths from outside of the area have tried to destroy the church."[43] His church at Kwararafa Cinema has benefited from his efforts. For example, we found this excerpt on his website:

> During the November 2008 crisis in Jos, an old Muslim man went to sit on the steps of the neighborhood Assemblies of God church in Kwararafa. Four times, he turned away angry youth who wanted to burn the church. The fifth time, the youth attacked him. Two weeks later he died of his wounds. Before he died, he told his wife, "You tell Pastor that he shouldn't worry. For what I have done for the church is for the sake of peace and the neighborhood and I love him very well." . . . Fighting for Peace challenges negative stereotypes heard so often of Plateau State and the north.[44]

God actually used the course to change his life. For instance, he told Prof. Danny McCain that before he went to New York he thought that the only thing that could change the minds of these Muslims was violence. He believed what many Nigerians express today because of decades of horrific violence; and that is "the only language they (Muslims) understood is

43. McCain, "Radical Peacemaker." Carmen McCain narrates how Rev. Pam was selected to be the chairman of the Plateau State Inter-Religious Committee. Through this committee, Rev. Pam began interacting with top leaders from the Muslim community and developed close relationships with Muslims for the first time in his life. After being selected as the chairman of the Inter-Religious Committee, Rev. Pam was transferred to a church in Kwararafa, a Muslim-majority area in Jos. The church building had been destroyed in the 2001 crisis and the church was in the process of rebuilding the structure. Because of the importance of the relationships he had developed with Muslims on the Inter-Religious Committee, Rev. Pam felt that he also needed to visit the Muslim neighbors around his church to develop relationships with them.

44. McCain, "Learning how to fight . . . peacefully." Last modified March 25, 2012. https://yacpif.wordpress.com/tag/jos-crisis/?blogsub=confirming#blog_subscription-3

force." However, his training course in New York and a subsequent follow up course convinced him that something should be done and that Muslims were indeed capable of and interested in peace.

Therefore, when he returned to Nigeria he started working to put together an organization called "Young Ambassadors for Community Peace and Inter-Faith Foundation." He got Solomon Lar, former governor of Plateau State, Professor Danjuma, the director general of Nigeria Institute for Policy and Strategic Studies (NIPSS) and the former governor of Kaduna State, Alhaji Ahmed Mohammed Maikarfi to become trustees of his peace organization. These are obviously well placed men who had some financial resources to help him start working to register the organization.[45] Rev. Pam had succeeded in training both Christians and Muslims youths as peacemakers. He told the story of how 24 of the Muslims youths he had trained protected his Kwararafa church during one of the crisis in Jos. Prior to the crisis, he had met and provided some training for 24 Muslim youths who live near his church, which is directly across the street from the Kwararafa Cinema, almost in the heart of the Muslim area in Jos. During the crisis, some Muslim youth came to burn his church. However, these 24 Muslim youths protected the church and even arrested one of the boys. After beating him very well, they turned him over to the police. This even encouraged Pam to do more. It also encouraged some of the people who were assisting Pam that perhaps some of his strategies might work.[46] Pam has been very instrumental in organizing training and peace talks between Muslims and Christians on the Plateau.

To appreciate the level of transformation that has taken place in Rev. Pam's life, we need to recall his past. For example, when the Plateau State crises turned worse in 2001, Reverend Pam was not personally affected by the violence. However, Rev. Pam describes himself as a Christian radical when the crises first began. "My view was quite straightforward, it was just an eye for an eye. Kill one Christian, kill one Muslim. We will retaliate." He turned down many invitations to meet with Muslim leaders to discuss peace because he did not believe there could be peace between Christians and Muslims. Today, however, Rev. Pam and a host of others on the Plateau have been making remarkable just peacemaking attempts with the hope that the situation can be neutralized for the best interest of all and sundry. In the search for a way forward, Pam and his colleagues have been able to bring Muslim and Christian youths together to talk at a round table to proffer

45. Ibid.
46. Ibid.

solution to the present impasse. The situations of violence in Jos and Bukuru have remarkably improved because of such efforts.[47]

In sum, the narrative of Crowther, Wuye and Ashafa, and Pam tell our story: the story of all human experiences. The truth is that all humans experience and express the sense of insecurity and fear. This is basically because of our inherent human nakedness: "I was afraid because I was naked" (Gen 3:10 NIV). To be a peacemaker therefore requires a radical transformation and transition from our human worldview and mindset to the worldview of the Prince of love and peace, the Master Peacemaker, Jesus Christ. In the apparent absence of checks and balances in Christianity, Christian just peacemakers still need to beware of the paradox of man.

Conclusion

Something is fundamentally wrong with the Nigerian Church. One of the problems Christians face in Nigeria is lack of systematic preaching and teaching on just peacemaking or on peace itself. Many a Nigerian is unaware of the debates in the West—pacifism, just war, crusade and the recent principle of just peacemaking—surrounding the issue of peace. Some seminaries in their Christian ethics classes do teach something about those debates; yet what they teach is not enough to prepare the students for the pulpit ministry. In fact both our missionary forbearers and our present crop of pastors and church planters tend to take teaching and preaching about the biblical doctrine of peace making for granted. Perhaps, they assumed that the matter of nonviolent resistance that Scriptures emphasize is a straightforward case and therefore does not need systematic analysis. All we need is to live it out as a way of life. The founding missionaries of the Church of the Brethren in Nigeria, which is part of the historic peace churches in the West, did not teach that biblical doctrine of peacemaking to Nigerians. When they came to Nigeria they chose not to talk about pacifism. The much they did was to teach members the matter of peace and reconciliation or of loving neighbors and living in peace with all people.[48] They, however, found it extremely unnecessary to teach Nigerians the biblical and theological doctrine of just peacemaking. We wonder why that was the case. Apparently, Filibus seems to have a plausible explanation. He explained thus,

> The truth is that, missionary churches were shaped by the situation in which the missionaries found themselves contextually, not by what the mother denomination believed. Thus it was not

47. Ibid.

48. Gwama, "Ekklesiyar Yan'uwa a Nigeria," 55–56.

surprising that the brothers and sisters who went to preach the gospel in Nigeria established a church not fully dependent upon the Brethren beliefs and practices, but upon what they felt the Holy Spirit was leading them to do in particular context.[49]

We have a problem with this explanation. We wonder what situation made it easy for the missionaries of the church of the Brethren to keep mute about preaching and teaching peacemaking. They were serving at an opportune time because the crises between Christian and Muslims were obvious and the possibility of perpetuating them was also clear. The northeast where they did their mission work was replete with crises and conflict between Muslims and the non-Muslims were the daily experiences of those people they were preaching the gospel to. Perhaps, a better explanation would be that they were ill-prepared or not well trained to handle the situation. They lack the wherewithal to teach and preach about peacemaking. Indeed, the way they understood the concept of peace became a blind spot to them. They understood peace thus:

> Peace was understood not primarily through preaching and teaching nonviolence, but through practical acts of loving and serving in life. Peace in Nigerian context is to know Jesus Christ. Peace is to love God with your entire mind, with all your soul, and your neighbor as yourself. Peace is to be free from poverty, hunger, disease, ignorance, and domination. Peace is not the absence of war; instead it is a war against evil and injustice. Peace is the refusal to compromise with injustice, sin or evil acts. Peace is courage to face evil in all its dimensions.[50]

With what is currently happening in Nigeria, we Christians cannot afford to have such kind of one-sided perspective on peace. We must teach and preach the concept of just peacemaking until members get its essential principles and strategies. The Nigeria church of today needs a strong dose of theological reflection on the meaning of just peacemaking. If the Master peacemaker, Jesus Christ took three chapters to teaching the principles of peace in Matthew why must we his followers shy away from teaching and preaching the disguise of blaming our context? Just peacemaking is not about the absence of weaknesses or about strength. But it is a matter of reverence obedience to the God of peace, love, and justice. It is remembering like Job that: "If it is a question of strength, He [God] is the strong One. If it is a matter of justice, who dares to summon Him [God] to court?"

49. Ibid. 56.
50. Ibid.

(Job. 19). Just peacemaking involves self-criticism, repentance, forgiveness, reconciliation and restoration to community with other fellow human beings. It requires the grace to overcome the assumption that I am the sinned against and therefore I am innocent sufferer of injustice. We too are caught cobweb of human *self-interest and the will-to-power.* That is, the whole situation Stott refers to as the *paradox of man.* Therefore we should like Job say: "For I know you will not find me innocent, O God. Whatever happens, I will be found guilty" (Job 9:28–29). What Job said to his miserable comforters help explain the emphasis in *just* peacemaking. Job says, "I could say [do] the same things if you were in my place" (Job. 16:4). This is what we mean by just peacemaking. That is, an honest realizing of the human condition. It is a recognition that we could possibly act in the same manner if we were in the place of the Muslims in Northern Nigeria. We seek peace not with the attitude of self-righteousness but as we way of our faith in Christ expressing itself in love. It is an act which emanates from a reverend obedience to the Holy Spirit whose guidance in our lives produces the fruit of: love, joy, peace, patience, kindness, goodness, faithfulness, gentleness, and self-control (Galatians 5:22–23). If Nigerian Christians do not initiate and engage in just peacemaking they will not escape the mutual destruction of each other that goes on in Nigeria or elsewhere!

Part 3

UNMASKING THE MISSION OF THE CHURCH

The problem of Nigerian society is not a lack of ardent religion. Rather, it is the problem of a surface, shallow religion; it is the problem of a godless religiosity. This is demonstrated by persistent corruption, injustice and the myth of redemptive violence. Our study so far has served to establish that the myth of redemptive violence appears in different shades and shapes: religious interactions, tribal wars and conflicts, and denominational misconception of public engagement. Based on the Servant Songs of Isaiah, how then should the Church respond to the challenge of the myth of redemptive violence through its understanding of mission? The early disciples understood the Servant Songs as critical to their mission (Acts 3:13–15). The body of Christ must understand Whose it is and what He expects from His body, the Church! The mission of the Church is the mission of its founder—Jesus Christ. In the last chapters of the book we focus on the mission of the Church, starting with a reflection on Acts 3–4.

Chapter 12

The Mission of the Church Distracted

Voices of the dead have homes in the living.

—AUDIE CORNISH

Introduction

As we read the account of the apostles' involvement in the mission of the church in Acts and other part of the New Testaments we see a pattern of distraction developing. This chapter examines the scenes of distractions in Acts and uses that to help Nigerian Christians understand how today's incessant violence can be linked to this pattern of distraction. We live and work in a world infested with various forms of distraction. No matter what your calling in life is, you will meet distractions. Missional distractions abound in the early pages of church history, particularly in the Acts of the Apostles. This chapter is about how terrorism is one of Satan's strategies to distract the Church from its mission: proclaiming the Good News of Christ. We particularly pay attention to the strategic nature of corruption in the scheme of things. In today's world, monetary and sexual values have over-shadowed the value of human dignity and integrity. Money, sex and power have become enormous factors that are even distracting the Church from her God-given mission. They are explicit illustrations of the work of Satan in this age.

As we reflect on what is happening around the world, we can recognize the obvious effort of Satan to use terrorism to threaten and silent the

Church. Islamic terrorism is a powerful tool in the hands of the enemy of the Church. Satan is literally saying to Christians today, "Shut up your mouths!" It is like a puzzle; which Acts 2, 3 and 4 seem to put together for us. Reading these three chapters has brought me to the conclusion that the reason why violent conflicts still persist today in the form of terrorism, jihad, Fulani-herdsmen attacks, ethnic clashes, humanist intellectualism and so on, is to stop the mission of the Church. These are the schemes of Satan. He is using different voices to shout down the preaching of the name of Jesus Christ. Nigerian Christians have been called to a mission that no situation is capable of stopping. For the truth is: "There is salvation in no one else. For there is no other name that is given by which men will be saved except the name of Jesus." Nigerian Christians today understand the notion of the mission of the Church variously. Some believe that it involves understanding and confronting injustice and alleviating suffering in a world of diverse challenges. Others, however, think that we ought to focus on evangelism without bothering ourselves with social matters. The mission of the Church as meant in this chapter is all-embracing. How can the Church destroy the work of Satan if it does not pursue both evangelism and social action? The primary goal of our mission is the proclamation of the birth, ministry, suffering, death and resurrection of Jesus Christ and its implication for the world. The secondary goal is engaging *the powers that be* by calling them to their responsibility to the people whom they are called to serve, through ensuring freedom, order and justice.

The Early Church Distracted from Its Mission

This section explores the salient and subtle evidence of scenes and signs of distraction from the mission of the Church at the beginning of her existence. It documents specific cases of distraction in the narrative of Luke, with a view toward helping modern readers evaluate the present evidence of distraction from the mission of the Church. It recognizes that with events in our contemporary globalized world, the question of the mission of the Church needs to be revisited. Acts scholars have concentrated on different aspects of the book. In this chapter, my approach is to trace the different voices and forces which tried to stop the advancement of the mission of the Church, and how the apostles carefully overcame those threats. I attempt to trace the evidence of distractions from the main thing: the full message of the name of Jesus Christ. To these we now turn. The narrator of the book of the Acts of the Apostles, Luke, carefully documented not only the signs and scenes of distraction from the mission of the Church, but also the manner in which the early apostles tackled and handled the problem in order to steadfastly remain in the business of the mission of the church. Luke tells of the fulfillment of the promise of the coming of the Holy Spirit, who was to help them in carrying out the mission of the Church in a hostile society. The Holy Spirit gave the disciples the power they needed to overcome all distractions and be able to get on with the task of preaching the full message of Jesus' resurrection to the very people who crucified Him. But the very powerful demonstration of the presence of the Holy Spirit at Pentecost entirely proved to be a distraction.

When everyone heard the disciples speaking in many different languages, some people charged the disciples with being drunk. They ridiculed the disciples, saying, "They're just drunk, that's all!" (2:1–13). This charge of drunkenness was a huge distraction to those who were waiting for an interpretation of the mission of the Church. Realizing that this was going to be an impediment to the people, Peter spoke out: when he stepped out with the other eleven apostles he shouted to the crowd, "Listen carefully, all of you, fellow Jews and residents of Jerusalem! Make no mistake about this. These people are not drunk, as some of you are assuming . . ." (Acts 2:14–15). In that way, Peter overcame Satan's distraction.

A further scene of distraction is when Peter and John healed the man born crippled from birth. The healing produced another moment of surprise and perplexity for the Jerusalem audience: "They were absolutely astounded! They all rushed out in amazement to Solomon's Colonnade, where the man was holding tightly to Peter and John" (3:9–11). Realizing that attention was being drawn to them and not to the Name of Jesus the Nazarene, Peter stepped out again and addressed the crowd, "People of Israel," he said, "what is so surprising about this? And why stare at us as though we had made this man walk by our own power or godliness?" (3:12). These words are evidence that Peter recognized the distraction involved. The distraction became crystal clear when Peter and John encountered the Sanhedrin after they healed a person. Because of their fear and jealousy, the Sanhedrin categorically tell them, "Shut up, Men!" In answer to their question, "By what power, or in whose name, have you done this?" Peter answered, "He was healed by the powerful name of Jesus Christ the Nazarene, the man you [Jewish leaders] crucified but whom God raised from the dead" (4:6–10). Luke tells of how the Jewish establishment, hearing the apostles' boldness, warned them not to speak or teach in the name of Jesus. But Peter and John would not obey this restriction. They asked the Sanhedrin, "Do you think God wants us to obey you rather than Him? We cannot stop telling about everything we have seen and heard" (4:19–20). The apostles overcame this distraction by deciding to be loyal to God, who had charged them with the mission of the Church.

Another sign and scene of distraction is the account of Ananias and Sapphira (Acts 5:1–10). In spite of all the distractions we have studied, the Church had been inaugurated. There was unity, a blooming practice of hospitality, and an awesome attitude of togetherness in all areas. Economic sharing was at its pinnacle. It was a situation where human dignity trumped all other values. Material goods were regarded with a deep sense of commitment to the common good. It was this context that enables us to understand how serious and grievous the sin of Ananias and Sapphira was. Ananias and Sapphira sought to achieve honor through a lack of integrity. Peter realized quickly that this could potentially lead to the destruction of the nascent community of the Name. Luke tells how Peter handled this poisonous distraction by confronting them with the true source of what they had done: "Ananias, why have you let Satan fill your heart? You lied to the Holy Spirit, and you kept some of the money for yourself . . ." To the wife he said, "How could the two of you even think of conspiring to test the Spirit of the Lord like this?" (Acts 5:1–9). This situation shows that human sin knows no borders. What happened was typical of what is in the human nature: Self-interest and deception. Christians can be a source of distraction too! Peter was cognizant of the inherent danger of hypocrisy and of the need to deal drastically with it for the sake of the spiritual health and nourishment of the Church.

The further sign and scene of distraction to the mission of the Church was the neglect of the Grecian widows in the running of the food distribution program. Again, Peter and the apostles realized that this would distract them from their primary task: preaching and teaching the word of God. In response to this distraction, the apostles said, "We apostles should spend our time teaching the word of God, not running a food program" (Acts 6:2). The apostles were able to go beyond this distraction to recognize that serving food was part and parcel of the mission of the church. So that was why the apostles asked that people be selected to focus on that mission task while they themselves focus on equipping believers for the wholistic task of mission. The execution of Stephen was also a sign and a scene of distraction. Stephen was to serve food and he realized that serving food was part of the mission of the church. Luke described him as "a man of God's grace and power, [and he] performed amazing miracles and signs among the people"

(Acts 6:8). These qualities made him a threat to the Jewish leadership that opposed the early Christians. Stephen became the first martyr of the Church. His execution was intended to shut the mouths of the earlier witnesses to the mission of the Church. But the Holy Spirit gave the early church the courage to keep preaching the Gospel. As one continues through Acts one notices other signs and scenes of distraction, including Simon the magician trying to bribe the apostles for the gift of the Holy Spirit (Acts 8:18–24); the execution of James and the imprisonment of Peter (Acts 12:1–18); the crisis of Paul and Barnabas (Acts 15:36–40); the healing of the cripple (Acts 14:8–20); and the issue of circumcision of Gentile believers (Acts 15:1–4). These scenes of distraction from the early church invite us to watch carefully the voices or forces of distraction in our contemporary generation that are trying hard to distract us from the mission of the Church.

Essentials in the Mission of the Church

The nature and depth of the mission of the Church is better grasped when we recognize God's involvement in mission. God is actively involved in this earth as a mission God, a mission Christ, and a mission Holy Spirit. That is, the God-head is mission. Since we, Christians, are also saved and called to serve the God-head, mission must be what defines us.

The Mission of the Church as the Mission of God

We have been struck by the way Acts describe the mission of the Church as the business of God. He is the One who has brought the Church into being. 1) God is the primary actor throughout Luke-Acts. 2) God directs the life of Jesus and the church by performing signs, wonders, healings, and exorcisms. 3) Epiphanies function to declare the divine will and divine guidance of history. 4) Divine purpose is emphasized through prophetic fulfillment (especially important in the passion narrative and the mission to the Gentiles). Finally, 5) divine necessity is inherent to Jesus' life, death, and the apostolic mission.[1] God is deeply involved in the affairs of humans. Just like God was involved in rescuing Israel from Egyptian slavery, God is yet involved in rescuing the entire human race.[2] God's involvement in the affairs of the entire human world illustrates His ownership of the entire creation, the Kingdom of God. So when Peter and John decided not to obey men, but

1. Salmeier, *Restoring the Kingdom*, 3.
2. Burnside, *God, Justice, and Society*, 15.

God, they were implying that God is King. This kingship is ultimately based on the divine creation of the world.[3]

The Mission of the Church as the Mission of Christ

Because Peter realized that there was intentional distraction, under the inspiration of the Holy Spirit he chose his words carefully. Peter's message was focused on the resurrection of Jesus. The Pentecost account and Peter's sermon on that day were programmatic, in the sense that it points to a summary of the book Acts: The resurrection of Jesus Christ. No resurrection, no church! "One of the main emphases of Peter's sermon is the exaltation of Christ. The crux of the sermon in terms of explaining the events of Pentecost, comes in Acts 2:33. Here it is spelled out that the coming of the Holy Spirit is a result of the exaltation of Christ."[4] As it were, Jesus reigns from the throne of David. Luke sees a connection between the ascension of Jesus to heaven and the birth of the Church.[5] In Acts, after the ascension Jesus continues to guide the church in its missionary efforts. He empowers the disciples to perform miracles.[6] In sum, the Church necessarily developed out of the Jesus story.[7] Christianity is a product of Christ's exaltation after the cross and resurrection. Christians are the fruit of Christ's willingness to absorb suffering nonviolently!

The Mission of the Church as the Mission of the Holy Spirit

Acts 2 tells of the birth of the Church through the instrumentality of the Holy Spirit. In the Greco-Roman world people spoke their native languages and could only communicate with others through the two commercial languages: Greek and Latin.[8] On the Day of Pentecost, however, we are told of the collapse of the language barriers that was caused in Genesis 11. God arranged an occasion that brought together His people all over the world for the inauguration of the Church. The Book of Acts has often been called "The Gospel of the Holy Spirit." Luke offers us, not a theological discussion of the Holy Spirit, but a practical demonstration of the Holy Spirit at work. For Luke, everything that happens in the life of the Church from the begin-

3. Thompson, *The Acts of the Risen Lord Jesus*, 88.

4. Thompson, *One Lord, One People*, 63–64.

5. Parsons, *Acts*, 35.

6. Ibid.

7. Marshall, *The Acts of the Apostles*, 53.

8. Shell, *Reading Acts*, 11–12.

ning to the end of his story is in one way or another controlled, inspired and furthered by the Holy Spirit. He sees the Church as the people of God advancing towards the fulfillment of God's incredible purpose for the world; not in their own strength, but in the power of the Holy Spirit. "It is a Spirit-filled Church, and its members are ordinary men and women who have been endowed with this unique gift from God."[9] Right at the beginning, the coming of the Holy Spirit upon the disciples is interpreted as power for witness to Jesus, and Pentecost event is seen as a fulfillment of the prophecy of baptism with the Holy Spirit. The initial group of disciples (all 120 of them are probably meant) receive the Spirit, and the event is marked by their bursting into praise of God in various languages. This is interpreted as one of the signs of the last days, and it is significant that the Spirit is now given to "all flesh." "The Spirit is given to the Church in various ways for the purpose of mission, directing the work and giving the capacity to speak and even to do mighty works"[10]—and to notice distractions and fight them. For instance, earlier we discussed the cases of Ananias and his wife, and the issue of the neglected widows.The coming of the Holy Spirit birthed the church. The basic event was a communal religious experience, as a result of which the Apostles embarked on the first stage of the Church's mission. "Luke, however, dramatizes this in terms of the 'wind' of the Spirit of God and the 'fire' of the Power of God together with the breaking down of the barrier of language, symbolizing the beginning of the reconciling power of the Gospel."[11] Nothing else could have transformed in the short space of thirty years an obscure Jewish sect into a world-wide religious movement.

The Mission of the Church is a Mission Assigned to Ordinary Humans

The mission of the Church is for all social classes. God has decided to use human beings to reach their fellow men and women. This is part of what it means to be created in the image of God; He created humans with the ability to be alternative creators and active participants in His mission. This is why no social group is exempted in the task of the mission of the Church.[12] That means that the mission of the Church is not for a selected few. It is a distraction to focus only on the wealthy.

9. Neil, *The Acts of the Apostle*, 52–53.

10. Marshall, *The Acts of the Apostles,* 66–67.

11. Thompson, *One Lord, One People*, 71.

12. Fiensy, "The Composition of the Jerusalem Church," 230.

The Mission of the Church as a Mission Focused on Uprooting Strongholds

In his first sermon, Peter reflects his conviction about the mission of the Church: preaching the gospel of Jesus' resurrection, which demonstrates that God has approved of His sacrifice on the cross. Peter's sermon reflects the basic certainty of the first Christians that all that had happened in the life, death and resurrection of Jesus was in fulfillment of God's revelation to Israel in the Old Testament Scriptures. The age of the Messiah, foretold by the prophet, had dawned: Jesus of Nazareth had been proved by what had happened to be that long-awaited Messiah; He was now exalted as Head of the New Israel, and had given the gift of the Spirit to His followers."[13] The Sadducees had for years claimed the sole prerogative to interpret Scriptures, the Sadducees also rejected belief in resurrection of the dead. Now Peter, an ordinary layman, is interpreting the scriptures and Jesus' resurrection! It was vexing for the Sadducees, therefore, to find the followers of Jesus—"unschooled, ordinary men" (Acts 3:13)—claiming the right to interpret the Scriptures, doing so both in the temple and in support of a doctrine that the temple hierarchy denied. For Peter and John were teaching in Jesus the resurrection of the dead (Acts 3: 2).[14] Anthony B. Robinson and Robert W. Wall observed that in Acts we see God at work to create a new people who are not to be defined by the old categories of race, language, gender, or social class, but a people united in the witness to the resurrection and in a way of life that embodies what we call "resurrection practices."[15] By being that new kind of community, they challenged the traditional practices (the old stronghold) of the time. Peter focused his energy on uprooting strongholds to the mission of the Church.

Christians and the Mission to the Contemporary Strongholds in Nigeria

The contemporary Nigerian church has an extremely difficult challenge to overcome in order to continue with the legacy of proclaiming the Good News to a dying and decaying world. Corruption presents a powerful challenge to the mission of the Nigerian church. In country, money/wealth, sex and power have become enormous tools that Satan is using to distract the church from its God-given mission.

13. Thompson, *One Lord, One People*, 74.

14. William, *Acts*, 78.

15. Robinson and Wall, *Called to the Church*, 79.

Corruption causes frustration to those who are deprived of their share of God-given resources and potentials to be dignified members of their societies. This frustration and humiliation leads to the desire to revenge those who are perceived perpetuators of economic and social hardships. And when those who feel disenfranchised get groups like Boko Haram or their associates, ISI, they easily become recruits to fight the system that is destroying their present and future. Satan takes advantage of such situation to target the church, thus indirectly using the outcomes of corruption to distract Nigerian Christians from the mission of the Church. Today, Satan uses the politics of human hostilities, which are rooted in self-interest, deception, lust for power, corruption and injustices to Christians from preaching the Good News. In order to help Christians stand firm and keep a strong grip on the mission of the Church, we need to ask the following salient questions: Why was Jesus Christ born into the world? Why was the incarnation necessary? There are two strong answers and convincing testimonies. First, the testimony of Jesus Christ Himself. In His interaction with Pilate during His trial, Jesus said, "'My kingdom is not an earthly kingdom. If it were, my servants would fight to prevent my arrest by the Jews. But now my kingdom is from another place.' Pilate said, 'So You are a king?' Jesus responded, 'You are right in saying I am a king. In fact, for this reason I was born, and for this I came into the world, to testify to the truth. Everyone on the side of the truth listens to me'" (John 18:37). The apostles realized that in His quest to testify to the truth, Jesus suffered, died and rose from the dead.

Second, we have the testimony of St. John, Jesus' disciple. He writes: "The reason the Son of God appeared was *to destroy the devil's work*" (1 John 3:8). Fundamentally, we have *two great testimonies*: Jesus said the reason he was born was to testify *to the truth*. John said, *The reason the Son of God appeared in the world was to destroy the devil's work*. These two testimonies not only reveal why Satan is mad at us but also the need for these testimonies to be carefully studied and understood as the mission of the Church. The Church is the body of Christ. Her mission cannot be different from her Master's and Lord's mission. It means therefore that the mission of the Church is mainly twofold: First, bearing witness to the truth—being on the side of the truth. Second, its explicit task is destroying the devil's work—the forces of corruption. Of course, corruption is not only what unbelievers do. Every human being, Christian or non-Christian, is a candidate for corruption. Corruption is in the human race. Third, Satan has decided to stop the preaching of the name of Jesus Christ by introducing another gospel, the gospel of wealth and wellness. Instead of promoting the preaching of "the powerful name of Jesus," the language of much of the Nigerian churches is "the blood of Jesus." We cover everything with the blood of Jesus. However, there is nowhere we read in the account of Acts those apostles using the blood of Jesus magically. For example, the apostles did not heal the crippled man with the blood of Jesus. So to stop the preaching in the name of Jesus we have adopted the language of war, with the blood of Jesus as our "weapon of self-defense."

Based on this understanding, the Church in Nigeria needs to intentionally create an alternative community—a community of faith, justice, love, forgiveness, reconciliation, restoration and peace. This redeemed community has to recognize that human corruption knows no borders. So it must understand why our world is being taken over by terrorists. It must be able to connect the dots between government corruption (money, sex and power) with terrorism. It must grasp the fact that government officials and their corrupt practices are fertile grounds for breeding terrorism. Corruption is a situation in which public officers take public resources for personal gain. Corruption is a situation in which members of a society are encouraged to pay a bribe for every transaction. Audie Cornish succinctly paints a picture thusly: "Imagine that every interaction you had ended with a demand for a bribe—postal clerks with your mail, police officers stopping you randomly, a bank clerk who refuses to sign off on your paperwork without a little extra cash."[16] Cornish interviewed Sarah Chayes, who had encountered the pervasive nature of the structure of corruption in the Middle East and in Africa. Chayes argues in her new book, *Thieves of State: Why Corruption Threatens Global Security*, that part of what is terrible about this practice is the amount of humiliation that accompanies it. It is money that is extorted from people, particularly the poor, who are face-to-face, with government officials who are treating them incredibly contemptuously.[17] This is not limited to cash. It also includes demands for sexual favors by judges. She cites the example of Nigeria, where there are situations in which a judge will ask a woman to have sex with him before he will agree to listen to her case. Chayes's study shows that young men who are discovering how their sisters have been raped by government officials are seeking revenge, and in the process they are told by groups like Boko Haram, al-Shabab, Al-Qaeda and ISI that corruption is happening because of the lack of a private moral code; if society were ruled by Islamic law, Shari'a, there would not be such evil perpetuated against the members of their families. Chayes paints a picture of the scenario thus:

16. Sarah Chayes, "'Thieves of State' Reveals Tremendous Power of Global Corruption," interview by Audie Cornish, *All Things Considered*, NPR, January 16, 2015, podcast audio, http://www.npr.org/2015/01/16/377780883/thieves-of-state-reveals-tremendous-power-of-global-corruption.

17. Ibid.

You get people who are indignant and personally humiliated in a country like Afghanistan and Nigeria and a significant numbers of them, especially males, are going to get violent. So if you have a violent movement that's around and looking to recruit people, there is a likelihood that they are going to really find people who have had an interaction like this—or five of them or 10 of them—that are ready to get some revenge. Thus, there is historically a really interesting intersection between acute public corruption and, I would say, militant puritanical religion, and that is in Christianity as well as in Islam. For example, go back and read Martin Luther and you will find that the "99 Theses" are largely taken up with issues of corruption. And I saw in Nigeria, for example, where I looked at northern Muslim areas, I also looked at some of the Pentecostal churches, which, although they are not violent now, have a lot of pretty violent rhetoric. And the connection seems to be that some people argue that the only way you can achieve public integrity is by way of a very strict code of private morality." Chayes' conclusion is that, "so long as people are being abused every day by their government, they will be joining the Taliban or joining Boko Haram every day."[18]

This is the social, political and religious context in which the Church is called by her Master and Lord to reach out in mission. Her challenge involves building an alternative community which is able to guarantee and foster human dignity even when it is nowhere granted in society. However, the Church always faces distraction. Satan knows that the Church is here to destroy his work, so Satan is battle-ready.

Conclusion

In the account of the apostles we see how human hostility and opposition target the mission of the Church. It says to Christians, "Shut up, Men!" similarly, Nigerian Christians face the challenge of opposition which has gradually metamorphosed to terrorists attacks. As such, the Nigerian contemporary society makes it difficult to preach the Good News of Christ Jesus, which is capable of bringing hope to a sick and dying nation. We have argued in this chapter that events in the world are not just isolated incidences. All events involving human hostility point toward the goal of distracting the Church from fulfilling her mission. For example, as we look at what Satan is doing presently across Nigeria, not only through Islamic extremists

18. Ibid.

but also through corrupt public officials and even corrupt Christian leaders and the laity, we can see that people of faith are often overwhelmed to the extent that the desire to live as witnesses of the Gospel of the risen Christ is abandoned. Satan and his agents know that if Christianity is left unhindered it will destroy the work of the devil. So they decide to stop its spread by any method possible. One way is to introduce another gospel, the gospel of wealth and wellness more than the name of Jesus Christ. Instead of promoting the preaching of "the powerful name of Jesus," the language of much of the Nigerian church is "the blood of Jesus." We cover everything with the blood of Jesus. Interestingly, the apostle did not heal the crippled man with the blood of Jesus. So to stop preaching in the name of Jesus we have adopted the language of war, with the blood of Jesus as our weapon of self-defense.

We have some good news: Satan and his agents will leave Christianity alone when they discover that the harder they hit Christians, the deeper they go! What will bring healing and restoration to the church in Nigeria is our willingness to live a life of faith in God, remaining faithful to the gospel of the resurrection of Jesus the Nazarene. The apostles never resorted to using the blood of Jesus as a weapon of self-defense! The next chapter addresses the question of how the Nigerian church understands her missions to the public arena. The study looks at the urgent need for the church to engage the public arena.

Chapter 13

The Church's Missions and the Public Arena

Introduction

In spite of the violent conflicts in Nigeria, the church still makes some appreciable level of contribution to the well-being of the nation. Yet, the distractions we discussed in the foregoing chapter happen at different levels in Nigeria too. A church that transforms society is a church that grasps the mission of the Church. It is not afraid to criticize itself, and when convicted, it repents. To assess the self-criticism level of the Church, this chapter evaluates Nigerian Pentecostal and Charismatic denominations' proactive or tangible social engagement in the public space in spite of the violence in the larger Nigerian society. The chapter elucidates the point of how Satan is specifically trying to distract the Nigerian church from its mission. It includes a review of Pentecostal and Charismatic social involvement, an overview of Pentecostals' political self-understanding and core values, an examination of the character of Pentecostal political engagement in the Nigerian public space and a conclusion. In fact, the violence in the Nigerian society has not deterred the Pentecostals and Charismatic denominations from engaging the public domain with innovative and creative activities.

That religion has been embedded in the historical narrative of Nigeria is not in doubt. What is in doubt is its social, moral, economic and political impact on the public sphere. The question that Nigerians and the rest of the global community need to ask is: How can Nigerian Christians translate their religious tenacity and resiliency into a social, economic, political and religious problem-solving mechanism in spite of the violent character of the Nigerian society? This question is necessitated by the fact that since the founding of Nigeria as a nation, Christianity and Islam, two major religions, have taken deep roots in the country. These two so-called foreign religions, plus the African Traditional Religions, have made Nigeria one of the most religiously conscious nations of the world. To various extents, in Christian communities across the country, entrepreneurially-minded persons name their business corporations (both large and small) after one or another member of the Godhead (e.g., "Water of God Computer Business"). Within such a vibrant religious context, one would expect religion to not only permeate all aspects of national life, but have concrete influence on its social, moral, economic and political life as well.

It is on this basis that this chapter will examine Nigerian Pentecostal and Charismatic denominations, with particular attention to the role they have played (and are still playing) in the public sphere. The basic obligation of Christians, according to Jesus, is to love God with all our heart, all our soul, and with our entire mind, and to love our neighbor as ourselves (Matt 22:37–39). But what does loving God and neighbor really entail? To love God is to commit ourselves to the fulfillment of God's intention for creation, in which love of neighbor is central.[1] Many a Christian denomination in Nigeria tends not to realize that the implication of this intention includes a preferential concern for the poor, the marginalized, and the voiceless members of society. It also includes commitment to long-term promotion and support of economic justice, human rights, social justice, compassionate love and charity. Nigeria's religious communities must pay attention to their role in the public sphere, because God is a personal God but not a private God. We must understand Nigerian religion, because "religion is the royal road to the heart of a civilization, the clearest indicator of its hopes and terrors, the surest index of how it is changing."[2]

The Popular Appeal of Pentecostalism

The time has come for Christian denominations in Nigeria and Africa at large to ask, "What is the mission of the Church in Africa?" How are economic and political injustices undermining the mission of the church? The Cape Town Commitment reveals the grimy context which necessitates this question. It shows that we live in a world where "the living God is denied in

1. Stivers et al., *Christian Ethics*, 77.
2. Cox, *Fire from Heaven*, 11.

aggressive atheism. The one true God is replaced or distorted in the practice of world religions. Our Lord Jesus Christ is abused and misrepresented in some popular cultures. And the face of the God of biblical revelation is obscured by Christian nominalism, syncretism and hypocrisy."[3] We must challenge the Church to fulfill its moral obligation to society by demanding an awareness of how economic, political and religious orientations in the past have often determined cultural views of work, city life, technology, cosmopolitan values, law, and political culture.[4] Nigerian Christians once came close to this awareness, but missed it by a one-sided emphasis. For example, "I Found It" was both a political and religious statement that characterized the 1970s. That revolutionary phrase became the impetus of the current wave and growth of Pentecostalism and Charismaticism;[5] it is no longer news to say that since the 1970s Pentecostal and Charismatic churches have remained the fastest-growing religious movements in the world. Scholars have argued that in Africa, Nigeria is one of the countries where the majority of the world's Pentecostals and Charismatics live. Indeed, Pentecostalism is the heartbeat of the contemporary religious quest in Nigeria and Africa at large. Speaking of the extraordinary and revolutionary significance of the Pentecostal movement in Nigeria, Ruth Marshall states, "Nigeria has been the site of Pentecostalism's greatest explosion on the African continent, and the movement's extraordinary growth shows no signs of slowing."[6] The church historiographer, Ogbu Kalu, adds that Pentecostalism in Africa "is simultaneously intense, pervasive, and multidirectional . . . African religious expression is a very alive universe in which all religious forms are exploding in numerical strength and have gained a voice in the public space."[7]

Our purpose here is to collate, examine, evaluate, determine and document the character of Pentecostal and Charismatic theology of public

3. Birdsall and Brown, foreword to *The Cape Town Commitment,* edited by Chris Wright, 11.

4. Stackhouse et al, *On Moral Business,* 12.

5. Burgess, *Nigeria's Christian Revolution,* 162. Richard Burgess draws our attention to the need to recognize the connection of this phenomenon as the direct result of the aftermath of the Civil War in Nigeria. He argues that the growth of Pentecostalism in Nigeria is the offshoot of the Igbo revivals of the 1970s: "The Biafran crisis exposed the deficiencies of existing religious options and created a favorable environment for a revival which was evangelical in its origins due to its Scripture Union roots, but quickly acquired a Pentecostal spirituality. The revival flourished because it adapted successively to new and challenging contexts. It resacralized the landscape in Christian terms by bringing renewal to existing churches, generating new theological emphases 'from below,' and precipitating fresh mission initiatives" (162).

6. Marshall, *Political* Spiritualities, 13.

7. Kalu, *African Pentecostalism,* 193.

engagement vis-à-vis how such involvement can translate into social, political, religious and economic problem-solving. Pentecostalism has gained and is still gaining a voice in public life; it is seen by its practitioners as a mighty force from heaven which has come to help ordinary humans take back their land from demonic agents who are holding it captive. We assume that the vision of total transformation—spiritual and physical—of Nigerian society is potent in the Pentecostal and Charismatic worldviews; but its practicability in public life may be more complicated and ambiguous than we perceive. This dilemma led Matthew A. Ojo to conclude, "Generally, leaders of Pentecostal and Charismatic movements have largely responded to political events, and have not formulated any critical opinion about governance."[8] He went on to explicate some of the contributions Pentecostals and Charismatics have made, particularly in the three fundamental debates that have charged the polity in Nigeria from the late 1970s to the 1990s. Such debates centered on Nigeria's political status (secularism), Shari'a criminal law, and Nigeria's illegal membership in the Organization of Islamic Countries (OIC).[9] All three issues centered on what Lamin Sanneh has characterized as the Muslim conviction that "Islam should not be gambled with in the cause of national sovereignty."[10] Pentecostals and Charismatics also have played an active role in confronting sectarian Islam, particularly during the Sheik Gumi led Shiite radicalism. They also spoke against the injustice of religious discrimination, especially discrimination against non-Muslim minorities in Northern Nigeria.[11] Ojo went on to assert that "Pentecostals and Charismatics have been concerned about the socio-political and economic situations of the country; [and to some extent] they have sought to intervene."[12] However, public life is not about just being concern and hoping

8. Ojo, "Pentecostal Public Accountability," 112. Apparently, there is overwhelming evidence that Pentecostals and Charismatics have made some landmark contributions to the stability of the country. But how concrete and sustainable have such contributions been? Can they say with Job, I have lived in a country of corruption and violence, "Yet my hands are free from violence and my prayer is pure?" Is the vision and mission of transforming society limited to the church leadership or trickled down to the grassroots? These questions are raised because of our recognition that to bring shalom transformation in a society requires a more robust way of doing Christian discipleship, whose primary aims will include raising Christians with a vibrant personal faith in Christ who will always and intentionally reflect their Christian values and virtues in public life.

9. Falola, *Violence in Nigeria*, 47.

10. Sanneh, "Shariah Sanctions as Secular Grace?," quoted in Ebenezer Obadare, "In Search of a Public Sphere," 181.

11. Ojo, "Pentecostal Public Accountability," 120.

12. Ibid., 121. Ojo recognizes that Pentecostals and Charismatics are still captive to "the linkage of the secular and the sacred" (123).

to intervene. Rather it is active and tangible engagement with a deep desire for "*transforming the* (seemingly) *untransformable*."[13]

In a socially and economically corrupt society, the Pentecostal and Charismatic churches in Nigeria need a deeper grasp of the full implication of Christian theology and Christology. When mention is made of our interaction or union with God, we need to have a clear grasp of this bond so that it can inspire "the love of righteousness [and justice] to which we are by no means naturally inclined."[14] John Calvin, who had a deep understanding of the implication of Christian faith for all of life, said that "if the Lord adopts us for his sons [and daughters] on the condition that our life be a representation of Christ, the bond of our adoption, then, unless we dedicate and devote ourselves to righteousness, we not only, with the utmost perfidy, revolt from our Creator, but also abjure the Savior himself."[15] Due to Christ's salvific work on the cross, God has claimed us as his sons and daughters. By implication, "God exhibited himself to us as a Father." It is therefore appropriate for us as Christians to equally reciprocate God's gesture to us by exhibiting ourselves as His children not only in private life but also in our public life.[16] To use the language of Walter Wink, Christian faith includes both the "inner" and "outer" reality of life. It is about consciously, concretely and tangibly engaging the powers that be in society as a whole.[17] It begins with the Church's ability to find its place in society as it obeys the biblical injunction, "Go and make disciples of *all* [or all spheres of] nations . . ." (Matt 28:19–20). Biblical discipleship shapes all of one's life, not just the private sphere.

Pentecostal and Charismatic Social Involvements in Nigeria

When one looks at some of the realities of Nigerian society, one could easily give up on the role of Pentecostal and Charismatic denominations in public life. But there is something that resembles "A cloud as small as a man's hand . . ." (1 Kgs 18:44) emanating from some Pentecostal and Charismatic public engagement. It is presently insignificant because it is one-sided. But one of

---

13. Okonjo-Iweala, *Transforming the Untransformable*, ix.

14. Calvin, "The Moral Law and the Christian Life," 182.

15. Ibid.

16. Ibid.

17. Wink, *Engaging the Powers*, 3. Here Wink argues, "The powers possess outer, physical manifestation (buildings, portfolios, personnel, trucks, fax machines) and an inner spiritual, or corporate culture, or collective personality . . . The powers, properly speaking, are not just the spirituality of institutions, but their outer manifestations as well."

the important lessons we can glean from the practitioners of tangible social change, such as Martin Luther King Jr. and Mahatma Gandhi, is this: "They know that you don't change a society by merely replacing one wet-fingered politician with another. You change a society by *changing the wind*."[18] They also knew that you do not change a society by focusing only on humanitarian activities or charity, which tend to perpetuate the culture of dependency.

Generally, what Pentecostal and Charismatic churches do in Nigeria stops at the level of charity and humanitarian actions. But charity is only one aspect of public engagement. If any Christian denomination is to make an enduring and tangible impact on Nigerian society, issues of public policy; understanding, confronting and dismantling systemic structures of social and economic injustice; and grasping issues of Christian love and just peacemaking and are important public matters that it cannot afford to ignore. In 2011, the Nigerian Pentecostal and Charismatic Research Center, Jos, Plateau State, undertook a survey of the presence and activities of Pentecostal and Charismatic churches across the country. The study focused on three basic areas: Pentecostal and Charismatic profile; phenomena; and socioeconomic and sociopolitical involvement in society. The writer of this paper participated in the group that focused on Pentecostal and Charismatic socioeconomic and sociopolitical involvement. In the course of carrying out the survey, the group discovered that there were basically two different strands of Pentecostals and Charismatics—conservatives and liberals (progressives)—in Nigeria. Some of the conservative Pentecostals and Charismatics are still apolitical, while some of the progressives show signs of public awareness and social activism.

An Example of the Conservative Strand

The Apostolic Church of Nigeria is a typical example of a conservative Pentecostal church. On July 28, 2011, my team visited the Territory Headquarters at Lawna International Convention Ground, Olurunda-Ketu, Ebute-Meta, Lagos. One of the apostles of the church was interviewed. He told the team that the headquarter church was founded in 1972. The church does not encourage its members to participate in politics, because politics is "a dirty game." Thus the church sanctions and disciplines any ordained pastor who ventures into politics. In terms of politics, the most the church can do is to encourage her members to vote. The argument used against political involvement is that the Bible says, "We are in the world but not of the world." The church does not believe in modern medicine. Rather, she

---

18. Wallis, *God's Politics*, 22.

believes in divine healing, and therefore she does not encourage members to take modern medicine or to set up hospitals. But the church is involved in other forms of social services such as sending funds to orphanages and other charitable organizations in Nigeria.[19]

An Example of the Progressive Strand

This section treats the question of what distinguishes the progressive Pentecostals and Charismatics from the conservative Pentecostals and Charismatics. In other words, what specifically do progressive Pentecostals and Charismatics do that shows a shift in their social and political discourses? Progressive Pentecostalism/Charismaticism is injecting a new way of viewing Christian life. Apparently, there are deliberate and intentional moves to engage in public discourse. For example, in an interview with Rev. Dr. William Okoye, the pastor and founder of All Christian Fellowship Mission (ACFM), Abuja on August 1, 2011, our team learned how he and his church spearheaded research that unraveled the secrecy of Islamic Banking in Nigeria, and thereby provided helpful information about the real issue at stake. The result of their research came after the national House of Representatives ignorantly endorsed the idea of Islamic Banking without carefully debating it and understanding the issues and implications involved. However, with the findings of the ACFM, the issue was brought back to the table for debate. This put ACFM on the frontline of attacks. Consequently, the Islamic sect Boko Haram attacked one of Dr. Okoye's churches in Suleja in April, 2011.[20] The willingness and courage of some Pentecostal churches to pay the price for political involvement shows a shift in political thinking.

1. Collaboration with Government

   Some Pentecostal churches are doing what other churches and communities usually ignore on the pretext that it is the government's responsibility to ensure the availability of basic social amenities to the citizenry. In our team's interview with Bishop John Praise Best of Dominion Chapel, Abuja, he told the team that his local church single-handedly constructed and tarred a road and also sank a borehole in the community to provide water free of charge. The church is doing this out of the realization that she is supposed to collaborate with the government in providing social services to the community. These acts

19. Jacob Akiyemi Akintola (Pastor), interview with the author, July 28, 2011.

20. William Okoye (Reverend, All Christian Fellowship Mission, Abuja), interview with the author, August 8, 2011.

of service are also seen as a wonderful expression of their love to their Lord and Savior Jesus Christ and to their neighbors.[21]

2. Conversion is no Longer Seen as a Private Decision and Practice without Public Implications.

There are some neo-Pentecostal churches and organizations in Nigeria who are no longer satisfied with converting and preparing members only for the world to come; they also train people for this life. This shift in thinking has necessitated the collapsing of the dichotomy between the secular and the sacred. Their major motivation is the fact that the Great Commission enjoined Christians to disciple nations. Therefore, individuals are saved for the transformation of whole nations.

3. Progressive Pentecostal/charismatic Churches' Specific Involvement in the Social life of the Community

As our team embarked on research on Pentecostal involvement in social life, we discovered a shining light of hope. For instance, in the team interview with the founder of Guiding Light Assembly Lagos, Parkview Estate Laki, Ikoyi, Lagos, on September 29, 2011, Pastor Wale Adefarasin, a businessman turned pastor, told the team that his local church had realized that "government cannot do it all. The church must participate with God in providing social services to humanity." It is this realization that has led the church to social action. The church has identified a community in Lagos and is doing several things to transform it. Obalande community in Lagos is a community of small businesses, tailoring and *yan suya* (those selling barbeque meats), harlotry, and so on. The church provides feeding, boreholes, garbage containers, renovation of dilapidated school buildings in the community, sending the children to school, providing food to the aged and medical services to the community. The church does not discriminate in its distribution of essential materials. Food distribution is both raw and cooked. It is done street by street and house by house. Beneficiaries are documented. He further observed that because "the church is the engine of change, the light needs to expunge the darkness." To do this, "We [Christians] need to encourage the members to go into politics." He sees danger coming if the church does not get it right: "The loss of sound biblical values will destroy our country."[22]

21. John Praise Best (Apostle, Dominion Chapel, Garki Area One and Abuja), interview with the author, July 31, 2011.

22. Wale Adefarasin (Pastor, Guiding Light Assembly Lagos, Parkview Estate Laki, Ikoyi, Lagos), interview with the author, September 29, 2011.

Furthermore, his engagement in sociopolitical issues was not out of ignorance. He is aware of the fact that the political terrain in Nigeria is very corrupt and has no room for godliness.[23] This realization has caused the church to step up its effort toward preparing members to be agents of transformation in society, resulting in the church actively training members for political activism. In helping government to fight corruption, the church is not just concerned about those who are in politics but all those who find themselves in public life in general. "The church is God's agent of transformation. Therefore, the church should encourage her members to carry God to the market, business, politics or any human endeavor . . ."[24] To inject biblical vision and virtue into the mindset of the members, the pastor explained how his church often organized seminars and workshops. For example, one was titled: "Church for change: Good governance." Five hundred leaders both within and outside the church attended the seminar. These leaders were trained on what to expect in public life.[25] The above case studies underscore specific things that some of the Pentecostal churches interviewed are doing to change the sociopolitical landscape of Nigeria.

The Contributions of Pentecostals/Charismatics to Democracy in Nigeria

From the above review, it seems appropriate to conclude that Pentecostalism and Charismaticism are apparently all-encompassing. Taking the above reports at their face value, the movement affects every facet of Nigerian society. It has gained access to the religious and political spheres of the nation. It seems its self-understanding as a "God-sent" agent of change and of meeting basic human needs has enabled it to politically influence society on a deeper level. In his article "Evangelicals and Politics in the Third World,"[26] Paul Freston writes: "The training needed for the third-world church now is not so much the conventional pastoral and evangelistic training but the formation of people who can interface with society in various areas of expertise."[27] Freston is suggesting a sort of discipleship training of members in local congregations which can help them effectively engage and transform the public space of Nigerian society. Danladi Musa states, "It is now generally accepted that one of the main ways that Christians can positively influence

23. Ibid.

24. Ibid.

25. Ibid.

26. Oladeji, *Understanding the Pentecostal Movement,* 25.

27. Gushee, *Christians and Politics Beyond Cultures of War,* 105.

society and make a difference is to get involved in politics, business and social action. By so doing, Christians will truly become the light and salt of the society."[28] Progressive Pentecostal pastors believe that evangelism and mission go hand in glove with social involvement.[29] The team interviewed the General Oversea of Ever Increasing Anointing Ministry International, Olabisi Olaitan Street Omolade Bus Stop Off Lasu Isheri Expressway Egan Lagos on 28/07/2011. Pastor Taiye Emmanuel Olayemi told the team that his ministry has existed for 16 years. The church is involved in the following social actions: supply of borehole water, to which the neighborhood has free access; and grading of the access road leading to the church and community. In terms of political involvement, he said that he encourages his members to go into politics because "when the righteous rule, the people rejoice," and that Christians are the salt of the world, and finally, it is only when Christians participate in voting that they can freely talk to the elected officials.[30] The founder of Gospel Light Redemption Church Garki Abuja, Rev. Oriakhia Isaac, said that the political terrain in Nigeria has no platform of godliness. Yet leaving it in the hands of unbelievers will make matters worse. As a result of the pastor's encouragement, the church has a serving senator in the present administration of President Jonathan. Isaac told the team that he encouraged his members to vote for Jonathan. The church is also teaching the members biblical values. Pastor Ben Nkonya Arabo, Beacon of Light Assembly Church, Garki Abuja encourages his members to exercise their civic responsibility by voting into power credible Nigerians. Over the years, he has discovered that the problem most members face when it comes to elections is that they hardly know the issues. He believes that teaching people sound biblical principles will help them to know what questions to ask when it comes to electing credible members of society to elective positions. He said, "We need to teach people how to demonstrate God's kingdom values on earth—love, justice, mercy, compassion, and so on." These core values, when adhered to, will transform Nigerian society, which is always characterized by "self-interest and the desire and will for power."[31]

---

28. Musa, *Christians in Politics*, 35.

29. Miller and Yamamori, *Global Pentecostalism*, 125.

30. Taiye Emmanuel Olayemi (Pastor, Ever Increasing Anointing Ministry International, Olabisi Olaitan Street, bus stop off Lasu Isheri Espressway, Egan, Lagos), interview with the author, July 28, 2011.

31. Niebuhr, *The Children of Light and the Children of Darkness*, 9.

Pentecostal Motivations and Theology of the Public Arena

It was Oliver O'Donovan who said that "the church in each age, lacking a political conceptuality that is native to it, simply deploys those current concepts which fit best its present tasks of worship, ministry and proclamation."[32] In view of such similar problems in the Pentecostals' and Charismatics' current situation, the big question to answer is, why do some Pentecostals and Charismatics who at first were apolitical suddenly became interested in politics? Undoubtedly, Charismatics' and Pentecostals' core values of evangelism, mission and social involvement have together resulted in its explosive growth beyond the shores of Nigeria. The Pentecostal and Charismatic churches in Nigeria apparently pay attention to a holistic vision of ministry. However, some of them seem to assume that if they engage in humanitarian activities or telling members to participate in politics or vote in an election, that is enough evidence of social and public activism.

For Nigerian Pentecostals and Charismatics to be effective in public life, beyond charity and encouraging people to vote, they must realize the inexhaustible power of Christianity. Luke's account of Jesus' resurrection has it that "after His suffering . . . He appeared to them over a period of forty days and spoke about the kingdom of God" (Acts 1:3). For Jesus Christ, what is at stake is the rule or reign of God in this broken and decaying world. To bring about the workings of the Kingdom of God requires a power that is more than flesh and blood: the power of the Holy Spirit. Luke characteristically stresses the Holy Spirit's work and enabling power (Acts 1:8; 2:4, 17; 4:8, 31; 6:3, 5; 7:55; 8:16; 9:17, 31; 10:44; 13:2, 4; 15:28; 16:6; 19:2, 6). By combining the subject of the Kingdom of God and the need to wait for the gift of the Holy Spirit (Acts 1:3–5), Luke draws our attention to the fact that God gave the Church the Holy Spirit not just for leading unbelievers to faith in Christ and raising an alternative community—the redeemed community—but also for the transformation of systemic structures of social injustice. In Luke, Jesus Christ condemned the Pharisaic systemic structures of injustice. He preached the in breaking of the kingdom of God (the rule or reign of God) in this generation. The Church needs to talk about the Kingdom of God—the rule and reign of God in all spheres of creation. God's rule and reign is both in the Church and in the world. The idea of the Kingdom of God gives the Church a profound public perspective: God is the ultimate Governor. That is:

- God is the ultimate source of the principles of all good government for the well-being of society.

32. O'Donovan, *The Desire of the Nations*, 15.

- To know God enables us to understand and influence our society.

- We must pray, rely on the power of the Holy Spirit and work with God for a better society.

- If we harmonize with his principles, God will bless our nation with peace and prosperity, but if we do not, God will judge our nation.[33]

The spirit of public engagement is one that knows the unlimited power of the Holy Spirit. He is given to enable Christians not only to lead unbelievers to Christ, but to make such redeemed individuals agents of social change not only in Jerusalem, Judea and Samaria but also "to the ends of the earth." It means "to grasp the principles by which God rules the nations of the world—in blessing and in judgment"; it also means that, "more Christians will bring the whole of their lives under the Lordship of Jesus Christ—to pray and work for the principles God wants in our society."[34] That realization starts with recognizing that all human beings deeply value a present life that holds hope for a pain-free future. Human hope is generally rooted in the ability to meaningfully participate in the affairs of one's society and generation as a dignified human being. Vernon E. Light writes:

> Humans sense that they must have purpose in life, a purpose that includes playing a part in restoring the world towards its intended purpose and design. Christianity through its "Great Commission and the Cultural Mandate," godly living and eschatology, offers such a life-purpose . . . It would be difficult to find a more significant, purposeful, meaningful and hopeful life than the redeemed, God-centered life offered in true Christianity.[35]

He summarizes the inexhaustible power of Christianity thus: "Christianity provides the key to understanding the realities and mysteries of life and the universe."[36]This key is embedded in the Bible. Light goes on to explain, "The story-line of the Bible is about morally transforming individuals and through them society."[37]If truly inner and divine transformation has taken place in a human's life it must bear fruit horizontally and vertically (upward and outward). For example, the Nigerian-born Bishop Sunday Adelaja of Ukraine (whom many Nigerian Pentecostal and Charismatic pastors see as their mentor) believes that God's intention in this world is the transformation of individual lives, who will in turn transform whole nations.

33. Adeyemo, *Christian Leaders in Society*, 5.

34. Ibid., 3.

35. Light, *Transforming the Church in Africa*, 26.

36. Ibid., 27.

37. Ibid., 24.

Adelaja states, "As believers, our first calling is to be part of the master's plan. National transformation is at the heart of the Great Commission. It is the primary calling of everyone who follows Christ."[38]Conceivably, it is this self-understanding of the Church's mission that has helped Adelaja to transform Ukraine and to influence world politics. In view of Adelaja's foregoing argument, certain key principles drive the political vision of Pentecostals:

1. The Great Commission happens outside the church. Ministry is what you do to bring your life and sphere of influence under kingdom rule.[39]

2. God holds the church responsible for societies.[40]

3. The church is responsible to train us to be Christ-like, to embody Jesus and His principles, so that in every area of life we may operate from a godly perspective. That's what the church is for. That's why we come to church on Sunday. That's why we preach, teach, and worship together.[41]

Adelaja's starting point is the Great Commission. In it, he rediscovers the fact that God cares about nations, not just the individuals in them. His reflection on Matthew 28:19–20 gives him a thick understanding of the Great Commission. He writes, "The Bible is very clear: God wants to redeem nations. His redemptive work on the cross is for nations and individuals. That's why He said to go preach the gospel to all nations and to disciple nations. God eagerly awaits the redemption of nations."[42] Adelaja's emphasis on the kingdom of God has impacted Nigerian Pentecostal pastors. For example, Pastor Yinka Ojo sees the concept of the Kingdom of God as a strategy for society transformation: the Church transforming every sphere of society, including the marketplace. Ojo writes, "God wants to invade the marketplace with His Kingdom through His children. The marketplaces of this world are the avenues, locations and positions where the people in their public life meet to interact and do business. This terrain is certainly outside of the four walls of our local church assemblies."[43]Another motivation is the belief in the anointing of the Holy Spirit, and what such anointing can do to a society. "The anointing is . . . not an emblem; it is an instrument

38. Adelaja, *Church Shift*, xxvii.

39. Ibid., 10.

40. Ibid., 11.

41. Ibid.

42. Ibid., 17.

43. Ojo, *The Kingdom and the Market Place*, 13.

for triumph," says David Oyedepo.[44] In other words, it is meant to enable Christians to accomplish things that ordinary people cannot accomplish. Oyedepo states:

> The time has come for the Spirit to dwell in us so much that we live perpetually under the influence of His anointing. Then shall we begin to do things that will make people wonder at us. Our results will be so staggering that men will be confounded. God desires that you and I become amazement to our world, just as it was with Jesus, who after the Holy Ghost descended on Him, the eyes of all men were fixed on Him. The eyes of all men will be fixed on us because of the exploits we will be doing. Men will come to recognize our new power and status . . .[45]

The idea of doing exploits in the world motivates Pentecostals to participate in the affairs of their nation. Oyedepo's definition is not limited to the four walls of the church, but to every sphere of human endeavor, and that includes politics. Although the political impact of the Pentecostal and Charismatic churches is not yet felt in Nigeria as it is in Ukraine, Nigerian Pentecostals and Charismatics believe that they are attempting great things for God in a corrupt and decaying society. For example, (1) Some of them continue to influence what happens at the grassroots level of the Nigerian economy through proactive social involvement in their communities; and (2) The political class patronizes their faith-prayer houses. For example, some Christian governors in Nigeria go to *Throneroom International Ministry*, Inc., Kafanchan, at the end of the month to be prayed for. In spite of all these positive things, I agree with the scholars who honestly believe that given their size and influence in Nigeria, the potential of the Pentecostal and Charismatic churches for grassroots political mobilization is not yet realized.[46] There is still some persistent ambiguity in their theology of public morality.

Public Morality and Machiavellianism in Pentecostal/ Charismatic Thought

The problem of moral ambiguity is not only true of Pentecostal and Charismatic churches but is a general cancer across denominations. Public discourse is often obscured by ambiguous and paradoxical perceptions of

44. Oyedepo, *Anointing for Exploits*, 559.

45. Ibid., 560–61.

46. Kunhiyop, *African Christian Ethics*, 157–60.

morality. Compartmentalization of morality has led to unnecessary hair-splitting. Consequently David Hollenbach points out that "the beginning of the twenty-first century confronts all religious communities with a fundamental challenge: how to relate their distinctive visions of the good human life with the growing awareness that all persons are linked in a web of global interdependence."[47] The situation described by Hollenbech requires Christians to be very clear about their moral and ethical obligations to the world. However, given that many Nigerian Christians, like their Western Christian counterparts, have been deeply influenced by the Platonic dualistic general perspective on morality (Plato's misguided separation of body from soul, matter from spirit, the secular from the sacred), their engagement in public life has often remained weak and ambiguous. This moral ambiguity is informed by the fact that there is significant tension between private and public morality. To resolve this tension is not impossible, but it is difficult. This difficulty has led to varying conclusions.

Nigerian Pentecostalism and the Self-Understanding of the Public Life

It could be argued that since African Pentecostalism and Charismaticism originated from the African Christian experience and encounter with Western Christianity, their public involvement cannot be limited to the political sphere only. In the real sense of African worldviews, there is no such thing as the dichotomy between the secular and the sacred, the church and state. The historiographer Ogbu Kalu states that African Pentecostalism is unique; it is a homegrown movement, a "made in Nigeria" movement, so to speak. Some of its groups were formed in reaction to the Western missionary Christian enterprise in Africa which uprooted Africans from their rich cultural heritage and left them dangling in mid-air. In other words, African Pentecostalism is a reaction to Western missionary church policies in Africa.[48]

But the fact that some Pentecostal and Charismatic groups originated in Nigeria does not necessarily make it true that they understand the public implication of their faith. Additionally, the fact that they are homegrown does not preclude the fact that they were indirectly influenced by Western missionary Christianity, which found roots in Africa before the Pentecostal phenomenon broke out in Nigeria. According to Musa Gaiya,

47. Hollenback, *The Global Face of Public Faith*, 3.

48. Kalu, *African Pentecostalism*, xiii. "Exercising a measure of agency, African Christians absorbed new resources generated internally and externally in reshaping their histories" (ibid., 170).

African Pentecostalism is "by all standards an outgrowth from missionary Christianity."[49] But it must be noted that there is a part of the movement that is indigenously and independently initiated. Kalu is aware that there are two types of Pentecostals and Charismatics: those who had Western missionary contact and those who did not. But in arguing that it is uniquely a Nigerian initiative, outside of the Azusa episode, he is critiquing the work of scholars[50] who argue that African Pentecostalism resulted from the Azusa Street revival. In some ways, Kalu's argument is reinforced by Paul Gifford, who asserts that African Pentecostalism is attractive to Africans because Pentecostals claim to have answers to peoples' existential problems and especially to their most pressing existential problem: economic survival.[51] I will argue that Nigeria's Pentecostals make this claim and even more. An overview of how Pentecostals view the public space illustrates this salient truth.

Nigerian Pentecostal and Charismatic perceptions of public life must be examined on their own terms. Any attempt to fit this definition into a Western mode of understanding will fail to grasp the depth of the Pentecostals' and Charismatics' involvement in public life, or limit it to what happens in political spheres. Generally, African Pentecostalism has grown because it is culturally fitted into indigenous worldviews, and is willing to pay attention to and respond to the questions that are raised within those worldviews.

Nigeria's Pentecostals and Charismatics have attempted to respond to Nigeria's challenges in diverse ways. Kalu identifies three interpenetrative publics which they respond to: "The village public, the emergent urban public, and the Western public that is represented by Multinational Corporations and international institutions."[52] In each of these publics, the Pentecostals' and Charismatics' primary task is rooted in their overall perception of the mission of the Church, which includes, among other things, conversion of unbelievers and the uprooting of spiritual forces of darkness that are at work in public systems, structures and institutions. It is on this basis that economic and political bondage are also seen as obstacles to human flourishing: Freedom from all that oppresses is the goal of life. This is not only a major reason why people are attracted to the movement. It is also true that

> ". . . the Pentecostal and Charismatic movements [have] created new theological and ideological discourse by bringing the concept of evil and spiritual warfare onto the agenda of political

49. Gaiya, "The Pentecostal Revolution in Nigeria," 1, 13.
50. Rodriguez, "Pentecostal Identity, Diversity and Public Witness," 54.
51. Gifford, Ghana's New Christianity, ix.
52. Kalu, African Pentecostalism, 169–70.

discourse, thus consolidating new forms of religious expression and political understanding.[53]

First, in addressing *the village public*, the movement speaks the language of the African mindset derived from the general worldview of what constitutes reality. Their worship is characterized by renunciation of the ancient covenants their forefathers made with the devil and breaking them down with a view of not only taking over the land, but also taking every thought captive and making it obedient to Christ's Lordship. This liturgical stance is also seen as a reaction to the activities of Western mission Christianity.[54] That is to say, due largely to their focus on the village public, Pentecostalism and Charismaticism in Africa pay close and careful attention to African worldviews. They take seriously the African mindset.[55]

Second, in dealing with *the emergent urban public*, African Pentecostalism is fully aware that every African is rooted in his/her cultural contexts, to the extent that no amount of Western education can erode the traditional beliefs that determine people's daily life. According to Kalu, the Pentecostals' effort to rid society of the schemes of the devil has led to the creation of a niche.[56] He further explains that "The argument here is that Pentecostalism is, in fact, colored by the texture of the African soil and derives idiom, nurture, and growth from its interior. It does not merely adapt, it gestates the resources of externality, transforming it to serve its needs."[57] In other words, Pentecostals' involvement in distinctively urban public life is rooted in their ability to take the African map of the universe seriously, by actually acknowledging that it is redeemable "to the praise of his [God's] glory." To take captive the urban realm and make it obedient to Christ, "they deploy four strategies: adopt a posture of spiritual warfare; use the covenant imagery to describe the relationship between human beings and the gods;

---

53. Ojo, "Pentecostal Public Accountability," 124.

54. Kalu, *African Pentecostalism,* 174.

55. Kalu, *African Pentecostalism,* 175. Kalu speaks of the Pentecostal reconstruction of the primal worldviews: "The Pentecostal goes through life keenly aware of the presence of evil forces just as the African does. Life is secured through a good relationship with the supernatural. The Bible, for instance, prescribes both obedience and active maintenance of the covenant with God; it, therefore, contains a diatribe against the competing covenants with other gods. These are imaged as snares and, therefore, the need for testing of spirits. The promise of land was a key component of the covenant. Similarly, when there is a drought or famine or social distress, Africans look to the land and to their relationship with the earth deity because the earth deity sustains the economic and moral order. The Pentecostals do likewise: They bring to the problem the importance of the land among the Israelites."

56. Ibid., 175.

57. Ibid., 189.

explore swaths of resonance between the Bible and African indigenous worldview; and reinvent a theology that reclaims God's rule over the whole inhabited earth."[58] By and large, it seems that Pentecostals and Charismatics understand and interpret the purpose of Christian public life, within certain lenses. These include, among other things, the notion of "break," or "radical reversal," the reality of hope, which makes sense of secular history and faith; and a sense that all of humanity and nature are mutually involved in the progress toward the apocalyptical end.[59]

Dynamism and Character of the Engagement

The foregoing overview of how Pentecostals' worldviews work vis-à-vis public life sets the agenda for discourse on the contemporary character of Nigerian Pentecostals' and Charismatics' theology of public engagement. We recognize that Pentecostalism and Charismaticism in Nigeria are part of the religious movement which paradoxically shares in the hopes and the terrors of the civilization in which it participates. Christianity is not only a private but also a public faith. Jesus categorically tells the Church, "You are the salt of the earth . . . You are the light of the world. A city built on a hill cannot be hid . . ." He also said to the individual members of the Church, "Let your light shine before others, so that they may see your good works and give glory to your Father in heaven" (Matt 5:3–16). Why then does the Church still pay little attention to the public arena? Perhaps she has forgotten that becoming the salt of the earth and the light of the world is not automatic; it requires preparation and training. This writer believes that it is the responsibility of every denomination (including the Pentecostals and the Charismatics) in Nigeria to prepare its members for both private and public life. To engage in public space means that many things must be clarified:

1. We must understanding the distinction between charity and economic justice. "One of the most obvious differences between justice and charity is how power is distributed. Justice distributes power so that the weak become stronger and better able to care for themselves. Charity meets people's immediate needs in ways that keep them dependent."[60] Justice rooted in love is effective. This effectiveness would include empowering those Jesus calls "the least of these" (Matthew 25:40, 45). Jesus' conception of church involvement is re-

58. Ibid., 178–79.

59. Clark, *What Is Distinctive About Pentecostal Theology?*, 90.

60. Stivers et al, *Christian Ethics*, 78–79.

vealed in that little phrase: "the least of these." It tells us what public engagement is not, and what it is. First, it is not about church leaders or members siding with and helping the political elite maintain the status quo, nor competing with the powerful to the detriment of "the least of these my brothers [and sisters]." Second, it is about recognizing that "living in poverty over time robs individuals and communities of the ability to make choices, to control their own lives and communities."[61] That is, realizing that "unless poverty and impoverishment are actively resisted by religious communities, it makes persons powerless and dependent. Inevitably this powerlessness and dependence wear away feelings of both dignity and self-worth and the ability to feel beloved by God and other persons."[62] Without a sense of dignity and self-worth, "communal bonds weaken and break." It is recognizing that "involuntary poverty is sinful and an affront [to] God our Creator . . . it kills and maims bodies and souls, individuals and communities."[63]

2. There are different forms of engagement in public life. Some engagement involves formulating antigovernment policies and protests against social injustice. Other forms include intercessory prayer, active participation in politics and/or filling the gaps of a failed state. We have shown above that conversion is a primary task of Nigerian Pentecostals and Charismatics. As such, some of them are not interested in serving tables and leaving this call to suffer. From all indications, church leaders and members do not often have a good grasp of the workings of the political sphere. This lack of understanding leads to what Kalu speaks of as Christian government officials' involvement with secret societies behind closed doors, and sometimes even in the open. According to Ojo, by and large, Christians' uncritical engagement has led some of them to soil their moral character; some have become materialistic and corrupt—worse than the public servants.[64] Kalu identifies four things that the foregoing analysis of the nature of politics in Africa can teach Pentecostals and Charismatics to watch, as they seek to make a meaningful and intelligent engagement in the Nigerian public space:

61. Ibid.

62. Ibid.

63. Ibid.

64. Personal communication during the author's presentation of a paper on this topic.

> First, it is important to enlarge the boundaries of our understanding of political engagement beyond overt activities such as political protest, party politics, and the electoral process. Second, we should be attentive to the magical substratum that underpins the political culture, and Pentecostal political response is embedded in the indigenous terrain and the religious foundations of the political culture . . . In the African terrain, the pneumatological approach is key to understanding the Pentecostal political theology and practice. Third, that the vast differences within the regions and countries within the continent compel attention and comparative perspective. Fourth, that the sacralization of political order and ethics in primal society informs the political culture in modern public space. The political elite tap the resources of primal religion in their competitions in the modern space; dynamics of modern politics. A legitimacy crisis merely intensifies the process in a religious space bedeviled with an occult explosion. Meanwhile, other religious forces are growing, with many political implications . . . Indeed, Pentecostals are implicated in the conflict generated by the Abrahamic religions in the political dynamics of Africa.[65]

Kalu's point is that public life is complicated. For fear of unknown invisible forces, public servants patronize occult agents. The Nigerian political culture is one that is saturated with "religious undercurrents."[66] The point of this chapter is that uncritical engagement in public life can easily lead to political alignment with the status quo. Instead of the church becoming a catalyst of transformation, she is converted to the status quo. Furthermore, often church leaders are naïve about the magnitude of the challenges their members face in public life. In such situations, it is difficult to help members become effective agents of healthy transformation in society. In 1944 (reprinted in 1960), America's renowned theologian, political philosopher, and social critic Reinhold Niebuhr wrote a book, *The Children of Light and the Children of Darkness*. He picked the title directly from Luke 16:8, which reads: "The children of this world are in their generation wiser than the children of light." As he explained the basic difference between them, Niebuhr profoundly observed the contradiction of each. He said,

> The children of darkness are evil because they know no law beyond the self. They are wise, though evil, because they understand the power of self-interest. The children of light are virtuous because they have some conception of a higher law

65. Kalu, *African Pentecostalism*, 199–200.
66. Ibid., 200.

than their own will. They are usually foolish because they do not know the power of self-will . . .[67]

According to Niebuhr, self-interest and the will to power drive all political ambition. It is rooted in the belief that in this world there are basically two operating political principles: "You are either dominated by others or you dominate others." Consequently, this conception of political life shapes the thinking of people at every level of social, religious, political and economic spheres. This insight helps us understand the continuing occultism and corruption of good morals and politics in the country that Kalu alludes to.[68] Power and authority over other fellow human beings and natural resources become the driving forces of public life. Niebuhr's analysis shows the political ignorance of church leaders and their members. In general, the Christian community does not recognize the problem of self-interest or group interest. Self-interest or group interest is a general problem of humanity and the major cause of religious, economic and political corruption. Today, the political class sees public funds as personal funds. This is why onetime U.S. Ambassador to Nigeria John Campbell pointed out that governance in Nigeria faces many challenges: "Nigeria is run by competing and cooperating elites supported by their patron-client networks, ethnic interests, big business, and the military . . ."[69] This is what is happening in a country where the growth of Pentecostalism is well and alive. Reinhold Niebuhr further asserts: "Man's capacity for justice makes democracy possible; but man's inclination to injustice makes democracy necessary."[70] Democracy worldwide is a system of governance which provides checks and balances of power. It promotes the use of public resources for the social and economic enhancement of the citizenry. Nigeria's public space is grossly managed by the few who in most cases recycle themselves in power; and in no way have the masses' interests at heart. They get immunity because there are no structures in Nigerian civil society which provide checks and balances. Niebuhr exposes the danger inherent in a democratic culture that has no checks and balances of power. According to him, in a crooked and depraved world, humans are often inclined towards evil. And to have a system that has no independent checks and balances of power is dangerous.[71] He argues, "If men are inclined to deal unjustly with their fellows, the

---

67. Niebuhr, *Children of Light and Childred of Darkness*, 10.

68. Ibid., 10–11.

69. Campbell, *Nigeria Dancing on the Brink*, xiv–xv.

70. Niebuhr, *Children of Light and the Children of Darkness,* xiii.

71. Ibid., xiii–xiv.

possession of power aggravates this inclination. That is why irresponsible and uncontrolled power is the greatest source of injustice."[72]

Understanding the Five Essential Levels of Public Involvement

Most Pentecostal and Charismatic churches are strategically located in urban areas where their members could effectively make positive contributions to politics and government. So, we give the following recommendations for formation of people for good political involvement.[73] First, *moral character*: The greatest public contribution a church can make is to help its members develop a strong ethical vision, and virtues such as human dignity, love, justice, honesty, hard work, humility, compassion, perseverance, creative initiative, the fear and love of God and so on, which will enable them to shape the character of society. In a society where people generally assume that every Nigerian is corrupt and dishonest, concrete lifestyle matters. Pentecostal and Charismatic churches can disciple their members in such a way that they are able to demonstrate honesty, integrity, justice and nonviolence in the church and in society. In a country where ethnic, political and religious prejudices and hatred characterize the larger society and startle citizens from all angles, Pentecostal and Charismatic members will do a great service to humanity if they consciously and persistently practice Christian core values in public space.[74] A great service that the Pentecostals and Charismatic churches owe all citizens of Nigeria is to raise up members who in their daily lives are able to demonstrate justice and nonviolence.[75]

To be effective in the public sphere, Christians in Nigeria need to pay attention to the dynamic economic, religious, social and political forces driving globalization today. From Friedman's analysis of the contemporary global situation, we can say with certainty that the world has changed. Therefore, Church leaders and members need to realize that the world has changed. But more than just knowing that the world has changed is the fact that this is a dreaded change because, "It is not only the software writers and computers geeks who get empowered to collaborate on work in a flat

72. Ibid.

73. These five criteria are distilled from Duane K. Friesen's book, *Christian Peacemaking & International Conflict*, 190.

74. Asamoa-Gyadu, "Religious Education and Religious Pluralism," 242.

75. Friesen, *Christian Peacemaking & International Conflict*, 207. Friesen observes that "In many respects the church is an alternative institution when its members live out a lifestyle of love, forgiveness, and peace, and through that example, witness to what could be, and convert others to that position."

world. It is also al-Qaeda and other terrorist networks."[76] Friedman notes that, "The playing field is not being leveled only in ways that draw in and superempower a whole new group of innovators. It is being leveled in a way that draws in and superempowers a whole new group of angry, frustrated and humiliated men and women."[77] Pentecostal and Charismatic denominations are to some extent already taking advantage of global contemporary technologies and innovations. But they still need to take advantage of the global opportunity individuals now have to collaborate with their next-door neighbors for a tangible transformation of the public sphere.

The second thing that Pentecostals and Charismatics have to offer Nigeria is, *provision of basic services*: Christian organizing institutions to meet human needs in society. There are Pentecostal churches that are already doing this in Lagos and Abuja and across the length and breadth of the country. This is a situation where a church "often organizes itself to do tasks that aim to meet the basic needs of people. It is an organizer of institutions, which are responsive to human needs such as poverty, ignorance, malnutrition, disease, and community disorganization. In this role the churches have been and continue to be the creators of numerous institutions—educational and health care institutions, programs for prisoner rehabilitation, agricultural and community development projects."[78]

Third, *positively influencing policy*: Pentecostal and Charismatic churches can engage the public space by consciously discipling their church members so they can in turn influence public policy. Policies promulgated in the public square have implications for every member of society. The Pentecostal and Charismatic churches in Nigeria will do a great service to the country if their members are able to push for bills that will meet the needs of the general public. Sometimes church leaders are good at polemics, but they do not know how issues are debated, let alone how to reorient their members on how to nonviolently engage other faiths or government on issues bordering on detrimental policies.[79]

Fourth, *vocation*: This entails teaching members to see their work as a "calling" or as part and parcel of the mission of God. If Nigerian Pentecostal and Charismatic Christians will take advantage of the opportunities God has given them to work in public places and in institutional settings and see their calling as not limited to evangelism and individual conversion, but also including changing structures of social and economic injustice, the impact

---

76. Friedman, *The World Is Flat*, 8.

77. Ibid.

78. Friesen, *Christian Peacemaking & International Conflict*, 208.

79. Ibid.

will certainly be much deeper than what it is currently. Currently, Nigerian Pentecostal and Charismatic Christians work in many institutions—business corporations, governmental structures, social agencies, schools and universities, and international organizations. In these vocations they can seek not primarily to serve their own interests but also to see their being there as an opportunity, a "calling" by which to try to further the interests of peace and justice in or through the institution or organization. For example, they can pay attention to the policies that are made by institutions, corporations, governmental structures, social agencies, businesses corporations, particularly on how they affect "the least of these my brothers."[80]

Conclusion

Every believer needs to grasp the notion that Christianity has a public face. Therefore, every denomination in Nigeria must see its responsibility to disciple and prepare its parishioners for life in the public arena. This will go a long way toward ameliorating the high rate of corruption and the resultant politically motivated violence in Nigeria. There is a good deal missing in Nigerian Pentecostal and Charismatic churches' theology of public engagement. It obviously lacks "grassroots mobilization." In the survey conducted, we found a general tendency in Pentecostal and Charismatic theology of public engagement that stops at the level of Christian charity, or mobilizing people to vote for political candidates during elections. Consequently, what Pentecostals and Charismatics call holistic engagement does not tally with what the Bible means when it says, ". . . teaching them to observe all that I taught you" (Matt 28:19–20). Due to this tendency, the existing public theology generally serves the agenda of the political elite who are afraid of freedom of the oppressed. Like their counterparts in mainstream Nigerian Christianity, Pentecostal and Charismatic churches have the tendency of aligning themselves with the status quo (the oppressors) rather than remaining committed to the plight of the least of these" (the oppressed) (Matt 25:40, 45). Undue attention is paid to those in leadership, not only to

80. Friesen, *Christian Peacemaking & International Conflict*, 216. Friesen writes: "A person can be an innovator, one who seeks to create an alternative vision of how institutions can better serve human need: a business corporation that designs and markets products to meet basic human needs rather than superfluous products with the primary motive of profit, a lawyer seeking to defend the cause of justice or civil liberties or working in behalf of the poor rather than defending the special privileges of the rich, a teacher who teaches science from a global framework rather than from a narrow nationalistic perspective, a social worker who helps to organize the poor to restore their dignity rather than simply cooperating with a demeaning social welfare system which dehumanizes people."

the detriment of the poor and marginalized, but also to the extent of being snared by elitist lifestyles.

Some Pentecostal and Charismatic church leaders compete with politicians and business tycoons who own personal bulletproof SUVs, private jets and personal security escorts or aides. As public officials grow fat on the culture of taking advantage of "the least of these," church leaders who are supposed to remind them of their divine responsibilities and vocations and the need to be voices of the oppressed, instead follow suit.

A theology of public engagement which this chapter advocates is one that takes its inspiration from the fact that after his suffering and resurrection, Jesus took forty days talking about the Kingdom of God to his disciples before sending them out to be his witnesses in Jerusalem, Judea, Samaria and the ends of the earth teaching the new disciples everything he taught them (Acts 1:3–5). This theology realizes that the task of public engagement is for those who believe that "with man this is impossible, but with God all things (including Christian public engagement) are possible" (Matt 19:26). Grassroots mobilization involves a belief in the unlimited power of God's rule in this age, through the power of the Holy Spirit. In other words, this belief sees the role of the Church as significantly seeking to create critical consciousness at all spheres of society, particularly at the grassroots level. This means helping the rural peasants, the marginalized and the silenced to learn and believe in themselves as agents of social change.

The Brazilian-born educationist, Paulo Freire, explains that creating critical consciousness is "learning to perceive social, political and economic contradictions, and to take action against the oppressive elements of reality."[81] That means, if the Church believes that "with God all things are possible," she will undoubtedly believe in the potential of people at the bottom of society, the grassroots. She will specifically believe that these people can be mobilized through training to be radical transformers of culture through identifying the two dangers of culture: the "culture of silence" and impunity and the "culture of fear of freedom."[82] We need churches who believe in God's Kingdom rule and that "with God all things are possible," and are thus willing to have a "direct engagement in the struggles to liberate men and women [at the grassroots level] for the creation of a new world [a new Nigeria]."[83] As Richard Shaull explains, "Freire is able to do this because he operates on one basic assumption: that man's ontological vocation (as he calls it) is to be a Subject who acts upon and transforms his world, and

81. Freire, *Pedagogy of the Oppressed*, 9.

82. Ibid., 10.

83. Ibid., 11.

in so doing moves towards ever new possibilities of fuller and richer life individually and collectively."[84] For Freire, the idea that "with God all things are possible" takes on new meaning, or new power: "It is no longer an abstraction or magic but a means by which man [human] discovers himself and his potential as he gives names to things around him." He succinctly puts it thus: "Each man wins back his right to say *his own word, to name the world.*"[85]

This is exactly what creating critical consciousness can cause at the grassroots level. It is a situation where those in power will not be afraid of the freedom of the so-called powerless. It is the belief that even if people are exposed to "specific situations of injustice," that exposure will not lead them to "destructive fanaticism" or to "a sensation of total collapse of their world."[86] Rather, creating critical consciousness in the peasant, "[E]nrolls them in the search for self-affirmation and thus avoids fanaticism."[87] In view of the foregoing analysis in this chapter, one can categorically say that this is not what is happening in the Pentecostal and Charismatic churches we have surveyed. The kind of theology of public engagement that we propose is one that does not confuse freedom with the maintenance of the status quo, but threatens to radically place that status quo in question.[88] In the contemporary socioeconomic, sociopolitical and socioreligious climates of Nigeria, particularly the rising sectarianism, the grassroots need what Freire calls radicalization as an alternative to sectarianism.[89] Christian radicalization is the realization that the enabling power of God is for radicals. In other words, the task of transformation is for radicals and not for sectarians.

The idea of the Kingdom of God is capable of transforming our society. The prayer that Jesus taught His disciples is a prayer that is meant to help us focus on the Kingdom of God and the doing of its heavenly will on planet Earth. The questions that the Church must ask itself are, How much do members learn every week that helps them hallow God in their weekly activities and endeavors? How are members taught to monitor their political activity of members who become politicians? To actually achieve the goal of training members for public life, theological seminaries need to introduce courses on political theology, church, society and law, good governance, public policy administration, implementation and evaluation. The

---

84. Richard Shaull, foreword to *Pedagogy of the Oppressed*, by Paulo Freire. 12.

85. Freire, *Pedagogy of the Oppressed*, 13.

86. Ibid., 20.

87. Ibid., 21.

88. Ibid.

89. Ibid., 21–22.

Church should help members realize that politicians are servants or ministers of God (Rom 13:4, 6). Christian politicians are pastors in the public arena. Pastors labor in the public arena; therefore, what Scriptures require of a pastor is also required of a politician. To keep them from straying from the faith, they should be reminded of their vocation and calling as public figures who recognize that they are must follow biblical values as politicians. Therefore, they should love righteousness and hate all forms of wickedness.

Finally, Jesus calls every denomination to be salt and light in a broken and decaying world. We must stop assuming that members will automatically become the salt and light of Nigeria. They need to be given the skills required to perform as expected of the Children of Light when they find themselves in the public arena as business individuals, civil servants, politicians, and in every human endeavor. As the Church does all these, she must remember that "People want change; but they themselves do not want to change." In the chapter that follows we offer suggestions that might help Nigerians not only to love change, but to actually change!

Chapter 14

Restorative Justice and Insurgency

People often hate each other because they fear each other;
they fear each other because they do not know each
other; they do not know each other because they cannot
communicate; and they cannot communicate because they
are separated.

—MARTIN LUTHER KING JR.

Introduction

In Nigeria's contemporary context, the vicious circle of violence and counter-violence is consequence of the vacuum created by lack of justice, and the celebration of injustice. Corruption perpetuated by Nigeria government officials has excluded many Nigerians from the seat of governance. Consequently, ordinary Nigerians' rights to life's abundance are denied. This situation has not only created anxiety but also concern about how to have access to justice. Some wonder whether it is possible to get justice in Nigeria today. They are often in doubt of whether they can get justice in the face of blatant systemic injustice. Asides, they are confused as to how they can go about finding justice through nonviolent means. The point is, if the Nigerian populaces see those who break the law getting what is due—justice—they probably would not take up arms and fight. In a situation where criminals pay their way out of justice the masses take the law into their hands.

This chapter discusses and pushes the boundary of possibility for re-habilitating and obliterating the birthing of would-be terrorists. We argue that since there will always be criminals, what is needed is the creation of a community-based system of restorative justice. We need to think deeply about the reasons why crimes are rampant in our communities. Something bigger than the symptoms—political, religious, ethnic violent conflicts—is happening. There are gaps that must be filled. As we have observed in chapter II about the paradox of man, we have to have structures in place that guarantee hope for a future for the people of Nigeria. The corruption of our moral values and visions produced by self-interest, deception and lust for power is dehumanizing us. Corruption of morality and ethics is not the monopoly of the Majority World government officials. It is an aggressive cancer destroying the human dignity of a generation of young men and women across the globe. The entire first, second and third worlds' government officials are involved in the practice of corruption and thereby exposing us to the ugly teeth of destructive human hostilities: terrorism. In other words, we are witnessing the collapse of social covenants, a context where social and cultural injustices hold sway, leaving us in a situation where many people feel alienated from the mainstream society and therefore easily get flared up. Money, sex and power have indeed become the sources of all evil and wickedness. By devaluing human dignity and integrity, supplanting them with monetary and sexual values, the human family has been increasingly dehumanized. The victims of the acts of corruption need urgent attention or else terror will continue to grip us. The wild living of people who eat us up by their corrupt practices is tearing us down. When I watched what is happening in my country Nigeria, I had an idea. I realized that it is not enough to empathize with the people who suffer loss, hurting and mourning. Rather I must seek to see that the perpetrators of those gruesome acts, are also victims of circumstances, they need to be recognized as members of the human family. One thought I had is that we must seek to do something more than use the military option. We must change their mindsets. This chapter offers some suggestions on how we might convince people who have perceived themselves as alienated by their society to feel that they belong again. They will need to be reassured of the community's willingness to take them back. The chapter argues that such communities need to first of all recognize them as part of them. Second, such communities must be creative enough to know what incentives to give those who are willing to come back into a community to which they once belonged. I found out that the Saudi Arabian government has created rehabilitation centers for ex-terrorists to be rehabilitated and reclaimed back to the mainstream society. The center is staffed by psychologists and counselors and Islamic Sheiks who have been trained from the West. These people work hard to rewire the mindset and disorient the ex-terrorists from jihadist ideologies. According to a report by American National Public Radio (NPR) of April 5, 2015, the center has had an eighty-eight percent success rate.

We should look at those who are part of our community and yet are harming us from the perspective of a nursing mother like Selinena Maritunga (not her real name) who told me of how her baby boy punches her in the face even when she is nursing him. Other times he bits her breast. All those actions cause pain. But she does not throw him away. We need to recognize that we are also broken. Just because I am a Christian doesn't mean that I have gotten it all together. As we have observed above, we live in a world where much dysfunctionality is happening. There is obviously so much disconnect. For example, families and the larger society are aggravating their children, and causing them to become discouraged with life in general. They are often made to feel alienated or estranged from the mainstream society. This attitude makes many people lack a sense of belonging. These kinds of children become easy prey to terrorist recruits and they often turn against us to harm us in order to assert their self-worth. Paul's advice is important: *Fathers, do not aggravate your children, or they will be discouraged"* (Col 3:20). To put this challenge in another perspective, the Lucan narrative of Jesus Christ's mission will provide some clue. Luke's account of the ministry of the twelve disciples in Luke 9:1–2 underscores two important facts about ministry in a hostile society. The text reads, "Then He called His twelve disciples together and gave them power and authority over all demons and diseases. He sent them to preach the kingdom of God and to heal the sick." Jesus gave His disciples "power and authority" in order "to preach the kingdom of God and to heal the sick." This is an interesting combination—power and authority plus preaching the kingdom of God and healing the sick.

Jesus gave them what he was to be given: "authority over the heavens and the earth" (Matt 28:18). This is a reminder that what Jesus has, ("power and authority") has also been given to us so that we can preach the kingdom of God, which includes among other things, justice. The next task is to heal the sick. This task of healing the sick encapsulates, among other things, the socially, psychologically, politically, economically and mentally sick. The concept of restorative justice fits the idea of the kingdom of God and the idea of healing the sick. The kingdom of God largely speaks of God's justice, love, peace and hope. Healing of the sick speaks of God transformation of social settings that are not favorable to human flourishing; and providing a humane society or community. Therefore as we discuss the task of living together in community, we need to see restorative justice as an important practice that might offer us hope. We are aware that the greatest challenge in the face of incessant violence is how to get people to believe that justice is possible, in spite of its apparent lack. In the Nigerian context we believe that what is most needed is justice which restores disconnected and estranged members of our society back to community with their fellow human beings. Restorative justice is a current concern of peacemakers across the globe.

Definition of Restorative Justice

There are several ways of looking at or defining the concept of restorative justice. "The Restorative Justice Consortium," whose members are national organizations and individuals interested in the promotion of restorative justice across the globe, uses the following definition on its leaflet: "Restorative Justice works to resolve conflict and repair harm. It encourages those who have caused harm to acknowledge the impact of what they have done and gives them an opportunity to make reparation . . ."[1]

Advocates of restorative justice are not just interested in punishing criminals but also in learning how the offender can be restored to his or her human community, where he or she will find a sense of human dignity again. It is taking tangible interest in the criminal to the extent that he or she has confidence that they are accepted back to community with other fellow humans. For example, there was a young man lost his parents and had nobody to care for him. He said that when he was a little boy two years of age, his mother died. When he was four, his father died. He had to live one place and then another; and he was a sinner. He was going to turn fourteen years old when he was caught committing a crime and charged to court. He tried to look at the judge. He felt so guilty. He didn't have any friends, and he was miserable. The court room was packed with people. They looked at him, and then at the judge. Their faces seemed to say, "Judge, give him the full penalty of the law and save us thee trouble later on." He felt as though the whole world was down on him. In a short while, a court clerk stood up and said, "This court is open." The judge said to a lawyer, I appoint you to take this boy's case." The lawyer took him to a private court room and talk to him privately. Young boy sank into a corner. He thought the lawyer was going to drag him to execution, and then the young boy saw tears under the lawyer's eyelashes. The lawyer sat down and slipped his arm around the young boy. The young boy said, "it was the most tender touch I ever felt and

---

1. Quoted in Liebmann, *Restorative Justice*, 25.

it drew to him." The lawyer then gave him a compassionate gaze in that by the time he asked, "My little friend, are you guilty of this crime?" the young man couldn't lie but tell the truth. He said, "Yes sir, I did and even more." While sobbing, the lawyer put his arm around the young man. The young man grabbed his coat to feel the warm embrace of a brother. Together, they walked back to the court room. When the case was called the defending attorney stood up with the young man. He spoke until silence filled every mouth. He spoke until the most beautiful language filled every corner of the court. He spoke until old men wept. He spoke until the policeman who arrested the young boy was brushing tears from his cheeks. The lawyer then looked at the judge and said, "If you will show compassion on this orphan child, I pledge, your honor, to look after his education and his upbringing, and give society a useful and productive citizen. I want to adopt him for my very own." The lawyer spoke until the young boy's heart nearly burst within him for love and admiration for his new found friend, the lawyer. And the young boy thought to himself, "If I could just put my ragged sleeves around his neck and kiss him just one time, they could have taken me out and hanged me, and I would have died happy." The young man was waiting for the judge to sentence him to prison. Then the greatest shock of all came. The lawyer spoke again to the judge and said, "Father" (that word, *father*, shot through the young boy like a bolt from the blue). Then the young boy suddenly reasoned, "The judge had appointed his own son to plead for me; surely he would have mercy on me.") "Father," the lawyer continued, "the intensity of my love for my little client comes from the fact that he is my brother." Then the judge stood up and said, "Rejoice, for the lost is found, and the dead is alive!"[2] The foregoing story illustrates what restorative justice is intended to achieve: It gives those who get estranged by their community and society a future with hope. Restorative justice holds hope for the Nigerian context which is characteristically a disconnected and fragmented society.

Proponents of restorative justice have discovered and recognized the tremendous potential that God has endowed the human community with the ability to bring healing in situations where people are broken. Lorraine Stutzman Amstutz tells of how "restorative justice has come to mean many things" but how those who are working in that field have undoubtedly realized that

> it provides an alternative way of viewing criminal justice and a different way of shaping a legal system to deal with crime. It is also a fresh way of responding to harm and wrongdoing in

2. This story is distilled from Ferguson, *Romans*, 109–111.

other—noncriminal, nonlegal—contexts. While the primary focus of restorative justice theory and work has been in the criminal justice arena, its principles and practices are being implemented outside that system. It is being adapted for use in schools, places of work, and churches, and it provides general principles to guide the work of living together in community.[3]

A new discovery has led to unprecedented attention on this subject. Proponents of restorative justice have discovered that prior to the coming of the modern era of colonization; traditional communities had a system of justice that worked like restorative justice. They were not just concerned about the punishment to be meted to the offender but also about how to restore him or her back to a communal life of participation.[4] To reduce the number of recruits for Boko Haram, Nigerian communities need to recover the methods of restorative justice which used to bring hope. Restorative justice is capable of transforming a "warped and crooked" generation into a humane society.

It should be seen from two angles: (1) preventive and (2) restorative. The former has been proposed by John Braithwaite. It fits the saying that prevention is better than cure. Braithwaite calls it a responsive regulatory approach. He writes, "The responsive regulatory approach is the framework for locating restorative justice in institutional spaces where it can best complement institutions of crime prevention, human and economic development, deterrence, incapacitation, and care and love for the land."[5] The primary reason why modern court systems were instituted was to regulate traditional cruelty. The legal definition of a crime is an act by the offender which violates another person. It is a violation of both person and relationship. In that case, when treating the case all parties involved should be given adequate attention. That is, the victim and the offender should both be of primary concern. This will involve making all offenders aware of the harm they have caused, to get them to understand and meet their liability to repair such harm, and to ensure that further offences are prevented. That is, the form and amount of reparation from the offender to the victim and the

---

3. Amstutz, "Restorative Justice," 24–30.

4 Ibid.

5. Braithwaite, *Restorative Justice & Responsive Regulation*, vii. The argument here is that restorative justice is good. But it must be realized that it has its flaws. Without checks and balances it can impose a punishment beyond that which would be imposed by the courts for that kind of wrongdoing (see ibid., 12). Braithwaite recognizes that the UN universal declaration has provided that regulation. The fifth article says, "No one shall be subjected to torture or to cruel, inhuman or degrading treatment or punishment."

measures to be taken to prevent re-offending should be decided collectively by offenders, victims and members of their communities through constructive dialogue in an informal and consensual process; and efforts should be made to improve the relationship between the offender and victim and to integrate the offender into the law-abiding community."[6]

Unlike retributive and distributive justice, restorative justice focuses on the "harmful effects of offender's action and actively involves victims and offenders in the process of reparation and rehabilitation."[7] Howard Zehr describes crime as a violation of people and relationships. It creates an obligation to make things right. Justice involves the victim, the offender, and the community in a search for solutions which promote repair, reconciliation, and reassurance. Therefore, Amstutz argues, "Restorative justice provides a framework for looking at justice through a set of values that includes respect, relationships, responsibility, and accountability to one another."[8] Unlike the contemporary justice system which ignores the need of the victim, restorative justice pays careful attention to the needs and interests of all involved, including the victim. The contemporary justice system focuses on what to do with the offender. It is offender-driven. The victim and the offender are both human beings with human dignity. They need to be seen beyond the crime. Practitioners of restorative justice have worked to address those concerns and seek ways to balance the needs of victims and offenders as well as the well-being of communities. Amstutz distilled what that entails: A key conviction of restorative justice holds that a just response to harm or wrongdoing must (1) work as much a s possible to repair the harm; (2) encourage taking appropriate responsibility for addressing needs and repairing the harm; and (3) involve those affected by harm or wrongdoing, including communities, in the resolution.[9]

Principles of Restorative Justice

Ethicists and theologians have distilled the following hallmarks of a restorative justice that are capable of altering the human condition and restoring humans back to wholesome community. (1) Victim support and healing is a priority: here the primary concern is the perceived and real needs of the victims. (2) Offenders take responsibility for what they have done: key concern here is to help the offender (s) to take responsibility for the wrong-doing

---

6. Johnston, *Restorative Justice*, viii.

7. Ibid.

8. Amstutz, *Restorative Justice*, 26.

9. Ibid., 24–30.

instead of merely "taking the punishment." (3) There is dialogue to achieve understanding: The intention here is to help the victims honestly tackle questions such as "why me? Why my house? Is it likely to happen again?" and so on, which they are wrestling with as the result of the crime. (4) There is an attempt to put right the harm done: here the offenders are encouraged to put things right, as far as is possible. (5) Offenders look at how to avoid future offending: This principle recognizes that what happened did not happen in a vacuum. It realizes that sometimes the offender felt offended or has problems that lead to offending, such as homelessness, drugs or alcohol. In such cases they may need considerable help to avoid future offending and build a different kind of life. They will need the resources that make it possible to avoid future occurrence. (6) The community helps to reintegrate both victim and offender: the sole purpose of restorative justice is to take the victim and the offender through a process of integration into the community. This involves, among other things, providing accommodation, jobs and relationships in order to enable them to become positive members of the community.[10]

Contemporary Examples of Restorative Justice

Following the ideas of restorative justice, practitioners of peacemaking have made remarkable contributions to peace building in Nigeria. According to Justin Welby, Archbishop of Canterbury, any genuine involvement in just peacemaking needs to focus on the prayer of Jesus, "Father, forgive, forgive, forgive" and "Love, love, love." He or she must like Andrew White who worked with Justin Welby in Nigeria for a while. White moved to Jerusalem and has been able to "inspire forgiveness and demonstrate love, both in word and above all in action." Like White and Welby did, whoever wants to build the Nigerian society must seek to "turn reconciliation into a lived-out reality." Just peacemaking practitioners are people who have come to the conclusion that "The Christian faith is based on the reconciliation of human beings with God through the self-giving love of Jesus."[11] This realization inspires action to be reconciled to one's rights.

Andrew Atherstone tells of how the International Center for Reconciliation (IRC) was founded after the German Luftwaffe obliterated Coventry city center during an intensive bombardment which marked an escalation in World War II and added a new verb to the dictionary, "to coventrate." More than 500 civilians were killed and the cathedral was destroyed

10. Liebmann, *Restorative Justice*, 26–27.
11. Welby, "Foreword," 11–12.

alongside many homes and factories. Instead of calling for revenge, Provost Dick Howard spoke of reconciliation and forgiveness. Amongst the rubble lay medieval nails from the cathedral's fallen roof, three of which were bound together in the shape of a cross. The cathedral rose again, built afresh by Basil Spence during the 1950s, but the shell of the old remained, symbolizing death and resurrection, devastation and renewal. The "ministry of reconciliation" (2 Cor 5:18) became a particular vocation of the cathedral community.[12] This is a great story that illustrates the importance of thinking about the victim and the offender, particularly how they can be reconciled and be restored to community with hope for a future free of crimes. Atherstone tells of Archbishop Justin Welby who became part of this ministry and worked in Nigeria, particularly in Kaduna and Jos, Plateaus State and in the Niger-Delta. Welby and his colleague Andrew White agreed to divide the work. Welby focused on Africa, especially in Nigeria while White focused on the Middle-East. Welby had worked with an oil company in Nigeria in the 1970s. He tells of how "Coventry diocese, had a particular relationship with Kaduna diocese, in central Nigeria, the location of intense tribal and religious violence between Muslim and Christian communities. Tensions were heightened by the implementation of Shari'a law in 2001 and by rhetoric surrounding the Miss World beauty pageant in Abuja the following year. In three days rioting in November 2002 several thousand people were killed and 25,000 left homeless. Three months earlier, Andrew White had brought together 22 senior Christian and Muslim clerics to sign the Kaduna Peace Declaration, modelled on the Alexandria Declaration. Whelby inherited this work, seeking to facilitate the implementation of the Kaduna Declaration.

One of his first involvements was a conference for Anglican clergy in January 2003 on the theme of reconciliation, based on the book of Jonah: "It was bitter and difficult, with many of the clergy very hurt by the events which they had seen, Churches had been burnt, parishioners killed and injured, they were seeking revenge not reconciliation." Welby quickly established a close friendship with Josiah Idowu-Fearon (Bishop of Kaduna from 1997 and the first Archbishop of Kaduna province from 2003), whom he praised as "a man of outstanding character, integrity and vision." Idowu-Fearon modelled for his clergy a passion to reconcile and willingness to dialogue with Muslim leaders. "As part of this peace-making ministry in 2004 Kaduna diocese launched Jacaranda Farm, 80 hectares with a health center attached, providing agricultural training for unemployed

---

12. See Howard, *Ruined and Rebuilt*; Spence, *Phoenix at Coventry*; Lamb, *Reconciling People*.

Christian and Muslim young men, who worked side by side. Its crops included mangos, cashew nuts, oranges, grapes, passion fruit, maize and sugar-cane."[13]Northern Ireland provides another great example of the efficacy and workability of restorative justice. Northern Ireland experienced a period of protracted war and violent conflicts. And in seeking a way out of the impasse, in 1985 an attempt was made by Extern (a voluntary organization) to provide a comprehensive scheme of restorative justice for Northern Ireland, which included among other things, "victim support, neighbourhood dispute service, juvenile and adult diversion, and court-based direct and indirect reparation." However, due to lack of adequate funding this attempt failed. Yet, the seed sown in 1985 was kept alive and well, resulting in the Ulster Quaker Service Committee (UQSC) organizing a conference late in 1994 "to learn about restorative justice and to consider possibilities for restorative justice in Northern Ireland criminal justice." Eventually, three initiatives started, based in statutory agencies during the late 1990s:

- A probation youth justice unit (ages 10 to 17)-post-court mediation (Davies 1999)

- Two police schemes (Royal Ulster constabulary) based on the work of Thames Valley Police: a restorative cautioning scheme in East Belfast and a retail theft initiative in BAllymena.[14]

Two large community restorative justice schemes developed in response to the political situation, following the ceasefire in 1994 and the subsequent Good Friday Agreement in 1998.[15] In short, given that Northern Ireland realized the elusive and salient shortcomings of the state criminal justice system, particularly in encouraging a sense of disconnect, "Considerable interest developed in restorative justice as an alternative way of dealing with anti-social behaviour, instead of the punishment beatings delivered by paramilitary groups."[16] It is clear that justice is associated with the basic requirements of life in community of hope. Basic needs are basic rights. Thus what is literally "the justice belonging to the needy" is properly translated as "the rights of the needy" (Jer 5:28; RSV). These rights, found by observing what matters are involved in the context of passages mentioning justice (cf. Job 24:1–12; 22:6–9; 23; 31:6, 17–19), include land (Ezek 45:9), food and clothing (Deut 10:18), and shelter (Job 8:6). Beyond the biblical context we have contemporary situations that have a lot to teach us about why injustice

---

13. Atherstone, *The Road to Canterbury*, 69–70, 73–74.

14. Liebmann, *Restorative Justice*, 47–48.

15. Ibid., 48.

16 Ibid.

occurs and what can be done. The Navajo tribe has discovered why people harm others. They claim that people largely harm others when they feel disconnected. What is responsible for this sense of disconnection? Several things may be involve. Restorative justice does not need lots of bureaucracy. That is why the state involvement in every aspects of the community social and cultural life has created a state of communal disconnect. There has been an assumption that the government facilities for justice are doing the job of restoring people to their relationship with the society.[17]

The point is that people who harm others do so because they have become so disconnected from the world around them, so disengaged from the people they live and work with each day, that they act no longer have a personal foundation. To remedy harm situations when they occur, to help those affected by a harm to begin upon the path of healing, historically the Navajo have taken steps that are consistent with their views on the "causes" of harm. They call upon the relatives of the persons responsible for the harm (as well as those of the person harmed) to come forth and help their kin reconnect with the community they live in or, as happens in the case of some, become connected to that community for the very first time. The Navajo call this process of connection and re-connection "peacemaking." It is a form of restorative justice an essential part of which is community members assembling to "talk things out" so that harmony might be restored to relationships that have been set on end.[18]

Biblical Israel and Restorative Justice

The Bible gives us every reason why we should take justice seriously. "As sacred texts, the Scriptures have offered Christians not only a moral compass but also a grand resource for envisioning an alternative world, one where peace prevails."[19] In exploring the aspects of law and legality in the Bible Jonathan Burnside (2011) distills ten top biblical texts which stress the importance of justice and how to pursue it. The key function of justice is to create a humane society. This is why Burnside observed that biblical law "is relational in character."[20] Burnside explains what he means by justice as relational: "One of the key turning points in the story of God and Israel is the Exodus, in which God rescues Israel from the condition of being enslaved to Pharaoh in Egypt (Exodus 12–13). Israel's experience of the

---

17. Sullivan and Tifft, *Handbook of Restorative Justice,* 9.

18. Ibid., 1.

19. Myers and Enns, *Ambassadors of Reconciliation,* 129.

20. Burnside, *God, Justice and Society,* 2.

Exodus becomes the motivation for obeying the law in Exodus 23:9."[21] Israel experienced social injustice and oppression in Egypt; they were expected therefore to understand what justice means. This also explains why the quest for justice is a primary concern of the Jews.

There are two key aspects to Israel's understanding of justice. "The call of justice has both an ideological and a practical aspect. First, Israel's ideology of adjudication is rooted in the central and overwhelming belief that God is the sole source of justice. All justice is therefore divine. Second, human judges are thought to be capable of mediating actual divine decisions."[22] The relational character of justice makes human relationships with God and with fellow human beings a covenant rather than a contract. Burnside stresses the importance of covenant. He explains that the word covenant can mean many different things in both the Bible and the ancient Near East (ANE). Basically, it consists of an obligation or an agreement between two parties. Covenants were an everyday fact of ancient life—like writing a check, making a promise, or doing a deal.[23] A covenant (*berit*) refers to "the binding commitment taken on by one or both the parties to an agreement, or even a unilateral decision." The obligatory nature of the agreement is reflected in the fact that one or both the parties swear an oath, although this is not always explicit.[24] The modern covenant is "an undertaking contained in a deed by which one party ("the covenantor") promises another party ("the covenantee") that he will or will not engage in some specified activity in relation to a defined area of land" (for example, the use of the a restrictive covenant to prevent building on land)."[25]

In order to pursue and maintain justice which could create a humane society, Israel was taught how to do it. Burnside lists ten top ways Israel was taught to pursue justice:

> Participants in Israel's judicial process should (1) believe that God is the ultimate source of justice [Gen 1:1—2:3; Deut 32:4]; (2) believe that judges have the potential to mediate actual divine decisions [Exod 18:19; Deut 1:16–17; 2 Chron 19:60]; (3) fight to overthrow the oppressor and liberate the oppressed [Ps 5:2; 72:4; 82:3; 146:7–9; Isa 32:1–2; 33:22]; (4) put things right—from God's perspective [Lev 25:23]; (5) put justice in the hands of the many, not the few [Exod 21:1; 24:12; Lev 10:11;

21. Ibid., 15.
22. Ibid., 103.
23. Ibid., 31.
24. Ibid.
25. Ibid., 33.

Deut 17:10–11]; (6) respect the position of provincial courts [Deut 17:8–13]; (7) involve a range of authorities in adjudication [Exod 23:1–8]; (8) sort out their own legal disputes [Prov 2:6–8; Exod 3; Isa 11:2]; (9) apply practical wisdom [Deut 17:18; 2 Chron 17:9; 19:10]; and (10) be inspired by a divine sense of justice [Exod 19:6].[26]

Israel needed to follow these ingredients of justice because she was to be an example to the rest of the global community. The above understanding is what the demand for justice is based. In the word of Dempsey and Shapiro, "God's people are called to liberate all creation from the bonds of injustice and maintain hospitality of heart for all, regardless of race, gender, creed, belief, status, orientation or condition in life."[27] For their part, Myers and Enns state that restorative efforts require "a deeper rehabilitation of human dignity and social equity."[28] A salient point in restorative justice is: Do not give up on people. The God we serve doesn't give up on us. He pursues us until he finds us and brings us back into community with himself. We need to imitate God who does not give up on any of us.

Restorative Justice in Traditional Nigerian Communities

Before the coming of the colonialists, various Nigerian communities had key ways of encouraging members of a community to belong and to remain resolute in ensuring restorative justice to erring members. But after the coming of the colonialists Nigerian governments developed what was known as customary court.[29] The colonialists came with their own cultural understanding of law and thought that the Nigerian traditional justice system was incompatible with industrialized societies' laws. This conclusion obviously led to the colonial "legal reformers" believing that "the informal network of relationships that characterize traditional justice were not compatible with industrial societies." It also led to certain ethnic groups (for instance the Igbo people of Eastern Nigeria) rejecting the new arrangement. Consequently Elechi described the situation thus:

> Colonial administration and the social and political institutions introduced affected the democratic character of the society. These were especially so with the imposition of warrant chiefs as custodians of the courts. These chiefs were blamed for

26. Ibid., 103–4.

27. Dempsey and Shapiro, *Reading the Bible*, 129.

28. Ibid.

29. Elechi, *Doing Justice Without the State*, 109.

inaugurating a painful era of political and social disharmony, political corruption, authoritarianism, and various forms of colonial oppression and exploitation.[30]

The colonial system deprived the community of the skills of restorative justice: reconciliation, restoration into community and rehabilitation. The native courts that warrant chiefs were handling gradually became disconnected in that the warrant chiefs eventually lost the confidence of the ordinary peasant. They became secured in their places by government backing and no longer subject to the former sanctions to which an African chief was liable at the hands of his people if he does not comport himself well, is losing them much measure of popular support and acceptance.[31] This is a very serious matter because when human beings feel disconnect they see that immediately as form of oppression and injustice which they must resist at all cost. Tanzania today has succeeded in maintaining peace, order and justice because the state has had an "interest in maintaining its presence in all aspects of the people's life." Thus Christie states, "the socialist government of Tanzania's sponsorship of alternative conflict resolution . . . should be understood in this respect. Here, local party officials with other villages organize themselves for the purpose of resolving conflicts amongst the people."[32] The traditional restorative-justice system has the idea of win-win. By and large, it is the Nigerian understanding of win-win in conflict resolution that led General Yakubu Gowon to state immediately after the Nigerian civil war ended in 1970, "No victor, no vanquisher."[33]

There is a grave inconsistency in thinking about the question of justice. Most Christians' understanding of our cycle of moral obligation is parochial. They want justice done to those outside their "circle of moral obligation" but are not equally willing to let justice take its course on those within their "circle of moral obligation" who erred against justice. Simply put, Christians want justice and peace but, like all other Nigerians, they are not ready to allow justice to take its course on their relatives who are arrested and charged in court for taking the law into their hand. Fear causes us to build walls instead of building bridges of human flourishing. Justice is a critical virtue in human relations. It guarantees the equitable distribution of God's given resources for the enhancement of human life. That is why social ethicists define it as what is owed to you or what you owe to other fellow men and women. It is rendering to everyone that which is his or her

30. Ibid., 107.
31. Ibid.
32. Ibid., 110.
33. General Yakubu Gowon, *Daily Trust*, November 4, 2013.

due. Some definitions of justice tend to distinguish it from equity. That is, they argue that while justice means merely the doing of what positive law demands, equity means the doing of what is fair and right in every separate case. Realizing that justice includes equity will help us think outside the box. It will enable us to grasp the bigger picture of what needs to be done. Isaiah is one of the prophets who privileged justice in their penetrating insights into Israel's moral history and journey with Yahweh, God. In his day, both God and the people of Israel looked for justice but they could not find it: "We look for justice, but find none, for deliverance, but it is far away" (Isa 59:11). The Lord, their God, also looked for justice only to be disappointed by its lack: "The LORD looked and was displeased that there was no justice" (Isa 59:15). Isaiah identified the absence of truth-telling as the major reason for the conspicuous absence of justice. He also drew his people's attention to the fact that the absence of truth-telling vis-à-vis justice is a theological problem. It is a symptom of how God's people have decided to stop listening to God. They described the whole process to include, "Turning our backs on our God, fomenting oppression and revolt, uttering lies our hearts have conceived. So justice is driven back, and righteousness stands at a distance" (Isa 59:13–15).On the one hand, lies and falsehood are direct opposite paths to justice. On the other hand, the paths of justice include, among other things, truth-telling, love, justice, mercy, compassion, peace, etc. It is essential that Christians pay careful attention to the following crucial issues in discussing justice: the author of justice, human agents of justice, foundation of justice, types of justice, focus of justice, and how to pursue justice nonviolently where there is an apparent absence of justice.

True Justice Belongs to God

God is the author of justice. "The biblical view of reality corresponds to the complexity of the reality in which we live."[34] Theologians and Bible scholars tell us that justice is one of the attributes of God. That is, it is his essence. We have noted that the Servant of the Lord song reveals that the mission of the Servant includes bringing justice to the nations. Isaiah's view of history demonstrates that "history unfolds according to how human society relates to the sphere of powers that is beyond it. YHWH's "strange work" is the divine response to the people's violation of the torah, and this "strange work" is the central content of the commission Isaiah receives in Isaiah 6:9–10."[35] By telling his audience that the Servant of the Lord will bring justice to the

34. Schroeder, History, Justice, and the Agency of God, xi.

35. Ibid., 3.

nation, the Prophet Isaiah infers that God is a God of justice: justice is God's nature. It also means that God is the Creator of all the nations. Therefore, His rules and decrees are binding on all nations, for "YHWH's power transcends all national borders and has a universal dimension."[36] In a context where the general social experience is absent of justice, we have good news. The good news is, God *is righteous in Himself and in all He does*. Justice is the moral character and virtue of God, *the righteousness of the divine nature exercised in his moral government*. When we experience an apparent lack of justice, it does not mean that human beings do not have a clue to what justice is. It just means that they have chosen to ignore their God-given moral agency.

The Human Agents of Justice

God has created every human being with a moral law, moral conscience and the potential for moral character. However, as we have noted in chapter II, the Fall has distorted this moral law that is supposed to help us render to each other what is rightly due. Human beings are today prompted to self-interest and the will to power, exploitation and domination. For this reason, God has instituted human government to serve as the custodian of his justice. He has given government the power and the responsibility of ensuring the rightful exercise of his justice on earth. Justice is therefore the standard through which the government distributes the benefits and penalties of living in society. For example, it is only the government that is permitted to carry out capital punishment. God ordains governments, and has given them the responsibility to provide basic community services, provide for the general welfare, provide social guidelines and punish those who will not live within them. These are some of the things that God has promised to provide for us. It is quite reasonable that God uses the government to provide for some of our needs. Imagine what life would be like to live with no government. Without the protection of social law, unrestricted sin would abound. There would be little or no possibility for God to work in the lives of people. Government, good or bad, has a purpose and responsibility under God.

There is a sense in which God expects every one of us to model his moral law in his or her interpersonal relationships, particularly to the vulnerable in society. Special attention to the poor and the weak characterizes God's justice; therefore, God expects a corresponding quality of justice of his

36. Ibid.

people (Deut 10:18–19). When we properly carry out justice, we are agents of the divine will (Isa 59:15–16). Consequently, Apostle Paul presents God's justice as a grace flowing into and through the believers to the needy (2 Cor 9:8–10). The demand of God for justice is so central that other responses to God are empty or diminished if they exist without it (Amos 5:21–24; Mic 6:6–8; Matt 23:23). The point is, justice is demanded of all the people, but particularly of the political authorities (Jer 21:11–12; Isa 1:10, 17).

Essential Elements in the Pursuit of Justice

Types of Justice

By types of justice, I am referring to the spheres of the application of justice in real life. There are different dimensions or spheres in which justice is applied. For the sake of space, I will briefly mention just a few. First, legislative justice: God's legislative justice is his requiring of his rational creatures conformity in all respects to the moral law. Second, distributive justice: God's distributive is his dealing with his accountable-creatures according to the requirements of the law in rewarding or punishing them (Ps 89:14). Third, remunerative justice: In God's remunerative justice he distributes rewards (James 1:12; 2 Tim 4:8). Fourth, vindictive or punitive justice: In God's vindictive or punitive justice he inflicts punishment because of transgression without of fear or favor (2 Thess 1:6).

The Focus of Justice

Given that many people are confused when it comes to pursuing justice, it is important to stress here that justice is closely related to love, compassion, mercy, grace and peace (Deuteronomy. 10:18–19; Hosea 10:12) rather than being a contrasting principle. It thus provides vindication, deliverance, and creation of community in addition to retribution. John Rawls tells us that need is the criterion for distributing benefits. This criterion does not in any away exclude ability as a criterion once this priority is met. Thus the focus is upon the oppressed—with particular attention given to specific groups, such as the poor, widows, the fatherless, slaves, resident aliens, wage earners, and those with physical infirmities (Job 29:12–17; Ps 146:7–9; Mal 3:5).

It has been very difficult for ordinary Nigerians to pursue justice nonviolently because law enforcement agencies create certain potential barriers. They have not allowed the rule of law and due process to take their course (Exod 23:1–3, 6–8). The context for the carrying out of justice is the creation of community and the preservation of people in it (Lev 25:35–36; Job 24:5; Ps 107:36; Luke 7:29–30). Whoever engages in the effort of seeking social redress must avoid repeating the wrongs of the oppressors. He or she must seek the deliverance of both the oppressed and the oppressor. He or she must be cognizant of the fact that God is both the God of justice and of love. That is why justice is a deliverance, rectifying the gross social inequities of the disadvantaged (Ps 76:9). It puts an end to the conditions that produce the injustice (Ps 10:18). In the final analysis, therefore, a Christian advocate of restorative justice, love and peace seeks the deliverance of both the oppressed and the oppressors. They recognize the fact that both are in captivity.

Conclusion

The focus on restorative justice is a critique of the state's approach to the matter of justice. Proponents of restorative justice argue that the state has created a situation where the community has been crippled to the extent that it no longer has the wherewithal to engage its members in the journey of forgiveness, reconciliation, restoration and reconstruction (transformation). Restorative justice provides a fresh understanding of the concept of dialogue and places it at the center of community discourse. To restore entails the process of bringing someone or something to its original state or to where it belongs. It means reinstating someone to hers or his human God-given dignity. By and large, dialogue as a concept and as part of the Christian comprehensive understanding of God's justice and love which necessitated the incarnation is yet to be fully implemented. We dialogue because we believe in justice, love and peace. We talk to the "other" because we see the "other" as our brother or sister, in the family of the human community. We dialogue with the "other" because we believe in justice and want the "other" to know that we care about justice, love, and peace.

Chapter 15

Violence and Christian Eschatology

Every trial endured and weathered in the right spirit
makes a soul nobler and stronger than it was before.

—JAMES BUCKHAM

Introduction

The end of all violent conflicts is in sight! Thus, Christian eschatology is supposed to inspire endurance, tenacity and hope in a world of universal hostility, change and decay. We have so far affirmed that African Christians and the entire global community face various problems of social existence—corruption, social injustice, poverty, violence, terrorism, instability and so on—which are in all respects the byproducts of the fallen condition of humans.[1] Therefore, in this chapter we conclude our discussion on when evil strikes: faith and the politics of human hostility by discussing Christianity and other faiths' notion of the eschaton and how that shape and form their present faith and praxis. For Christianity, two or more fundamental reasons necessitate this: First, if you take way the eschaton in Christian worldview and morality the Christian present or future life will be utterly empty and incredibly miserable. The idea of the end of time and space will be a source of crippling fear, paranoia and hostility, instead of hope. Second, with

1. Katongole, *A Future for Africa*, xi.

secularism and naturalistic humanism lethally colonizing public sphere in the West and North America, eschatological perspectives which sustained and stabilized Christian ethics and hopes are being eroded. Third, eschatology is extremely important in forming Christian beliefs, ethics and morality. A Christian eschatological perspective is rooted in the essence of Christian quest for transformation of the mind and taking it captive so that it become totally obedient to Christ in this life. Thus it requires turning away from a life of wickedness to a life of right living, which is characterized by a way of life that honours and respects God's revealed truth.[2] Therefore, this book cannot overemphasize the importance of taking eschatology seriously.

The Nature and Scope of Christian Eschatology

Christian eschatological orientation is often expected to produce moral and ethical templates that guide its adherents in any given generation. Eschatology requires Christians who are now living to know what will happen in the future. It inspires hope for the present and the hereafter. For example, St. John writes: "Dear children, now we are children of God, and what we will be has not yet been made known. But we know that when he appears, we shall be like him for we shall see him as he is. Everyone who has this hope in him purifies himself, just as he is pure."[3] Eschatology is the belief about the final outcome of human life, value, belief and practice—good or bad—and the rest of God's creation. It is about the link between the present and the future, particularly what the future holds in store for all humans and all of God's creation.[4] Christian eschatology is generally defined as the doctrine of the last things, the end of the present world of time and space. Some proponents of this perspective have tended to see eschatology as independent from the Christian doctrine of creation. Eschatology is both and individual and a corporate idea. It is both cosmic (universal) and particular. Its major theoretical and ideological concerns are not only about the end of times and space but also about the present. It is a belief that is rooted in the Judeo-Christian Scriptures which gives a positive picture of the end of this present

2. John writes: "This is the message we have heard from him and declare to you: God is light; in him there is no darkness at all. If we claim to have fellowship with him yet walk in the darkness, we lie and do not live by the truth. But if we walk in the light, as he is in the light, we have fellowship with one another, and the blood of Jesus, his Son, purifies us from all sin" (1 John 1:5–7). He further said, "We know that we have passed from death to life, because we love our brothers. Anyone who does not love remains in death" (1 John 3:14). See also 2 John 4–5 NIV.

3. 1 John 3:2–3.

4. Hiebert, *Transforming Worldviews*, 45.

earth and the galaxies and the ushering in of a new heaven and new earth. From the vintage point of humanity the present body will be translated into a celestial body, mortality to immortality, the end of suffering and death and the experience of permanent joy, peace, security and freedom. In the Christian Scripture there are beliefs known as "the millennial beliefs," which, as Ojo observed, are generally sustained by four major factors:

1. Firstly, there is a dualistic worldview in which the world is seen as a battleground between good and evil, and we the faithful often side with God.

2. Secondly, events are interpreted in time perspectives and very often particular dates can be set, i.e., the entry points into a millennium, as had happened in 2000.[5]

3. Thirdly, certain sensational events have fuelled apocalyptic prophecies, particularly when they are interpreted as historical events leading towards the consummation of the end. A revelatory understanding of world social and political events or the power to attempt allegorical or symbolical interpretations all that are needed in selecting, interpreting and applying certain events to human lives.

4. Lastly, millennial groups often conceive salvation within the collective realm. The individual functions only within the group expectation, and the millennialist vision often looks towards the end time when all the faithful will be redeemed. Consequently preparations for the millennial end are done collectively. Within this context, charismatic leaders with messianic beliefs often thrive well. The salvation hoped for could be interpreted culturally, politically or religiously.[6]

Ojo is addressing only one group of people whose understanding of eschatology shapes their worldview and impacts their ethics and praxis. Millennialists are not the only group of Christian people who belief in eschatology, as Brian E. Daley demonstrates below. In his extensive study of the eschatological faith of the early Church, Daley noted that eschatological faith finds expression in different dimensions.

---

5 Jesus said regarding the time of his return, "No one knows about that day or hour, not even the angels in heaven, nor the Son, but only the Father" (Matt 24:36. Cf 25:19). Yet, Christians across the centuries have tried to predict the following dates: 1248, 1306, 1689, 1792, 1836, 1844, 1914, 1936, 1960, 1974, 1981, 1988, 1989, 1992, 1994, and 2011. See Frank Viola, "Rethinking the Second Coming of Christ," *Beyond Evangelical* (blog), July 1, 2013, http://frankviola.org/2013/07/01/secondcoming/.

6. Ojo, "Eschatology and the African Society," 95.

1. For people living under oppression or persecution, eschatological hope has often meant simply the overriding, radically optimistic sense that the present intolerable order of things is about to end. This sense of crisis, of challenge and promise, has usually been expressed by Christians in apocalyptic images: dramatic expectations of cosmic violence that will destroy the world and its institutions completely and let God begin again, powerfully saving his own.

2. For people living in times of social or economic strain, eschatological hope has meant a similarly strong conviction that the world is "growing old," running out of resources, facing depletion from within, and a similar trust that the end of its natural processes will mean the beginning of a new world, and for humanity a fresh start.

3. For others, living in periods of great public security and of individual freedom and competitiveness, eschatological hope has often been something quite difficult: an ordered doctrine of the "last things," personal expectation of final justice and retribution, personal longing for rest and satisfaction in a new life that will begin at death.

4. For the philosophical cultivate believer, eschatology can be the expression in future terms of underlying assumptions about the true nature of the mind, the person and the material world.

5. For the intensely religious person—the ascetic or the mystic—it can mean a trust that union with God in knowledge and love, which has already begun in this present life of faith, will someday be consummated in an existence free from all the limits and shadows.[7]

Daley's analysis underscores the fact that eschatology is fundamentally a doctrine that touches all cultures and contexts of human existence. His analysis lends credence to the claim that eschatology is not uniquely a Christian innovation. All humans have some sense of eschatology in their worldviews. This leads to the question, what is "hope" as it pertains to humankind in the midst of suffering? What are the implications of our Hope being an omnipotent God who promises to be with us always? Most importantly, "Is Christian eschatology a source of fear, paranoia, hostility or hope?" To answer these questions one needs to acknowledge that every human being born into this world has perception of the end of life. The desire for happiness, security, peace and freedom from a life of suffering or pain causes us to look forward to a time when these human desires and needs could be perfectly realized. The Christian doctrine of eschatology fits

7. Daley, *The Hope of the Early Church*, 15–16.

this desire to see the end of a broken and decaying world, which brings with it all forms of hardship and disappointments. It also has the idea of the last judgment and final punishment that will send people to their eternal destinations: hell or paradise. A true believer in Christ knows that he or she will not be condemned to hell because Jesus Christ has paid the price for his or her sins. But those who have no hope in the salvation of Christ have no other choice than to face the fear of the last punishment. "The one who fears is not made perfect in love." In the next section we discuss how the eschatological belief functions across religious cultures.

The Role of Eschatological Beliefs across Cultures

All eschatological hopefuls have shared understanding. They center on how the present life has implication to the life to come: the end of life, the afterlife and the judgment that results. This judgment is specifically on what one has done with the body while in this life.

The Eschatology of Ancient Judaism

As the chosen people of God, the Jews received God's special revelation. When they think of the future they are likely to go back to the biblical text to study what their prophets have told them about what God has said will happen. But there are times that they still have to face the challenge of living in a world of human limitation and doubt. Therefore, to give them a future with hope, they employ the concept of resurrection as one of the beliefs that encourages them to go on in spite of lack of certainty. N. T. Wright observed, "The Jewish hope burst the bounds of ancient paganism altogether by speaking of resurrection."[8] According to Wright, the second temple Judaism had developed a concept of resurrection to help it figure out the eschatological incentives that were needed to survive the occupation of their land by the Romans. Wright says that the term "resurrection" in both paganism and Judaism refers to the reversal, the undoing, the conquest of death and its effects.[9] Resurrection, in other words, means being given back one's body, or perhaps God creating a new similar body, sometime after death.[10] In the Jewish socio-cultural and socio-religious contexts, it is not everybody that agrees with the conception of resurrection after death.[11]

8. Wright, "Sketches," 42.
9. Ibid.
10. Ibid.
11. Ibid.

The Eschatology of the Early Christians

The early church is a shining illustration of how the Christian eschaton inspires hope. Of course, in the early church, eschatological language was ingrained in thoughts of a contrast between imminence and transcendence. Because of the presence of evil in the world, there is always a quest for paradise which produced disillusionment, fear, paranoia and despair.[12] The first century Christians saw their era as "the last hour." In his writings St. John categorically asserts, "This is the last hour" (1 John 2:18 NIV). He further said, "The world and its desires pass away, but the man who does the will of God lives forever . . . And now, dear children, continue in him, so that when he appears we may be confident and unashamed before him at his coming" (1 John 2:17, 28 NIV). In short, for the first century Christian eschatology entails the facing out of the old world of human passion and desires which are not in line with God's purposes. They believed that Jesus was going to return immediately.[13] They needed such a strong dosage of conviction and belief to sustain them through the turbulent years of persecution.

The eschaton helped early Christians to endure persecution. We catch a glim of what their take on eschatology was from the writings of the Apostles. In talking with his son in the Lord, Timothy, Paul states,

> For God has not given us a spirit of fear and timidity, but of power, love and self-discipline . . . By the appearing of Christ, our Savior . . . He broke the power of death and illuminated the way of life and immortality through the Good News. And God chose me to be a preacher, an apostle, and a teacher of this Good News. That is why I am suffering here in prison. But I am not ashamed of it, for I know the One in whom I trust, and I am sure that He is able to guard what I have entrusted to Him until the day of His return. (2 Tim 1:8–12 NLT)

In this text, there is a firm belief in the Trinitarian theology (theology, Christology and pneumatology) which inherently and coherently connects the past, the present and the future together. The interplay of the past, present and future have a huge influence on the present ethics and morality is created: power *with*, love and self-discipline. These ethical and moral traits play a significant role in our perspectives on present experiences of sufferings and disgraces. In the past, God broke the power of death. God called

12. Lincoln, *Paradise Now and Not Yet*, 16. Lincoln points out that "the issue of a transcendent dimension still plays a major role in the cultural and religious scene, is integral to contemporary theological debate and is crucial for determining the life-style of both the Church and the individual Christian" (ibid., 18).

13. Daley, *The Hope of the Early Church*, 17.

and chose people to be preachers, apostles and teachers of the Good News: The appearing of Christ, our Savior. In the future our Savior Jesus Christ will return. So as we live in this present life, nothing can intimidate us, humiliate us, threatens us. Beyond Paul's and the other apostles' generation, we have evidences of the early Christians continuing to count their lives worth nothing than to suffer for Christ's sake. "Yes, and everyone who wants to live a godly life in Christ Jesus will suffer persecution" (2 Tim 3:12).

Josiah W. Leeds tells of how because of Christ's salvific act on the cross, eschatological perspective was not just a hope for the future but hope for what is possible now. Leeds paints a picture of how the early believers did not see eschatology as something that has to do with the future only but as a concept that keeps faith alive and well even in the present. In their genuine portrayal of hope for a future we see a thread: the eschaton gives hopes for present possibilities of change. This hope makes it much easier for the Christians to endure persecution. They saw themselves as a profound witness to the truth that God has called us to be the true light that shines in the darkness that stands between the present age and the new heaven and the new earth that we are asked to "wait, watch and hasten."[14] Leeds draws from the writings of the early fathers. For example, in the writings of Justin Martyr this revelation is very poignant. "Justin Martyr was born at Neapolis, of Samaria—the modern Nablouse—about AD 114. He was diligent in studying the various philosophies, especially those of Stoics, Platonists and Pythagoreans; but finally, having discovered the emptiness of them all, was converted to Christianity. He travelled much, and hence was well-informed as to that whereof he wrote. At Rome, in the year 165, and in the reign of the Emperor Marcus Aurelius, he suffered martyrdom."[15] Before his martyrdom however, Justin Martyr wrote two significant apologies.

The first Apology was addressed to the Roman Emperor Antoninus Pius and the people; the second Apology, to the Roman Senate. The extracts which follow are from those writings. These extracts are very revealing. The extracts illustrate the significant role eschatology played in the life of the early Christians. Justin Martyr writes:

> And when you hear that we look for a kingdom, you suppose, without making any inquiry, that we speak of a human kingdom; whereas, we speak of that which is with God, as appears also from the confession of their faith made by those who are charged with being Christians, though they know that death is the punishment awarded to him who so confesses. For if we

<del>

</del>

14. Moltmann, *Ethics of Hope*, 6–8.
15. Leeds, *The Primitive Christian Estimate of War*, 5.

looked for a human kingdom, we should also *deny our Christ,
that we might not be slain;* and we should strive to escape de-
tection, that we might obtain what we expect. But, since our
thoughts are not fixed on the present, we are not concerned
when men cut us off: since also death is a debt which must at all
events be paid.[16]

Justin's writing illustrates how the coming of Christ created a biblical Christianity which provides its adherents with a richer worldview. This
worldview enables hope for a transforming present and a peaceful future.
This hope enables Christ's adherents to collapse the present with the future.
That is, "In hope we link far-off goals with goals within reach."[17] This worldview is comparably different from a non-Christian worldview, which is
characterized by the idea of a future with fear and paranoia. To some extent,
fear and paranoia are not necessarily evil. But like Moltmann argues, they
"are early warning systems of possible dangers and are necessary for living.
As long as potential dangers can be discerned and named, they give rise to
fears which impel us to do what is necessary in good time, and so to avert
the dangers."[18] However, the Christian fear and paranoia are different from
those of unbelievers or pagans. The hope that eschatology inspires comes
from a radical transformation that has taken place. Justin Martyr alludes to
that when he argues:

We who hated and destroyed one another, and on account of
their different manners would not live with men of a different
tribe, now, since the coming of Christ, live familiarly with them,
and pray for our enemies, and endeavor to persuade those who
hate us unjustly to live conformably to the good precepts of
Christ, to the end that they may become partakers with us of
the same joyful hope of a reward from God, the ruler of all. And
when the Spirit of prophecy speaks in this way: "For out of Zion
shall go forth the law, and the word of the Lord from Jerusalem.
And he shall judge among the nations, and shall rebuke many
people; and hey shall beat their swords into plowshares, and
their spears into pruning-hooks: nation shall not lift up sword
against nation, neither shall they learn war anymore." And that
it did so come to pass we can convince you. For from Jerusalem
there went out into the world men, twelve in number, and these
illiterate, of no ability in speaking: but by the power of God they
proclaimed to every race of men that they were sent by Christ

16. Ibid.
17. Moltmann, *Ethics of Hope*, 3.
18. Ibid.

to teach to all the word of God; and we who formerly used to murder one another, do not only now refrain from a king war upon our enemies, but also, that we may not lie or deceive our examiners, willingly die confessing Christ. but if the *soldiers* enrolled by you, and who have taken the military oath, prefers their allegiance to their own life, and parents, and country and all kindred, though you can offer them nothing incorruptible, it were verily ridiculous if we, who earnestly long for incorruption, *should not endure all things,* in order to obtain what we desire from Him who is able to grant it.[19]

The forgoing quote implies that what is happening now heralds God's future, "So that Christian action, inspired by hope, become the anticipation of the coming kingdom in which righteousness and peace kissed each other."[20] The period between Jesus Christ's incarnation, suffering, death, resurrection, ascension and the second coming or returning to earth is intrinsically linked. In other words, "God's coming unfolds a transforming power in the present."[21] Thus Justin Martyr writes:

And we who we *filled with war and mutual slaughter,* and every wickedness, *have each through the whole earth changed our warlike weapons*—our swords into plowshares, and our spears into implements of tillage—and we cultivate piety, righteousness, philanthropy, faith and hope, which we have from the Father himself, through him who was crucified. Now, it is evident that no one can terrify or subdue us who have believed in Jesus over all the world, . . . but the more such things happen [persecutions and deaths], the more do others and in larger numbers become faithful, and worshippers of God through the name of Jesus.[22]

It is instructive to note that Justin Martyr reads the Isaiah prophecy not as something that is going to happen only in the future but also as a reality that is already happening in the Christian community across the globe. Our past life was a life of fear, paranoia, hostility and even war. We were afraid of something as simple as human differences. We hated those who were different from us. We were headhunters but now, in view of what Christ has done on the cross and what we hope for ahead; we have turned our swords to plowshares and our spears into pruning-hooks. That is our minds have been renewed and transformed. We are even enabled to absorb pains, sufferings

19. Leeds, *The Primitive Christian Estimate of War,* 5.

20. Moltmann, *Ethics of Hope,* 4.

21. Ibid., 7.

22. Leeds, *The Primitive Christian Estimate of War,* 6–7.

and death because we have incredible hope in an "uncorruptable future life.." For the early Christians therefore, there was nothing like eschatology causing paranoia or fear. For like Moltmann observes, "Christian hope is founded on Christ's resurrection and opens up a life in the light of God's new world."[23] An eschatology that inspires fear and paranoia is one that is overwhelmed by present crises to the extent of not seeing the chances and opportunities and possibilities in the crises.[24] What inspires hope in Christian eschatology is the idea of the present in-breaking of the rule of God in all of life. In His public ministry, the kingdom of God was a central pierce of Jesus' proclamation. Of course, he proclaimed the arrival of the kingdom of God at time that it was difficult for his audience to understand it. The Israelites who had been living under foreign power were looking forward to a human Messiah, a Davidic figure, who will restore Israel to an earthly kingdom. Jesus brought Good News that makes the future expectation of Israel a present reality. He made it his personal goal to reveal the present reality of the rule of God (kingdom of God). This is illustrated in the prayer Jesus taught his disciples. When his disciples asked him to teach them how to pray, Jesus used the occasion to offer a moral vision that encapsulates the idea of the present reality of the kingdom of God. Roland Chia tells of how in teaching the disciples how to pray, Jesus places the petition for the coming of the kingdom between two other petitions, "the one for the hallowing of the name of God and the one concerning obedience to his will (Matt 6:9–10). The coming of the kingdom therefore has to do with man's worship of God and his obedience to God's word—the carrying out of the divine will, on earth as in heaven."[25]

Jesus points his disciples to the reversal that comes with the arrival of the kingdom of God. In his table fellowship, he included the tax-collectors, prostitutes, sinners, and lepers (all the outcasts). In eating with these categories of the people, Jesus was pointing to the present reality of God's reign. The reality of the reign of God is here and but also not yet. And because the reign of God has been inaugurated, we cannot longer live as if God does not exist. Chilton and McDonald describe how an ethics of the kingdom of God shapes our present life as we look forward to the future consummation of the kingdom of God. They argue that Christian perspective on eschatology creates a new morality which Chilton and McDonald have summarized as follows:

23. Moltmann, *Ethics of Hope*, 5.

24. Ibid., 4.

25. Chia, *Hope for the World*, 51.

1. The reversal of worldly values and a new lifestyle of service, servant-hood and humility;

2. Receiving the yoke of the kingdom in childlike fashion;

3. Sacrificing human reliance on worldly support-systems;

4. Being healed from [moral] blindness and following Jesus' way with faith-perception;

5. Seeking justice and surrendering false values such as wealth, status-seeking and power.

6. The focus of the new obedience is found in the twin commandments to love.[26]

The inauguration of the Kingdom of God and the unveiling of God's character are an open invitation to all believers in Christ to participate in the present reality of the Kingdom of God or the reign of God. The ethics of the kingdom recognizes that God is the ultimate source of morality.

Islamic Eschatology

Islam was founded during the turbulent era of Christianity and the catastrophic influence of Zoroastrianism. So as Christianity and Judaism, Islam places premium on eschatology. As a matter of fact there is no way one can become a true Muslim without belief in the Last Day.[27] That is to say, belief in the Last Day is one of the five pillars of the Islamic faith. To be a genuine Muslim one must believe in Allah, the Last Day, Angels, Scripture, and Allah's Prophets. In Islam, the signs of the Last Day are divided into two: Major and minor signs. The minor signs are those signs which precede the major signs. They are like what Jesus called "the beginning of birth pang" in the Gospels. Muslims—Sunnis and Shiites—are divided in their belief about the Last Day. What I have here is specifically on the belief of Sunni Muslims who are the largest Muslim group in the world. For lack of space, I will state one of the things that Sunni Muslims believe about the Last Day: Crossing the Bridge.[28] Sunni Muslims believe that after the appearance of

26. Chilton and McDonald, *Jesus and the Ethics*, 53, 73, 86–87, 91–92, as cited by Stassen and Gushee, *Kingdom Ethics*, 21.

27. From the Quran we read: "It is not righteousness that ye turn your faces to the East and the West; but righteous is he who believeth in Allah and the Last Day and the angels and the Scripture and the prophets . . ." (Surah 2:177, Pickthall translation).

28. For further details on Islamic eschatology see Warren F. Larson, "Islamic Eschatology: Implications for Christian Witness," last updated November 11, 2011. http://www.ciu.edu/faculty-publications/article/islamic-eschatology-implications-christian-witness

the Antichrist and the terrible suffering that will ensue, Jesus Christ will defeat the Antichrist and then proclaim Islam as the true religion and all Christians will convert to Islam, while all other faiths will be condemned. "The Hour" or the Judgment Day will take place after the resurrection. After the judgment, to enter paradise everyone has to cross a bridge that spans the gulf of Hell. Mohammed will be the first person to cross. Those who are condemned will fall from the bridge into Hell. The faithful will be able to cross to the other side. But there is no guarantee that they will not fall into Hell. This is because Allah is an arbitrary god. Therefore, even the faithful will cross in fear, hoping He does not change His mind.[29] This kind of eschatological belief is a source of fear and paranoia. One of the fearful things in Islamic eschatology is crossing the bridge. If there was anything one could do to avoid crossing the bridge that would have been great. The Islamic teaching on jihad, martyrdom meets this crucial need. It provides this eschatological incentive. Jihad is generally a war fought by Muslim faithful to promote the religion of Islam. David Bukay observed that in Islamic beliefs and practices, the martyr is one killed in jihad. He is entitled to special status in paradise and on the Day of Judgment.[30] Young Muslims are often given a fair dose of Islamic eschatology so that they will not even dream of leaving Islam. They often live in constant fear and paranoia. The only way they can alleviate their fear and paranoia is to participate in jihad. Their Koranic teachers always inform them that when they die while fighting for the religion of Allah to reign in the world, they will not have to cross the dreadful bridge. Instead they will have all the goodies of paradise, including having access to seven beautiful virgins. Anonymous Muslim who got converted to Christianity share this testimony:

> I lived my younger years wanting only one thing: martyrdom. I wanted to die in battle, in the name of Allah . . . I was conditioned from a very young age to think like this. My father believed that there was nothing nobler than to fight and be killed in jihad . . . Talking about the suffering and torment that awaits the unbelievers in the afterlife made me live in complete terror of losing my faith.[31]

From this story we can deduce that in Islam, as in other religious faiths, eschatology is a subject that brings fear and paranoia because it concerns

---

29. David C. Reagan, "Islamic Eschatology: What are the End-time Prophecies of Islam?" *Lamplighter,* May–June, 2010. http://christinprophecy.org/articles/islamic-eschatology/

30. Bukay, "The Religious Foundations of Suicide Bombings," 27–36.

31. Ibid.

what will happen in the afterlife. But there is also an element of incentive that gives an element of hope. In Islamic beliefs and practices, the concept of a holy war, jihad, meets this need. The picture of a terrible world of sin and evil which will have to face severe judgment and condemnation in hell, in contrast to paradise, a world of blissfulness, peace and security, make ji-had a welcome theme in Islam; and it provides eschatological incentive and hope. Both the Koran and the Hadith have something to say that provides eschatological incentives. For example, Harun Yahya tells of Surat al-Kahf which contains the signs of the end of time. This surat speaks of hell and what one should do when he or she found himself or herself in hell. Yahya notes, "Many prophetic hadiths connect Surat al-kahf with the End Times. In one of them our Prophet (SAW) said: 'Whoever enters his (the Dajjah's) hell, let him seek refuge with Allah and recite the opening verse of Surat al-kahf, and will become cool and peaceful for him, as the fire become cool and peaceful for Abraham (Ibn Kathir).'"[32] The teachings of the Koran and the Hadith are tremendous sources and fuels of hostilities across the Islamic World.

The Eschatology of African Traditional Religions

In African worldviews human beings are the center of creation. Unlike the Jews who believed in the resurrection, Africans belief in reincarnation. Ojo explains, "Africans generally conceive the world and life as cyclic—being born, living, dying, and being re-born."[33] That is to say, there is no end per se. The idea of an abrupt end to human history and ushering complete new heaven and earth is foreign to the African mindset. Of course, Africans have the idea of death and punishment and after life. But this is not the same with the biblical view of afterlife. "The cyclic view of the world by Africans sees their world as good, where everyone desires to live and return to. This concept calls for living well with people in the society, fulfilling one's re-sponsibility to the society within the communal bonds and seeking to die in a ripe old age and then be transformed as an ancestor."[34] The fact that

32. Yahya, *Signs of the End Times*, 10.

33. Ojo, "Eschatology and the African Society," 97.

34. Ibid. In most African societies burial rituals are performed for the dead with the intention of facilitating their process of transition "into the ancestral world and . . . veneration." There is a deep sense of collective responsibility of maintaining the society. This sense is due to the fact that the dead are still regarded as part and parcel of the living. They are the living dead. There is therefore connection between the world of the ancestors and the world of the living. The dead are "playing a form of guardianship role to the living."

life is cyclical means that there is no finality to human existence. This is underscored by the names Africans give their children. Among the Moro'a ethnic group of southern Kaduna, the name *Bobai*, literary means "he died and came back to life again." It is a name that is usually given to a child who was born preceding the death of a child.[35] In sum, eschatology is hope in God for God's glory

a) It is hope in God for the new creation of the world.

b) It is hope in God for the history of human beings on earth.

c) It is hope in God for the resurrection and eternal life of human beings.[36]

The Fundamentals of Christian Eschatology

Christian eschatology will be a total disaster if its primary focus is other-worldly, "the endgame." The Hebraic apocalyptic movement makes sense only when read with the lens of the New Testament eschatological perspective. Richard Hays has contributed to a richer and clearer understanding of the present significance of the doctrine of Christian eschatology.[37] His careful analysis of the matter shows the centrality of this subject to all Christian beliefs and practices. Hays pays considerable attention to the synergy between the present Christian experience of salvation and the future consummation of salvation which is generally known as eschatological hope. Hays is one of the biblical theologians and ethicists whose hermeneutical interpretation of eschatology has brought fresh insight into an understanding of the nature and character of Christian eschatology. He convincingly argues that there are three important elements that give a richer sense of hope ingrained in Christian eschatology.

The Redeemed Community

Christian eschatology shapes the worldview of contemporary Christians. It gives us ample reasons why we should remain dedicated and committed to walking in love that respects and honors the truth in the presence life. This involves daily turning away from sin, serving the true and living God and humanity, and eagerly waiting for his coming. According to Hays, all materials on Christian eschatology must be read through focal lenses of

35. Ojo, "Eschatology and the African Society," 98.
36. Moltmann, *The Coming of God*, xvi.
37. Richard Hays, *The Moral Vision of the New Testament*, 337.

community. Only when that happens will Christians recognize the significance of the church in a broken and decaying world. He writes: "The church
as a whole is called to live the way of discipleship and to exemplify the love
of enemies."[38] This shifts the concept of Christian eschatology to the present
concern: love, justice, forgiveness, peace and reconciliation. Christian belief
in the end of the world does not in any way invalidate the present relevance
of eschatological ideas. There is an intrinsic connection between *the already*
and *the not yet*. This is why Jesus through the Gospel writers and the writers
of the epistles urge the church to pay considerable attention to its present
vocation: "Matthew's call to be the light of the world, Paul's call to embody
the ministry of reconciliation, Revelation's call to the saints to overcome
the dragon through the word of their testimony."[39] Therefore as a redeemed
community, whose calling is to exemplify eschatological reality in the present scheme of things, "The church is called to live as a city set on a hill, a city
that lives in light of wisdom, as a sign of God's coming kingdom."[40]

The Cross

Hays gives Christian readers a second element that can help them arrive
at a definitive answer to the main question posed in these later days. Hays
points out that the *cross* is a very vital element in the Christian concept
of eschatology; it gives a healthy and hopeful view of eschatology (1 Cor
1:18–2:5). Here Hays explains that the cross presents the community with
a roadmap, a redemptive model of how to successfully portray the eschatological vision in the present world, regardless of corruption and social
injustices and all forms of human excesses. Hays states that in the cross, God
revealed "the other wisdom in light of which the community lives, [which]
is the paradoxical wisdom of the cross . . . The passion narrative becomes the
fundamental paradigm for the Christian life."[41] It is a costly vision, as, "the
community is likely to pay severe price for its witness: persecution, scorn,
the charge of being ineffective and irrelevant."[42] In his analysis of the cross
as an important element in Christian eschatology, Hays is able to illustrate
the point that Christian morality and ethics are central to biblical view of
eschatology.[43]

38. Ibid.
39. Ibid.
40. Ibid.
41. Ibid.
42. Ibid., 338.
43. Ibid.

The New Creation

The third element is *the new creation.* Christian eschatological hope is rooted in the idea of a new creation. This hope does not make Christians fearful, paranoid or full of despair. Instead, behind the idea of a new creation is the belief that "the nonviolent, enemy loving community is to be vindicated by the resurrection of the dead."[44] In that perspective of the world,

> Death does not have the final word; in the resurrection of Jesus the power of God has triumphed over the power of violence and prefigured the redemption of all creation. The church lives in the present time as a sign of the new order that God has promised. All the New Testament texts, dealing with violence, must therefore be read in this eschatological perspective.[45]

The idea of a new creation presents a hopeful picture instead of a despairing, fearful and paranoiac present or future. For example, Jesus' teaching on "turn the other cheek" which has generally been misread and misinterpreted can only make sense if it is "read through the lenses of the image of a new creation."[46] Without such an approach, Christian eschatology cannot avoid been a source of despair, fear, and paranoia. Hays argues that if that were not the case, "Jesus' directive in Matthew 5:38–48, to "turn the other cheek" will only become a mundane proverb for how to cope with conflict. But this will be ridiculous. For if the world is always to go on as it does now, if the logic that ultimately governs the world is the immanent logic of the rulers of this age, then the meek are the losers and their cheek-turning only invites more senseless abuse. As a mundane proverb, "Turn the other cheek" is simply bad advice."[47] The only way such action can make sense is "if the God and Father of Jesus Christ is actually the ultimate judge of the world and if his will for his people is definitely revealed in Jesus."[48] Christian eschatology that holds out hope for the present-life-experience is the language of Matthew's Gospel; "turning the other cheek makes sense if and only if it is really true that the meek will inherit the earth, if and only if it is really true that those who act on Jesus' words have built their house on a rock so that it will stand in the day of judgment. Turning the other cheek makes sense if and only if all authority in heaven and on earth has

44. Ibid.
45. Ibid.
46. Ibid.
47. Ibid.
48. Ibid.

been given to Jesus."[49] It makes sense only if Christ eschatology is not just a source of fear, paranoid but also of hope in a God that is capable of doing what he says he will do and carrying out all his eternal purposes and plans.

Additionally, Hays observes that Paul's exhortation "that we should bless our persecutors, eschew vengeance, and give food and drink to our enemies" makes sense if and only if it really is true that "the night is far gone, the day is near" (Rom 13:12)—the day when all creation will be set free from bondage (Rom 8:18–25)."[50] The whole point is that eschatology is critical to the Christian present way of life, belief and moral values. The New Testament concept of eschatology means that the church is called to stand as a sign of God's promised future hope and glory even in the present reality of a dark world. Once Christians grasp this truth, their way, however difficult, will be brightened and result in pure joy. "The Apocalypse" compares this hope with the imagery of the marriage of the Lamb, depicting the eschatological consummation of all things (Rev 19:6–9).[51]

Eschatology and the Nigerian Christians

Nigerian Christians are coming out of a worldview that used to understand eschatology as death, the end of this life and transition to the life beyond this life, where the ancestors were ready to welcome you home. I recall when I was growing up in the early 1960s I use to dread death. I did not one to hear of any of my neighbours or relations dying. However, in 1964, our dearest neighbour, Mr. Yashim Mangai, died. I was very saddened and devastated by his death. I wished he was not death. But now that he was death, I wished he could come back to this life again. My parents and I were still pagans and adherents of a tribal cult known as *abwoi*. The worship of *abwoi* requires adherents to participate in frequent rituals and an annual communal worship. During these cultic practices worshippers receive oracles about critical issues that require the attention of the community. Few days after our neighbour whom I knew very well died, the high priest of *Aboi* gave an oracle in which my mother reported that the oracle said our neighbour Mr. Mangai who died a couple of weeks then will return to earth again. The news of his returning back to life after several days gave me refreshing hope and peace. From then on, I used to think of the *abwoi* cult as the alpha and omega of our community. I thought that the *abwoi* was capable of protecting us from harm in this life and even able to bring us back from

49. Ibid.
50. Ibid.
51. Ibid., 338, 364.

the dead. I remember during the Biafran war in Nigeria, whenever we were told that the Igbos were coming to drop bombs on the Northern region, I will be consoling myself by thinking that the *abwoi* will swallow us and take us to where no bomb can reach us. Therefore, the idea of eschatology has traditionally served as concept that brings hope in a situation of fear, paranoia and hostility.

Nigerian Christians are largely grounded in the African mindset, which was originally rooted in the African traditional religions. This mindset believes that death is more than the physical end of earthly life. Death is the end of the earthly history of a member of a human community. For African traditional religions, death is a transition into another form of life. The spirit of the dead survives and acquires a superhuman status of ancestor communicating with the living and helping them in their needs. The evidence of afterlife in Christian Scripture and Tradition is based on the death and resurrection of Jesus, the true human in whom shines all Divinity. The afterlife in Christian perspective is the extension of the resurrection of Jesus to his disciples participating in the divine nature. Nigerian Christian theology advocates for an eschatology of life and solidarity flourishing on earth in a culture of life and solidarity. The new heaven and the new earth are a re-created world of life and brotherly solidarity brought about by the return of Christ and the end of mourning, sorrow and pain.[52] Nigerian Christian eschatology gives a picture of a world in which all events in this life are linked with the ultimate end. God's love and compassion has led to God sending Jesus Christ to preach repentance and to offer us forgiveness through His blood shed on the cross. The Nigerian Christian teaching on eschatology focuses on the idea of the end of this earthly life and the universe as humans know it. It is the doctrine of the end times which brings the Christian understanding of the world into the picture of God, present and future.[53] Nigerian Christian eschatology focuses on the reign of God which Jesus and His disciples taught and preached. In Nigerian Christian eschatology, human beings are not destined to die and be sent to hell; but hope in the risen Christ for the new creation and the end of history. Nigerian Christians are Pre-Millennialists. Most Nigerian Christians believe in a bodily return of Jesus Christ for the church. That is, they believe that the church will be raptured before the tribulation. Whenever most Nigerian Christians discuss the Christian doctrine of eschatology they include such issues as death, judgment, the intermediate state, heaven and hell. They gleaned these

52. Jean-Marie Hyacinthe Quenum, "Eschatology in an African Christian Perspective," Academia.edu, April 2010. https://www.academia.edu/1555470/Eschatology_in_an_African_Christian_Perspective. Accessed May 23, 2015.

53. Ibid.

theological concepts from their reading of the Judeo-Christian scriptural canon. In view of this, scriptural passages such as Hebrews 10:32–36, can help man a Nigerian Christian positively respond to hardship and pain. The writer of Hebrews writes:

> Remember how you remained faithful even though it meant terrible suffering. Sometimes you were exposed to public ridicule and were beaten, and sometimes you helped others who were suffering the same things. You suffered along with those who were thrown into jail, and when all you own was taken from you, you accepted it with joy. You knew there were better things waiting for you that will last forever. So do not throw away this confident trust in the LORD. Remember the great reward it brings you! Patience endurance is what you need now, so that you will continue to be in God's will. Then you will receive all that He has promised. (Heb 10:32–36 NLT)

Like the early church, eschatological expectations used to provide a moral template for Nigerian Christians. The belief in eschatology serves as a moral anchor to the Christian life and practice. Eschatology is very crucial to the Nigerian church which is one of the persecuted churches in the world. In His earthly ministry, Jesus of Nazareth used apocalyptic patterns of thought for his hearers. Thus, the expectation of a future with hope, is capable of bringing a new reorientation to the present situation it feels like saying "if you slap me I will slap you back; God doesn't care." Nigerian Christians Christian eschatology is based on God's larger purpose for creation. It is a doctrine that realizes the reason why God strategically placed Jesus Christ at the center of his interaction with his creation; Christ is the all in all of creation. Nigerian Christian eschatological hope begins with the incarnation. Through Christ's incarnation, God is working towards accomplishing his purpose for creating humanity and the entire creation. That is why the Bible itself emphasizes a Christo-centric idea of creation. All human beings are created by God's Word. God has given Christians his divine power (Holy Spirit), not for them to destroy themselves, but to redeem them, transform them into his likeness, so that they can participate in the divine nature and thereby be in communion with God. "By Christ becoming human (the Incarnation), he shows his willingness to be called their brother" (Heb 2:11). This perspective helps Nigerian Christians to grasp Christian eschatology in all its truths.

Paul tells believers that everything that has ever been made has been made through Christ, in Christ, and for Christ. Eschatology looks with refreshing hope at both the present and the future realities of our world: God indwelling all of his creation. Paul sees this metaphor as culminating in Christ; the Holy Spirit transforms Christians "into his likeness," as he puts it in his second letter to the Corinthians. Jesus is called the "visible image of the invisible God," assuming bodily form to give a unique revelation of God's purpose for humanity. This idea is intrinsically rooted in the package of Christian faith and practice. For instance, people often believe in Jesus Christ because he offers them hope for the present and the future life and reality. Paul describes the Thessalonian Christians: "[Y]ou turned to God from idols to serve the living and true God, and to wait for his Son from heaven, whom he raised from the dead—Jesus, who rescues us from the coming wrath" (1 Thess 1: 9–10 NIV).[54]

Indeed, any savvy reader of the writings of the Apostles of the New Testament will realize that the God who promised (vowed) to be with Christians till the end of the age is not a liar.[55] Events in the world are not outside his eternal plan for humanity and all of creation. The big picture of God's unfolding drama of salvation includes the transformation of all created things to their original intent. Grasping this big picture, Paul explains that in times of human hardship—suffering, pain and even death—the essence of Christian eschatological hope is to strengthen "the faith of God's elect" and enhance their "knowledge of the truth that leads to godliness—a faith and knowledge resting on the hope of eternal life, which God, who does not lie, promised before the beginning of time, and at his appointed season he brought his word to light through the preaching entrusted to me (Paul) by the command of God our Savior"(Titus 1:1–3). Christian eschatology is rooted in "the hope for eternal life, which God . . ." promised all those who truly believe in Christ (Titus 1:2). It will seem logical to say that the idea of God promising eternal life ought to give Christians hope and not paranoia or fear. If God does not lie nor die then he can be trusted to fulfill his promises to Christians. The idea of God not lying is an immense truth. It shows that God cannot promise what he cannot give. It is also rooted in the hope of a time of perfect peace and security, when no one will make Christians afraid any longer (Jer 46:27).

54. First Thessalonians 1: 9–10 NIV.
55. Heb 6:18 reads, "It is impossible for God to lie."

Throughout human history, one can catalogue different reactions to human sufferings and pains. In apocalyptic expectation, both the Old and New Testament paint a picture of grand events of a violent world whose end will usher in a new heaven and a new earth. In the effort to fast-track eschatological hope, apocalyptic reading of the Bible has led to a distortion of the concept of Christian eschatology, thereby causing trepidation. Regardless of this, eschatological beliefs are fundamental to Christian faith, belief and practice. As we have noted in this essay, the biblical language of eschatology is rooted in the whole spectrum of creation, especially of human life from conception, birth, life, death, judgment, the "after life" and the ushering in of a new heaven and new earth. However, misinterpretation of these ideas leaves the hearers with different psychological responses and reactions—fear, paranoid, or hope. The psychological response that results in fear and paranoid is caused by a so-called Christian eschatological perspective that has tended to see the world running its course without God. It eliminates the goal of Christian faith: Living as if tomorrow is today; a future with hope. It is caused by failure to recognize that it is God who has brought about this universe in the hope of realizing a specific purpose, which is the doctrine of creation. His intent is to guide the universe towards this realization, i.e. the doctrine of eschatology. If one grasps the doctrine of Christian eschatology, one will realize that creation is not just about what happened in Genesis, about origins; which is deism. Rather, it is about God continuing to interact with his creation even after the Fall of humankind. Hope comes when one recognizes that every moment of the universe implies a creative act by God. God upholds His innovative creation throughout time, and his decision to sustain the universe at each moment is one of creativity. Similarly, eschatology is not only concerned with the end, but with the realization of God's purpose in each moment of creation. Genuine Christians live the eschatological event now! "people who expect God's justice and righteousness no longer accept the so-called normative force of what is fact, because they know that a better world is possible and that changes in the present are necessary."[56]

Christian eschatology is critical to Nigerian Christian present way of life, belief and moral values. In a hostile world with diverse threats and their enslaving fear, the hermeneutical interpretation of Christian eschatology is inseparable from the idea of Christian sufferings and pains: martyrdom. But unlike Islam, Christianity does not encourage us to fight a holy war, jihad.

---

56. Moltmann, *Ethics of Hope*, 7.

Rather it encourages Christian resilience, to absorb the impact of hostility and endure hardship out of love for the enemy and for God. Thus Nigerian Christian eschatology cannot afford to continue to encourage a situation of paranoia and fear. But how can we not fear when we face the challenge of terrorism and aggression? Love is the way of the cross that we are called to bear. Love is stronger than death. That is why Jesus said, "All this I have told you so that you will not go astray" (John 16:1). To avoid straying from the faith, Paul proposes that we overcome evil with good (Rom 12:21). Earlier on he said: "Be . . . patient in affliction, faithful in prayer . . . Bless those who persecute you; bless and do not curse . . . do not repay anyone evil for evil. Be careful to do what is right in the eyes of God" (Rom 12:12). Jesus stresses love as the language of the Christian community. Love language is difficult to come by in times of crisis. But this is what Christian discipleship demands. Love never fails; it does not give up on God; it perseveres. For this to happen, Paul says that Christian "love must be sincere. Hate what is evil; cling to what is good" (Rom 12:9). God's will in Christian suffering and pain cannot be determined if love is not genuine. Christian suffering and pain are sometimes part of God's will for his children. St. Peter tells Christians:

> Do not be surprised at the painful trial you are suffering, as though something strange were happening to you. But rejoice that you participate in the sufferings of Christ, so that you may be overjoyed when his glory is revealed. If you are insulted because of the name of Christ, you are blessed, for the Spirit of glory and of God rests on you . . . If you suffer as a Christian, do not be ashamed, but praise God that you bear that name. (1 Pet 4:12–16)

It was because Paul understood the intrinsic connection between eschatological hope with the secret of Christian suffering and pain that he prayed and sought the privilege of participating in them. He prayed, "I want to know Christ and the power of his resurrection and the fellowship of sharing in his sufferings, becoming like him in his death, and so, somehow, to attain the resurrection from the dead" (Phil 3: 10–11). Many Christians want to know Christ. They may even resonate with Paul in this prayer. But they are not willing to suffer for the sake of Christ. How can Christians have the privilege of enjoying the fellowship of sharing in his suffering if their attitude to suffering and pain is completely negative? This attitude will not help them appreciate the fact that God is capable of using even terrorism to accomplish his eternal purposes. Jeremy Taylor rightly says, "Whatsoever we beg of God, let us also work for it." Therefore, if we pray like Paul we should be willing to experience suffering and pain. Suffering and pain are God's will for his children. Peter concludes: "So then, who suffer according to God's will should commit themselves to their faithful Creator and continue to do good" (1 Pet 4:19).

Conclusion

In a world of enormous human hostility, the Christian idea of eschatology strikes an important cord. It provides a positive motivation for Christians to participate with God in creating an alternative moral vision than what the modern world faiths offer. For as Hans Küng observed, "In the modern world, religion is a central, perhaps the central force that motivates and mobilizes people . . . What ultimately counts for people is not political ideology or economic interest. Faith and family, blood and belief are what people identify with and what they will fight and die for."[57] For a Christian, however, the idea of eschatology is a liberating idea. It gives Christians the wherewithal to reverse the vicious cycle of violence perpetuated by those who do not know that God's power is incomparably great to the extent that he does not need any one of us to fight for him. God holds the present and the future. He has inaugurated his kingdom reign through Jesus Christ's incarnational birth, ministry, trial, death and resurrection. He who can conquer death can also usher in the eschatological kingdom.

Christian eschatology gives us every reason to hope for a better future in spite of the present reality of a world of a moral failure and its resultant extreme hostility and destruction. The in breaking of God's Kingdom which Jesus and his disciples proclaimed is a foretaste of what is coming. So, the idea of an eschatological future has some concrete implications: neutralizing the human tendency toward return hate with hate, mistrust with mistrust, and destruction with destruction. Our nonviolent response to the conflict violence that abounds in our global village depends largely on the Christian theology of eschatology.

Jesus brought us good news that gives us a glimpse of what God has in store for us in this life and the life to come. A healthy eschatological vision produces a healthy lifestyle in this life. It collapses the dichotomy between the present and the future. In Christ the future and the present are inseparable. So we have to live our lives today as if tomorrow is already here.

---

57. Küng, *A Global Ethic for Global Politics and Economics*, 117.

Chapter 16

Conclusion

WE HAVE ELABORATED WHAT happens when darkness strikes and faith encounters the politics of human hostility. Our study has brought us face to face with the embedded roots of human hostility. It revealed an interesting irony: the paradox of the human condition demonstrates that all humans are capable of tremendous good and tremendous evil. The psalmist puts it thus: "They praise me to my face but curse me in their hearts" (Ps 62:4c). The straight forward thesis of the book is: All humans—Christians, Muslims and other religious adherents—possess good and evil in their nature. Therefore, no human being has the monopoly of violence or wickedness or evil. However, because of "the great mystery of our faith," the cross, (1 Tim 3:16 NLT), Christians can possibly live a way of life that is above human excessive self-interest, deception and the lust for power, which, since the Fall, hold our world captive.

Our promised to help the reader understand what happens when evil strikes and what exactly should be a Christian appropriate reaction to evil: human hostility has been achieved. We have situated evil in the territory where it belongs: the human heart and mind. We have argued that evil entered the human race via Adam and Eve opting for personal autonomy versus dependence on God. We exposed and highlighted the hidden roots of human hostility in order to debunk definitions and interpretation of the phenomena of human fragility and hostility that are grossly inadequate. The Bible doctrine of human original sin provides a biblical framework within which to grasp the roots of human evil. We made it clear that no human is completely evil or completely good. Rather, all humans possess within their nature both good and evil, dignity and depravity, self-love and group hatred. Our conclusion therefore is that hostility is part and parcel of the narrative of the human race. As the British born theologian and ethicist, John Stott, puts it, all human beings, without exception, are capable of doing tremendous good and by the same token capable of doing tremendous evil. Thus the human family is paradoxically characterized by compassion and wickedness, love and hatred, peace and war, development and stasis. This characterization buttresses the fact that human hostility is intrinsically ingrained in our human essence, which involve, among other things, our choices and responsibilities. Although this was not how God created us, evil has become part of who we are the moment Adam and Eve decided for autonomy instead of dependence on God. In vying for autonomy humans have rejected and opposed any demand for complete loyalty to God. We are capably good and yet pathologically evil.

The narrative of the human paradox is nowhere clear like in Nigeria. However, Nigeria's narrative of human hostility knows no monopoly. It is part and parcel of human brokenness in a world that is under siege by sin and death. This is why other contexts are mentioned and discussed in this study. Muslim-Christian relationships in Nigeria have largely portrayed the ludicrous nature and scope of human violence or hostility. Muslim and Christian communities have continued to demonstrate that good and evil coexist in the human nature. We have been able to unravel the fact that Nigerians, like other humans across the globe, tend to define and interpret evil within the confines of religious, economic, tribal and ethnic dimensions. We have also discovered how the global community, (through the United Nations) assumes that socio-economic development is all we need to overcome human hostility. In so doing, the human family failed to grasp the big picture of where the problem lies: The human heart and mind which both manufacture self-interest, deception, lust for power. Knowing what we now know about the paradox of humanity, we have fundamentally concluded that human hostility does not have prejudice of where to perpetuate itself. It is the narrative of Nigerian Christians, Muslims and African Traditional Religionists together. By and large, it is the narrative of the human family. Therefore, since this is the narrative of the human family, we have offered some suggestions on how the Nigerian situation of human hostility and violence should be seen with the eyes of justice, love, peace and compassion so that those who hate and even harm us will be restored to their position of membership in the human family.

On the whole, we have identified some of the roots of bitterness that easily turn to poisonous sentiment and endanger healthy relationships which are necessary for human flourishing. All human beings have needs and desires that drive them to action in order to fulfill their perceived and real needs. In the course of trying to find fulfillment humans get carried away by their perception. They invariably perceive other fellow humans as blocking their chances or way to self-fulfillment. This is why we have zeroed in on the pathology of human hostility, which is often eternized against those who are perceived as standing in the way of getting what is wanted or desired by others. Religious communities as well as the general public fight and kill each other simply because human beings are blind to the symbiotic relationship that exists between them. If not for anything, the fact that God has given all humans the earth to inhabit shows that God has given all humans what they will need to survive on earth. So, no one religion or tribal group has the right to deny others the right to live, right to participate in dignifying and lively community through the exercise of their God-given full potentials. To open the eyes of Nigerians to this reality, we have made it categorically clear that there is a symbiotic interaction amongst all the three religions in Nigeria. We have drawn the attention of Nigerian to the fact that our identity does not start with religion. Rather, it starts with our creation in the image and likeness of God. We are human beings first before becoming religious people. Religion and ethnicity cannot take away what makes us truly humans: the image of God in the human family. In order to enjoy our symbiotic relationship as Nigerians—ATR members, Muslims and Christians—must embrace the reality of our participation in one habitable earth and in God's one humanity. As a nation of ethno-linguistic groups, Nigeria is not for a tribal group or people of one religious affiliation. Nigeria is God's own country. Irrespective of our religious and ethnic affiliations, Nigeria is for all us.

Among the crucial issues this study unraveled and discussed is the fact that in Nigeria no religion has a monopoly of violence and hostility. In fact, every religion—ATR, Islam or Christianity—has its enthusiasts. This is why is necessary for all the religious communities to seek justice and peace together. Ironically, all governmental administrative regimes in Nigeria have had to work hard at bridging the gap that religious and ethnic animosities and fault lines create. Religious divides are arguably detrimental to the positive development of the nation. However, government officials equally ignore what contributes to this problem: corruption. Thus, we have made it categorically clear that a lot of what is happening in our country and other countries in the global community has much to do with corruption spearheaded by the elite in society. They invariably immortalized corruption. We hereby conclude that people who immortalize corruption do so because they hate peace. They indirectly hate the language of peace and justice. The primary reason is they actually benefit from violent conflicts. It gives them more opportunity to steal public funds. In this context, matters so much to emphasize the fact that God is "the God of peace" (Heb 13:20a). Thus, if anyone hates peace he or she hates God. By and large, corruption, as we have shown in this study is causing enormous pressure and stress on our national life. That is, the growing level of corruption is not only producing Islamic terrorism and aggression but also producing a culture of impunity. Corruption has become a way of life that determines the course of contemporary history for all of us. This corruption of our morals has affected our tribal relationships in that our sense of neighborliness is disappearing. In Nigeria, like the rest of Africa, tribal and ethnic sentiments are trumping moral values which are significant sources of human flourishing. Yet, the fact still remains; Nigerians and other Africans make sense of the world through tribes and tribalism. Ironically, however, they tend to be blind to the fact that other tribes are their cousins, neighbours and members of the human family. Our study of the subject of tribes and tribalism has enabled us to conclude that, tribes and tribalism should not be seen as a threat in Nigeria. The important thing we need is to learn to accept our diversity and difference. To reiterate, Nigeria belongs to all tribes. Tribal diversity and differentiation can be fun, if Nigerians are willing to embrace and embody Jesus' ethics of loving other tribes as our own tribe.

In a country where we have people who are socially and spiritually derailing, social safety network is the responsibility of all of Nigerians. Thus we have advocated restorative justice for those Nigerians who have concluded that they will harm us because they don't belong. There is the need to help our communities with the skills they need to handle cases of social and moral challenges. Those who harm us must be given a second chance. For example, we have the members of Boko Haram sect who have continued to cause enormous havoc and destruction. We must leave the door open for those of them who would want to give up their violent practices and embrace peace as a way of life. One of the ways we have suggested is rehabilitation. Nigerian Muslims can learn from Saudi Arabia where rehabilitation centers have been created and staffed with erudite liberal Qur'anic imams who talk the would-be terrorists out of it. The truth is that people who harm us still have potentials of been reformed and transformed. It is therefore our responsibility to work at helping them to embrace the idea of repentance, reconciliation, restoration, restitution and so on. Those of us who are still in our senses must work at helping them to live in peace and love, rather than giving up on them. In this way of thinking, we should try to push our government security agents to think outside the box. The government must demonstrate creativity by fashioning other ways of obliterating the danger of a growing insecurity. They must work hard at blocking the chances of the sect continuing to get recruits in any part of Nigeria or Africa.

Furthermore, our study has considered and discussed the matter of self-defense. The desire for self-defense is potent in Nigeria. Nigerian Christians feel the pressure and stress of a society where they are often despised, treated as target for slaughter or destruction with impunity. However, Nigerian Christians must realize that self-defense has its limits. If Christians decide on self-defense they should not forget that the God they serve is called "the God of peace." Therefore, their primary goal should be to work at living in peace and in holiness with everyone. The quest for self-defense should not cause Nigerian Christians to get distracted from the mission of the church. Rather, the mission of the church should be seen as Christian's best method of self-defense. Therefore, as Nigerian Christians worry about what to do to defend themselves, they must also focus on the mission of the church.

Satan is working tirelessly against Christians so that they will ignore the mission of the church. They must not give in to Satan's strategy to distract the church from its mission. Like Peter and the apostles refused to give in to Satan's tactics, the Nigerian church should be mindful of Satan's strategy and not allow itself to be distracted. This argument becomes necessary because of what we observed in the narrative of the Nigerian Pentecostal and Charismatic churches. Many of them are doing tremendous good in terms of building and equipping the lives of their members for public life. Yet, they have elements of distraction from the mission of the church. They are doing tremendous good in the public sphere. Yet, at the same time they are distracted by the desire to adopt the lifestyle of public leaders and servants. This problem is in no way limited to the Pentecostals and Charismatic. Rather, all Christian denominations in Nigeria are facing the temptation to mimic the political system of the day.

Self-defense is not the primary concern of the Christian community. Rather, love and peace are. We have proved that Nigerian Christians are capable of living in peace with others. They are capable of engaging in peacemaking that is just. The biographical account of Bishop Samuel Ajayi Crowther who was the first black Bishop of CMS in Africa lends credence to that story. Other contemporary Christians in Kaduna and Jos, Nigeria have also shown that it is possible to work at living in peace with the Muslims. In spite of the jihad rhetoric in the Qur'an, we have argued that Muslims are capable of engaging in genuine peacemaking. As we reflect on human hostility, we have tried to examine how eschatological ideas might necessitate the perpetuation of violence. We addressed the issue by comparing the Nigerian Christian eschatology with other faiths in the country in order to gauge which eschatology perspective causes paranoia, fear, hostility or hope. In examining the Christian perspective, we concluded that Christian eschatology has the potentials of helping us to work at living in peace with others as well as living in holiness in a corrupt society, like Nigeria. Therefore, we suggested that eschatology in general, and Christian eschatology in particular is capable of sustaining and keeping the Christian faith alive and well, in spite of persecution. The history of the early church and contemporary contexts prove that to be the case. The subject of Christ returns makes Christians "too good for this world." For Christian eschatology is meant to keep us focus on what Christ has done and on the hope of His coming back with rewards.

Fundamental Implications of the Present Study

Today, the greatest challenge Nigerian Christians, and indeed Christians across the globe face is how "to live a life worthy of His (God's) call" in a hostile global community. That is, how can they work at living in peace with everyone as well as equally working at living in holiness? We have pointed out the crucial need of the church today is understanding how to live to live a life that proclaim God's glory and displays his holiness in a hostile society. This Christian perspective has the following implications:

1. Living a way of life that honours God and our Lord Jesus Christ in a world of enormous corruption, which fuels hardships and persecutions requires constant dependence on God's grace. It equally demands a genuine change of heart and mind rather than outward progress and development. If our hearts and minds are not converted and transformed all physical development we may achieve will be destroyed by us.

2. Nigerian Christians need to recognize that by virtue of their confident trust in the Lord Jesus Christ, they are too good for this world (Heb 11:38). In other words, the Christian life is a higher calling. That is why Christians are asked and encouraged to ". . . strip off every weight that slows us down, especially the sin that so easily trips us up. And let us run with endurance the race God has set before us. We do this by keeping our eyes on Jesus, the champion who initiates and perfects our faith. Because of the joy awaiting Him, He endured the cross, disregarding its shame. Now he is seated in the place of honour beside God's throne. Think of all the hostility He endured from sinful people; then you won't become weary and give up" (Heb 12:1–3).

3. The role of prayer in the schemes of things cannot be underestimated. Prayer include, among other things: "Asking our God to enable you

(Christians) to live a life worthy of His call . . . to give you power to accomplish all the good things your faith prompts you to do" (2 Thess 1:11). The goal of such a way of life and prayer is: God's honour and glory. "Then the name of our Lord Jesus will be honoured because of the way you live, and you will be honoured along with Him" (2 Thess 1:12).

4. Humanity before the fall was in perfect peace and joy. We read, "In the beginning was the Word . . ." (John 1:1). This is a way of reminding Christians of the original plan of God. However, the self-ambition and lust for power have now taken over, creating a condition of comparison, competition and corruption.

Corruption in Nigeria (like in other nations) is perpetuated by the elites who indulge in loose and extravagant ways. Corruption is grievously destructive. President Muhammadu Buhari of Nigeria once observed, "Unless Nigeria kills corruption, corruption will kill Nigeria." He further stated, "Corruption has no political party, no religion and no ethnic group."[1] Indeed, if Nigerians do not urgently confront corruption head-on it will kill the country. Biblical history is replete with accounts of how ancient empires who were involved in loose and extravagant living and corruption literally disappeared from the face of this earth. Such examples include Babylon, Assyria and the Roman Empire, to mention but a few. They are no more! In fact, indulging in loose and extravagant ways will kill any nation, no matter its political fame. One hour is enough to bring it down (Rev 18:16–17). Therefore, in a corrupt nation, like Nigeria, Christians need to imbibe the life of public integrity. That is, living a life that is above private and public reproach. To live this sort of life is to live under the constant awareness that it is only God's grace that can make this possible: "This is all made possible because of the grace of our God and Lord, Jesus Christ" (2 Thess 1:12). This grace enables Christians to walk in the step of Jesus Christ. Jesus Christ walked in obedience to God's will and God's original intention for humanity. Jesus walked as the Prince of peace.

5. Christianity has Good News for its adherents. The good news is: God is the God of mysteries. Therefore, in spite of what is happening in Nigeria at present, the church needs to still hope for a great harvest. Corruption and the resultant persecution are scattering us; but they are also giving us a great door of opportunity to harvest souls for God's

---

1. See Isiaka Wakili, "My anti-graft war not partisan—Buhari," *Daily Trust,* Monday, August 10, 2015.

kingdom. Therefore, it is important to note that complexity of conflict can be met with complexity of God's resources at our disposal.

6. In trying to bring new out of the old life we need to appreciate the broad human context and not just the Nigerian context. Peacemaking needs you to manage your emotions so that you can be creative. You need to raise your standard up above the current situation. It is saying to yourself: I must do this because it is "to the praise of his glory" (Eph 1:12, 14).

7. Nigeria is a multiethnic and multi-religious nation. These two realities are a gift to the nation and not a curse. However, ignorance of God's involvement in the creation of Nigeria as a nation and His continuing interaction with the diverse ethnic and religious groups has caused Nigerians to continue to despise each. This state of affairs hinders a broad understanding of the significance of ambiguity and complexity of the Nigerian situation.

8. Ultimately, we need to recognize the fact that we have a phenomenon of violent conflict. This situation is not limited to a present phenomenon. It is a historical reality that goes back to the legacy of our ancestors: Creation and Fall, good and evil, dignity and depravity. Hence, violent conflict, persecution and hatred are not the monopoly of a certain religious community; rather they are part and parcel of the human essence, the mega narrative of the human family.

9. Finally, the church enjoys the full benefits of Christ salvific work and its reward (Eph 1:15–23). A persecuted church needs a refreshed vision of God's love and friendship (Ps 73:22–24). It needs to realize that whenever, "Love and faithfulness meet together; righteousness and peace kiss each other." And whenever, "Faithfulness springs forth from the earth, and righteousness looks down from heaven; the Lord will indeed give what is good, and our land will yield its harvest. Righteousness goes before him and prepares the way for his steps" (85:10–13). Righteousness is a biblical concept that has not be adequately grasped by humans. In the Hebrew sense of the word, it is about right living with God and one's neighbors. In other words, righteousness is not living in isolation of the other. Thus the Christian community as God's glorious inheritance and hope can be truly a game changer in a world of human hostilities.

Bibliography

Abdu, Hussaini. *Clash of Identities: State, Society and Ethno-Religious Conflicts in Northern Nigeria.* Kaduna, Nigeria: DevReach, 2010.

Adelaja, Sunday. *Church Shift: Revolutionizing Your Faith, Church, and Life for the 21st Century.* Florida: Charisma, 2008.

Adeyemi, Sam. *We Are the Government.* Lagos, Nigeria: Pneuma, 2010.

Adeyemo, Tokumboh, ed. *Christian Leaders in Society: Making a Difference.* Nairobi, Kenya: Association of Evangelicals in Africa, 1997.

Agang, Bobai Sunday. *The Impact of Ethnic, Political and Religious Violence on Northern Nigeria, and a Theological Reflection on Its Healing.* Carlisle, UK: Langham Monographs, 2011.

The American Heritage Dictionary of the English Language. 5th Edition. Boston: Houghton Mifflin Harcourt, 2011.

Amstutz, Lorraine Stutzman. "Restorative Justice: The Promise and the Challenges." *Vision: A Journal for Church and Theology* 14, no. 2 (Fall 2013) 24–30.

Asamoa-Gyadu, J. Kwabena. "Religious Education and Religious Pluralism in the New Africa." *Religious Education* 105, no. 3 (2010) 238–244.

Atherstone, Andrew. *The Road to Canterbury: Archbishop Justin Welby.* London: Darton, Longman & Todd, 2013.

Awolalu, Joseph Omosalde. "Continuing and Discontinuity in Africa Religion: The Yoruba Experience." *Orita* 13 (1981) 3–20.

————. "The Encounter Betweeen African Traditional Religion and Other Religions in Nigeria." In *African Traditional Religion: In Contemporary Society,* edited by Jacob K. Olupona, 8–20. St. Paul, MN: Paragon, 1991.

Banks, Robert. "Neighbor." In *Baker's Dictionary of Christian Ethics*, edited by Carl F. H. Henry, 451–52. Grand Rapids, MI: Baker, 1997.

Baron, David. *The Servant of Jehovah: The Sufferings of the Messiah and the Glory that Should Follow: An Exposition of Isaiah LIII.* London: Marshall, Morgan & Scott, 1954.

Barth, Karl. *Der Römerbrief.* Munich: Kaiser, 1992.

Bauckham, Richard. *The Bible in Politics: How to Read the Bible Politically.* Louisville, KY: Westminster John Knox, 1989.

Berman, Marshall. *All That Is Solid Melts into Air: The Experience of Modernity.* New York: Penguin, 1988.

Best, Shadrack Gaiya. "Religion and Religious Conflicts in Northern Nigeria." *University of Jos Journal of Political Science* 2, no. 3 (December 2011) 60–75. https://www.

researchgate.net/publication/43939960_Religion_and_Religious_Conflicts_in_
Northern_Nigeria.

Beyer, Bryan E. *Encountering the Book of Isaiah*. Grand Rapids, MI: Baker Academic, 2007.

Bingham, Richard. *The Gospel According to Isaiah, Lectures on the 53rd Chapter of the Prophet*. Cambridge: Tyndale, n. d.

Birdsall, Doug, and Lindsay Brown. Foreword to *The Cape Town Commitment: A Confession of Faith and a Call to Action,* edited by Chris Wright. The Third Lausanne Congress. Bodmin, UK: Printbridge, 2011.

Blocher, Henri. *Songs of the Servant: Isaiah's Good News*. London: InterVarsity, 1975.

Bock, Darrell L. *Luke 1:1–9:50*. Grand Rapids, MI: Baker, 1994.

———. *Luke: The IVP Application Commentary*. Grand Rapids, MI: Zondervan, 1996.

Bock, Darrell L., and Mitch Glaser, eds. *The Gospel According to Isaiah 53: Encountering the Suffering Servant in Jewish and Christian Theology*. Grand Rapids, MI: Kregal, 2012.

Boer, Jan H. *Christians: Why We Reject Muslim Law*. Studies in Christian-Muslim Relations 7. Vancouver, CA: Essence, 2008.

———. *Muslims: Why We Rejected Secularism*. Studies in Christian-Muslim Relations 4. Vancouver, CA: Essence, 2005.

———. *Nigeria's Decades of Blood*. Studies in Christian-Muslim Relations 1. Vancouver, CA: Essence, 2003.

Bonhoeffer, Dietrich. *Cost of Discipleship*. New York: Simon & Schuster, 1995.

Braithwaite, John. *Restorative Justice & Responsive Regulation*. Oxford: Oxford University Press, 2002.

Bruce, F. F. *The Book of the Acts: The New International Commentary on the New Testament*. Revised edition. Grand Rapids, MI: Eerdmans, 1988.

Bukay, David. "The Religious Foundations of Suicide Bombings: Islamic Ideology." *Middle East Quarterly* 13, no. 4 (Fall 2006) 27–36.

Burgess, Richard. *Nigeria's Christian Revolution: The Civil War Revival and Its Pentecostal Progeny (1967–2006)*. Oxford: Regnum, 2008.

Burnside, Jonathan. *God, Justice, and Society: Aspects of Law and Legality in the Bible*. Oxford: Oxford University Press, 2011.

Cadbury, Henry J. *The Book of Acts in History*. London: Black, 1955.

Caillois, Roger. *Man and the Sacred*. Translated by Meyer Barash. Glencoe, IL: Free Press, 1950.

Caird, G. B. *The Gospel of Saint Luke*. Harmondsworth, UK: Penguin, 1965.

Calvin, John. "The Moral Law and the Christian Life." In *On Moral Business: Classical and Contemporary Resources for Ethics in Economic Life,* edited by Max L. Stackhouse et al., 180–186. Grand Rapids, MI: Eerdmans, 1995.

Cameron, David R., Gustave Ranis, and Annalisa Zinn, eds. *Globalization and Self-Determination: Is the Nation-State under Siege?* London: Routledge, 2006.

Campbell, John. *Nigeria Dancing on the Brink*. Ibadan, Nigeria: Rowman & Littlefield, 2010.

Caner, Ergun Mehmet, and Emir Fethi Caner. *Christian Jihad: Two Former Muslims Look at the Crusades and Killing in the Name of Christ*. Grand Rapids, MI: Kregel, 2004.

Çapan, Ergün, ed. *Terror and Suicide Attacks: An Islamic Perspective*. Somerset, NJ: Light, 2006.

Cartwright, David. *Peace: A History of Movements and Ideas.* Cambridge: Cambridge University Press, 2008.

Chayes, Sarah. "'Thieves of State' Reveals Tremendous Power of Global Corruption," interview by Audie Cornish, *All Things Considered,* NPR, January 16, 2015. http://www.npr.org/2015/01/16/377780883/thieves-of-state-reveals-tremendous-power-of-global-corruption. Podcast audio.

———. *Thieves of State: Why Corruption Threatens Global Security.* New York: Norton, 2015.

Chia, Roland. *Hope for the World: The Christian Vision.* Downers Grove, IL: Inter-Varsity, 2006.

Chouin, Gerard. Foreword to *Boko Haram: Islamism, Politics, Security and the State in Nigeria,* by Marc-Antoine Pérouse de Montclos, viii–ix. Leiden: African Studies Centre, 2014.

Climenchaga, Alison Fitchett. "Heathenism, Delusion, and Ignorance: Samuel Crowther's Approach to Islam and Traditional Religion." *Anglican Theological Review* 96, no. 4 (Fall 2014) 661–681.

Clines, David J. A. "I, He, We, and They: A Literary Approach to Isaiah 53." Journal for the Study of the Old Testament Supplement Series 1. Sheffield, England: JSOT Press, 1976.

Clough, David L., and Brian Stiltner. *Faith: A Christian Debate about War.* Washington DC: Georgetown University Press, 2007.

Coady, C. A. J. *Morality and Political Violence.* Cambridge: Cambridge University Press, 2009.

Collins, John J. *Does the Bible Justify Violence?* Minneapolis: Fortress, 2004.

Committee on Society, Development, and Peace. *Peace—The Desperate Imperative: Baden, Austria, April 3–9, 1970.* A SODEPAX Report. Geneva: The Ecumenical Center, 1970.

Conteh, Prince Sorie. "Traditionalists, Muslims and Christians in Africa: Interreligious Encounters and Dialogue." Cambria Press. http://www.cambriapress.com/cambriapress.cfm?template=4&bid=292. Accessed November 13, 2014.

Cooper, Terry D. *Dimensions of Evil: Contemporary Perspective.* Minneapolis: Fortress, 2009.

Cox, Harvey. *Fire From Heaven: The Rise of Pentecostal Spirituality and the Reshaping of Religion in the Twenty-First Century.* Reading, MA: Addison-Wesley, 1995.

Craigie, Peter C. *The Problem of War in the Old Testament.* Grand Rapids, MI: Eerdmans, 1978.

Cross, F. L., and E. A. Livingstone, eds. *The Oxford Dictionary of the Christian Church.* 3rd edition. Oxford: Oxford University Press, 2005.

Crowther, Samuel. *Experiences with Heathens and Mohammedans in West Africa.* London: np., 1892.

Crowther, Samuel, and James Frederick Schön. *Journals of the Rev. James Frederick Schön and Mr. Samuel Crowther, Who, with the Sanction of Her Majesty's Government, Accompanied the Expedition up to the Niger.* London: Hatchard & Son, 1842.

Crowther, Samuel, and John C. Taylor. *The Gospel on the Banks of the Niger.* London: Church Missionary, 1859.

Culliton, Joseph T., ed. *Nonviolence—Central to Christian Spirituality: Perspectives from Scripture to the Present.* New York: Mellen, 1982.

Daley, Brian. *The Hope of the Early Church: A Handbook of Patristic Eschatology.* Cambridge: Cambridge University Press, 1991.

Davis, Charles. *Religion and the Making of Society: Essays in Social Theology.* Cambridge: Cambridge University Press, 1994.

Debki, Bitrus V. Z. "Crisis in Kaduna." In *Seeking Peace in Africa: Stories from African Peacemakers,* edited by Donald E. Miller et al., 88. Geneva: World Council of Churches, 2007.

Decorvet, Jeanne, and Emmanuel Oladipo, eds. *Samuel Ajayi Crowther: The Miracle of Grace.* Lagos, Nigeria: CSS Bookshops, 2006.

Dempsey, Carol J., and Elayne J. Shapiro. *Ambassadors of Reconciliation: New Testament Reflection on Restorative Justice and Peacemaking.* New York: Orbis, 2009.

Deng, Francis Mading. *War of Visions: Conflicts of Identities in Sudan.* Washington, DC: Brookings Institution, 1995.

DeYoung, Curtiss Paul. *Reconciliation: Our Greatest Challenge—Our Only Hope.* Valley Forge, PA: Judson, 1997.

Donald, Miller E., and Tetsunao Yamamori. *Global Pentecostalism: The New Face of Christian Social Engagement.* Berkeley: University of California Press, 2007.

Dow, Philip E. *Virtuous Minds: Intellectual Character Development.* Downers Grove, IL: InterVarsity Academic, 2013.

Dreyer, Elizabeth A. "The Soul's Journey into God." In *Christian Spirituality: The Classics,* edited by Arthur Holder, 9–15. London: Routledge, 2010.

Driver, John. *How Christians Make Peace with War: Early Christian Understandings of War.* Scottsdale, PA: Herald, 1988.

Duffey, Michael K. *Peacemaking Christians: The Future of Just Wars, Pacifism, and Nonviolent Resistance.* Kansas City: Sheed & Ward, 1995.

Easton, M. G. *Easton's Bible Dictionary.* Oak Harbor, WA: Logos Research Systems, 1996.

Edwards, Mark. "Origin's Two Resurrections." *Journal of Theological Studies* 46, no. 2 (1995) 502–18.

Ehret, Christopher, ed. *The Civilizations of Africa: A History to 1800.* Charlottesville, VA: University of Virginia Press, 2002.

Elechi, O. Oko. *Doing Justice Without the State: The Afikpo (Ehugbo) Nigeria Model.* New York: Routledge, 2006.

Erickson, Millard J. *Christian Theology.* Grand Rapids, MI: Baker Academic, 2013.

Falaranmi, James Olatoso. "The Nigerian Islamic View of the State and Its Effects on the Mission of the Christian Church in Nigeria." DMiss diss., Reformed Theological Seminary, Jackson, MS., 1995. ProQuest.

Falola, Toyin. *Violence in Nigeria: The Crisis of Religious Politics and Secular Ideologies.* Rochester, VA: University of Rochester Press, 1998.

Falola, Toyin, and Matthew Hassan Kukah. *A History of Nigeria.* Cambridge: Cambridge University Press, 2008.

Fiensy, David A. "The Composition of the Jerusalem Church." In *The Book of Acts in Its First Century Setting, Vol. 4: Palestinian Setting.* Edited by Richard Bauckham. Grand Rapids, MI: Paternoster, 1995.

Fiere, Paulo. *Pedagogy of the Oppressed.* New York: Seabury, 1970.

Floristan, Casiano, and Christian Duquoc, eds.. *Forgiveness.* Concilium 184. Edinburgh: T. & T. Clark, 1986.

Frame, John M. *The Doctrine of the Christian Life: A Theology of Lordship.* Phillipsburg, NJ: Presbyterian & Reformed, 2008.

Friesen, Daune K. *Christian Peacemaking & International Conflict: A Realist and Pacifist Perspective.* Scottsdale, PA: Herald, 1984.

Gaiya, Musa A. B. "The Pentecostal Revolution in Nigeria." Occasional Paper. Centre of African Studies, University of Copenhagen, July 2002.

Gandhi, Karamchand Mohandas. *Non-violent Resistance (Satygraha).* New York: Schochen, 1951.

Gifford, Paul. *African Christianity: Its Public Role.* Indianapolis: Indiana University Press, 1998.

———. *Ghana's New Christianity: Pentecostalism in a Globalizing African Economy.* Bloomington, IN: Indiana University Press, 2004.

Girard, Rene. "Mimesis and Violence: Perspectives in Cultural Criticism." *Berkshire Review* 14 (1979) 9–19.

Gladwin, John. *God's People in God's World: Biblical Motives for Social Involvement.* Downers Grove, IL: InterVarsity, 1979.

Glaser, Ida. *The Bible and Other Faiths: What Does the Lord Require of Us?* Downers Grove, IL: InterVarsity, 2005.

Goldingay, John. *God's Prophet, God's Servant: A Study in Jeremiah and Isaiah 40–55.* Carlisle, UK: Paternoster, 1994.

———. *The Message of Isaiah 40–55: A Literary-Theological Commentary.* London: T. & T. Clark, 2005.

Goldingay, John, and David Payne. *Isaiah 40–55: A Critical and Exegetical Commentary.* International Critical Commentary Series. Vol. 1. London: T. & T. Clark, 2006.

Gowfen, Rotgak I. *Religion and Peacebuilding in Northern Nigeria.* Kaduna, Nigeria: Human Rights Monitor, 2004.

Grant, Edward. *God and Reason in the Middle Ages.* Cambridge: Cambridge University Press, 2001.

Greider, Kathleen J. *Reckoning with Aggression: Theology, Violence, and Vitality.* Louisville, KY: Westminster John Knox, 1997.

Gruchy, John W. de. *Reconciliation: Restoring Justice.* Minneapolis: Fortress, 2002.

Gülen, M. Fethullah. "In True Islam, Terror Does Not Exist." In *Terror and Suicide: An Islamic Perspective,* edited by Ergun Capan, 7–22. New Jersey: Light, 2006.

———. *Toward a Global Civilization: Love & Tolerance.* Clifton, NJ: Tughra, 2011.

Gupta, Dipak K. *Understanding Terrorism and Political Violence: The Life Cycle of Birth, Growth, Transformation, and Demise.* London: Routledge, 2008.

Gushee, David P., ed. *Christians & Politics Beyond the Culture Wars: An Agenda for Engagement.* Grand Rapids, MI: Baker, 2000.

———. *Righteous Gentiles of the Holocaust: Genocide and Moral Obligation.* St. Paul, MN: Paragon, 2003.

Gutierrez, Gustavo. *Spiritual Writings.* Selected and with an introduction by Daniel G. Groody. Maryknoll, NY: Orbis, 2011.

Gwama, Filibus. "Ekklesiyar Yan'uwa a Nigeria" [Church of the Brethren in Nigeria]. In *Seeking the Peace of Africa: Stories from African Peacemakers,* edited by Donald E. Miller et al., 55–56. Geneva: World Council of Churches, 2007.

Hackett, R. I. J. "Charismatic/Pentecostal Appropriation of Media Technologies in Nigeria and Ghana." *Journal of Religion in Africa* 28 (1998) 258–77.

Hamerton-Kelly, Robert G. *Sacred Violence: Paul's Hermeneutics of the Cross*. Minneapolis: Fortress, 1992.

Hastings, Adria. "Religion." In *The Oxford Companion to Christian Thought: Intellectual, Spiritual and Moral Horizons of Christianity*, edited by Adria Hasting, Alistair Mason, and Hugh Pyper, 604. Oxford: Oxford University Press, 2004.

Hauerwas, Stanley. *A Community of Character: Toward a Constructive Christian Social Ethic*. Notre Dame, IN: University of Notre Dame Press, 1981.

Hawker, Sara, and Waite Maurice, eds. *Oxford Dictionary & Thesaurus*. Oxford: Oxford University Press, 2007.

Hays, Richard. *The Moral Vision of the New Testament: A Contemporary Introduction to New Testament Ethics*. New York: HarperCollins, 1996.

Hick, John. *God and the Universe of Faiths*. London: Font, 1977.

Hiebert, Paul G. *Transforming Worldviews: An Anthropological Understanding of How People Change*. Grand Rapids, MI: Baker Academic, 2008.

Hollenback, David. *The Global Face of Public Faith: Politics, Human Rights, and Christian Ethics*. Washington, DC: Georgetown University Press, 2003.

Holmes, Arthur F., ed. *War and Christian Ethics: Classic and Contemporary Readings on the Morality of War*. 2nd edition. Grand Rapids, MI: Baker Academic, 2005.

Howard, Richard T. *Ruined and Rebuilt: The Story of Coventry Cathedral, 1939–1962*. Coventry, UK: Council of Coventry Cathedral, 1962.

Hubbard, D. A. "Ethiopian Eunuch." In *New Bible Dictionary*, 3rd edition, edited by D. R. W. Wood et al., 346. Leicester, UK: InterVarsity, 1996.

Hughes, R. B., and J. C. Laney. *Tyndale Concise Bible Commentary*. Wheaton, IL: Tyndale, 2001.

Human Rights Watch, "Criminal Politics: Violence, 'Godfathers' and Corruption in Nigeria." *Human Rights Watch* 19, no. 16(A), October 11, 2007. http://www.hrw.org/en/node/10660/section/1

Hunt, Leslie. "Good Neighbor." In *Baker's Dictionary of Christian Ethics*, edited by Carl F. H. Henry. 267–68. Grand Rapids, MI: Baker, 1973.

Hunt, Robert. *Muslim Faith and Values: What Every Christian Should Know*. New York: General Board Ministries, 2003.

Huntington, Samuel P. *The Clash of Civilization and the Remaking of World Order*. London: Simon & Schuster, 1997.

Ilesanmi, Simeon O. *Religious Pluralism and the Nigerian State*. Athens, OH: Ohio University Press, 1997.

Ironside, H. A. *Expository Notes on the Prophet Isaiah*. New York: Loizeauz Brothers, 1952.

Isaak, Paul John. "Luke." In *African Bible Commentary: A One-Volume Commentary*, edited by Tokumboh Adeyemo, 1248–49. Nairobi, Kenya: WordAlive, 2006.

Jackman, David. *Teaching Isaiah: Unlocking Isaiah for the Bible Teacher*. Fearn, Ross-Shire, UK: Christian Focus; London: Proclamation Trust Media, 2010.

Jatau, Peter Y., and Saidu Dogo. "A Position Paper by Christian Association of Nigeria." Paper presented at Northern State Governor's Forum, Gen. Hassan Katsina House, Kawo, Kaduna, May 7, 2009.

Jenkins, Philip. "Third World War: The Real Showdown Between Christian and Muslim Isn't in the Mideast." In *The American Conservative*, April 1, 2010.

Jewett, Paul K. *God, Creation and Revelation: A Neo-Evangelical Theology*. Eugene, OR: Wipf & Stock, 2000.

Johnston, Gerry. *Restorative Justice: Ideas, Values, Debates.* Cullompton, Devon, UK: Willan, 2002.

Juergensmeyer, Mark. *Terror in the Mind of God: The Global Rise of Religious Violence.* Berkeley: University of California Press, 2003.

Jürgen, Moltmann. *Ethics of Hope.* Minneapolis: Fortress, 2012.

Kalilombe, Patrick. "Race Relations in Britain: Possibilities for the Future." In *A Time to Speak,* edited by Paul Grant and Raj Patel, 11. Nottingham: Russell, 1990.

Kalu, Ogbu. *African Pentecostalism: An Introduction.* Oxford: Oxford University Press, 2008.

Kässmann, Margot. *Overcoming Violence: The Challenge to the Churches in All Places.* Geneva: WCC, 1998.

Katongole, Emmanuel M. *A Future for Africa: Critical Essays in Christian Social Imagination.* Scranton, PA: University of Scranton Press, 2005.

Keener, Craig Stephen. *Acts: An Exegetical Commentary: Introduction and 1:1–2:47.* Grand Rapids, MI: Baker Academic, 2012.

———. *The IVP Bible Background Commentary: New Testament.* Downers Grove, IL.: InterVarsity, 1993.

Kellett, Peter M. *Conflict Dialogue: Working with Layers of Meaning for Productive Relationship.* Wheaton, IL.: Sage, 2007.

Kemeny, P. C. ed. *Church, State and Public Justice: Five Views.* Downers Grove, IL: IVP Academic, 2007.

Kimball, Charles. *When Religion Becomes Evil.* New York: HarperCollins, 2002.

King, Martin Luther, Jr. *Strength to Love.* Philadelphia: Fortress, 1981.

Korieh, Chima J., and G. Ugo Nwokeji, eds. *Religion, History, and Politics in Nigeria: Essays in Honour of Ogbu U. Kalu.* Langham, MD: University Press of America, 2005.

Kukah, Matthew Hassan. *Religion, Politics and Power in Northern Nigeria.* Ibadan, Nigeria: Spectrum, 1993.

Küng, Hans. *On Being a Christian.* Translated by Edward Quinn. New York: Doubleday, 1976.

———. *A Global Ethic for Global Politics and Economics.* Oxford: Oxford University Press, 1998.

Kunhiyop, Samuel Waje. *African Christian Ethics.* Nairobi, Kenya: Hippo, 2008.

Lamb, Christopher A., ed. *Reconciling People: Coventry Cathedral's Story.* Norwich, UK: Canterbury, 2011.

Lapidus, Ira M. *A History of Islamic Societies.* 2nd edition. Cambridge: Cambridge University Press, 2002.

Lederach, John Paul. "Cultivating Peace: a Practitioner's View of Deadly Conflict and Negotiation." In *Contemporary Peacemaking: Conflict, Violence and Peace Processes,* edited by John Darby and Roger Mac Ginty, 36–44. New York: Palgrave Macmillan, 2003.

Lee, Ilchi. *Earth Citizen: Recovering Our Humanity.* Sedona, AZ: BEST Life, 2009.

Leeds, Josiah W. *The Primitive Christian Estimate of War and Self-Defense.* New Vienna, OH: Peace Association of Friends in America, 1908.

Legenhausen, Muhammad. *Islam and Religious Pluralism.* London: Al-hoda, 1999.

Liebmann, Marian. *Restorative Justice: How it Works.* London: Kingsley, 2007.

Light, Vernon. *Transforming the Church in Africa: A New Contextually-Relevant Discipleship Model.* South Africa: South African Theological Seminary Press, 2012.

Lincoln, Andrew T. *Paradise Now and Not Yet: Studies in the Role of the Heavenly Dimension in Paul's Thoughts with Special Reference to his Eschatology.* Cambridge: Cambridge University Press, 1981.

Loh, I-Jin, and Howard A. Hatton. *Handbook on the Letter from James.* New York: United Bible Society, 1972.

Loimeier, Roman. "Boko Haram: The Development of the Militant Religious Movement in Nigeria." *Afrika Spectrum* 47 nos. 2–3 (2012) 137–155.

Macchia, Frank D. "Terrorists, Security, and the Risk of Peace: Toward a Moral Vision." *Pneuma: The Journal of the Society for Pentecostal Studies* 26, no. 1 (Spring 2004) 1–7.

Macquarrie, John. *The Concepts of Peace.* Wiltshire, UK: SCM, 1973.

Mahaney, C. J. *Humility: True Greatness.* Colorado Spring: Oasis, 2005.

Mangalwadi, Vishal. *The Book that Made Your World: How the Bible Created the Soul of Western Civilization.* Nashville: Nelson, 2011.

Marshall, I. H. *The Acts of the Apostles.* Sheffield, UK: JSOT Press, 1992.

Marshall, Ruth. *Political Spiritualities: The Pentecostal Revolution in Nigeria.* Chicago: The University Chicago Press, 2009.

Marshall-Fratani, Ruth. "Mediating the Global and the Local in Nigerian Pentecostalism." *Journal of Religion in Africa* 28 (1998) 278–315.

Marson, Gary Saul, ed. *Politics, Law and Morality.* New Haven: Yale University Press, 2013.

Martin, J. A. "Esther." In *The Bible Knowledge Commentary: An Exposition of the Scriptures,* edited by John F. Walvoord & Roy B. Zuck, 199–265. Wheaton, IL: Victor, 1985.

———. "Luke." In *The Bible Knowledge Commentary: An Exposition of the Scriptures,* edited by John F. Walvoord and Roy B. Zuck, 199–265. Wheaton, IL: Victor, 1985.

Mavalla, Ayuba. *Conflict Transformation: Churches in the Face of Structural Violence in Northern Nigeria.* Oxford: Regnum, 2014.

Mbiti, Stephen John. *African Traditional Religion and Philosophy.* Oxford: Heinemann, 1969.

McCain, Carmen. "Radical Peacemaker" published by Weekly Trust, March 31, 2012.

McCullough, Michael E. *Beyond Revenge: The Evolution of the Forgiveness Instinct.* San Francisco: Jossey-Bass, 2008.

McEntire, Mark. *The Blood of Abel: The Violence Plot in the Hebrew Bible.* Macon, GA: Mercer University Press, 1999.

McGrath, Alister E. *Christian Theology: An Introduction.* Oxford: Blackwell, 2001.

McKenna, David. *Mastering the Old Testament: A Book-by-Book Commentary by Today's Great Bible Teacher, Isaiah 40–66.* Edited by Lloyds J. Ogilvie. Dallas, TX: Word, 1982.

McKenzie, P. R. *Inter-religious Encounters in West Africa: Samuel Ajayi Crowther's Attitude to African Traditional Religion and Islam.* Leicester Studies in Religion 1. Leicester, NC: University of Leicester, 1976.

Merton, Thomas. *Faith and Violence: Christian Teaching and Christian Practice.* Notre Dame, IN: University of Notre Dame Press, 1968.

Miller, Donald E., and Tetsumao Yamamori. *Global Pentecostalism: The New Face of Christian Social Engagement.* Berkeley: University of California Press, 2007.

Mills, John O. "New Heaven? New Earth?" In *New Heaven?: New Earth? An Encounter with Pentacostalism,* edited by Simon Tugwell, 69–118. London: Darton, Longman & Todd, 1976.

Mohammed, Kyari. "The Message and Methods of Boko Haram." In *Boko Haram: Islamism, Politics, Security and the State in Nigeria,* 9–31. Leiden: African Studies Centre, 2014.

Moltmann, Jürgen. *The Coming of God: Christian Eschatology.* Minneapolis: Fortress, 1996.

———. *Ethics of Hope.* Cambridge: Cambridge University Press, 2012.

———. *God in Creation: A New Theology of Creation and the Spirit of God.* Minneapolis: Fortress, 1993.

———. "Political Theology and the Ethics of Peace." In *Theology, Politics, and Peace,* edited by Theodore Runyon, 41. New York: Orbis, 1989.

———, ed. *The Politics of Discipleship and Discipleship in Politics: Jürgen Moltmann Lectures in Dialogue with Mennonite Scholars.* Edited by Willard M. Swartley. Eugene, OR: Cascade, 2006.

Mott, Charles Stephen. *Biblical Ethics and Social Change.* New York: Oxford University Press, 1982.

Mugambi, J. N. K. "Missionary Presence in Interreligious Encounters and Relationships." *Studies in World Christianity* 19, no. 2 (August 2013) 162–186. http://www.eupublishing.com/doi/abs/10.3366/swc.2013.0050 (pdf document)

Mugambi, J. N. K., and Laurenti Magesa, eds. *The Church in African Christianity: Innovative Essays in Ecclesiology.* African Challenge Series 1. Nairobi, Kenya: Initiatives, 1990.

Musa, Danladi. *Christians in Politics: How Can They Be Effective.* Bukuru, Plateau State: African Christian TextBooks, 2009.

Myers, Ched, and Elaine Enns. *Ambassadors of Reconciliation: New Testament Reflection on Restorative Justice and Peacemaking.* Maryknoll, NY: Orbis, 2009.

Nafi, Basheer M. "The Rise of Islamic Reformist Thought and its Challenge to Traditional Islam." In *Islamic Thought in the Twentieth Century,* edited by Suha Taji-Farouki and Basheer M. Nafi, 28. London: Tauris, 2004.

Nathan, Ronald. "Issues for the Black Minister." In *A Time to Speak,* edited by Paul Grant and Raj Patel, 10–15. Nottingham: Russell, 1990.

Newman, Paul. *The Etymology of Hausa Boko.* Nanterre: Mega-Chad Research Network, 2013.

Niebuhr, Reinhold. *The Children of Light and the Children of Darkness: A Vindication of Democracy and a Critique of Traditional Defense.* New York: Charles Scribner's Sons, 1960.

Neil, William. *The Acts of the Apostles: New Century Bible.* London: Marshall, Morgan & Scott, 1973.

Nussbaum, Barbara. "Ubuntu: Reflections of a South African on Our Common Humanity." *Reflections: The SOL Journal* 4, no. 4 (2003) 21–26.

Nystrom, David P. *The NIV Application Commentary on James.* Grand Rapids, MI: Zondervan, 1997.

O'Donovan, Oliver. *The Desire of the Nation: Rediscovering the Roots of Political Theology.* Cambridge: Cambridge University Press, 1996.

Oftedal, Emilie. "Boko Haram: A Transnational Phenomenon?" Masters thesis, Department of Political Science, University of Olso, 2013.

Ojo, Matthew A. "Eschatology and the African Society: The Critical Point of Disjunction." *Ogbomosho Journal of Theology* 11 (2006) 30–45.

———. "Pentecostal Public Accountability." *Ogbomosho Journal of Theology* 13, no. 1 (2008) 112–127.

Ojo, Yinka. *The Kingdom and the Market Place: A Strategy for Society Transformation.* Lagos, Nigeria: Triumph, 2006.

Okonjo-Iweala, Ngozi. *Reforming the Unreformable: Lessons from Nigeria.* Cambridge, MA: MIT Press, 2012.

Oladeji, Moses Olatunde. *Understanding the Pentecostal Movement.* Ibadan, Nigeria: Bounty, 2005.

Olsen, Ted. "Bishop Before His Time." *Christian History* 79 (2003) 9–16.

Ondigo, Yahya M. A. *Muslim-Christian Interactions: Past, Present and Future.* Nairobi, Kenya: Abut Aisha Stores, 2005.

O'Neil, J. C. *The Theology of Acts in Its Historical Setting.* 2nd edition. London: SPCK, 1970.

Onuoha, Freedom. "Why Do Youth Join Boko Haram?" United States Institute of Peace, Special Report 348, June 2014. http://www.usip.org/publications/why-do-youth-join-boko-haram (pdf document)

Orr, James. *The Christian View of God and the World.* Grand Rapids, MI: Eerdmans, 1954.

Oyedepo, David O. *Anointing for Exploits.* Lagos, Nigeria: Dominion, 2005.

Paden, John. *Faith and Politics in Nigeria. Nigeria as a Pivotal State in the Muslim World.* Washington, DC: US Institute of Peace, 2008.

———. *Muslim Civic Cultures and Conflict Resolution: The Challenge for Democratic Federalism in Nigeria.* Washington, DC: Brookings Institution, 2005.

Parsons, Mikeal C. *Acts.* Grand Rapids, MI: Baker Academic, 2008.

Pennenberg, Wolfhart. "Constructive and Critical Functions of Christian Eschatology." *Harvard Theological Review* 77, no. 2 (April 1984) 119–139.

Pinkares, Servis. *The Sources of Christian Ethics.* Washington, DC: The Catholic University of America Press, 1995.

Procter, Paul, et al., eds. *Longman Dictionary of Contemporary English.* Harlow, UK: Longman, 1992.

Puniyani, Ram. *Religion and Violence: Expression of Politics in Contemporary Times.* New Delhi, India: Sage, 2005.

Ramachandra, Vinoth. *Faiths in Conflict?: Christian Integrity in a Multicultural World.* Downers Grove, IL: InterVarsity, 1999.

Reader's Digest Oxford Complete Wordfinder. Oxford: Oxford University Press, 1993.

Reichberg, Gregory, Henrik Syse, and Endre Begby, eds. *The Ethics of War: Classical and Contemporary Readings.* Oxford: Blackwell, 2006.

Rice-Oxley, Richard. *Forgiveness—The Way of Peace.* Bramcote, Nottingham: Grove, 1989.

Robinson, Anthony B., and Robert W. Wall. *Called to Be Church: The Book of Acts for a New Day.* Grand Rapids, MI: Eerdmans, 2006.

Rodin, David. *War and Self-Defense.* New York: Oxford University Press, 2003.

Rodney, Walter. *How Europe Underdeveloped Africa.* Abuja, Nigeria: Panaf, 2009.

Rodriguez, Dario Lopez. "Pentecostal Identity, Diversity and Public Witness: a Critical Review of Allan Anderson's An Introduction to Pentecostalism." *Journal of Pentecostal Theology* 16, no. 1 (2007) 54–67.

Roman, Peter. *Proclaiming the Peacemaker: The Malaysian Church as an Agent of Reconciliation in a Multicultural Society*. Oxford: Regnum, 2012.

Rule, K. "Religion, Religious." In *The Evangelical Dictionary of Theology*, edited by Walter Elwell, 426. Grand Rapids, MI: Baker, 1991.

Ryan, John A. "The Church and the Workingman." In *On Moral Business: Classical and Contemporary Resources for Ethics in Economic Life*, edited by Max L. Stackhouse, Dennis P. McCann, and Shirley J. Roels, 298–300. Grand Rapids, MI: Eerdmans, 1995.

Salmeier, Michael A. *Restoring the Kingdom: The Role of God as the Ordainer of Times and Season in the Acts of the Apostles*. Eugene, OR: Pickwick, 2011.

Sanda, Julie G. "Nigeria's Global Role in Peacemaking: From the Congo Through Lebanon to Bosnia Hezegovina." In *Nigeria at Fifty: Contributions to Peace, Democracy & Development*, edited by Attahiru M. Jega and Jacqueline W. Farris, 79. Abuja, Nigeria: The Shehu Musa Yar'adua Foundation, 2010.

Sanneh, Lamin. "Shariah Sanctions as Secular Grace? A Nigeria Islamic Debate and Intellectual Response." *Transformation* 20, no. 4 (October 2003) 236–440.

Schaefer, Glenn E. "Peace." In *Baker's Evangelical Dictionary of Biblical Theology*, edited by Walter A. Elwell. Accessed on biblestudytools.com. http://www.biblestudytools.com/dictionaries/bakers-evangelical-dictionary/peace.html

Schroeder, Christopher O. *History, Justice, and the Agency of God: A Hermeneutical and Exegetical Investigation on Isaiah and Psalms*. Leiden: Brill, 2001.

Schwager, Raymond. *Must There Be Scapegoats?* San Francisco: Harper & Row, 1987.

Shaull, Richard, and Waldo Cesar. *Pentecostalism and the Future of the Christian Churches: Promises, Limitations and Challenges*. Grand Rapids, MI: Eerdmans, 2000.

Shiell, William David. *Readings Acts: The Lector and the Early Christian Audience*. Boston: Brill Academic, 2004.

Sindima J., Harvey. *Religious and Political Ethics in Africa: A Moral Inquiry*. Westport, CT: Greenwood, 1998.

Smith, William. *Bible History of World Government and a Forecast of Its Future from Bible Prophecy*. Westfield, IN: Union Bible Seminary, 1955.

Soloviev, Vladimir S. *Politics, Law and Morality*. Translated by Vladimir Wozniuk. New Haven: Yale University Press, 2013.

Soyinka, Wole. *Climate of Fear: The Quest for Dignity in a Dehumanizing World*. Ibadan, Nigeria: Bookcraft, 2004.

Snaith, Norman H. *The Distinctive Ideas of the Old Testament*. London: Epworth, 1944.

Spence, Basil. *Phoenix at Coventry: The Building of a Cathedral*. London: Bles, 1962.

Spencer, Scott F. *Journeying through Acts: A Literary-Cultural Reading*. Peabody, MA: Hendrickson, 2004.

Stackhouse, Max L., Dennis P. McCann, and Shirley J. Roels, eds. *On Moral Business: Classical and Contemporary Resources for Ethics in Economic Life*. Grand Rapids, MI: Eerdmans, 1995.

Stassen, Glen, ed. *Just Peacemaking: Ten Practices for Abolishing War*. Cleveland, OH: Pilgrim, 1998.

———. *Living the Sermon on the Mount: A Practical Hope for Grace and Deliverance*. San Francisco: Jossey-Bass, 2006.

———. "The Unity, Realism, and Obligatoriness of Just Peacemaking Theory." *Journal of the Society of Christian Ethics* 23, no. 1 (2003) 171–186.

Stassen, Glen, and David Gushee. *Kingdom Ethics: Following Jesus in Contemporary Context.* Downers Grove: InterVarsity, 2003.

Stivers, Robert L., et al. *Christian Ethics: A Case Method Approach.* New York: Orbis, 2000.

Stob, Henry. *Ethical Reflections: Essays on Moral Themes.* Grand Rapids, MI: Eerdmans, 1978.

Stone, John, and Rutledge Dennis. *Race and Ethnicity: Comparative and Theological Approaches.* Berlin: Blackwell, 2003.

Storr, Anthony. *Human Aggression.* New York: Athenaeum, 1968.

Stott, John R. W. "Christian Responses to Good and Evil: A Study of Romans 12:9–13:10." In *Perspectives on Peacemaking: Biblical Options in he Nuclear Age,* edited by John A. Bernbaum, 43–56. Ventura, CA: Regal, 1984.

———. *Issues Facing the Contemporary World.* Grand Rapids, MI: Zondervan, 2006.

———. *The Message of Acts: The Bible Speaks Today.* Downers Grove, IL: InterVarsity, 1990.

Suberu, T. Rotimi. *Ethnic Minority Conflicts and Governance in Nigeria.* Ibadan, Nigeria: Spectrum, 1999.

Suchocki, Marjorie Hewitt. *The Fall to Violence: Original Sin in Relational Theology.* New York: Continuum, 1994.

Sullivan, Dennis, and Larry Tifft, eds. *Handbook of Restorative Justice: A Global Perspective.* London: Routledge, 2006.

Swindoll, Charles R. *The Tale of Tardy Oxcart: And 1,501 Other Stories.* Nashville: Word, 1998.

Temple, William. *Christ and the Way to Peace.* London: Student Christian Movement, 1935.

Thompson, Alan J. *The Acts of the Risen Lord Jesus: Luke's Account of God's Unfolding Plan.* Downers Grove, IL: InverVarsity, 2011.

———. *One Lord, One People: The Unity of the Church in Acts in It's Literary Setting.* London: T. & T. Clark, 2008.

Thompson, Dennis F. *Political Ethics and Public Office.* Cambridge, MA: Harvard University Press, 1987.

Tonti-Filippini, Nicholas. "Self Defense and Just War Theory." John Paul II Institute for Marriage & Family. http://jp2institute.org/Portals/39/Documents/NTF_Self_Defence_and_Just_War_Theory.pdf. Accessed March 23, 2015.

Turaki, Kabiru Tanimu. "Better Equipment, Pay for Security Agencies." *Daily Trust,* November 6, 2013.

Turaki, Yusufu. *The British Colonial Legacy in Northern Nigeria: A Social Ethical Analysis of the Colonial and Post-colonial Society and Politics in Nigeria.* Kaduna, Nigeria: Baraka, 1993.

———. "Christianity and African Traditional Religion, Vol. 2." Unpublished manuscript, last modified 2008.

———. "The Institutionalization of the Inferior Status and Socio-Political Role of the Non-Muslim Groups in the Colonial Hierarchical Structure of the Northern Region of Nigeria." PhD diss., Boston University, 1982.

———. *The Trinity of Sin.* Nairobi, Kenya: WordAlive, 2011.

Tutu, Desmond. *No Future without Forgiveness.* London: Rider, 1999.

United States Conference of Catholic Bishops. *The Challenge of Peace: God's Promise and Our Response.* USCCB, May 3, 1983.

Wainwright, Geoffrey, ed. *Keeping the Faith: Essays to Mark the Centenary of Lux Mundi*. Philadelphia: Fortress, 1988.

Waliggo, John Mary. "The African Clan as the True Model of the African Church." In *The Church in African Christianity: Innovative Essays in Ecclesiology*, edited by J. N. Kanyua Mugambi and Laurenti Magesa, 111. Nairobi, Kenya: Initiative, 1990.

Walker, Andrew. "What is Boko Haram?" Special Report 308. Washington, DC: United States Institute of Peace, 2012.

Wallis, Jim. *God's Politics: Why the Right Gets It Wrong and the Left Doesn't Get It*. San Francisco: HarperSanFrancisco, 2005.

Walls, Andrew. "Samuel Ajayi Crowther, 1807–1891: Foremost African Christian of the Nineteenth Century." In *Mission Legacies: Biographical Studies of Leaders of the Modern Missionary Movement*, edited by G. H. Anderson et al. Maryknoll, NY: Orbis, 1994.

———. "A Second Narrative of Samuel Ajayi Crowther's Early Life." *Bulletin of the Society for African History* 2 (1965) 14.

Walzer, Michael. *Just and Unjust Wars: A Moral Argument with Historical Illustrations*. 3rd edition. New York: Basic Books, 2000.

———. "Terrorism: A Critique of Excuses." In *The Morality of War: Classic and Contemporary Readings*, edited by Larry May, Eric Rovie, and Steve Viner, 297–305. Upper Saddle River, NJ: Pearson Prentice Hall, 2006.

———. "Terrorism and Ethics." In *The Ethics of War: Classic and Contemporary Readings*, edited by Gregory M. Reichberg, Henrik Syse, and Endre Begby, 642–52. Oxford: Blackwell, 2006.

Webb, Barry. *The Message of Isiah*. Downers Grove, IL: InterVarsity, 1996.

Weiss, Johannes. *Die Predigt Jesu vom Reich Gottes*. Edited by Ferdinand Hahn. 3rd edition. Göttingen: Vandenhoeck & Ruprecht, 1964.

Welby, Andrew. Foreword to *Father, Forgive: Reflections on Peacemaking*. Oxford: Monarch, 2013.

Werbner, Richard, and Terence Ranger, eds. *Postcolonial Identities in Africa*. Atlantic Highlands, NJ: Zed Books, 1996.

White, Andrew. *Father, Forgive: Reflection on Peacemaking*. Grand Rapids, MI: Monarch, 2013.

Wiersbe, Warren W. *The Bible Exposition Commentary: New Testament*. 2 vols. Wheaton, IL: Victor, 2001.

Williams, Rodman J. *Renewal Theology: Systematic Theology from a Charismatic Perspective*. Three volumes in one. Grand Rapids, MI: Zondervan, 1996.

Wilson, Colin. *A Criminal History of Mankind*. London: Granada, 1984.

Windass, Stanley. *Christianity Versus Violence: A Social and Historical Study of War and Christianity*. London: Sheed & Ward, 1964.

Wink, Walter. *The Domination Systems*. Philadelphia: Fortress, 1999.

———. *Engaging the Powers: Discernment and Resistance in a World of Domination*. Minneapolis: Fortress, 1992.

Wiseman, John. *The SAS Self-Defense Handbook: A Complete Guide to Unarmed Combat Techniques*. Guilford, CT: Globe Requot, 1997.

Wright, N. T. "Sketches: Jesus' Resurrection & Christian Origins." *Stimulus* 16, no. 1 (February 2008) 41.

———. *Surprised by Hope: Rethinking Heaven, the Resurrection, and the Mission of the Church*. New York: HarperCollins, 1989.

Yahya, Harun. *Signs of the End Times in Surat al-Kahf.* New Delhi, India: Goodwork, 2003.

Yeatts, John R. "Peace in the Old and Testament." In A Peace Reader, edited by E. Morris Sider and Luke L. Keefer, 15–21. Nappanee, India: Evangel, 2002.

Yong, Amos. *In the Days of Caesar: Pentecostalism and Political Theology.* Grand Rapids, MI: Eerdmans, 2009.

Yuar, Francis Ayul. "A Critical Evaluation of Christian Moral Response to the Blood Ethnic Conflicts Between the Dinka and the Nuer of the Upper Nile Region of Sudan." MTh thesis, South African Theological Seminary, 2011.

Zinn, Howard, ed. *The Power of Nonviolence: Writings by an Advocate of Peace.* Boston: Beacon, 2002.

Zuck, R. B. *A Biblical Theology of the Old Testament.* Chicago, IL: Moody, 1991.

Zuhur, Sherifa. *Precision in the Global War on Terror: Inciting Muslims through the War of Ideas.* Carlisle, PA: Strategic Study Institute, 2008.

Sunday Bobai Agang's Bio

Sunday Bobai Agang is both a Langham and a ScholarsLeaders scholar. He lives and works in Nigeria. He is married to Mrs. Sarah. The Lord has blessed their marriage with five children:

1. Mrs. Nancy Alex Zemo

2. Mrs. Esther Paul Moses

3. Late Miss Nisama Sunday

4. Master Kent Sunday

5. Miss Dorcas Sunday

Agang is Professor of Christian Ethics, Theology and Public Policy. AGANG was a onetime Academic Dean of one of Africa's premier theological seminaries in Africa, ECWA Theological Seminary Jos (JETS) and currently the Provost of ECWA Theological Seminary Kagoro (ETSK). Agang holds a BA (JETS), MDiv (Palmer Theological Seminary, Philadelphia, Pennsylvania), and PhD in Christian Ethics, systematic theology of public policy (Fuller Seminary, Pasadena). He has published several articles on various theological issues as well as being a regular contributor to Christianity Today.

An ordained minister with the Evangelical Church Winning All (ECWA) as well as a member of the Institute for Global Engagement; he is founder and chair of the International Foundation for Entrepreneurial Education (IFEE) and co-founder and Vice President of Ganty's Aid to Widows, Orphans and Needy (GAWON). He is also the Secretary of ECWA Scholars Fellowship (ESF) and President of ECWA Theological Seminary, Jos, Alumni Association. Agang is a just peacemaking advocate. He is concerned with the impact of religions violence, HIV and AIDS and public policy on Nigerians. His research work on The Impact of Ethnic, Political, and Religious Violence on Northern Nigeria, and a Theological Reflection on Its Healing was published by Langham Monographs in 2011. His new book on No Cheeks to Turn, is in the process of being published by HippoBooks in 2016. He has presented papers on HIV and AIDS at Tearfund and World Council of Churches seminars and workshops in Nigeria, respectively.